DATA ANALYTICS, DATA VISUALIZATION & COMMUNICATING DATA: 3 BOOKS IN 1

LEARN THE PROCESSES OF DATA ANALYTICS AND DATA SCIENCE, CREATE ENGAGING DATA VISUALIZATIONS, AND PRESENT DATA EFFECTIVELY

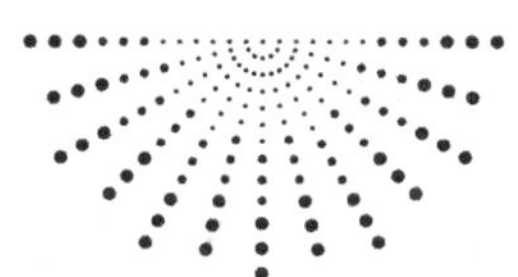

ELIZABETH CLARKE

TABLE OF CONTENTS

EVERYTHING DATA ANALYTICS: A BEGINNERS GUIDE TO DATA LITERACY

BEGINNERS GUIDE TO DATA VISUALIZATION

HOW TO WIN WITH YOUR DATA VISUALIZATIONS

A Free Gift From Me to You!

The Winning
Data Visualization Checklist

Make sure every visualization you create has all the elements that lead to a successful presentation!

Scan the QR code or visit
ElizabethSClarke.com
to get yours Free!

Download Here!

ELIZABETH
CLARKE

Everything Data Analytics

A Beginner's Guide to Data Literacy

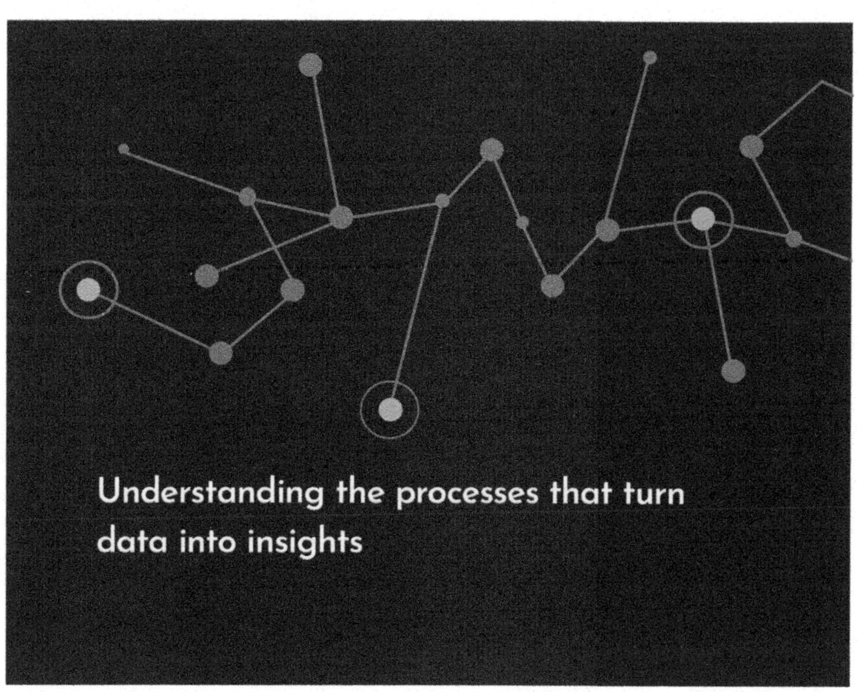

EVERYTHING DATA ANALYTICS: A BEGINNERS GUIDE TO DATA LITERACY

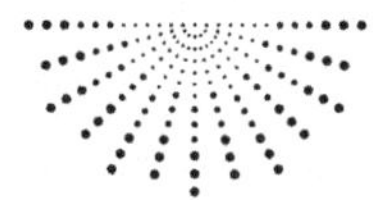

UNDERSTANDING THE PROCESSES THAT TURN DATA INTO INSIGHTS

INTRODUCTION

Data.

Just four letters, yet such a powerful word. Data is all around us. It is the foundation that every business sits on and without proper storage, development, analysis, and summarization of that data, that business's foundation will not hold strong. Data allows companies to make projections and develop goals for the future.

This is why over 74 zettabytes of data were produced in the year 2021 alone. 1 zettabyte is 1,000,000,000,000,000,000,000 bytes of data! That yearly figure is expected to grow to 175 zettabytes by 2025. This is because businesses revolve around data and its analysis and billions of dollars are being pumped into that industry. In fact, by the year 2023, it is expected that the data industry will be worth approximately $77 billion.

There are a few troubling statistics, though:

- About 80% of all data collected by companies are uninstructed and have not been interpreted for proper use.
- On average, most companies only analyze a little over 10% of the data that they receive. More than 80% of that data goes

> unused! So much insight remains unseen, which means, so much money is being left on the table.

Even though this industry is already worth billions of dollars, there is still so much room left for growth, improvement, and spending. That is where data professionals come together - to drive business decisions from structured data and make unstructured data pliable for companies to use in decision-making.

We have touched lightly upon why data is essential to every single organization in existence, but now the question is – why is it important to you, a blooming data professional? Hearing the word data can incite yawns in many people, but you are made of tougher stuff. You become excited, don't you? Because you see the value of this topic. Not only can you be one of the people filling the seats that need to be filled with the abundance of jobs in this industry, but you would also be paid handsomely to do so as there is so much demand. Data is everywhere, and someone needs to do the work of deciphering it and presenting it to other people in an easy-to-understand format. That is never going to change and therefore, there is so much potential for growth as a data professional. Not only can a career in this field be exciting, it can also offer a big incentive.

However, taking advantage of that opportunity can be challenging if you do not know where to start or how to gain the momentum you need. This book was written to give you that direction. Think of it as your compass to develop data literacy and guide you to gaining the skills that you need to be efficient and assured in your abilities.

However, we are getting ahead of ourselves and speaking about your future self, a confident and accomplished data professional. Currently, you might be feeling the pain of looking at career options and feeling intimidated. You may already be in a position, wanting to take that next step to excel in your career. You are not alone, and your feelings of trepidation are perfectly valid.

Yes, indeed, it can all seem overwhelming, take a moment and breathe. Take a deep inhalation and a slow exhalation. This book is going to take away that overwhelming sensation by taking all these unknowns and breaking them down into small, digestible pieces that allow you to take definitive steps in the right direction.

From the first chapter, you will gain valuable insights into what it means to be data literate and make a successful career out of data analytics. We will then touch on a familiar term known as "Data Science" and why it keeps getting thrown around. Before we get into the analysis process, we will cover fundamentals like "variables" and "data management systems." Once those systems are in place and the collection process begins, we can move into one of the most common tasks of the average data scientist, cleaning data. Only clean data has the capabilities to be appropriately analyzed, which will shortly follow the cleaning process. We will cover an exciting topic and an extremely useful tool known as "Business Intelligence (BI)," and much more, including machine learning algorithms for analysis, data visualization, big data, and job opportunities.

This book was written with the aim to give you everything you need to know about these aspects of data analytics and so much more. I am truly geeked out and fascinated by the way the world of data works. So, I have taken my fascination and many years of experience as a reputable marketer (where I analyze data and use data visualizations on a quarterly basis) to provide you with a compact guide for understanding and navigating this world of wonders.

I get it. I get *you.* I was overwhelmed when I first started wading through millions of bytes of data when I began my career. I didn't know where to start and I didn't know how to make them relate or connect. I certainly did not know how to find the causation for their existence. Learning what it all meant seemed an impossibility, mainly because it was so hard to find literature at the time that simplified the processes involved.

Through the confusion, I stuck with it because I was fascinated by how it all worked and how rewarding it would be to be one of the few people who understood what it all meant. The world of data amazes me, and I sense you feel the same way. Keep that passion for data. It will serve you well and guide you through that confusion. It has, after all, guided you to opening this book and reading so far.

That passion is why the book was written - my passion for helping other people who are also intrigued by data analytics. It was written to help people who are just starting out in this field and need easy-to-understand tools at their disposal to keep from being dissuaded from pursuing data analytics. It was written to be a simple yet effective guide for anyone to gain the data literacy they need and keep from being overwhelmed by all these bytes of data generated every day. It was created to let people who love data know what career options are available and what is required to pursue those careers.

No matter the global climate. No matter what the local economy says. No matter the current issues that plague a company, data analytics is always a vital part of engineering the way forward and you can be part of the few that pave the way. You can be someone who makes a positive impact from data.. Data analytics is always here to save the day, and you can be a hero in your own right. Best yet, there is an entire culture composed of people just like you here to support you. Turn the page to start your data analytics training!

1
GETTING STARTED WITH DATA ANALYTICS

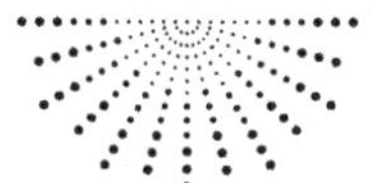

"Information is the oil of the 21st century, and analytics is the combustion engine."

— PETER SONDERGAARD

Data analytics is the broad term for turning data into insights. Formally defined, it is a network of processes and techniques focused on the analysis of raw sets of data so that concrete conclusions can be arrived at based on the information provided by that data. However, there is not one way to turn data into insights, there are many sub-disciplines that make this possible. There are three main components that make up data analytics:

Data analysis

Data analysis is a process of inspecting, cleansing, transforming, and modeling data with the goal of discovering useful information, informing conclusions, and supporting decision-making.

Data science

Data science is an interdisciplinary field that uses scientific methods, processes, algorithms and systems, to extract knowledge and insights from noisy, structured, and unstructured data and apply knowledge and actionable insights from data across a broad range of application domains

Big data

Big data is a field that treats ways to analyze, systematically extract information from, or otherwise, deal with data sets that are too large or complex to be dealt with by traditional data-processing application software.

If data analytics is the pie, then data analysis, data science, and big data are the fruit inside. You need to be familiar with each of these components no matter what direction you go in this industry.

This chapter serves as an introduction to the field of data analytics and the tools, processes, and techniques that drive its functionality.

What Exactly is Data Literacy?

I'm sure you've seen this term thrown around, including in this book. Data literacy is the ability to collect, manage, analyze, and communicate data effectively to gain better business insights, leading to better business decisions.

Processes of Data Analytics

All businesses need to partake in the practice of data analytics. This examination of raw data allows companies to develop better strategies for pushing that business toward the ultimate goal of all companies: to grow, develop, and maximize profits. To that end, when data analytics is done correctly, it helps:

- Market more effectively
- Uncover business opportunities
- Make better decisions

- Find trends to follow
- Predict actions, triggers, or events that will affect the company

These benefits are only possible if those organizations follow the steps involved in the data analytics process. These steps include:

- Collect, organize, and manage the data

Companies are collecting data every single minute of the day. More than they can process, in fact, but you can never have enough when it comes to data. Knowing your customer can be the difference between significant gains or big losses. Companies collect data in many different ways, but internet tracking, social analytics, and transactional data are more common. This uncovers everything from customer purchases, interests, location, or behavior. The data collected needs to be organized to make the analysis process as easy as possible. Proper data management and storage are essential, especially in larger companies, when amassing incredible amounts of data every day. Systems need to be in place to keep everything running smoothly.

- Clean the data

Uncleaned data is data whereby certain details overlap or are missing. Such data is not helpful as it does not provide a complete picture that allows for sound decision-making to occur. Anything that overlaps needs to be rectified, and incomplete information must be supplemented with whatever is missing. There is also the aspect of eliminating any mistakes that might have happened during the data collection and organization processes. Data can be considered clean and useful only after these processes have been done.

- Analyze the data

Understanding and engaging the bytes of information sets the foundation for dissecting this data. This process of dissection is analyzing the data. Analyzation allows for the shift of focus from collecting the data to discovering insights available from the data. Many techniques and processes can be learned to find information from large sets of data. Some include machine learning techniques like classification or clustering. The goal is to find patterns, trends, outliers, or anything else that will give you valuable information. We will cover some common techniques in chapter 8.

- Interpret and visualize the data

Data is simply that, data. Bytes of information, numbers, statistics. What does it mean? Without understanding it, there isn't much use for it. After the analysis, you will be left with insights and outliers that only some will understand at a glance. (Most likely still in a spreadsheet of data) Data visualization is how you can turn a set of numbers into an understandable presentation from which employees can take action. With this understanding, better business decisions can be made.

When these steps are followed correctly, companies can make educated decisions based on facts and not guesses. For example, companies can monitor customer behavior and preferences and ensure they continue to provide them with similar products or services to keep them happy and engaged. Similar to what Netflix does with your show suggestions or Amazon with your product suggestions.

This book will take you through the processes of data analytics and help you enhance your data literacy to strive in such an important industry.

2
WHAT EXACTLY IS DATA SCIENCE?

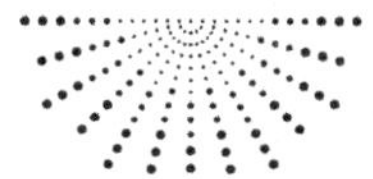

"Data science is all about asking interesting questions based on the data you have, or often the data you don't have."

— SARAH JAVIS

Many terms are being thrown around in the world of data, and data science is one of them. I'm sure some of you are wondering what this means and why you keep seeing it. Well, Data science is a field of study that uses algorithms, systems, statistics and more to extract insights from data. For reference, a data analyst usually works with structured data to solve business problems and gain insights using Python, and SQL. Well, a data scientist tends to be off in the unknown, using more advanced techniques to make predictions for the future from raw data. They could potentially set up unsupervised machine learning algorithms or predictive modeling processes (these terms will become more familiar as you read on). I like to consider a data scientist an upgraded version of a data analyst. They still analyze and work with data, just in a more advanced way. Data scientists usually work for larger companies and work with larger sets of unstructured Big Data. Let's briefly go through the main components of data science so you have a better understanding of this common term.

5 MAIN COMPONENTS OF DATA SCIENCE

There are a few basic concepts we need to understand that make up this field of study. It will also help you wrap your head around some common terms to better understand the concepts of this book. These components are as follows:

1. **Structured and Unstructured Data**

Structured data refers to organized and formatted data that is easily searchable through machine language. Examples of data items in this category include addresses, names, and dates.

There is a subset of structured data called semi-structured data. This type of data does not conform to the typical tabular structure of structured data. Still, it contains features that make it fit within a database—email databases, web pages and HTML fall under this type of data structure.

Unstructured data refers to information that is not arranged to a specific data model and cannot be stored in a traditional database. The processing of unstructured data needs a bit of human intuition and opinion. Examples of unstructured data include video clips, social media activity, audio clips and text messages.

For now, we are only skimming the surface of structured and unstructured data to understand the terminology. We will look at some examples and get a better understanding in chapter 3, data storage.

1. **Machine Learning**

As mentioned previously, machine learning is essentially algorithms that allow the processing of sets of data without human handling. These systems are driven by algorithms or rules that allow large volumes of data to be processed and refined in a uniform and structured way.

Machine learning is used to analyze patterns, make predictions, and give recommendations. We will focus more deeply on machine learning later.

1. **Statistics and Probability**

Statistics refers to the mathematical application of collecting, analyzing, interpreting, and presenting data in a numerical form. Probability speaks to the extent to which something is likely to occur. Probabilities are measured with ratios to show that extent. These applications provide insight and likelihood and thus, provide the numerical foundation that drives decision-making and strategic planning in data science. Although not necessary to master right away, there is a bonus chapter on statistics at the end of the book if you would like to understand it a bit more.

1. **Programming Languages**

Data is largely processed by computers in this day and age, and these computers speak their own unique languages. These languages include:

SQL

SQL stands for structured query language. It is a programming language used most often to manage tabular or relational databases.

This programming language is the opposite of NoSQL, which is a language that allows for the storage and processing of data that falls outside of that tabular structure.

Examples of SQL databases are Oracle, Access and Microsoft SQL server. Learning SQL is an essential skill for a data scientist.

Python

This is the most popular programming language among data scientists. Even though this is a high-level language, its popularity is attributed to its high readability and the ease with which it can be used in both large-scale and smaller projects. In other words, it is a great tool for beginners to use. One of the features that make this a beginner-friendly tool is that it is object-oriented. This means that everything created in Python is perpetrated as an object. All of these objects have different properties, making them easy to identify and operate.

Another feature that makes this easy to use is that its system uses English words and basic symbols. Users do not have to be an expert at coding languages to learn this.

It is also cost-effective as it can be integrated with other software and third-party components like API (Application Programming Interface) as well other programming languages like C++, Rust and Java. Python is also easy to integrate with existing databases like customer lists as most people and businesses are not starting from scratch when they start using this programming language. As a result of this seamless integration across so many platforms, Python can be the glue that holds it together. It is a far better alternative to attempting to piece everything together or dumping it all to use one brand's products.

Python is often used to develop websites, software, and apps in addition to conducting data analysis. If a data scientist or business is indeed starting from scratch, Python can be used to create databases. Other uses include:

- Conducting simulations
- Automating reports
- Creating predictive models
- Doing academic research

If you are a beginner to Python but want to get your feet wet quickly, here are a few things that I would advise you to learn:

Data Types

These are the classification of data items. Data types in Python include:

- Integers, which are a number classification with no maximum limit to the value of the number. These are whole numbers.
- Strings, which are lines of characters represented by single, double, or triple quotes. (NORWAY, XX777, 12/12/2024)
- Floating point numbers, which is a number classification that uses decimal points to show no maximum limit to the value of the number.

Loops and Conditionals

Despite the extreme readability of python, it's recommended that you understand what loops are (the execution of blocks of code several times) and what conditions are (the commands that tell loops when to stop repeating).

Learn How to Manipulate Data

The best way to do this is to learn how to read the data stored in the Python program. Despite the fact that this tool makes it easy for you, you will want to get down and dirty with cleaning up data, doing calculations, and doing all the other work that goes into manipulating data. Do not let the use of technology turn you into a lazy data scientist!

Although I can't make you a Python and SQL expert in this book as we have a broad array of topics to cover, it's worth investing in a program or course with hands-on projects. This is the best way to learn Python and SQL, in my opinion. There are many jobs in data, some with interchangeable skills and some with fewer entry barriers. It's necessary to assess your career goals, what skill sets are required for said goals, and then decide what is worth investing in and what isn't.

Guidelines to follow when learning python programming

Step 1: The basics

You should start by learning the basics of the language, libraries, and data structures. A great way to do this is to take an online course through Udemy or Coursera. They offer great beginner to advanced programs on many data related topics.

. . .

Step 2: Learn regular expressions in Python

You will need to use them for data cleansing, especially if you are working on text data. There are also great online courses specifically specializing in regular expressions.

Step 3: Learn Scientific libraries in Python – NumPy, SciPy, Matplotlib, and Pandas

Here is a brief introduction to the various libraries:

- Practice NumPy thoroughly, especially NumPy arrays. This will form a good foundation for things to come.
- Next, look up SciPy Tutorials. There is a lot of free content available. Find an introductory course to learn the basics and go from there.
- Finally, let us look at Pandas. Pandas provides DataFrame functionality (like R) for Python. This is also where you should spend a good time practicing. Pandas would become the most effective tool for all mid-size data analysis. Start with a short introduction, then move on to more advanced/hands-on training. Either through free content online or the many courses available. There's no shortage of data science-related content online nowadays.

Step 4: Data visualization

Learn how to create effective data visualizations, to turn your insights into valuable information. There will be more information on various programs to use in chapter 10.

Step 5: Learn Scikit-learn and machine learning

Although this is more advanced, Scikit-learn is the most useful library on python for machine learning. It's also great to go through lectures/courses with assignments attached. Supervised learning algorithms like regressions and non-supervised learning algorithms like clustering. (Which we will briefly cover later).

Step 6: Practice!

Work on a variety of different projects to expand your knowledge.

If you need a guideline on where to get started for more advanced training, Join my email list at ElizabethSClarke.com and reply to the first message with your needs. I will happily guide you in the right direction with some great free content and course suggestions.

Although this is a brief introduction, I hope it points your compass in the right direction and gets you started on your python journey.

5. Big Data

We have come to the 5th main component of data science, which is big data. The definition of big data is revealed in the name. It is data that contains a wide variety of information, coming at an increase in velocity. Big data is larger and more complex than your run-of-the-mill data. Examples include social media websites and stock exchanges. Large companies like Netflix or Meta are good examples, as they collect unfathomable amounts of data every day.

Big data consists of unstructured, structured, and semi-structured data and it is used for driving machine learning projects, data modelling, and advanced analytics applications.

We will focus more deeply on big data later in the book.

3
UNDERSTANDING VARIABLES

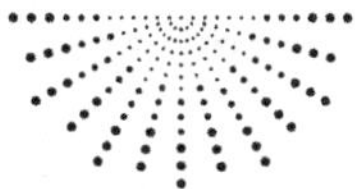

"Errors using inadequate data are much less than those using no data at all."

— CHARLES BABBAGE

In the world of data analytics, there are some fundamentals everyone must know. Variables are one of them. We know that data can be structured, unstructured, and semistructured, but if we dive deeper into the details of that data, you'll find they are made up of numerical and categorical values, which we call variables. Variables identify the data to be understood by algorithms and accessed for future analysis.

Variables can be length, time, price, diameter, date, strength, temperature, and more. Let's look at this customer order spreadsheet for reference.

Customer No.	Order No.	Order Date	Product Sku	QTY	Product Cost	Total
00865	708900	6-Feb-22	ZG011AQA	2	$49.99	$99.98
00779	708901	6-Feb-22	GH77HRU	7	$29.95	$209.65
00669	708902	6-Feb-22	ZG011AQA	3	$49.99	$149.97
00079	708903	7-Feb-22	JJ955RUR	1	$139.99	$139.99
00447	708904	7-Feb-22	JK88JJM	19	$14.50	$275.50
00125	708905	8-Feb-22	GH77HRU	6	$29.95	$179.70
00777	708906	8-Feb-22	LL65LLK	17	$19.95	$339.15

FIGURE 3.1 Everything in this table is considered a variable

Independent and Dependent Variables

As we dove into the details of data to discover it is made up of variables, you'll learn they are either independent or dependent if you dive even deeper. Independent variables (Known as X) are responsible for determining the value of the dependent variables (Known as y). If you're analyzing a student's average test score (dependant variable), the result is determined by how much the person studies (independent variable). Understanding the relationships between the variables allows you to make desired changes and predict certain outcomes. As we go further into data science, you'll learn that this is the basic model for machine learning and algorithms. The independent variable is considered the "Input," and the dependant variable the "Output." Machines learn the relationship between these two and run "models" to predict future outputs.

Types of Variables

There are four main types of variables in data analytics that one must be familiar with.

1. Categorical
2. Numerical
3. Date/Time
4. Boolean

Categorical Variables

Categorical Variables can be divided into two main subcategories:

1. Ordinal
2. Nominal

As they sound, ordinal variables have a natural categorical order to them. Examples of ordinal variables would be income level (40-70k, over 100k) rating (satisfactory, good, great), days of the week, or anything alike. Nominal variables, however, are the opposite, with no order associated with them. This could be gender, city names, operating systems, zip codes, eye color, etc. Although categorical variables are strings of letters, they can sometimes be expressed as a number for the purpose of statistics. Still, these numbers won't have the same meaning as a numerical value. E.g., medicine 1, medicine 2, zipcodes, etc.

Numerical Variables

As categorical variables are divided into two subcategories, numerical variables do the same. They are divided into:

1. Discrete
2. Continuous

Discrete numerical variables contain only a discrete quantity known as integers. This would be a whole number (1, 11, 111). Examples include the number of houses someone owns, the number of purchases from a customer, or the number of products a company sells. Continuous variables, however, fill in the void. Showcasing continuous quantities or fractional quantities. E.g., Customer transactions ($725.67) or average time customers spend on a website (14.76 seconds).

Quick Tip: "Categorical" and "date/time" variables are generally categorized as "Discrete" values.

Date/Time

Date/time variables are relatively simple. They mark the date or time. Examples would be transaction history (Date of order), clock in time of an employee, birthdates, etc.

Boolean Variables

A boolean variable is a variable that can be 1 of 2 outcomes (0/1, true/false, yes/no)

They can often be overlapped with categorical variables. For example, if you're determining who owns which vehicle, you could categorize Audi as (0) and Lexus as (1), as long as you compare only two values. This can also make it easier for algorithms to analyze large data sets.

Having a general understanding of variables will give you a strong foundation that will be necessary for many data-related tasks you may come across.

4
DATA COLLECTION

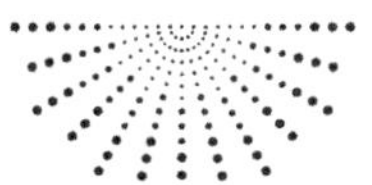

"With data collection 'The sooner the better' is always the best answer."

— MARISSA MAYER

Hoarding.

This sounds like an unpleasant word to my ear. That might be because it incites an image of junk threatening to bury anyone who dares to walk by it. The word incites the same image in my head regarding data collection - one where the data analyst mentally gets buried by tons of information. Not every single byte of information is useful for reaching conclusive insights. That is the data collection process needs to be approached in a way that makes the data professionals' job more accessible rather than one where they will need help to become unburied.

The Goal of Data Collection

There needs to be an end goal for the collection process. This can be decided at the analyst level before infiltrating some databases or at a big business level when they set up data management systems to encapsulate customer information. To determine that end goal, you need to ask yourself a few questions. Answering these questions will help define what your goal for data collection is. Such questions include:

- What is the current situation and where is it happening?
- Why is this situation occurring?
- What is the data going to be used for?
- Why is it being collected?
- How will it be useful?
- Whom will it be useful to?

Answering these questions will allow the development of a plan of attack for approaching the data collection to support these questions. It allows for awareness of the problem or opportunity. It defines that problem or opportunity instead of having a vague or obscure notion of why you engage in this process. To be clear, a problem and an opportunity have something in common, and that is they represent the difference between the current situation and desired outcome. You would like to move from point A to point B. Data collection is the vessel that moves you between these points. But first, there needs to be a brainstorming session that presents possible routes for moving between these two points. Only after this brainstorming session occurs can you then move on to how this vessel will be designed. The design of this vessel is the particular method of data collection that will be used. This is why Netflix collects data such as time spent watching a show, so they know to recommend more of what you are actually watching, not recommendations based on shows you tried out but didn't like. Collecting the right data is important.

Different Types of Data Collection

Data collection is not a one size fits all kind of deal. What might be appropriate in one instance might lead to a headache in another instance. For example, falling back on your vessel analogy, let's say you want to take a leisurely boat ride across a pond, a cargo ship will not be suitable. It might even destroy the setting because of its size and power. However, a rowboat will certainly be more effective in creating the end goal which is a relaxing ride.

The same applies to data collection. The method of collection needs to align with the goal of its collection. The first step in choosing the right method of data collection is to know what the options are. Let's discuss these options now.

There are two main forms of data collection. They are:

- Primary data collection
- Secondary data collection

Primary Data Collection

Let's look at primary data collection first. This type of data collection is the one where the data is collected directly from the source about which that data is being developed. There are two types of primary data collection methods. They are:

- Qualitative research method
- Quantitative research method

The qualitative research method measures the intangible components of the data gathered. Such tangible items include feelings and sentiments. There are no figures included in this data collection method, so this method is developed around descriptions instead of numeric values.

An example of qualitative data collection is a customer's review after buying a product. This customer might say they loved, hated, or simply had a satisfactory experience using the product. As a result, the data collected is not easily measured; there is no real measure of a person's feelings toward the product.

So how is qualitative data useful?

The answer to this is that this kind of data is great for finding the causation of the data received. The customer is likely not to express only their feelings about the product but also why they feel that way.

Where qualitative data falls short, quantitative data picks up the slack. Quantitative data are measurable items given in figures, numbers, and quantities. The quantitative aspect would be the customer's product rating (e.g., 4 stars). Other quantitative data items will be how long this customer spent on the website if this shopping experience happened on an e-commerce store, how many other customers have also bought this product and how the product scores compared to similar products.

Qualitative data is excellent so you can uncover information about the customer. In contrast, the measurable qualities provided by quantitative data allow for gaining an objective insight into which reliable decision-making can be done. Quantitative and qualitative data go hand in hand. Quantitative data sets the foundation with figures and other measurable items, which is supplemented with the why these measures exist with qualitative data. As should be noted, both of these types of data are collected directly from the source. The customer is a direct source of information about their feelings about the product purchased. The website analytics of the e-commerce store is a direct source of information about visitor behavior.

Secondary Data

Secondary data is qualitative or quantitative data previously gathered by another person, institution, or organization, in the past, usually for a different purpose, such as reporting or research, which will most likely be kept in a database that you can access. If you need to gather secondary data, there are some things you need to consider.

1. Evaluating and stating the purpose of getting this supportive data. There needs to be a clearly stated understanding of why the collection of this data is being pursued. This prevents data hoarding and gives clear direction in the collection process.

2. The development of a data design plan. This plan needs to include:

- Where the data will be sourced.
- The type of data that will be sourced, quantitative or qualitative.
- The method by which the data will be collected.
- The tools that will be used for the collection.
- How the collected data will be analyzed.

3. The development of research questions will validate the secondary data collected. This step is necessary for authenticating the data collected as relevant, reputable, and unbiased.

4. Locating the secondary data. With the design plan and research questions in hand, you can then identify the secondary data. This location is vital as only reputable sources need to be used. Also, it needs to be clear whether or not the data source is quantitative, qualitative, or both.

5. Evaluation of the secondary data collected. The stage serves to validate the data gathered to note whether or not it has fulfilled its intended purpose.

Data Collection Methodologies

Whether the data type is primary or secondary, there are a few standard methods by which data is collected. It is important first to understand the systems in place that are built to manage large quantities of data that companies collect everyday. A data architect's primary role is to create blueprints for data management systems. After they assess a company's data sources (internal and external), architects put together a plan that effectively integrates, centralizes, protects and ultimately maintains the system. Their goal is to allow employees to access crucial company information with ease. Effective data management follows a particular pathway. Different businesses and organizations have their own particular needs and need to cater that pathway to reach their goals, but a general pathway looks like this:

The data architecture

The data architecture describes the collection, organization, integration and storage plan. It is introduced at the beginning of the data analysis process as it sets the stage for everything else that will follow. Just like you will not build the foundation or the roof of a building without the architectural plan in place, the same applies to data. The architecture sets a precedent for everything else.

The data model

This describes how the structure of a database will be modeled. Data models define how the data relate to one other, how it processes and where it gets stored within the system.

The data integration system

Data integration is how data from all different business systems and formats get combined into a single unified view. This then gets stored in a data warehouse.

The quality check system

The quality check identifies and removes inconsistencies and errors in the data that have been collected. This part of the system will also ensure that no information is missing, and if this is found, that information will be promptly sourced. This pathway of the data management process activates cleanup tasks.

The data governance system

The governance system is the pathway that sets the rules that will guide the entire analysis process management. It ensures that consistency remains from start to finish and that the parameters of the data gathering, collection, integration and storage processes are obeyed. It also determines who has authority and control of the data and its use. As a data scientist or data analyst, you will simply be gaining access to this data to make sense of it.

The process usually starts with the data architect designing the blueprint for the system. It then moves to the data engineer, which brings the blueprints to life. For the data scientists and analysts to access this data, the data engineers move and transform it into data "pipelines" that get the data to the scientists and analysts. Data pipelines transfer data between a source system and a target repository.

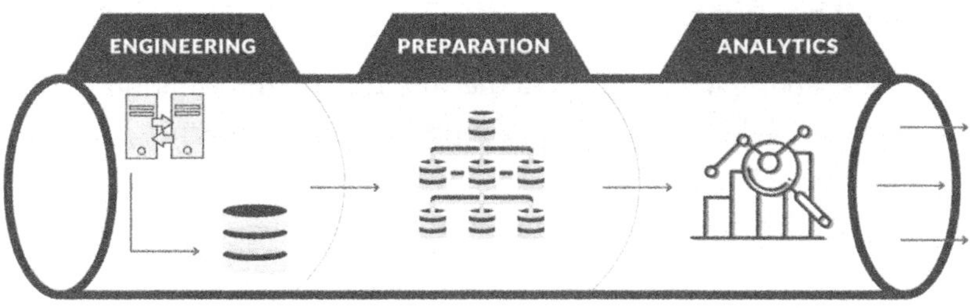

FIGURE 4.1

Now that we understand the systems that allow companies to keep track of their data, how are they collecting it? Some data collection methods include:

Online Forms and Questionnaires

Widely used because it is so effective at collecting both quantitative and qualitative data, forms and questionnaires facilitate the collection of data by asking questions in an effort to gain key insights through unbiased answers. Examples of tools used in this methodology of data collection are Google Forms and Type-form. It is more typical to see closed-ended questions used in forms and questionnaires as this places parameters around the data collected. For example, if a form asks *How satisfied are you with the product?* The possible answers for this include may include:

1. Very satisfied
2. Satisfied
3. Somewhat satisfied
4. Dissatisfied

This prevents the collection of data that is irrelevant to the intended purpose of gathering that set of data. This also limits the cleanup process necessary for making this data usable.

Internet Tracking

If we think about it too deeply, the amount of information gathered about everyone who uses devices connected to the internet is alarming. Someone's social media activities, the websites they frequent most often and the type of content they enjoy watching and reading are just a few of the data points accumulated as we enjoy using them.

This data is useful to us in many contexts as it allows more relevant content to come up on our social media feeds and as the recommended items on many of our most loved internet activities. It is also an excellent avenue for companies to understand individual and consumer needs. These companies can gather this data using tools known as cookies and tracking pixels. It should be noted that you do have the option to disable at least some of the functionalities of such tools in your internet browsers.

Web-Based Marketing Analytics

Marketing without tracking the reactions of the intended consumer is highly ineffective as it does not allow for fine-tuning the processes to better reach and entice the target market. In the day and age that we live in, billboards and posters are not the only avenues for reaching target markets and often they are not the most efficient for getting the audience to act as desired. Web-based marketing techniques like the use of social media are far more efficient. Selling a product to a consumer or getting a person to sign up for a newsletter is just one click away.

As a result of this, there is a plethora of data that can be gathered based on consumer behavior and how they respond to particular web-based marketing techniques. Such data includes how frequently a specific ad gets clicked on, the times of day it's viewed, regions where it gets most visibility and how long the viewer engages with the ad.

The great thing is that social media platforms and personal web development allow you to easily access this information with an analytics feature. As easy as can be, the data, which is more often quantitative, is right there at the data professional's fingertips.

Social Media Monitoring

Social media is a major part of the marketing focus of any company in this digital day and age. Qualitative data is available in statistical, percentages and numeric forms. They provide data on how often content is engaged with. From these metrics tailored marketing, consumer retention, and audience outreach strategies can be developed to ensure higher conversions.

Qualitative data can also be derived from comments and remarks.

Transactional Data

Transactional data can benefit a company as it tells them exactly what people buy. This information can be used for email campaigns so 1:1 outreach is more effective with targeted discounts. It can also determine a campaign's success, your best and worst customers and everything in between. This makes targeting lookalike customers easier, which is essential to creating loyal customers, not one-time buyers.

Collecting consumer data helps a wide range of companies better understand their customers to provide better services for those customers. Now that we've collected the data, I think it's time we understand how to store it.

5
DATA STORAGE

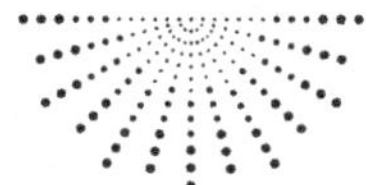

"Data that is loved tends to survive."

— KURT BOLLACKER

Data is comparable to having gold in the business world. This is why so much of it is collected; because every byte of it has the potential to fatten up many bank accounts and continue to do so for decades and centuries after it was collected. Therefore, just like you would not leave a nugget of gold just sitting out in the open for anyone to potentially pick up, businesses also should not leave data where anyone can grab it and disappear with it.

Storage is one of the first steps that needs urgent consideration when it comes to data security. Before we get that, though, let's get into a formal definition of data storage. Data storage is the physical means used to hold data to remain accessible when needed.

Efficient data storage gives a healthy balance between security and accessibility. It does no good to data analysts and other business professionals who use this data if they feel like they have to jump through hoops just to access it. Before we find out about storage methods, we must first understand the three main categories of data and their characteristics. These 3 are Unstructured, Semi-Structured, and Structured data.

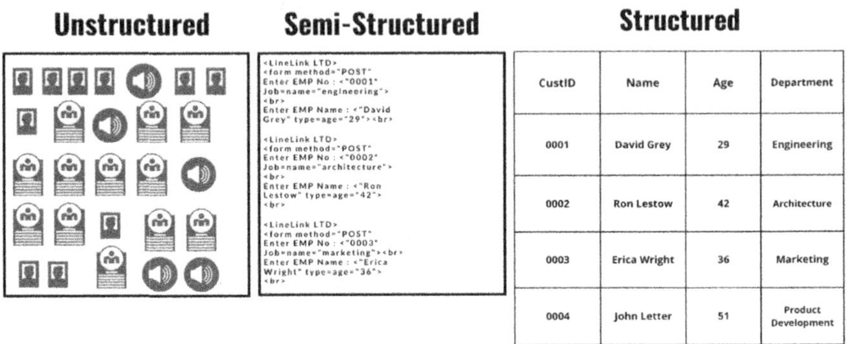

CustID	Name	Age	Department
0001	David Grey	29	Engineering
0002	Ron Lestow	42	Architecture
0003	Erica Wright	36	Marketing
0004	John Letter	51	Product Development

FIGURE 5.0

Unstructured Data

Unstructured data is exactly how it sounds, data that is in multiple formats and has no specific organization or structure to it. Unstructured data is essentially any data that doesn't fit nicely into a spreadsheet. Anywhere from videos clips to pdfs, images and audio files. Unstructured data is challenging for a computer to make sense of. This is why data scientists will often use more advanced techniques and even AI (Artificial intelligence) to organize and make sense of this data. Unstructured data can be stored in applications such as NoSQL. This database is non-tabular and therefore perfect for holding this type of data. A non-tabular or non-relational database is a database that does not use standard columns and rows. It uses a storage model with specific requirements based on the data being stored. Another example of this would be a data lake.

Unstructured data makes up 80% of all data. Although difficult to work with, unstructured data is widespread and essential to businesses. New processes and techniques are being implemented consistently to work with this type of data efficiently.

Semi-Structured Data

Semi-structured data falls right in the middle. It's not as organized as structured data but isn't as chaotic as unstructured data. It doesn't entirely obey the tabular structure of databases the same way structured data does. Still, it does contain tags or other markers to separate essential elements and categorize the information roughly. An example could be data in an HTML format. The information is there, but it is not in as organized of a format as it should be and is not quite readable by algorithms. It needs some slight processing.

Structured Data

Structured data refers to organized and formatted data easily searchable through machine language (algorithms , etc). A well-organized excel spreadsheet is a great example. The reason structured data is so valuable to data professionals is they can easily use it for data visualizations, data analytics and machine learning models without any extensive preprocessing. It is often in tabular form, storing it in tables and rows where you can update multiple rows simultaneously. This can be useful for removing commas or anything that isn't easily read by machine learning algorithms. It also proves helpful when you want to designate a specific feature, such as people living in a particular area or country. You can filter out anyone who doesn't meet your desired requirements. Although structured data is desired, it only makes up about 20% of all data.

TYPES OF DATA STORAGE

Relational Database

A relational database organizes structured data into tables linked based on pre-defined relationships. The tables will be linked using keys. A primary key will identify each row. This key can be added to another table, making it a foreign key. The relationships between the primary key and foreign key form the basis of how the database works. This allows you to retrieve data from multiple tables with a single query (a query is a request for data or information from a database table or combination of tables.) It can be advantageous when companies want to understand better relationships among data and gain valuable insights that lead to better decision-making.

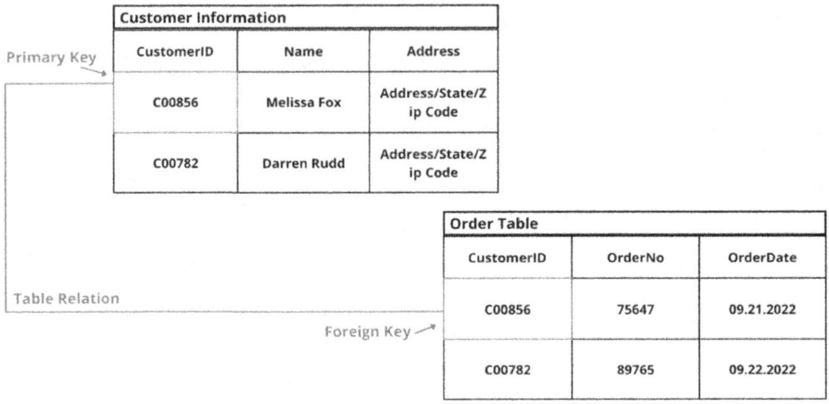

Customer Information

CustomerID	Name	Address
C00856	Melissa Fox	Address/State/Zip Code
C00782	Darren Rudd	Address/State/Zip Code

Primary Key

Table Relation

Foreign Key

Order Table

CustomerID	OrderNo	OrderDate
C00856	75647	09.21.2022
C00782	89765	09.22.2022

FIGURE 5.1

A great example would be company transactional data. There may be a table with customer information and separate tables with different transactions for different products. This could look something like a customer table (with customer information), orders table (with customer orders), and product tables (separating the different products.) Your query can then pull information from the separate tables simultaneously based on the specific information required. Customer 001, order #7754, product X.

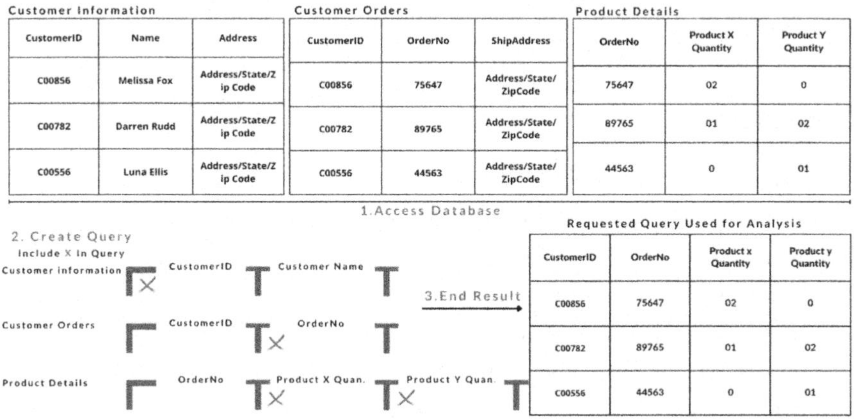

Customer Information

CustomerID	Name	Address
C00856	Melissa Fox	Address/State/Zip Code
C00782	Darren Rudd	Address/State/Zip Code
C00556	Luna Ellis	Address/State/Zip Code

Customer Orders

CustomerID	OrderNo	ShipAddress
C00856	75647	Address/State/ZipCode
C00782	89765	Address/State/ZipCode
C00556	44563	Address/State/ZipCode

Product Details

OrderNo	Product X Quantity	Product Y Quantity
75647	02	0
89765	01	02
44563	0	01

1.Access Database

2. Create Query
Include X In Query
Customer information: CustomerID, Customer Name
Customer Orders: CustomerID, OrderNo
Product Details: OrderNo, Product X Quan., Product Y Quan.

3.End Result

Requested Query Used for Analysis

CustomerID	OrderNo	Product x Quantity	Product y Quantity
C00856	75647	02	0
C00782	89765	01	02
C00556	44563	0	01

FIGURE 5.2 Relational database query example

Hierarchical Database

This database management system is so named because it resembles the traditional hierarchy where items are ranked above others. There is a primary source of data called a parent or owner in the data-related context. It forms one-to-many relationships with other data sources that will be integrated into this data management system. As a result, all other data items integrated into this architecture will be related to the parent in some way or the other.

This system is used in very specific instances. For example, data may need to be connected and thus, analyzed about sea creatures. Sea creatures would be the parent data item, and other data items like saltwater and freshwater would be linked to the parent. Saltwater and freshwater would both have items linked underneath them. This would ultimately create a structure that looks like a tree. This differs from relational databases because relational database tables must be manually connected using keys, while hierarchical is all connected.

The data items need to be defined prior to gathering information for this system to work. Being at the top of this system, the parent and the items directly linked to the parent are easy to access and update.

The system has a few downsides. Relationships other than that with their parents are not allowed. Also, the lower down items come on the system, the harder they are to access or update. The fact that there can only be one parent can also serve as a disadvantage.

Network Database

This system is more flexible than a hierarchy model, even though there are similarities between the two systems. The network system has a tree-like formation, but multiple parents can be integrated instead of just a single parent. Also, many-to-many relationships are allowed in such a system. This makes the system easier to navigate as information is easy to look up, no matter where it is linked or the type of relationship to other items.

The downside to using this type of system is the same thing that makes it beautiful. There are so many relationships that can be formed in multiple directions, which causes complexity to arise. As such, updates are tricky to perform as manipulating one data point can lead to changes across the board.

Data Warehouses

A data warehouse is a relational database solely meant to perform queries and analyses. They often contain large amounts of historical data. It is stored in an extract, transform, and load process (ETL). This means information is extracted from its origin, transformed into high-quality data, then loaded into the warehouse ready for analysis. Data warehouses are ideal for online analytical processing (OLAP), allowing users to perform multi-dimensional analysis on high volumes of data.

Data Lakes

Data lakes are another way to store unstructured data. While data warehouses are usually built on relational databases and only comprise of structured data, data lakes are generally home to a vast amount of structured, semi-structured, and unstructured data. Data lakes can be created in the cloud or on-premise with in-house data storage capabilities. Typically, data warehouses store data in hierarchical dimensions and tables, while a data lake uses a flat architecture to store data, mainly in files or object storage.

Cloud Data Storage

Small and medium-sized businesses and organizations often use this method of data storage because of its inexpensive nature. No investment in expensive equipment is necessary as the data is stored on a cloud service. A cloud service is a solution that provides a remote network of servers hosted on the internet for the intended purpose of storing, managing, and processing data. The servers used in this type of data storage are not owned or managed by the data owners. Instead, they belong to the company that provides the cloud service. Because the data owners have handed over full responsibility of data storage to another entity, the cost for storing that data becomes much less. None of the equipment, special software, housing, or other infrastructure needs to be purchased. These benefits come at a predictable premium that the data owner is obliged to pay to continue using the service.

There are other benefits apart from the lowered cost of using a cloud service. One of these is that the solution is quite easily scalable. If the business or organization needs more storage space, it is simply a matter of paying an increased premium or switching service providers.

No matter the type of data storage or storage devices used, the importance of data storage remains and one needs to be picked. Luckily, the future for data storage is bright as demand grows in keeping with the growth of data that is always being created. After all, it is expected that the digital data created by businesses and organizations all around this green and blue ball that we live on will exceed 160 zettabytes. The capacity to store and manage this data needs to be in place before that time arrives. Who knows? Maybe, in the future, there may be an option that does not mean having to choose between cost, security, or smooth authorized accessibility to stored data.

6

CLEANING YOUR DATA

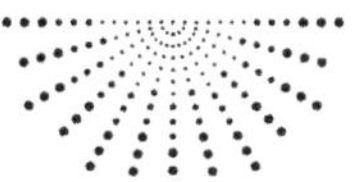

"No data is clean, but most is useful."

— DEAN ABBOTT

The results you gain from using data are only as good as the quality of data that you use in the pursuit of achieving your goal. If your data metaphorically resembles a dump site, you will get garbage results. On the other hand, if you use high quality data, your result will also favor that characteristic. Good data always outweighs fancy algorithms.

Think of it as keeping up our health, with a little exercise, a clean diet, plenty of water, you'll be functioning great. Data needs to be treated with the same determination to keep up its good health. This chapter is about showing you how to get off on the right foot so that you not only begin the data sourcing process in a way that allows for sourcing as many bytes of clean data as possible. It also depicts how you can take data that has already been through the wringer and bring it up to that pristine quality. Good quality data equals good-quality decision-making, after all.

What is Data Cleaning?

No data gathering procedure produces data that is 100% clean. The more data being collected or sourced, the higher percentage of data that will need to be put through the cleaning cycle. This is why it is important to double-check and triple-check data before using it. This checking process is also called data cleaning.

Data cleaning is a process that entails procedures that correct or remove corrupt, mislabeled, poorly formatted, duplicate, or incomplete data items within the data set as a whole. Data cleaning might seem boring to some, but don't be fooled. Better data quality means better insights, better decisions, more profits, and more promotions for the one managing the data.

The higher the quality of the data, the more valuable it becomes. Making decisions based on poor quality data typically leads to an unfavorable outcome. The last thing you want is for a group of executives to point out your analysis flaws because you didn't clean the data correctly. Or even worse, they trust you and make crucial decisions based on your discovery that may be slightly off. A very costly mistake you don't want to be a part of.

However, decision-making grounded on good quality data more than likely leads to increased productivity, faster results, more efficient operations, and access to greater resources, which are all conditions that allow businesses and organizations to thrive.

This leads to the benefits of this high-quality data:

- Better informed decision-making.
- Boosts results and revenue
- Saves money
- Saves time and increases productivity
- Gives companies a competitive advantage

The 6 Characteristics of Good Data

How are you supposed to clean your data if you don't know what good data looks like? Understanding The 6 characteristics of good data is crucial, let's go through them:

Accuracy and Precision

The first characteristic of good data is that it needs to be accurate and precise and as close to true values as possible. This means ensuring the sources are credible if you're sourcing secondary data and ensuring the data your company has collected is accurate based on the parameters set.

Legitimacy and Validity

Remember, there are parameters set during the data collection process so that only data that falls within those confines are collected. Clean data adheres to these rules and ensures that the information is valid for use and achieving the ultimate goal of collecting that data. For example, if there are parameters for collecting data about a particular bee species, including the bees' size, color and flying habits within a certain area. Then including information about a separate bee species in that area would be invalid and thus hinder achieving the goal of collecting that data.

It is also essential to consider how the data obey these constraints and rules. This is to limit the type of data that can go into a table to ensure the values are accurate and consistent. Constraints can be column level or table level. Some constraints are:

- **Unique Constraint:** All values in a column or field are different across a dataset.
- **Mandatory Constraint:** Specific columns cannot be empty
- **Set-Membership Constraints:** Column values must be enum values. E.g., Predefined constants such as NORTH, SOUTH, EAST, or WEST.
- **Range Constraints:** Dates and numbers should generally fall within a specified range.

- **Data-Type Constraints:** Values must be of a particular data type. E.g., numeric, date.
- **Expression Patterns:** Text that must be a specific pattern, e.g., date formats, may be required to be mm/dd/yyyy
- **Foreign Key:** This enforces referential integrity. If a column value X refers to column value Y, then column value Y must exist—reference *relational databases* in the previous chapter for a refresher on keys.

Making sure your data confines to these parameters ensures that it can be accessed properly and run through algorithms without errors.

Reliability and Consistency

In a perfect world, data would be collected from one source so that time and effort would be conserved and so that the results would be consistent across the board. However, we do not live in a perfect world and data often needs to be collected from different sources to gain a complete picture. As a result, there need to be systems in place to ensure that data collected from differing sources do not conflict with each other. For example, having data collected in different measurements such as inches vs centimeters can lead to inconsistent results. Cleaner data does not have inconsistencies.

Timeliness and Relevance

The time at which data is collected is also relevant to how useful it is and therefore, how clean it is. For example, if the information is being collected about current fashion trends, collecting data about the future wants of consumers can lead to having information that is not valid. Data needs to be collected at the right time to ensure proper usefulness.

Completeness and Comprehensiveness

If you thought using incorrect information was bad, you have never encountered the situation of using incomplete data. Having unfilled fields leads to a skewed view of what this data conveys. As a result, decision-making is flawed. A lot of the time, the algorithms you use will cause an error and won't be able to analyze data with missing values.

Granularity and Uniqueness

The purpose of the collection of data will determine how detailed it needs to be. However, having too much detail or too little detail can lead to problems of confusion and inaccuracy. Clean data has the appropriate level of depth for the intended purpose.

How to Clean Data (Data Scrubbing)

Let's say that your data does not have these 6 qualities. Not all is lost. Inaccurate, incomplete, and inconsistent data can be cleaned using the following steps:

Remove Duplicate or Irrelevant Observations

This step involves removing data items that do not fall within the parameters set for the data collected as well as items that are duplicated across the set. Irrelevant and duplicate items are often a problem faced when data is collected from multiple sources. Taking the time to remove these duplicate or irrelevant items saves data analysts time and energy during the analysis process. Before removing duplicates, always copy your original data to another worksheet, so you don't accidentally delete important insights.

To filter for unique values in Excel: Click Data > Sort & Filter > Advanced

To remove duplicates in Excel: Click Data > Remove Duplicates, and then Under Columns, check or uncheck the columns where you want to remove the duplicates. In some instances, you might need all values. E.g., there might be $0.00 in sales for multiple products in February. Although duplicates are in the column, you wouldn't want to remove them as they are all relevant information to the analysis.

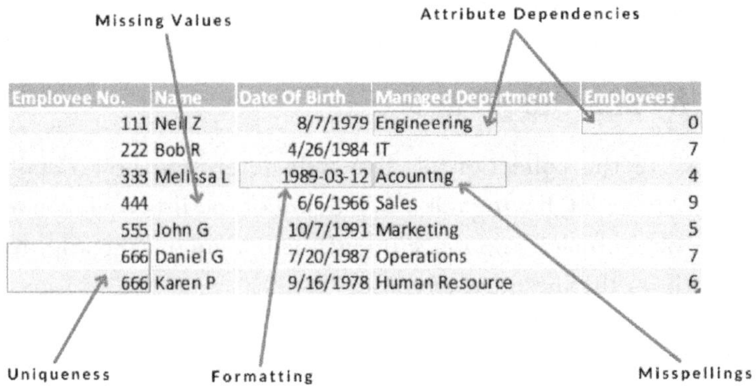

Employee No.	Name	Date Of Birth	Managed Department	Employees
111	Neil Z	8/7/1979	Engineering	0
222	Bob R	4/26/1984	IT	7
333	Melissa L	1989-03-12	Acountng	4
444		6/6/1966	Sales	9
555	John G	10/7/1991	Marketing	5
666	Daniel G	7/20/1987	Operations	7
666	Karen P	9/16/1978	Human Resource	6

FIGURE 6.1

Syntax Errors

Syntax: "the arrangement of words and phrases to create well-formed sentences in a language."

A syntax error is an error in the syntax of a sequence of characters, some examples are:

- **Typos:** A string (any series of characters that are interpreted literally by a script, e.g., "Norway," "66HKLZ8") can usually have many different abbreviations that are all necessarily correct but will cause an error if not formatted to be the same. E.g.,

Gender:

Male

M

Female

Fem.

F

- **Pad Strings:** Strings are generally padded in some way or the other. E.g., numerical codes usually need to be the same number of digits, so 488 would be 000488, if the string has six digits.
- **Remove spaces:** Remove unwanted spaces " November " > "November"

Structural Errors

Not only are you spotting the typos, but ensuring each value is in a standardized format.

This includes:

- ensuring the values are either upper or lowercase in all strings.
- Make sure measurement units for numerical values stay consistent (cm to inches, etc.)
- Ensure dates are in the correct format based on company specifications and location (the US will have a different format than Europe.) To simplify, just keep everything consistent.

Filter Unwanted Outliers

An outlier is a data item that differs from the rest of the set. More often than not, an outlier is a one-time observation that does not fit particularly well with the rest of the data set. Of course, there are times when this one-off observation is valid, but if it is not valid for achieving the goal of the data collection, it needs to be removed so that it does not impede the analysis process. Remember though that outliers are not necessarily incorrect so there needs to be a thorough consideration process as to whether or not the outlier should be kept or removed.

A simple way to find outliers is through data visualization. Once the data becomes visual, it will be evident if any points are out of place. Some effective visualizations to use:

Box plot: A box plot defines outliers as a data point located outside the whiskers of the box plot. It sets parameters based on the data and considers anything over or under the determined values, an outlier, making it very easy to spot them (we will learn more about the characteristics of a box plot in Chapter 10.)

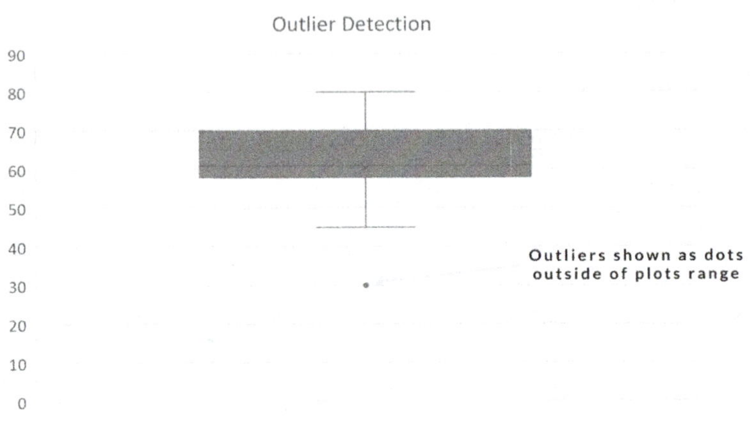

FIGURE 6.2 Outlier detection with a box plot

Scatter plot: Scatter plots can also be useful to spot outliers. Keep in mind that scatter plots can also make it a bit more challenging to distinguish what is an outlier and what is just a high value, so make sure you double-check specific points so you're not removing key values.

There are some more advanced ways to remove outliers, such as interquartile ranges or standard deviation, but these methods are a bit out of reach for this book. Feel free to look into them if you get the chance.

Handle Missing Data

Remember that having incomplete data sets is just as bad or even worse than having incorrect data. This needs to be corrected immediately, and there are three options for doing so.

The first option is to simply discard data items that have missing values. However, this needs to be done mindfully as this may create holes in your data set as a whole. So, ensure that the data item is unnecessary for the analysis process before discarding it.

The second option is to conduct further data collection to input the missing values.

The third option is to flag it for the algorithm to know about. The missing value might have significance to your analysis. Do this with a "0" for numeric values or "missing" for categorical data. E.g., the same question in a given survey could have been skipped by multiple candidates. Why was it skipped?

It is essential to note the terminology used for incomplete values to correct them. E.g., Values like "0", "NA", "Null", "Not applicable", or "None", can all mean the same thing. The value is missing.

Validation

The final step of the clean-up process is to indeed ensure that the data is valid for use. This involves asking a few questions that need to be ticked off before sending this data for analysis. These questions include:

- Is this data logically sound?
- Does the data follow the rules set by the parameters in the initial collection process?
- Does the data bring any insight to light?
- Does the data support achieving the ultimate goal for its collection?
- Are there any trends developed from the data collected?

If the answer to any of these questions is not satisfactory then you need to restart the clean-up process. You need to do so until the data achieves the appropriate cleanliness that is fit for its use in the data's analysis.

Data Transformation Techniques

After the data is clean, you can do a few things to make the data more readable for algorithms and analysis to gain more information. These include:

data binning/bucketing. Binning is used to reduce the effects of minor observational errors. It is a way to group data into smaller variables such as "bins" to be understood more effectively by algorithms and analysis. An example of this would be compiling ages into categories such as "10-20, 21-30, 31-40." Another example would be changing dates into desired categories such as "90s, 80s, 70s" or "March, April, May."

Name	Date Of Birth
Neil Z	8/7/1979
Bob R	4/26/1984
Melissa L	3/12/1989
Alex M	6/6/1966
John G	10/7/1991
Daniel G	7/20/1987
Karen P	9/16/1978

→

Name	Date Of Birth
Neil Z	70's
Bob R	80's
Melissa L	80's
Alex M	60's
John G	90's
Daniel G	80's
Karen P	70's

FIGURE 6.3

Indicator Variables: This transforms categorical data into boolean values. For example, we can transform Male and Female into "0" and "1". This can be read easier by algorithms.

Name	Gender
Neil Z	M
Bob R	M
Melissa L	F
Alex M	F
John G	M
Daniel G	M
Karen P	F

Name	Is Female?
Neil Z	0
Bob R	0
Melissa L	1
Alex M	1
John G	0
Daniel G	0
Karen P	1

FIGURE 6.4

Grouping Outliers: When you have a variety of outliers, you can categorize them as one. Such as "Others" which makes for less clutter and cleaner analysis.

Name	Country		Name	Country
Neil Z	United States	→	Neil Z	United States
Bob R	United States		Bob R	United States
Melissa L	United States	→	Melissa L	United States
Alex M	United States		Alex M	United States
John G	United States	→	John G	United States
Daniel G	United Kingdom		Daniel G	Other
Karen P	Canada	→	Karen P	Other

FIGURE 6.5

TOP 7 DATA CLEANING TOOLS

Cleaning data can be a tedious process. Many tools exist in this day and age to help you remove inconsistencies and inaccuracies as well as fill in incomplete items. An entire book can be written on this, but I will give you a brief rundown of some of the most popular and efficient data cleaning tools. Feel free to research some on your own and expand your knowledge. I also recommend learning SQL and Python, as they are essential for data cleaning and data analytics in general. Most business professionals will work in Excel, which is also capable of cleaning data. Some other applications include:

OpenRefine

Formerly going by GoogleRefine, this powerful data cleaning software allows you to transform data from one format into another and clean the data. Some of the advantages of using this particular software are that it is open source and free to use, which translates into zero cost to you and constant updates by developers to make the software better. It also allows for sharing and collaborating during the process.

Trifacta Wrangler

This is a cloud-based platform that allows for data cleaning—because of this, sharing and collaborating during the clean-up process is easy. Being a cloud platform makes easy access for multiple people and fast work for larger projects. However, this does come at a cost, as the platform is not free to use.

Winpure Clean and Match

This software, like OpenRefine, boasts features like enhancing data quality by de-duplication, matching items to ensure consistency and cleansing information. It is also user-friendly without a steep learning curve. Unlike OpenRefine, though, its robust features come at a cost.

TIBCO Clarity

This tool comes with additional features like data collection and data profiling. This could be the solution for you if you want more out of your data cleaning tool apart from its cleaning features.

Melissa Clean Suite

This data cleaning tool claims to fight "dirty data" by verifying, correcting, amending and improving the consistency of data records. This cleaning tool is created to help sales teams and best serve customer relationship management (CRM) information.

IBM Infosphere

This highly robust tool is especially useful for cleaning heterogeneous data. Heterogeneous data are records that are highly variable in format and structure. This makes it highly probable that there will be incomplete items, duplication and inaccuracy. Therefore, if you have a high volume of data collected from several sources, this just might be the tool for you.

Data Ladder

This data cleaning tool is most suitable for larger businesses and IT users with larger volumes of data that need to be cleaned.

Excel

If you're like many business professionals and find yourself in Excel daily, a lot of your data cleaning needs can be filled within the software. Familiarizing yourself with the relevant commands will make it that much easier. Not everyone needs to access large databases and sift through terabytes of data. Assessing your day-to-day needs is essential to finding the most efficient process for your needs.

As I mentioned before, all of these data cleaning tools are great in their own right. I would recommend that you do a bit further research on each one - and others - to find which one best suits your criteria and will help you accomplish your specific goals.

7
ANALYZING DATA

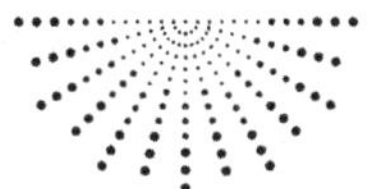

"Data is a tool for enhancing intuition."

— HILARY MASON

Your data is now squeaky clean. So, what do you do with it now? You use it to come up with conclusions that will align with your goals. Think of any lightbulb moment and you will know what I mean. But how does this happen? This chapter is the explanation that shows how data is used to gain insights.

Data is made to be presented to others. There would be no point to its collection if that was not true. The issue that arises is that it needs to be translated to most audiences for that purpose to come to fruition. That translation comes in the form of charts and graphs called data visualization. Data visualizations build a story so that audience can have a narrative to anchor them to what the data is conveying. Remember that lines of values and raw data generally incite headaches, but when that data is simplified with lines on a graph or sections of a bar chart, head-nodding to indicate understanding is more commonplace.

However, to meet that ultimatum of presentation, the data needs to be analyzed to present something coherent and educational. That is where analyzing the data that has been collected and cleaned is a necessary step. The first thing that needs to be understood is the different ways that you can approach data analysis. That approach defines what conclusions you will reach and ultimately how that data will be presented. We briefly looked at these data analysis types in chapter one, but the section below will take a deeper dive.

TYPES OF DATA ANALYSIS

Descriptive Analysis- "What Happened"

This is the simplest form of data analysis that any data analyst will come across. Does this method seek to provide the answer to *what happened?* The focus during data collection is on information about the past. There are two data-intensive processes highlighted in this method of data analysis. First comes data aggregation, which is the process of first gathering data and then presenting it in a summarized format so that the notable points are highlighted.

Once this application has taken place, then we move on to data mining. Data mining is the process that involves scanning large databases to pinpoint and gather specific data items so that new information can be derived from that stored collection by noting relationships and patterns between these data points. There are different techniques used to locate those specific data points, as the use of the word 'large' to describe these databases is by no means an exaggeration.

These techniques include:

- Classification analysis
- Clustering analysis
- Regression analysis
- Outlier detection
- Associated rules

We will go deeper into understanding these techniques in the following chapter. No matter the method used, this historical data will be analyzed to find and highlight trends and draw conclusions about what is likely to happen in the present or the future. One of the most classic uses of descriptive analysis is to track how a business is performing and thus, how actions like marketing and product development can be fine-tuned to build on past performance. Monthly revenue reports and sales lead overviews are examples of descriptive analysis.

Diagnostic Analysis - "Why did this happen."

Data professionals do not have to limit themselves to only one type of analysis. After using descriptive analysis to find out what happened in the past, the data analyst can build on this by asking *why* it happened—the question of why is answered through the use of diagnostic analysis.

Diagnostic analysis builds on the insights gained from descriptive analysis to drill down on causation. Finding the cause of data's existence is just as important as the data itself. For example, a business may note historic steady growth in sales of a particular product over the last five years. Of course, the news of this development is excellent but understanding why can allow the business to leverage that performance to increase it even more.

Diagnostic analysis is particularly useful when outliers appear during the data collection process. Unfortunately, anomalies often mean a negative impact on businesses and organizations. Understanding the cause of why these anomalies arose in the first place puts companies and organizations in a position where they can adequately address these issues rather than putting a band-aid over them with only short-term solutions or, worse yet, guessing at how this should be fixed.

One of the biggest benefits of performing diagnostic analysis is that it allows you to be prepared in case the same problem or a similar problem arises in the future. It prompts the gathering of detailed information about the problem. Having that information already at hand is cost-effective and great for time management when future problems arise. Diagnostic analysis can be done manually, using an algorithm, or with statistical software (such as Microsoft Excel)

Predictive Analysis - "What might happen in the future."

As the name hints, predictive analysis answers what is most likely to happen in the future. This type of analysis builds on the techniques used in descriptive and diagnostic analysis. The effectiveness of predictive analysis relies on a high-quality descriptive analysis, followed by the large amounts of data that would have been collected as a result of the diagnostic analysis.

Predictive analysis is not as commonly used as descriptive or diagnostic analysis. Rather, predictive analysis often comes in handy when a business or organization is facing difficulty and needs to develop a solid plan on how to proceed so that this difficulty is nullified most effectively. Risk analysis, such as those used by insurance companies, is a commonly referenced example of predictive analysis. Other examples of predictive analysis at work include analytics reports highlighting predictions about customer behavior in response to the release of a new product and sales forecasting.

Prescriptive Analysis - "What should we do next."

Prescriptive analysis is a combination of all the other above-described types of analysis. It considers what happened, why it happened, and how problems can be fixed so that decision-making is effective at present and in the future. Whereas the other types of analysis are more heavily focused on monitoring data, this analysis process is more action-oriented. It uses the insights provided by the data monitoring in descriptive, diagnostic, and predictive analysis to implement solutions and strategies.

Prescriptive analysis is commonly used in science and mathematics communities. Artificial intelligence (AI) is the product of prescriptive analysis. The system that drives artificial intelligence uses large amounts of data to continuously learn and adapt so that this information is used to make more educated decisions. AI systems use these decisions to develop actionable plans.

As technology grows and provides more and more data, these systems become more adaptable and more advanced. This is why data-driven companies like Facebook and Apple are making such huge strides currently and are projected to bring bigger and better things to the table in the future.

As CAN BE SEEN, these types of analysis have an interdependent relationship. As such, no one type of analysis should be disregarded by data analysts. They all bring something unique to the table and serve different purposes, but none of the insights are less valuable. While predictive analysis and prescriptive analysis require a little more technical know-how than descriptive analysis and diagnostic analysis, they should not be disregarded by any business or organization, as the solutions and actionable steps derived from them are invaluable. The value of descriptive and diagnostic analysis should not be discounted either, as predictive and prescriptive analysis cannot occur without their existence.

8
DATA MINING AND MACHINE LEARNING ALGORITHMS

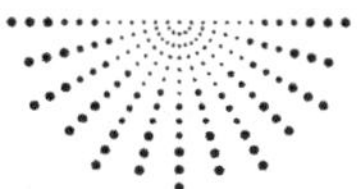

"If you torture the data long enough, it will confess to anything."

— RONALD COASE

It is interesting to note that one of the biggest, real-world examples of machine learning is something that billions of people on this planet use on a daily basis. The social media platform Facebook is that example. Facebook uses a variety of algorithms that allow the platform to analyze user behavior and make recommendations for what articles and posts will appear on each user's feed. Other familiar examples include the recommendation systems that power websites like Spotify and Netflix, search engines like Google, and voice assistants like Alexa and Siri. These applications can only work as well as they do by collecting data about users. The engine drives these applications to use that data to make predictions about what you want to view in the future or what words best match the decibels you emit in the case of Siri and Alexa. Although machine learning and data mining can both be essential to a company's success with its data, understanding what makes them unique is critical.

Data mining

Data mining is the process of searching, extracting, and analyzing a large amount of data to gain valuable insights and uncover trends about that data. This leads to more effective marketing strategies, increased sales, decreased costs, and many other benefits. Data mining is a tool that is used and monitored by humans.

Machine learning

Meanwhile, machine learning is a method that automates analytical model building. The use of algorithms allows for the learning, identifying of patterns, and decision-making with minimal human involvement. Essentially an automated version of data mining. Not only is machine learning responsible for making your online activities as enjoyable as possible, but it is responsible for the majority of artificial intelligence developments that will come across your news feed. While such technology can seem unrelated to some people, artificial intelligence, Facebook, and Alexa all have a common ground: the use of machine learning technology that drives the systems to find and repeat patterns.

Understanding The Difference

Data mining and machine learning are both a subset of data science, making the terms often interchangeable in many instances. Both processes utilize the same essential algorithms for discovering data insights and patterns, but their end result ultimately differs. Simply put, there are 2 main differences between the two:

1. Purpose: data mining is used to determine an outcome from an existing data set. While machine learning trains systems to execute complex tasks and predict future outcomes based on preexisting data.

2. Human Factor: Data mining relies on human interaction and is repeated constantly to gather insights from data. However, the main purpose of machine learning is to teach itself and not rely on any human influence. After the initial algorithms are set up, machine learning will

continue to work independently. While data mining will need consistent interaction.

Deep Learning

Deep learning is a technology that gives machines the ability to find and enhance those patterns. This technique of detection and amplification is known as a deep neural network. The word 'deep' describes how many layers of computation go into detecting and amplifying even the smallest patterns. This technique uses past data to predict the future.

The neural networks that power deep learning are reminiscent of the way the human brain works. Every time we learn something new, our brains are wired to factor that learning into how we proceed with the future and make decisions. For example, suppose we fall because we stepped in a particularly muddy area. In that case, our brain becomes rewired to adjust our footing if we happen upon this terrain or similar terrain in the future. It is also trying to map out other paths that we can take that might be safer. The brain has used past information to make predictions about how we can best proceed in the future to avoid a problem or make life better.

The neural networks that power the deep learning technology work in much the same way as they continuously rewire themselves to adapt to the new information they receive.

Supervised, Unsupervised and Reinforcement Learning

Deep learning, and thus machine learning, happens in three ways. They are supervised, unsupervised, and reinforcement learning. There can be many subsets of machine learning and algorithms, which can get quite confusing. Before diving deep into some essential algorithms and analysis, familiarize yourself with this graph to understand how they relate.

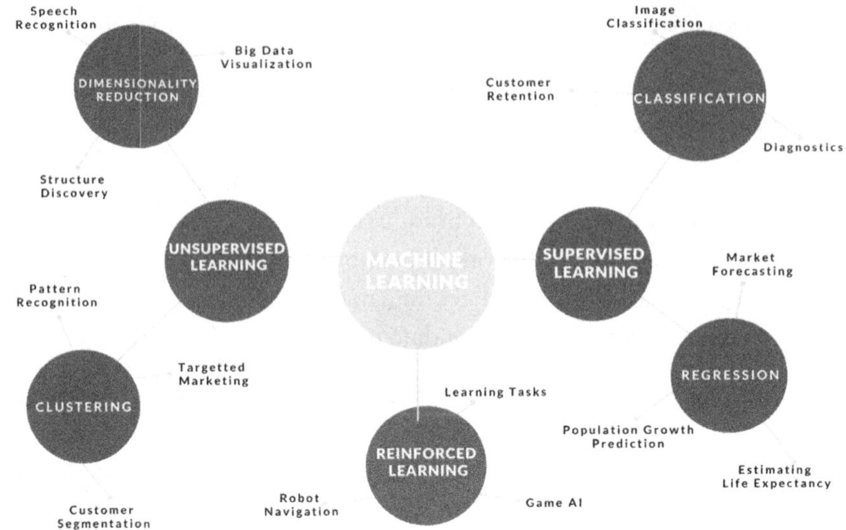

FIGURE 8.1

Supervised Learning

These algorithms are reliant on obtaining specific target outcomes based on rules that govern a given set of independent variables. It maps an input to an output based on example input-output pairs. The two main types of supervised learning are classification and regression. An example of supervised learning would be text classification. The goal is to predict the class label of a piece of text.

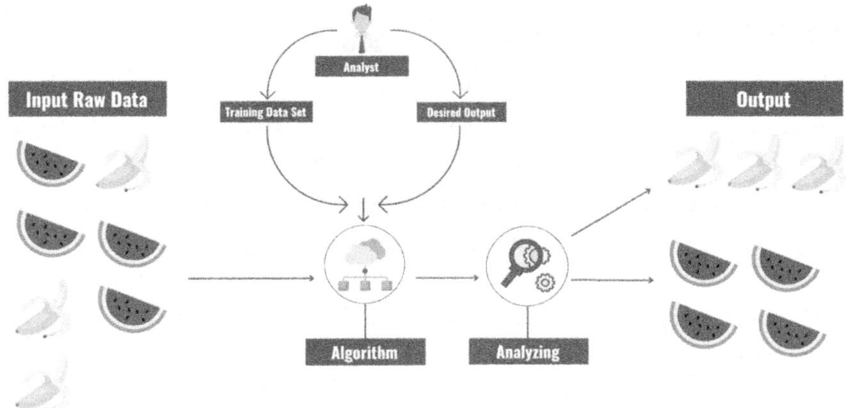

FIGURE 8.2 Supervised Learning- **Goal:** Perform tasks as good as humans. **Task:** Clearly Defined (with desired output). **Training Data Set**: Yes

Unsupervised Learning

Unsupervised learning uses machine learning algorithms to analyze and cluster unlabeled datasets. They can discover patterns and group similar items without any human involvement. It is known as "Unsupervised" as it doesn't have a training output to reference. The most common unsupervised learning tactic is known as "Clustering" which is used to group similar values in a data set.

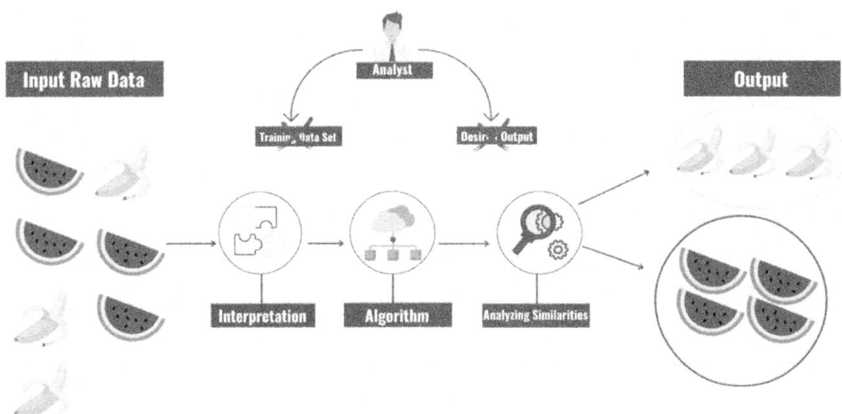

FIGURE 8.3 Unsupervised Learning- **Goal:** To find structure in the data. **Task:** Vaguely Defined. **Training Data Set:** No

Reinforcement Learning

Reinforcement learning is the most advanced out of the three. It trains machine learning models to learn in an interactive environment using trial and error feedback from its actions and experiences. In the simplest form, it takes action, fails, learns from the failure, and attempts to act correctly the next time. Although prominent in robotics and AI, it is a relatively new concept in data science. I'll keep reinforcement learning brief as it is a fairly advanced technique. We don't want to stray away from significant information for a method that you will rarely, if not ever, use until later in your career.

TYPES OF ALGORITHMS

Regression (Supervised Learning)

Regression analysis is the process of first identifying and then analyzing the relationship between the variables that may link or differentiate data items. This technique is instrumental in making predictions and forecasts as it allows whoever is working with the data to note how variables are dependent and interdependent. You're essentially trying to find a line or curve representing the patterns in the data. An example would be medical researchers often use linear regression to understand the relationship between drug dosage and blood pressure in patients. The researchers would administer several dosages of a particular drug to patients and observe their blood pressure response. With a simple regression model, they would use dosage as the predictor variable and blood pressure as the response variable. Some important regression algorithms to know are:

- Linear Regression

Linear regression predicts an outcome based on continuous features. It establishes a relationship between dependant and independent variables by fitting a "best line,", commonly called the regression line. The variable you are predicting is the dependent variable (aka the response variable.) The variable you are using to predict the value of that variable is called the independent variable (aka explanatory or predictor variable.) The simple formula to remember for a linear regression line is Y = a + bX.

Y is the Dependant variable (that represents the Y-axis,) and X is the independent variable (which is plotted on the X-axis.) "b" represents the slope line, thus determining its steepness, and the "a" is the intercept (value of "Y" when "X" = 0.) Let's look at an example. In this case, we are comparing advertising cost (independent variable) to the number of conversions (dependant variable.) Let's plot this data.

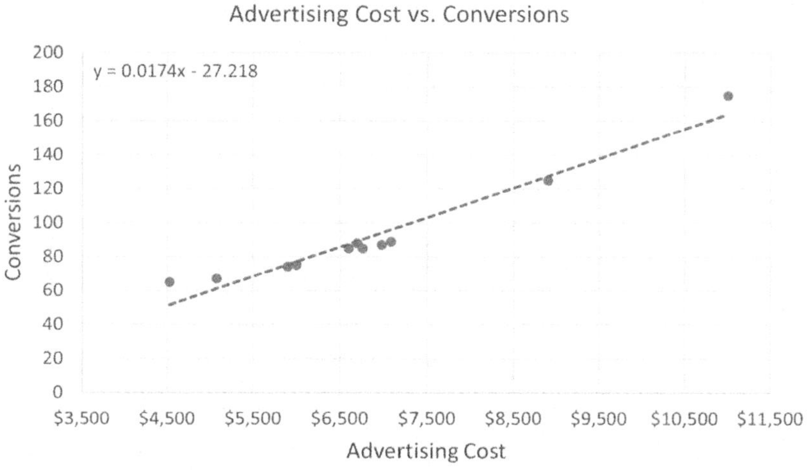

FIGURE 8.4 Linear Regression

We have 12 data points to showcase the 12 months of the year, showing the ad spend and the number of conversions for each month. The given change in the independent variable determines the dependant variable's value. We can use the relationship between the independent and dependent variables to predict the trajectory of the data and conversion rate.

The goal of linear regression is to create a line that creates the least amount of distance between the points and the line, so it represents the true trajectory of the data.

- Non-linear Regression

When a set of data doesn't follow the rules of a linear model, then it is essentially a non-linear model. Nonlinear regression is similar to linear regression as it relates two variables (X and Y) just in a non-linear (curved) relationship.

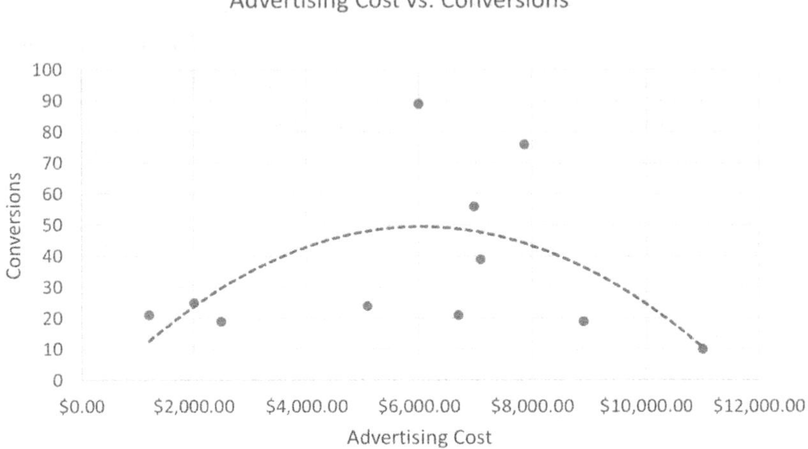

FIGURE 8.5 Non-linear regression

An example of this would be exponential regression. Exponential regression is the same concept as linear regression: finding a trajectory regression line that best fits the data. An extreme spike in the data makes it non-linear, rendering a linear regression line ineffective. The line is more of an exponential curve. An example of exponential data would be bacteria growth/decay, population growth/decline, or investment growth/decline. These data sets rapidly increase and decrease more significantly than a linear model.

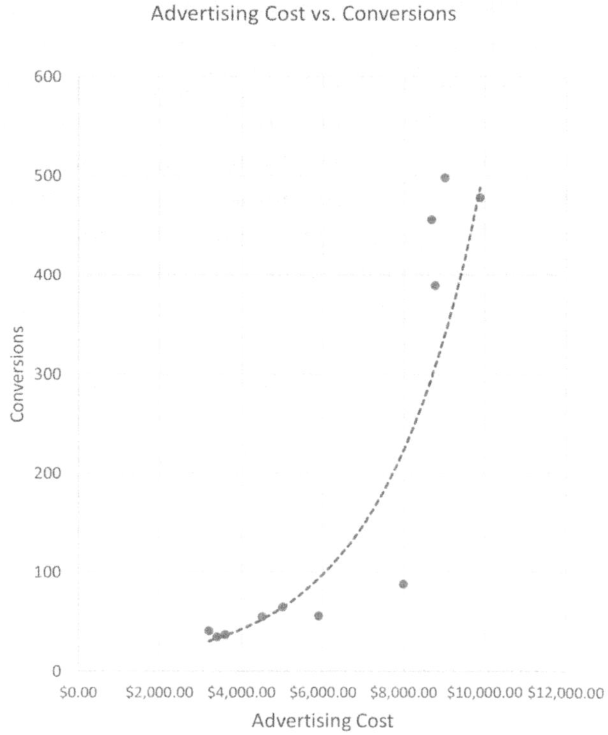

FIGURE 8.6 Exponential regression

Classification (Supervised Learning)

Classification is essentially an algorithm recognizing objects and categorizing them accordingly. It helps us separate vast quantities of data into discrete values. E.g., 0/1, True/False, or pre-determined output labels. Some important classification algorithms to know are:

- Logistic Regression

Logistic regression is used to estimate discrete binary values such as yes/no, true/false and 0/1 based on a set of independent variables. Essentially, it predicts the probability of the occurrence of an event by fitting the data into a logistic function or logistic curve. For example, categorizing tests passed based on hours studied. Logistic regression fits an S-shaped logistic function instead of fitting a line to the data. The curve tells you the probability of passing a test, based on hours studied. If you have many hours studied, there is a high probability you will pass the test. If you have a medium amount of time spent studying, there is only a 50% chance you will pass the test. There's only a small probability you will pass the test if you have minimal hours studied. Although logistic regression determines a specific outcome, it is used for classification. For example, if the probability of passing the test is greater than 50% (based on hours studied), it will be classified as passed. If it is below 50%, it will be classified as failed.

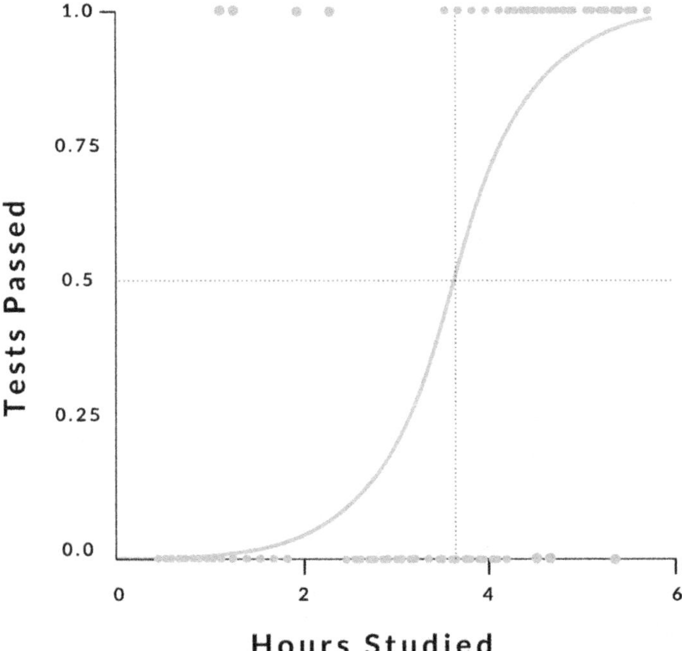

FIGURE 8.7 Logistic regression

Based on this analysis, we can determine that the students who studied for more than 3.7 hours had a much higher rate of passing a test.

- Decision Trees

A decision tree is a type of supervised learning mainly used for classification problems. It works for both categorical and continuous input and output variables. It splits the sample into two or more sets based on the most significant splitter/differentiator in input values. This algorithm takes the entire data set and progressively places it in smaller groups. It differentiates these groups by specific features. Think of it as a tree with several branches coming from one stem. A simple example of this would be dictating if you will go on a hike based on the weather.

Day	Outlook	Temperature	Humidity	Wind	Hike?
1	Sunny	Mild	Normal	Strong	Yes
2	Sunny	Hot	High	Strong	No
3	Overcast	Hot	High	Weak	Yes
4	Overcast	Mild	High	Strong	Yes
5	Rain	Cool	Normal	Weak	Yes
6	Rain	Mild	High	Strong	No
7	Overcast	Cool	Normal	Strong	Yes
8	Sunny	Mild	High	Weak	No
9	Sunny	Cool	Normal	Weak	Yes
10	Rain	Mild	Normal	Weak	Yes
11	Rain	Mild	High	Weak	Yes
12	Sunny	Hot	High	Weak	No
13	Overcast	Hot	Normal	Weak	Yes
14	Overcast	Hot	High	Strong	No

FIGURE 8.8

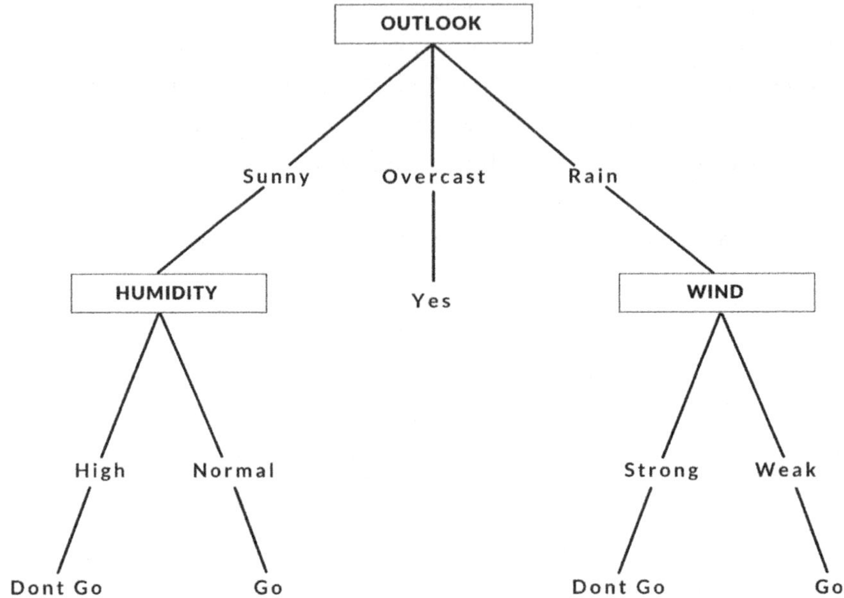

FIGURE 8.9

Clustering (Unsupervised Learning)

A cluster is a collection of data that share similar qualities and thus, can be grouped based on these characteristics. This type of analysis is similar to classification, as data is placed in like groups. The difference is that classification derives these groups from predetermined characteristics. On the other hand, the groups derived from clustering develops without prior knowledge of grouping systems. They develop more organically. Let's go through some essential clustering algorithms.

- K-Means

K-means is a clustering algorithm responsible for finding groupings within data. The number of groups is represented by the variable K. The algorithm repeatedly runs and assigns each data point to one of the K-groups based on their feature similarity. This repetition will continue until data items do not change the cluster they belong to. There are many instances where K-means can be extremely useful for a business. One good example would be during a new product launch. When it comes time for advertising campaigns, you can group customers into clusters based on similar interests and deliver a different advertisement to each group of people that matches their interests.

To begin the algorithm you start out by determining the value for K (amount of clusters) then select an initial centroid (center of each cluster.)

1. Assign each observation to its nearest centroid (cluster.)
2. Update the centroids to be the center of their new observations.
3. Repeat these steps until the data points cease to change clusters.

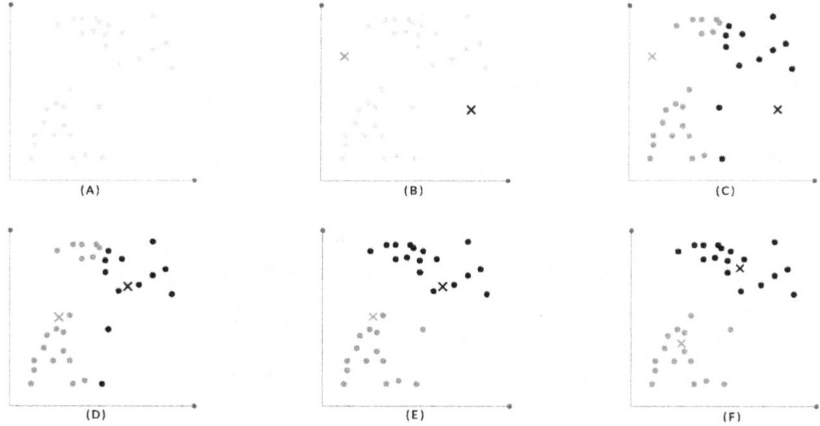

FIGURE 8.10

Some more common algorithms worth familiarizing yourself with over time:

- SVM Algorithm

SVM stands for Support Vector Machine. This type of algorithm is used to classify items in a data set by plotting particular variables of that dataset and linking those items based on those variable features. This supervised learning technique is mainly used for classification but can also be useful in regression analysis.

- Naive Bayes Algorithm

This particular algorithm comprises a family of smaller algorithms that share a particular rule whereby variables are interdependent. Based on this principle, finding a variable that does not belong is easy. This is a supervised learning technique.

- kNN Algorithm

kNN stands for k-nearest neighbor. This unsupervised machine learning algorithm is one used for classification by estimating how likely a data item is dependent on its nearest neighbor in that data set.

- Random Forest Algorithm

This is a supervised learning algorithm that makes use of several decision tree learning algorithms to classify data items. New data items are classified within particular trees based on how well it fits onto a 'branch' of that tree.

- Dimensionality Reduction Algorithms

This is an unsupervised learning technique. This particular algorithm aims to reduce the number of variables within a particular data set. It does this by reducing the number of variables. Reducing the number of pixels in a picture to make it smoother is an example of this particular algorithm at work.

- Gradient Boosting Algorithm

This algorithm is used when faced with large volumes of data. It uses data models and combines them to make an overall higher accurate prediction of what the next data model that will be included in the set will be. This is a supervised machine learning technique.

Many of these algorithms won't be useful until you are further into a data science career. If you are starting to get sweaty palms, don't fear, there are many career options available that don't require you to be well versed in this complex stuff day to day, like a business analyst. It's essential to have a clear roadmap of where you want to go (or at least an idea) to efficiently spend your time learning what's useful and avoiding what isn't. That leads us to our next chapter and a potential career field, business intelligence.

9
BUSINESS INTELLIGENCE

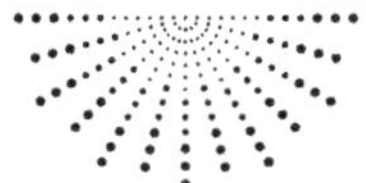

"BI is about providing the right data at a the right time to the right people so that they can take the right decisions."

— NIC SMITH

In the world of data analytics, many companies utilize their gathered information to predict future outcomes and make better business decisions. Now, you're probably wondering why everyone is focused on the future and not on the "now," which inevitably creates the future. Well, that's where business intelligence comes in. Business intelligence (BI) provides insights into the current state of the business. BI is an integrated system that allows businesses to manage, track and analyze critical business information such as key performance indicators (KPIs,) financial statements, customer transactions, etc. Implementing BI allows essential metrics to be stored in one place, which many employees can access and analyze regardless of their technical background.

BI vs. Data Analytics

It can be difficult to differentiate all of these terms while they're being thrown around. In its simplest form, BI is descriptive. It tells us what's happening now and what happened in the past to create our current state. Usually through company analytics and reports (sales reports, customer information, website traffic.) BI aims to deliver a precise picture of the current state of affairs to business executives. Data analytics, however, is predictive. It's the processing of raw data to predict future outcomes and decide what can be done to achieve or avoid those outcomes. It requires data scientists to analyze and interpret raw data.

Another defining characteristic of BI is that it can be a lot more user-friendly, as there is minimal technical analysis and a lower barrier to entry. BI tools have come to be very intuitive and user-friendly. Today, it is prevalent to have non-technical individuals use BI tools to produce reports based on their companies' metrics. Although having minimal knowledge in data analytics or modeling, many marketing, finance, and operations experts can rely on BI tools to give them the information and insights they need.

BI Strategy

BI is generally a system that gets integrated into your business to track critical data—as with data analytics, having a strategy is essential to an efficient system. You want to create a clear roadmap for smooth integration into your business. There are many ways to approach a potential BI strategy. Let's look at a straightforward 4 step plan to get your feet wet.

Step 1 - Get Input From Your Team

It is important you get input from various sources such as executives or managers to find out important details that may affect your BI system. Some details include who will be accessing the system? what specific tasks will it need to perform? What budget is available? What workloads will the software take over? As well as anything else that is relevant. An overlooked yet vital thing to consider is will the software be able to integrate into your current system without any modifications. You don't want to spend a large sum just to be at the same place you started because the tool doesn't work with your servers.

Step 2 - Determine Goals for the System

Determining what exactly you want the system to deliver is a crucial task. You have to ask yourself and your team questions such as what insights you require from the system? What KPIs are essential to track? This will also help you determine other factors down the line, like what platform will be best for your business.

Step 3 - Determine Your Budget

Most software comes with different bells and whistles, with varying prices. Determining a budget enables you to find the best system within your range. This also allows you to have any wiggle room for any extra costs down the line.

Step 4 - Select a System

Now that you have the requirements, goals, and budget, you should be able to assess the multitude of software available and select the most efficient program to integrate into your system. From there, employees can track important data, create dashboards for visualization purposes, and monitor your business's metrics and KPIs.

How BI Can Transform A Business

Implementing a BI strategy into your business is a proven way to maximize revenue and stay competitive. Let's walk through a few quick examples to gain a better understanding.

CASE STUDY #1

A biotech company needs to develop a more strategic marketing plan for the upcoming year. They want to increase market share and overall profits. Their company lacks processes and systems essential to capturing and analyzing customer data.

Goal: Uncover high-value customers and marketing opportunities.

Problems:

- They have no way of categorizing their customers based on key parameters for specific targeting.
- They have no marketing campaign analytics or ways to track their impact.
- They don't have an integrated data collection system.

Possible solution:

The company can implement a BI platform, which collects and integrates multiple metrics into a single place. They can calculate specific marketing metrics needed and segment the data for future targeted campaigns. Resulting in lower expenses, higher conversions and the discovery of high-value customers.

CASE STUDY #2

New York Shipping Exchange (NYSHEX)

New York Shipping Exchange is a shipping-technology company that improves shipping processes overseas.

Goal: Streamlining their data for easy access and analysis.

Problems: NYSHEX would manually extract data from its various locations and import it into Excel for data analysis. It was a labor-intensive project which rendered the data only accessible to a select few, causing the engineers to be overwhelmed with requests.

Solution: NYSHEX implemented BI, which centralized its data into one system while giving the entire company access. Even those with no technical experience could access, analyze and visualize the data. The company was able to triple its shipping volume between the United States and Asia in 2019.

WHATEVER BUSINESS REQUIREMENTS YOU HAVE, a BI system can drastically improve the effectiveness of your day-to-day operations. You can save time and money, create productive and happy employees, and gain a competitive edge over your competition.

10
INTRODUCTION TO DATA VISUALIZATION

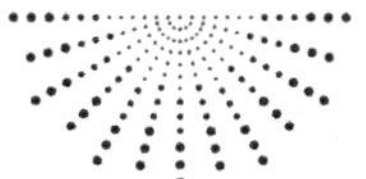

"The goal is to turn data into information, and information into insight."

— CARLY FIORINA

Your data is cleaned and analyzed to give you clear insights. However, this is only valuable to the data professional that brought it to light. It needs to be shared with the right people to make effective business decisions. This leads to data visualization.

If data was easy for everyone to understand, most people could claim to be data experts. However, data professionals are of an advanced skillset. They possess the ability to effectively translate data into understandable pieces of nuggets for other people to absorb.

Data translated into visualizations that others can understand is called data visualization. This chapter dives into exactly what data visualizations are and how we can use them effectively.

It's important to understand that even the best visuals won't make up for a poorly planned presentation. Knowing what information to present is essential for creating effective data visualizations. For example, let's say your team is about to launch a new product, and you're determining a price point. You've researched similar products and their pricing over the past five years and came up with a launch price based on the competitor average. You now have to present these findings to the product manager. Considering they already have a lot of in-depth knowledge of the product, presenting this might entail a simple line graph, showcasing similar product pricing over time while highlighting the average price of competitors and where the product should be priced. Now, If the product manager has to present why they selected this price point to the executives or even the CEO, They would have to be a little more in-depth—adding an additional graph showcasing the profit margins. This shows the executives that the price point is competitive, profitable and in alignment with company goals. It is crucial that you always consider your audience and what information they need, so you can avoid an unfinished presentation.

Let's look at a brief snippet from my book "How To Win With Your Data Visualizations" to get a better idea of what a good data story entails.

"With the many, many bytes of information available for relating to other people, how do you decide which ones deserve precedence and should be added to your slides? That is a fundamental question when approaching data storytelling. If this question has come to your mind, you have set yourself up with the right mindset to present data in the most digestible way to your audience. The answer of which bytes of information you will relate to your audience depends on your final goal of the presentation. Too many business professionals get stuck on the visual aspects of the presentation and leave the information that needs to be relayed as an afterthought. But it is truly the other way around. The visuals do not matter if your audience cannot follow a defined path from the initial insight to a solution.

A narrative is about developing a language that allows for augmenting data in the most effective way to deliver to an audience so that the people in the audience are not left confused and trying to piece together these bytes of information. The narrative is the vehicle that conveys insights on the data that has been collected to the audience. There are 3 main components of a great narrative. The what, The who, and the how.

The What: *What is the goal of your presentation? What insights do you need to convey? What solutions do you need to guide your audience toward? The "what" is arguably the most important part of any data story. Without having a goal in mind, you will not know what insights to bring forward and how you will effectively present them.*

The Who: *Who are you presenting to? Knowing this is essential when presenting data because you need to know what they already know, and what they don't. What you present to your product manager vs. the CEO is very different. Finding out who you're presenting to will allow you to determine what you need to present and how you will present it. This will be covered more in-depth in chapter 2.*

The How: *Now that you know what you're presenting and who you're presenting it to, how you will do it should come naturally. Based on what you've already learned, you can select specific insights with supporting information and transmit them through beautifully crafted data visualizations in a favorable sequence. Of course, the bulk of the book shows you exactly how to do this, so I will not go any more in-depth here. Keep reading!"*

Scan the QR code below, or click the link (for kindle readers) if you'd like to check out "How To Win With Your Data Visualizations". It goes more in-depth with the presentation process and teaches you how to create visualizations that are effective and aesthetic. How To Win With Your Data Visualizations

USE THE RIGHT VISUALS

Inputting the right visual for conveying data allows data professionals to take complex information and relay it in a simple form that is easy for people of all expertise levels to understand. There are many different types of data visualizations.

The first step in using data visuals to the fullest advantage is actually choosing the right visualization appropriate for the circumstance. That choice boils down to questions that you must ask yourself. Such questions include, what type of data are you trying to represent? Is it data that is part of a whole or different data sets? Is it data that shows the relationship between two or more data sets? The answers to these questions allow you to drill down on the type of data visualization that makes the most sense for that portrayal.

The four main categories of charts are:

Comparison Charts

Comparison charts allow for the comparison of at least two sets of data. This comparison can either highlight the similarities or the differences between these data sets. Some of the best charts for making comparisons include bar charts, column charts, and line charts.

Composition Charts

Composition charts allow for showcasing the different parts of one whole set of data and how these parts changed over time. Some of the best charts for portraying composition include pie charts, pyramids, stacked column charts and area charts.

Relationship Charts

Relationship charts are used to show the connection between at least two variables in data sets. Some of the best data visualizations for portraying relationships between data sets include bubble charts and scatter plots.

Distribution Charts

Distribution charts are used to identify trends and outliers by highlighting how variables are distributed over time. Some of the best charts for highlighting distribution include scatter plots, area charts and line graphs.

TYPES OF CHARTS

Let's go through some important visualizations you can utilize:

Infographics: Sometimes, your boss or executives want a quick rundown of multiple KPIs in your company. This is where infographics come in handy. Infographics are used to showcase a lot of information quickly and clearly. They are ideal for showing the bigger picture of a lot of data instead of critical specific insights. If you've done extensive analysis to find some crucial insights, a single visualization per insight and a proper presentation might be a better option.

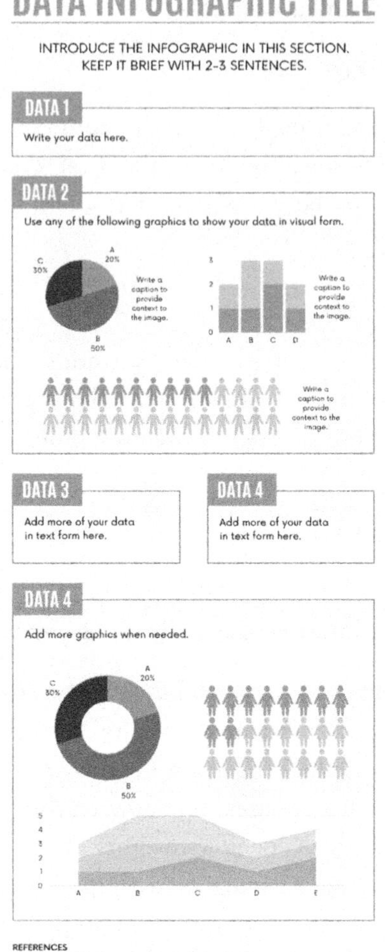
DATA INFOGRAPHIC TITLE
INTRODUCE THE INFOGRAPHIC IN THIS SECTION.
KEEP IT BRIEF WITH 2-3 SENTENCES.
DATA 1
Write your data here.
DATA 2
Use any of the following graphics to show your data in visual form.
A 20%
C 30%
B 50%
Write a caption to provide context to the image.
A B C D
Write a caption to provide context to the image.
Write a caption to provide context to the image.
DATA 3
Add more of your data in text form here.
DATA 4
Add more of your data in text form here.
DATA 4
Add more graphics when needed.
A 20%
C 30%
B 50%
A B C D E
REFERENCES
Place the source of the information you've gathered and used here.

FIGURE 10.1

Technology's Impact on Child Development

Recent surveys show that 85% of parents allow their young children access to technology: tablets, smartphones, televisions, and computers.

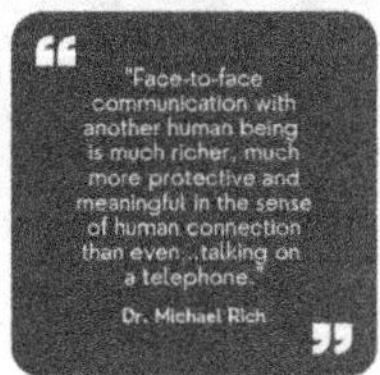

Children have more difficulty understanding sounds from devices such as smartphones and tablets as opposed to hearing the voice of an actual person trying to communicate.

Parents satisfied with technology's effect on their children.

They associate their children's strong comprehension of literacy with tablet use.

Parents concerned with technology use.

Screen time includes inappropriate content, affects sleep, and takes away from outdoor time.

Parents who do not allow screen time at home.

There is zero access to devices and more outdoor time and face to face interaction is encouraged.

The duration of screen time is crucial in homes that allow children access to smartphones, tablets, televisions, and computers. Child development experts emphasize the importance of consciousness —that screen time should not replace what is most essential for child development: human interaction.

FIGURE 10.2

Bar Graph: Bar graphs, horizontal bar graphs and stacked bar graphs are all the tried and true visualization methods in business. They work great for comparing values like sales figures by month or website traffic by country—they're ideal for conveying quick and clear insights to your team.

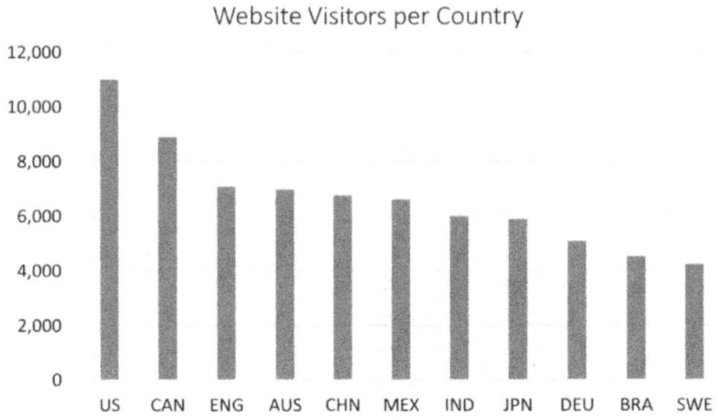

FIGURE 10.3

Line Graph: Another common chart is a line graph, which are great for showcasing trends over time. Whether it's revenue for the year or housing prices over the last ten years. Line graphs are also useful for reviewing numbers, whether quarterly, yearly, or monthly, to monitor spikes and dips to better understand business performance.

FIGURE 10.4

Scatter Plot: Scatter plots are used to display and compare values from two variables. Scatter plots are great because they report individual values, but when absorbed as a whole, you can spot patterns and trends. Identification of correlational relationships is a common practice for anyone using scatter plots. When given a particular horizontal value, we can adequately predict the vertical value. The horizontal axis is known as the independent variable, while the vertical axis is the dependent variable. Relationships between variables can come in many forms: positive or negative, strong or weak, linear or non-linear.

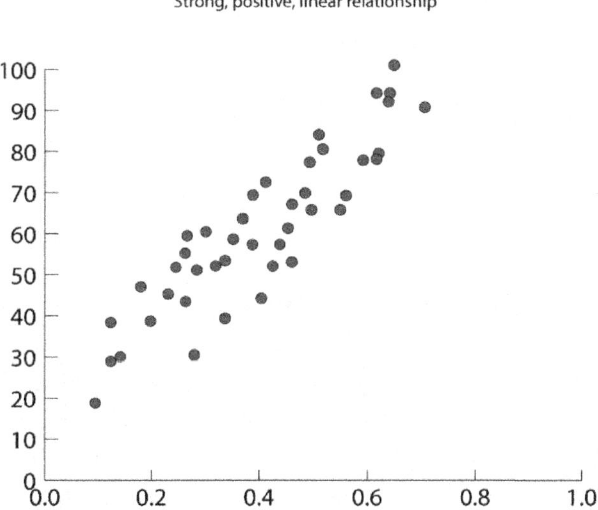

FIGURE 10.5 Scatter plot

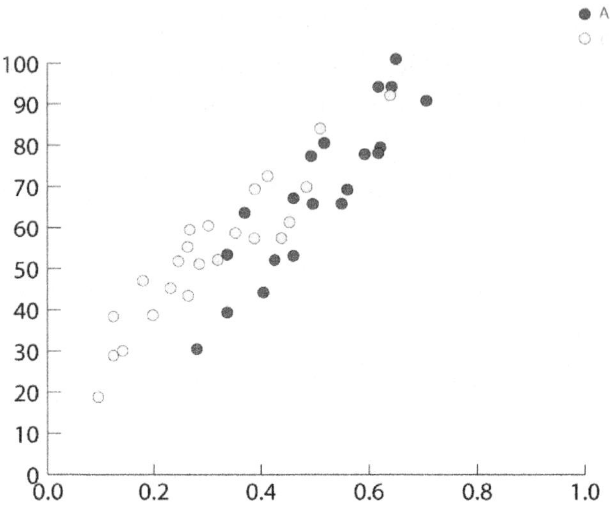

FIGURE 10.6 Scatter plot comparing two variables

Box Plot: A box plot is a graphical rendition of statistical data. It is a standardized way of displaying the distribution of data based on a five-number summary minimum. First quartile, median value, third quartile and maximum value. With the "Mean" Value representing the average of the dataset. Essentially, it compares the distribution of a data set.

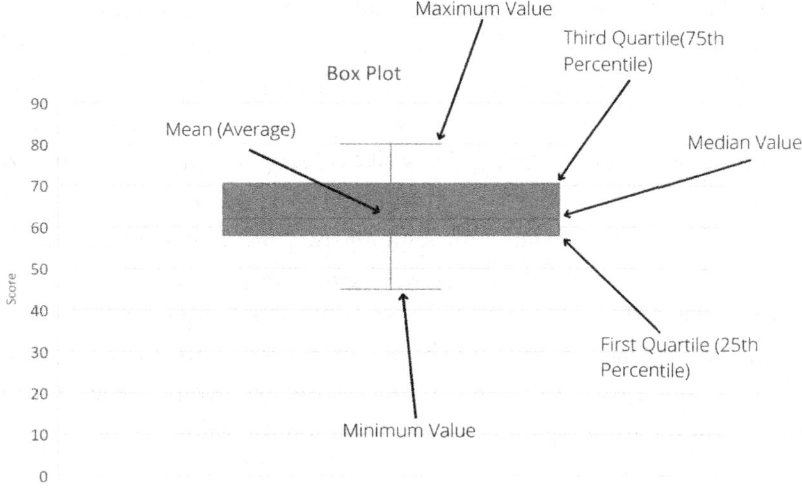

FIGURE 10.7

You can also compare data sets and their distribution.

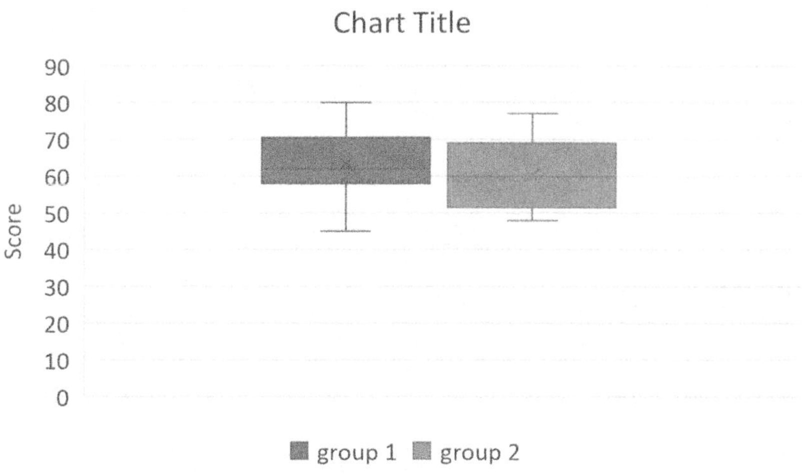

FIGURE 10.8

Heat Map: A heat map is a data visualization where a color represents the numerical figures of each value. A light color usually means less and dark color means more. This can also be referred to as a "sequential" color palette. A great example would be a map of America, showcasing the population of cities. The color will be very dark in high population areas and fade out as the population gets smaller. The same concept would apply to website traffic throughout the world. Heat Maps can also be helpful with a table that shows figures from multiple marketing campaigns over the years—highlighting which campaigns made the most revenue so you can easily spot the top performers. In this case, green would be showcasing the highest values, and red would showcase the lowest values, fading lighter or darker based on the value.

FIGURE 10.9

	Q1	Q2	Q3	Q4
Campaign 1	$50,000	$85,000	$75,000	$98,000
Campaign 2	$75,000	$79,000	$65,000	$86,000
Campaign 3	$100,000	$110,000	$90,000	$125,000
Campaign4	$56,000	$59,000	$50,000	$67,000
Campaign 5	$43,000	$69,000	$60,000	$65,000
Campaign 6	$78,000	$70,000	$77,000	$82,000
Campaign 7	$68,000	$67,000	$60,000	$77,000
Campaign 8	$55,000	$50,000	$56,000	$62,000

FIGURE 10.10

Although there are a plethora of visualizations you can use, it's important to start with the essentials and not overwhelm yourself. These charts can cover almost all of your bases, but as you excel in your career, continue trying new methods to tell the most effective data stories.

Once you have chosen your particular visualization, it is time to get to the design phase. Some people are tempted to use bright, bold and colorful charts, but doing so will only serve to mislead or confuse the audience. Design must be approached carefully and should be clean, concise and clutter-free.

To ensure that your data visualizations are clutter-free, here are a few tips:

- Ensure that the chart is appropriately labeled and legible. Your audience should not have to squint to note what is labeled on your chart or have to scratch their head when they connect the dots.
- Do not use uppercase text unnecessarily. Just like adding big clunky furniture to a small space, uppercase letters will clutter your visualizations. Limit using uppercase text to instances where you are trying to call attention to a particular element on a chart or a title.
- Ensure that the charts are not misleading by doing any of the following:

- Omitting the baseline, which is the zero value at the vertical axis.
- Manipulating the y-axis with disproportionate scales.
- Cherry Picking favorable sets of data to highlight in your charts. All relevant data should be represented without bias.
- Using the wrong type of chart to display information, such as using a pie chart to highlight comparisons. (the information can easily get lost with all the slices being similar sizes. A horizontal bar chart would be better for this. Rank the values in order from highest to lowest.)
- Do not overuse bright, bold colors as they can detract from the message you send. When such colors are used, ensure that the use is relevant to bring attention to particular details on the chart.
- Do not use dark grid lines. Using gridlines is meant to make charts easier to read, but if they overpower the rest of the chart, that defeats the purpose of the use. When it is necessary to use gridlines, use soft grey ones but my advice is to eliminate their use when possible.

DATA VISUALIZATION TOOLS

New data visualization software is coming out all the time. But there are a few dependable programs that won't be going anywhere anytime soon. My top 3 data visualization tools would be:

Excel

Excel is widely known and used by many. It's also very user-friendly and easy to create beautiful visualizations. If you're the average business professional, writing quarterly reports and tracking metrics, Excel is all you'll ever need. It's very intuitive and can quickly turn a set of data into a chart and that chart into an engaging visual with some slight customization.

Power BI

Power BI is the older brother of Excel. It has that extra processing power to work with larger sets of data. Their dashboards are also more interactive and customizable than those in excel. You can also argue they're prettier. Power BI excels in comparison between tables, reports, and data files. It's used prevalently in business intelligence, hence the BI.

Power BI is a fan favorite. It can connect to many different file data sources, including Excel and CSV, as well as database sources like Oracle, SQL Server, IBM and much more. It also makes it easy to export your reports as JPGs or PowerPoint slides, so you can seamlessly go from reporting to visualizing.

Tableau

We are now at higher levels of data visualization. Tableau can visualize even the most extensive data sets without limitations on the number of data points or row size. It is faster and provides extensive features for visualizing data and creating intricate dashboards. When you want to visualize big data, Tableau will not fall short. Of course, the more elaborate the program, the higher the cost, which is a tradeoff.

Python and R

I'll toss in a bonus option for any aspiring data science nerds. With the ability to code in Python or R, you also can create complex data visualizations. Python visualization libraries such as Matpoltlib or Seaborn allow you to turn your data into engaging, interactive charts with one line of code. If you plan to learn any of these languages, learning these skills is recommended.

By mastering these tools, you'll be set up to visualize any set of data, at any time. Pair that with some killer presentation skills, and you're well on your way to a fantastic career as a data or business professional.

We are only scratching the surface of data visualization in this book. If you'd like to go more in-depth, check out my first book, "How To Win With your Data Visualizations," I mentioned earlier, or join my email list at ElizabethSClarke.com for future updates on new projects and content.

11
GETTING FAMILIAR WITH BIG DATA

"Data is the new science. Big data holds the answers."

— PAT GELSINGER

If you're going into the world of data science, you're going to need to know a little more about big data. As stated earlier, big data is not your average data. The name implies it and it is quite true; big data is larger than the scope of regular data and so entirely deserves its own field of study. This chapter is about helping you understand what big data is, what makes it different, and why it requires big data analytics.

What Exactly is Big Data?

Big data describes large amounts of raw data obtained from multiple sources. This data aims to make a bold statement and not creep in. Rather, it comes in with a bang at a high velocity and so, it requires a lot of computing power to collect and process.

This type of data is collected through computers, the internet, mobile devices, social media and other electronic and digital means. You and I contribute to the creation of this big data every time we use our smartphones or our computers. These are only a few instances that we contribute to this collection daily. Watching your favorite series on Netflix, ordering food to be delivered to your home and taking an Uber also count as data items collected toward big data collection. All of this data is aimed at one specific purpose - to help businesses with strategic business planning and decision-making.

Before we get down to the nitty-gritty of what big data is, let's take a brief moment to outline the history of big data. Big data has not been around all that long. In fact, it is only about 70 years ago that big data made an emergence into this big, beautiful world of ours with the launch of the first data centers and with relational databases. Still, it had a slow start to being acknowledged. Around 2005, people saw how much unstructured data was generated through social websites like YouTube and Facebook, and other online services did acknowledgment of big data begin. This also led to the development of NoSQL to store data that was not searchable.

Big data continues to make strides because it allows businesses and organizations to gain complete answers that are not available just through processing structured data alone. These answers allow for more well-rounded decision-making as well as the provision of more perspectives on solving difficult problems.

The Five V's of Big Data

Let's break down what big data means with the five characteristics that differentiate it from your average data. These characteristics all begin with the letter V and so, they are called the three Vs of big data.

Volume

Volume is defined as the amount of space something occupies. If something has a small volume, it occupies a small amount of space, and the reverse is true for something that has a large volume. The sheer amount of data matters in defining big data as what it is. Big data is most often stored in data lakes. A data lake is a large storage location that houses vast amounts of raw, unprocessed data. Once this data has been processed, it is then moved to a data warehouse, which is a location where data that has already been processed is stored. Big data moves from both of these locations, whose sole existence is to store large amounts of data.

But what is defined as a volume of data large enough to be described as 'big'? Once data becomes too large or too complex for your ordinary computer to process, it has moved into big data. Therefore, big data is a term relative to what current technology can compute on an ordinary basis. In 1999, just 1 gigabyte of data would have been considered big data. That is not even the size of a good-quality movie these days. However, we have computers that far exceed this processing power in our homes in this time and age. Therefore big data only becomes so if it larger than a person or business can store easily, which is around 100 terabytes. Most organizations process hundreds, if not thousands of TB of data.

Velocity

The next quality that differentiates big data as such is the velocity at which it is received. Velocity describes how quickly something is moving in a given direction. Big data needs to be received quickly and likely be processed just as quickly to fall into that category of data. Therefore, waiting just a few minutes for data to be received from one end to the other might demote this from big data. On the other hand, a computing speed of a few seconds would categorize big data. An example of this ideal speed is when you post a message on Facebook. Almost as soon as you post that message, billions of other people can find it on their feed.

The velocity of the big data is largely dependent on the speed of the internet, which allows for real-time or near real-time receiving of data from one end to the other. This is why there are high-speed internet connections available.

Variety

Variety is the quality of being diverse or being different. It takes away the monotony of sameness. Big data encompasses that by having data collected from a variety of different sources and having many types of data encompass its data sets. Traditionally, data was structured neatly and organized in tabular databases. But we live in a time where unstructured and semi-structured data gives as much insight as structured data with proper processing.

Unstructured and semi-structured data types are also encompassed in big data sets along with structured data. This means that big data needs additional processing power to derive meaning from unstructured and semi-structured data types such as audio, video, and text.

Remember that big data has only been around for the last few decades, and it is still evolving as an entity. Therefore, we are still learning about its usefulness. As this education continues, big data has been further differentiating itself from other types of data over the last few years with the addition of two more V's, and they are:

Bonus-Veracity

Veracity describes how true something conforms to the facts. In other words, it is about how accurate or how truthful the data is. The value gained from data is only as true as strongly as you can rely on it. Data that has high veracity can be analyzed in a meaningful way that contributes to overall more valuable results in decision-making and planning.

The accuracy of data can get lost in the high volume, high variety and high velocity that is the characteristic of big data. Therefore, it is necessary that the truthfulness of this data be maintained. Structures are being put in place to ensure this, and therefore, this is another characteristic that differentiates big data from traditional data.

Big Data Analytics vs. Data Analytics

Data analytics is applied to big data just as it is applied to any other type of data. This data needs to be processed and analyzed. Otherwise, how else would it provide valuable insight to companies and organizations?

How else would the decision-makers reach conclusions from this raw data? But since it stands to reason that if big data is not like average data, the big data analytics process will be different. So, how does big data analytics differ from your typical data analytics? Let's look at those differences now.

1. Nature

Big data analytics is the elevated version of data Analytics. Because of the sheer amount of data being received –processing, analyzing, and interpreting this data needs to be enhanced so that solutions are easier to find. Whereas analytics of traditional data allows the uncovering of answers in a more seamless process, big data analytics needs to dig deeper with more complex processes to uncover the information that is being sought, especially since that message can be lost when new data is constantly coming in at a high speed.

2. Structure of data

Traditionally most data is structured. This type of data is structured to fit a format that was determined before it was collected. It is also easily manipulated. This is why the use of SQL databases, with rows and columns, is used to support the storage of this data. The easily manipulatable nature of structured data and the structure in which it is stored make it easy and straightforward to analyze.

Big data consists of structured, unstructured and semi-structured data that are not as easy to manipulate or as easy to store. The analysis of such data is not as straightforward as they cannot be arranged into tables where they would be easily searchable. Traditional data analytics tools are not equipped to handle unstructured and semi-structured data format and complexity. As a result, more complex data analytics tools are necessary. Such tools can include artificial intelligence-powered machines.

3. Tools being used

Predictive models and statistical models are the tools used in data analytics with traditional, structured data. These tools are ideal to use in this instance because the relational, tabular nature of structured data makes the data items easy to search out and move between rows and columns.

More complex technology is needed to work with big data. Examples of such tools include parallel computing tools and automation tools. Parallel computing tool refers to machine-powered processes that allow for several calculations or analyses to be done simultaneously. This allows for the acceleration of certain tasks, which is necessary with big data as new data is constantly being added to the data set. Automation tools are software that allows data analytics processes to run with as human interference as possible. The software generates insights and data scientists work with those conclusions.

4. Types of industries using big data analytics

There are certain industries where generating terabytes and terabytes of data is commonplace. That is not true for all industries, though. Industries, where it is common for big data to be generated, include healthcare, banking, retail, and IT. Therefore, such industries help pioneer the way forward in the way big data analytics are used.

Other industries that generate fewer bytes of data are less associated with these big data advancements.

Benefits of Big Data

Any business or organization that generates big data has many activities going on daily. That is the only way such large amounts of data will be generated and received quickly and in so many formats. The data analytics associated with these instances of big data need to keep up with the volume, velocity, and variety of the data being collected.

Once this data analytics process has been fine-tuned, the organization or business will benefit. Such benefits include:

Cost Savings

Analyzing big data allows for noting unnecessary costs and thus, implementing strategies that will minimize these costs. This allows the business to operate more efficiently and cost-effectively. Big data also allows for a better understanding of a company's customer base to provide better services, which equates to more profit.

Product Development

Product development is often done after years of study of the target market. This patience is required because releasing a product the target market does not want is a recipe for loss and disappointment. Analyzing big data allows companies to drill down on what customers truly want, s, they are more likely to develop a winning product.

Market Insights

All too often, companies are making blind assumptions about what their target consumer base wants out of products. These blind assumptions often lead to missed sales and opportunities. However, companies do not have to lowball themselves in this manner. They can use big data about consumer behavior and marketing trends to stay ahead of the curve and note opportunities that their competition has not noticed yet. The success of Fenty Beauty is a prime example of this, as the executive noticed a shortfall in the beauty industry and provided a more diverse product to fill this gap. They use models from many ethnicities and have a wide range of typically hard-to-match skin tones, developing new formulas that work for all skin types and pinpointing universal shades. Making them known as the "new generation of beauty."

JOB RESPONSIBILITIES OF BIG DATA PROFESSIONALS

One of the best solutions for solving many of the problems listed above is hiring a big data professional. The job description of big data experts is similar to that of data analysts. The similarity exists because both of these professionals analyze large volumes of data to give insights to businesses and organizations so that concise conclusions are met. Big data professional job descriptions are often more weighted with additional responsibilities such as collecting, interpreting, analyzing and reporting on a larger scale in addition to helping companies and organizations maintain software and hardware that allow for higher levels of accessibility, usability and security of big data. Data scientists are usually at the forefront of working with big data.

To break it down further, the responsibilities of big data professionals include:

- The analysis of real-time situations. Big data always comes in quickly and constantly and leaving this data sitting neutral will be of no value to businesses and organizations. This data needs to be processed as soon as possible, oftentimes as immediately as they are collected. Big data professionals are the ones who help businesses and organizations stay on the ball by making use of this data as they facilitate the analysis and interpretation of real-time situations so that conclusions are met without delay.
- The development of systems that allow the processing of data on a large scale. Remember that big data is composed of structured, unstructured, and semi-structured data. This collection of a multitude of types of data needs to be stored and processed so that all of it is easy to retrieve and interpret. This storage and processing need to be comprised of both software and hardware components that are best suited for the particular needs of businesses and organizations. Big data professionals help develop well-rounded systems that better analyze all types of big data received so that better decisions are made.
- The detection of fraudulent transactions and outliers. We live in a time where fraudulent activity is commonplace and ever-increasing. These fraudulent activities are often detected in big data collection, but that is only possible if this big data is monitored data. Big data professionals help data owners, especially in industries such as the banking and security sectors that handle sensitive content, detect fraudulent activities and transactions. The monitoring of big data also allows for the detection of outliers that can mean a change in the direction of decision-making for businesses and organizations.

Top 10 Big Data Tools You Should Know About

Big data cannot be adequately stored or processed through your traditional data analytic means. Special tools are needed for all the processes that allow for the ultimate use of this big data.

Whether you are a big data owner or a big data professional, you need to become familiar with a few common tools to store, process, and analyze big data with as much efficiency and accuracy as possible. Don't worry. You don't have to learn them all at once. Different companies use different tools, so you'll slowly gain familiarity throughout your career. Some of these tools include:

- **Apache Hadoop**, which is open-source software that boasts several functions that allow the storage, processing, and resource management of data. It is written in the programming language Java and is one of the most popular big data processing tools. There is a major drawback to this tool, it does not allow real-time data processing.
- **Apache Spark**, which is a tool that is equally as popular as Hadoop. This is because it overcomes the drawbacks of the previous software with real-time processing. It also allows batch processing of data just like Hadoop does.
- **Apache Storm**, which is also an open-source big data tool. It's popularity is attributable to the fact that it allows for the processing of unbounded streams of data, which refers to data that is constantly coming in with no definitive end.
- **Apache Cassandra**, which is a database that is perfect for processing all data types. With this tool, you do not have to worry about storing structured, unstructured, and semi-structured data types in different locations.
- **MongoDB**, which is a NoSQL database data analytics tool that is user-friendly and cost-effective. It is written the programming languages JavaScript, C, and C++ and is great for use in big data infrastructures that are cloud-based.
- **Apache Flink**, which is a data analytics tool that is used for both bounded (data that comes in with a definitive end) and

unbounded data streams. It is also open-source and quick to recover from faults that occur in the data architecture.

- **Apache Kafka**, which is a streaming platform that allows for the output of big data with guaranteed zero downtime. LinkedIn launched this open-source platform in 2011.
- **Tableau,** which is a data visualization tool that quickly turns raw data into valuable insights. It is user-friendly and does not require any programming or technical skills to use.
- **Rapidminer**, which is a tool that facilitates machine learning, data analytic processes, and data science processes in one powerful tool. This is an open-source tool that can be integrated with cloud services and APIs
- **R programming**, written in the open-source programming language R, this tool allows for the computation of complex statistical operations to enhance data analysis.

12
CAREER GUIDANCE

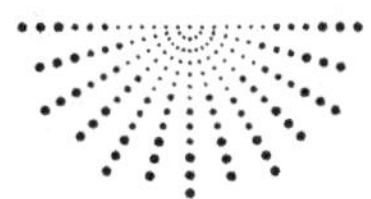

"Data will talk to you, if you're willing to listen"

— JIM BERGESON

The world of data holds a wealth of opportunities for anyone brave enough to delve in and make learning a priority. From the tree of data science, there are several paths that you can take to develop a career. If you're still in the process of finding a career and want to dive deeper, this chapter discusses some of the leading career paths and allows you to analyze which one of these might be right for you. It's possible to land a career as a data analyst with knowledge in SQL, Python, Excel, etc. However, many higher-level jobs such as data scientists require some level of higher education such as a bachelor's in math, statistics, computer science, economics, engineering, or anything similar. Due your due diligence and find out what is required for your desired field. If you're already working in data and are happy with your path, feel free to skip to the conclusion.

DATA ANALYST

Average Salary: $63,456 (Source: Payscale.com as of 2022)

There is no doubt about it. Becoming a data analyst is one of the most common directions that any person interested in the field of data first thinks of. If you:

- Like working with numbers
- Understand the mechanics of coding with languages such as Python or R
- Understand the significance of communication skills in this field just as importantly as you understand the vital contribution of mathematics toward data

...then becoming a data analyst might just be the career path for you.

But what exactly is it that data analysts do? Let's break it down. There is actually quite a lot involved in this career and some of the tasks include:

- Gather data
- Clean data
- Model data
- Present data

To simplify things, data analysts transform data into clear, concise insights that are used to make decisions and plan strategies. This means the presentation of data visuals is a vital part of this career. Because of this, data analysts need to develop expert-level skills when it comes to the manipulation of data fit for communication to others by using all of the tools available to them. Excel is one of the most commonly used tools, so understanding and deriving information from spreadsheets quickly and efficiently is a must.

The use of Microsoft Excel is one of the first steps that many startup companies take to start the development of databases. Excel is typically adequate as they have not accumulated as much data as bigger companies and organizations. Excel is equipped with enough features that allow for storage of moderately-sized databases in addition to quick data analytics. Learning to use Excel is typically one of the first steps that data analysts take. Once they have mastered this, they move on to more advanced database start-ups like SQL, Python, and R programming.

Other must-have skills of data analysts include:

Programming Languages

SQL: Many companies and organizations use SQL databases to store, access, and manage data. For example, payroll is handled in such a database. Retail companies store information about products in such databases as well.

Python or R (even both): Both of these programming languages can perform advanced data analytics on large sets of data. Knowledge of either of these programs is well respected in the world of data.

As stated earlier, Python is more user-friendly and easier to learn but learning either or both of these two programs is suitable when pursuing a career as a data analyst.

Critical Thinking

Data is of no use to anyone if the data analyst cannot view this with a critical eye and ask the right questions to find possible answers to the problems a business or organization might face. Therefore, to be successful as a data analyst, you need to develop your critical thinking skills.

Data Visualization

Remember that a huge part of a data analyst's job is to make data presentations to other people to aid in decision-making. As a result, this person needs to be able to develop a great narrative and tell a compelling data story that mobilizes the audience to act on the solutions provided with a problem. My recommendation for this is Tableau's visualization software. This tool allows the creation of attention-grabbing charts and graphs to enhance your data story.

Presentation Skills

Your data visualizations will fall flat if you do not have the presentation skills to enhance them. Don't be alarmed if presenting to groups of people doesn't come naturally to you. It does not to most people. Luckily, this is something that you can work on and improve so that you can become more comfortable as time passes by. There are plenty of courses and classes to help with this but nothing beats experience. The more you do it, the better you will become at it.

DATA SCIENTIST

Average Salary: $97,665 (Source: Payscale.com as of 2022)

Being a data scientist involves a mathematical, statistical and programming background to develop the skills necessary for analyzing data and creating mathematical models that can be applied to data collection, storage and processing. Becoming a data scientist involves using analytic skills to develop trends and manage data collection and processing. Data scientists typically develop these skills in a niche-specific way to specialize within that industry. For example, some data scientists develop skills that are particular to the healthcare industry, while others develop skills best suited for the IT industry. No matter what industry a data scientist specializes in, their role within an organization or business is to develop a contextual understanding of the data accumulated in that industry and that specific company for more effective decision-making and the development of strategic plans.

With typical majors such as mathematics, computer science, physics, and economics, even if a data scientist develops niche-specific skills, all data scientists start off learning the same skills. The skillset required of data scientists is more than those required of a data analyst. Must have skills of data scientists include:

- Fluent in Python and R programming languages
- SQL Databases
- Big Data storage and processing programs
- Machine learning

- Data visualization and software need to make winning presentations
- Business strategy
- Math and statistics
- Data modeling

We have already discussed most of these and their application to a data career above. Let us touch on those we have not discussed yet; business strategy, big data programs for storage and processing, and data modeling.

Business Strategy

To help companies and organizations create the most effective business strategies, a data scientist must understand business-specific problems, conduct analysis of those problems, and spearhead the way to engineering solutions to solve these problems. Encompassed within the development of business strategy skills, acquiring other skills is necessary and that list includes analytic skills, problem-solving skills, communication skills, and planning and management skills. Data scientists need to get a handle on all of these as they are the foundation for thinking with a strategic business mindset. Luckily, all of these skills can be developed with time by asking strategic questions, learning to take a step back and observing data, learning to leverage opposing ideas to reach the common, beneficial ground and of course, embracing the development of formal skills.

Big Data Programs for Storage and Processing

With so much big data being generated every single day, collecting and processing big data is something every data scientist will encounter if he or she hopes to grow within this field. As a result, learning to make use of the tools that streamline collecting and processing big data is a must. We have discussed many of these in the previous chapter, such as Hadoop and Spark. My suggestion is to pursue becoming familiar with each of the programs listed in the previous chapter. Do not overwhelm yourself. Take pursuing this education one platform or software at a time if possible.

Data Modeling

Data modeling describes the process of finding and analyzing the parameters necessary to support the collection and processing of data that supports the overall achievement of a business or organization's goals. This process needs to define how data sets relate to each other and how the resulting insights are generated. Without the provision of these parameters, chaos will ensue and obtaining concise, helpful insights from that data will become impossible. Data scientists are tasked with developing these parameters and locating the tools that will ensure that these parameters are kept no matter how much data is collected or how quickly that is done.

Because data scientists tend to need a broader set of skills but to encompass aiding businesses and organizations with the theory, implementation, and communication of data systems, they tend to be compensated higher than data analysts.

DATA ENGINEER

Average Salary: $93,623 (Source: Payscale.com as of 2022)

Data engineers specialize in creating software solutions that surround the collection and processing of big data. This means that data engineers are responsible for paving a way to ensure that big data is usable and accessible to the right persons. They are the ones responsible for ensuring that data is secure and adds value to companies and organizations. They are the ones who are able to transform all types of big data into usable insights. Whereas data scientists focus on extracting value from data, data engineers are the ones who develop the infrastructure that allows the extraction of this value. Data engineers focus on the architecture of data generation as well. This is a contrast to data scientists whose tasks focus more on advanced mathematics and statistical processes that transform the data generated by the infrastructure and architecture data engineers develop. Even though data scientists are constantly engaged with interacting with this data infrastructure and architecture, data engineers claim praise for building and maintaining systems.

Still, the skillsets needed in these careers tend to overlap. Must-have skills that they share include:

- Knowledge of both SQL and NoSQL database systems
- Knowledge of programming languages such as Python and R.
- Understanding the basics of distributed systems
- Understanding the basics of machine learning and the related algorithms and data structures

Soft skills such as collaboration skills, presentation skills, and communication skills

It should be noted that data engineers tend to rely on additional programming languages such as Java and Scala. Java Is an object-oriented, general-purpose programming language that is designed to have a smooth implementation. Scala works in a similar way. Therefore, learning both or either of these programming languages will benefit data engineers greatly.

Additional skills that data engineers need include:

Understanding and Implementing Data Warehousing Solutions

A data warehouse is a database where big data has accumulated from a wide range of sources. Such as system relies on efficient reporting and data analysis so that this big data is ultimately used to generate meaningful insights. Data engineers need to be able to implement both the software and hardware components that go into efficiently creating such a system.

Implementing ETL Tools

ETL stands for extract, transform and load. This is the process that is used to copy data from one location or source into another while ensuring that the integrity of this data is maintained. This is a vital database function used for data cleaning and the combination of data from several sources. Data engineers set up the parameters of this function to ensure that this integrity is maintained.

Understanding and Implementing Data APIs

As a reminder, API stands for application programming interface. This is the software architecture that allows accessing data and the applications that go into its management. APIs are the protocols that allow data to be transmitted between different software products without compromising the data's integrity. Data engineers aid in setting up these data APIs.

DATA ARCHITECT

Average Salary: $123,754 (Source: Payscale.com as of 2022)

Data architects are the ones who envision and design the framework to manage a business or organization's data needs and conceptualize how these needs will be fulfilled. This means this person helps with the planning, specification of parameters, enabling, maintenance, access, cleaning, control, and more of the data systems. Think of data architects as the ones who translate the wants of businesses into the data specifications that it will take to fulfill these needs. Envision it just like with the design of a house. Structural architects take the requirements of the house owners that need to be built, such as the layout and the number of bedrooms, and translate those needs into plans that the engineers can understand and thus, turn into reality.

This means that data architects work closely with data engineers. While the data architect is responsible for creating the blueprint for the data systems, the data engineers are the one who builds it.

Because the world of data is still evolving, the role of the data architect is also still changing. Many data architects are still learning on the job. But there are still some basic skills that data architects must have. They include:

- Knowledge and development of SQL and NoSQL databases.
- Knowledge and development of systems development life cycles. A system development life cycle looks like this:
- Planning

- System analysis
- System design
- System development
- Implementation
- Integration
- Testing
- Operations
- Maintenance
- A data architect needs to oversee and implement all of these parts of a data systems development life cycle.
- Proficiency of data modeling and design of the systems that encompass that.
- Proficiency in predictive modeling. This means developing predictions about future events based on trends and insights gained from data collected. Data architects develop systems to make this as efficient as possible for enhanced decision-making.
- Knowledge of programming languages such as Python and Java. Acquiring knowledge of additional programming languages such as C, C++, and Perl is also a plus. Perl is feature-rich and has been around for over 30 years. C and C++ are general-purpose languages that support advanced statistical operation as well the input of structured data.
- Knowledge of NLP (natural language programming.) This programming language is a subfield of computer science, linguistics and artificial intelligence. This subfield focuses on studying the interaction between human languages and machines. As it relates to data, the focus is on how computers process data input in the form of natural human language. The development of this field is to make it so that computers can efficiently analyze the unstructured data input of human speech.
- Proficiency in text analysis. This involves developing and maintaining processes and systems that can obtain relevant data from text data like emails and tweets. This is a machine learning technique.

- Project management approaches and requirements. The task of designing the blueprint for an entire data system is no small feat. The normal person will get lost in the nuances that go into this and quit. However, data architects need to be able to design a plan for moving from one step to the next effortlessly. That is where being efficient at project management comes in clutch.

More Careers

The career titles listed above are only a few more sought-after jobs available in the world of data. There are so many more that you can branch off into. It is best to explore and find the one that appeals to you and tailor your education and experience towards achieving that discipline. Some of the other job titles within the data career include:

Business Intelligence Analyst

Average Salary: $71,493 (Source: Payscale.com as of 2022)

BI Analysts focus on utilizing data and information to improve an organization. After they gather, organize and analyze internal and external company data, they use that information to identify trends, issues, and patterns to turn their analysis into actionable strategies the business can implement.

Senior Business Analyst

Average Salary: $87,131 (Source: Payscale.com as of 2022)

One of the most pursued sub-careers in data analytics is business analytics. Business analysts focus their efforts more on the business applications in data and actions that can enhance the efficiency and productivity of businesses and organizations. Their efforts give insight into how companies should make investments, approach marketing, and product development, to name a few. Essentially, Business analysts use data and current business metrics to make strategic business decisions.

Data analysts gather data, manipulate it, identify useful information, and transform their findings into digestible insights.

Marketing Analyst

Average Salary:$58,375 (Source: Payscale.com as of 2022)

Marketing Analysts help their company better understand their market. They tend to analyze data sets, do market research, customer surveys, and monitor purchasing trends to identify their target market. They then can develop strategies to help companies better meet and connect with new and existing customers. They then present these findings to leadership and managers through reports and visualizations.

Machine Learning Engineer

Average Salary: $112,792 (Source: Payscale.com as of 2022)

This career is related to creating and implementing software solutions to solve problems related to data storage and processing.

General Data Analysis Courses
Link:imp.i384100.net/DataAnalysis

SQL Courses
Link:imp.i384100.net/SQLCourse

Excel For Data Analysis Courses
Link:imp.i384100.net/ExcelData

Machine Learning Courses
Link: imp.i384100.net/MachineLearningData

Python For Data Analysis Courses
Link: imp.i384100.net/PythonForData

Data Visualization with Tableau
Link:imp.i384100.net/Tableau

Full Data Science Certificates
Link: imp.i384100.net/DataScienceSpecialization

CONCLUSION

There are instances where just one byte of data is more valuable than a brick of gold. Imagine the value that can be derived from zettabytes of data being generated every year. Technology is growing fast and with it, the bytes of data are streaming in faster and faster and in formats and volume that could not have been interpreted just a few decades ago.

Businesses and individuals worldwide have recognized that data is not what it used to be - confined to rows and columns in tabular form. Instead, voice notes, tweets, text, videos and so many more data forms also contribute to the makeup of all these zettabytes of data. These forms of data are outside of the convention and they are a large reason why the value of data is climbing every single day.

However, all of this data is useless until it is transformed from its raw state into insights that lead to reasonable decision-making and plans that translate into the billions of dollars that this industry is now worth. This value is still growing every single year. Remember that the data industry is expected to exceed $77 billion by the end of 2023. Imagine the global value of this industry as big data and data analytics are just part of the data world. Now imagine the value that cannot be measured. The value that comes from the piece of making decisions is based on sound research and information. Imagine the security of knowing that these decisions are based on facts and trends instead of mere hunches and assumptions.

As a data analyst, data engineer, data architect, or carrying any of the other career titles in this industry, imagine how you can be part of developing that value.You can be a part of the revolution that allows for the use of all of this data, since more than 80% of it remains unused and therefore, without developed value. In this day and age of the ever-increasing advancements made in technologies like artificial intelligence, machine learning and more, there is no limit to the possibilities of what we can achieve by using data and thus, developing each byte to its fullest potential.

You can help move this industry towards growth and prosperity and be part of one of the most important decades for data.

13
BONUS CHAPTER - INTRODUCTION TO STATISTICS AND PROBABILITY

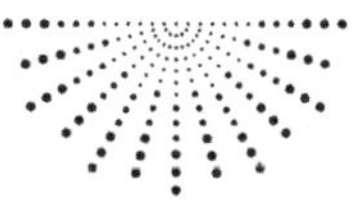

"I keep saying that the sexy job in the next 10 years will be statisticians, and I'm not kidding"

— HAL VARIAN

For any of you dedicated folks wanting a quick introduction to statistics read on!

Part of the numerical literacy that every data scientist must have is knowledge of statistics and probability. Not only that, but every data scientist must know how to apply those numerical functions. The first step to getting to that height is to understand what each of these terms means and how they are applied in the world of data. So, jump right into those explanations.

First up, let's take a look at statistics. Statistics revolves around collecting, analyzing, interpreting and presenting data. The entire point of using statistics is to show how the data that has been collected, analyzed, interpreted and presented can be used to solve a particular problem. We have plenty of statistics on world poverty. Why? To ultimately solve the problem of world poverty. Companies have statistics on customer retention and how well marketing campaigns are working. Why? To improve sales.

Population and sample are two of the most frequently used terms in statistics. Population refers to a data set whose features and variables need to be analyzed. Samples are subgroups within the population. Samples are used to gain the most accurate information to highlight the qualities of the population as a whole. Therefore, samples need to be chosen effectively.

Luckily, to achieve this sample as best as possible, you are not left up to your own devices, nor do you have to play a game of eeny, meeny, minee, moe. Instead, you can use the techniques known as probability sampling or non-probability sampling.

When using probability sampling, samples are chosen using the theory of probability. That leads to an explanation on what probability is. Probability describes the characteristic of how likely something is to happen. Therefore, these techniques of sampling rely on that characteristic. There are three main types of probability sampling are:

- **Random sampling**, which is based on the theory that any data item of the population has an equal chance of being selected to represent this population in that sample. Data items are selected at random to make this representation.
- **Systematic sampling**, which is based on data items being chosen based on a certain characteristic to be part of the sample. For example, data items may be chosen based on whether they are an odd number or an even number to be part of the sample.
- **Stratified sampling**, which is based on picking data items to be part of the sample based on a stratum. A stratum is a subgroup within a population that shares at least one feature in common. Once that subgroup is determined, then random

sampling is used to determine the final number of data items that will be part of the sample.

Non-probability sampling does not give data items on the population an equal chance of being selected for analysis. Non-probability sampling is in a whole other ballpark and very complex. Therefore, we will not go into much detail about it in this book.

There are two main types of statistics. They are:

Descriptive Statistics

This type of statistics describes certain characteristics of a set of data and thus, giving short summaries about the sample used to represent the population. Words that you will come across frequently used to make these descriptions include average, minimum, and maximum.

Inferential Statistics

This type of statistics is used to make predictions about a population based on the sample taken to make their representation. Rather than giving precise descriptions, inferential statistics make generalizations about the population and use probability to back the conclusion made. Therefore, you may hear more vague descriptions such as small, medium and large, used in creating conclusions based on inferential statistics.

LET's take a moment to look at the relationship between statistics and probability. The two areas are related as probability shows the prediction of the likelihood of events happening in the future, while statistics allows the production of this probability by analyzing the frequency of past events. Probability is the engine that drives the vehicle of statistics. Therefore, to solidify your understanding of statistics, it is only right that we delve deeper into what probability is.

I have stated that probability is a measure of how likely something is to happen. Still, in business, probability is more aptly defined as how likely the desired outcome is compared to the total number of outcomes possible. The formula for this looks like this:

(desired outcomes) / (total outcomes)

Unfortunately, sometimes outcomes cannot be predicted absolutely and that is known as a random experiment.

Other terms that you will come across in your study of probability include:

- Sample space is the total number of outcomes possible in a random experiment.
- Event, which describes one or more outcomes that are possible with an experiment.
- Disjoint event, which is a type of event described as not connected. That is, events that cannot happen at the same time. An example of this would be to toss a coin and get heads and tails simultaneously, which is an impossibility.
- Non-disjoint event, which is a type of event that has common outcomes. An example of this would be a basket player throwing the ball 25 times to make a basket every time.
- Probability distribution, which describes all the possible outcomes that may occur with a random event within a given set of parameters.

There are three main probability distribution functions: probability density function, normal distribution and central limit theorem.

Probability Density Function

This describes the likelihood of a continuous random variable occurring within particular parameters of the sample. Continuous random variables speak to the quality of having an infinite number of possible values. Because of this, the probability density function is often used to gauge the risk/reward probability of investments such as stock and ETFs.

Normal Distribution

This describes the continuous probability distribution around a central peak. This peak shows the mean or average distribution of variables within that sample. Averages on either end of this distribution are less dense, showing a lesser likelihood to occur. When depicted on a graph, this type of probability is bell-shaped to show a higher concentration around the mean. An example of normal distribution can be the average height of 30 boys within a particular grade in elementary school. More than likely, the heights of these boys will be centralized around a mean peak while there will be a few boys who are shorter or taller than this average. This also goes by the name Gaussian distribution.

Central Limit Theorem

This describes the theory that if a large population is divided into several samples, then these samples' average will be equal or almost equal. In other words, the central limit theorem describes the characteristic of normal distribution perpetrating itself regardless of how large this population gets.

THANK you for sticking around this long! Make sure to grab your free checklist by joining my email list at ElizabethSClarke.com and stay up to date with all future releases!

RESOURCES

Akhtar, Z. (2020, August 17). 5 basic components of data science. Retrieved from https://databasetown.com/basic-components-of-data-science/

Bad data costs the U.S. $3 trillion per year. (2016, September 22). Retrieved from https://hbr.org/2016/09/bad-data-costs-the-u-s-3-trillion-per-year

A complete tutorial on statistics and probability. (2020, April 24). Retrieved from https://www.edureka.co/blog/statistics-and-probability/#What%20Is%20Statistics

Corporate Finance Institute. (2021, July 27). Data analytics. Retrieved from https://corporatefinanceinstitute.com/resources/knowledge/other/data-analytics

Data analytics vs data analysis: What's the difference? (n.d.). Retrieved from https://www.bmc.com/blogs/data-analytics-vs-data-analysis/

Data collection: Purpose, methods, and tools for great decision making. (2019, November 20). Retrieved from https://upskillnation.com/data-collection/

A data literacy guide for D&A leaders. (n.d.). Retrieved from https://www.gartner.com/smarterwithgartner/a-data-and-analytics-leaders-guide-to-data-literacy

Guide to data cleaning: Definition, benefits, components, and how to clean your data. (n.d.). Retrieved from https://www.tableau.com/learn/articles/what-is-data-cleaning

Hao, K. (2018, November 17). What is machine learning? Retrieved from https://www.technologyreview.com/2018/11/17/103781/what-is-machine-learning-we-drew-you-another-flowchart/

Machine learning for data analysis. (2020, August 7). Retrieved from https://www.udacity.com/blog/2020/08/machine-learning-for-data-analysis.html

Machine learning: Applications of artificial intelligence to imaging and diagnosis. (n.d.). Retrieved from https://www.ncbi.nlm.nih.gov/pmc/articles/PMC6381354/

Requirements of data visualisation tools to analyse big data: A structured literature review. (n.d.). Retrieved from https://www.ncbi.nlm.nih.gov/pmc/articles/PMC7134219/

Seven characteristics that define quality data. (2018, November 30). Retrieved from https://blazent.com/seven-characteristics-define-quality-data/

Types of data analysis. (2018, February 23). Retrieved from https://chartio.com/learn/data-analytics/types-of-data-analysis/

What is data management and why is it important? (2019, October 30). Retrieved from https://searchdatamanagement.techtarget.com/definition/data-management

What is data science? (2021, October 25). Retrieved from https://ischoolonline.berkeley.edu/data-science/what-is-data-science/

Why is data visualization important? What is important in data visualization? · Issue 2.1, winter 2020. (2020, January 31). Retrieved from https://hdsr.mitpress.mit.edu/pub/zok97i7p/release/3

Z. (2020, May 19). *4 Examples of Using Linear Regression in Real Life.* Statology. Retrieved March 31, 2022, from https://www.statology.org/linear-regression-real-life-examples/#:%7E:text=Linear%20Regression%20Real%20Life%20Example%20%232,how%20their%20blood%20pressure%20responds.

Singh, J. (2019, October 8). *7 Real-Life Examples of How Business Intelligence Can Transform a Business [Update]*. RTS Labs. Retrieved March 31, 2022, from https://rtslabs.com/7-real-life-examples-of-how-business-intelligence-can-transform-a-business/

deBara, D. (2021, February 2). *Data Professionals Are in High Demand—Here Are 8 Jobs You Should Consider.* The Muse. Retrieved February 31, 2022, from https://www.themuse.com/advice/data-and-analytics-jobs-careers

Digital Vidya. (2021, April 23). *8 Ways To Clean Data Using Data Cleaning Techniques.* Retrieved February 31, 2022, from https://www.digitalvidya.com/blog/data-cleaning-techniques/

Morris, A. (2021, April 16). 23 *Case Studies and Real-World Examples of How Business Intelligence Keeps Top Companies Competitive.* Oracle NetSuite. Retrieved March 31, 2022, from https://www.netsuite.com/portal/resource/articles/business-strategy/business-intelligence-examples.shtml

PCMag. (n.d.). *Definition of relational query.* Retrieved February 31, 2022, from https://www.pcmag.com/encyclopedia/term/relational-query

Morrow, M. M. (2020, November 4). *How Businesses Use Transactional Data to Drive Growth.* Hubworks. Retrieved March 31, 2022, from https://altametrics.com/en/sales-forecast/transactional-data.html

Trevino, A. T. (2016, December 26). *Introduction to K-means Clustering.* Oracle AI & Data Science Blog. Retrieved March 31, 2022, from https://blogs.oracle.com/ai-and-datascience/post/introduction-to-k-means-clustering

Z. (2020b, October 26). *Introduction to Simple Linear Regression.* Statology. Retrieved March 31, 2022, from https://www.statology.org/linear-regression/

P. (2021, August 26). *K Means Clustering | K Means Clustering Algorithm in Python.* Analytics Vidhya. Retrieved March 31, 2022, from https://www.analyticsvidhya.com/blog/2019/08/comprehensive-guide-k-means-clustering/

Jeffares, A. (2021, December 12). *K-means: A Complete Introduction - Towards Data Science.* Medium. Retrieved March 31, 2022, from https://towardsdatascience.com/k-means-a-complete-introduction-1702af9cd8c

S. (2020a, December 2). *Linear vs Logistic Regression | Linear and Logistic Regression.* Analytics Vidhya. Retrieved March 31, 2022, from https://www.analyticsvidhya.com/blog/2020/12/beginners-take-how-logistic-regression-is-related-to-linear-regression/

Agrawal, A. (2020, February 14). *Logistic Regression. Simplified. - Data Science Group, IITR.* Medium. Retrieved March 31, 2022, from https://medium.com/data-science-group-iitr/logistic-regression-simplified-9b4efe801389

Yi, M. (2019, October 16). *A Complete Guide to Scatter Plots.* Chartio. Retrieved March 31, 2022, from https://chartio.com/learn/charts/what-is-a-scatter-plot/

Smallcombe, M. (2020, June 17). *Structured vs Unstructured Data: 5 Key Differences.* Integrate.Io. Retrieved March 31, 2022, from https://www.integrate.io/blog/structured-vs-unstructured-data-key-differences/#:%7E:text=The%20term%20structured%20data%20refers,it's%20within%20an%20RDBMS

%20structure .

Elgabry, O. (2019, February 28). *The Ultimate Guide to Data Cleaning - Towards Data Science.* Medium. Retrieved March 31, 2022, from https://towardsdatascience.com/the-ultimate-guide-to-data-cleaning-3969843991d4

Dawar, H. (2021, May 25). *Types of Variables in Data Science! - Geek Culture*. Medium. Retrieved March 31, 2022, from https://medium.com/geekculture/types-of-variables-in-data-science-eb347395 89b2

E. (2020a, July 24). *Understanding K-means Clustering with Examples*. Edureka. Retrieved March 31, 2022, from https://www.edureka.co/blog/k-means-clustering/

A. (2020a, July 18). *Understanding The Linear Regression!!!! - Analytics Vidhya*. Medium. Retrieved March 31, 2022, from https://medium.com/analytics-vidhya/understanding-the-linear-regression-808c1f6941c0

Kovačević, A. (2021, June 10). *What Is a Relational Database?* Knowledge Base by phoenixNAP. Retrieved March 31, 2022, from https://phoenixnap.com/kb/what-is-a-relational-database

Fruhlinger, P. M. J. K. (2019, October 16). *What is business intelligence? Transforming data into business insights*. CIO. Retrieved March 31, 2022, from https://www.cio.com/article/272364/business-intelli gence-definition-and-solutions.html

Gramlich, M. (2022, September 9). *What is structured, semi structured and unstructured data? › Michael Gramlich*. Michael Gramlich. Retrieved March 31, 2022, from https://www.michael-gramlich.com/what-is-structured-semi-structured-and-unstructured-data/

Piech, C. P. (n.d.). *CS221*. Stanford Cs221. Retrieved March 31, 2022, from https://stanford.edu/%7Ecpiech/cs221/handouts/kmeans.html

Saini, A. (2021, August 31). *Decision Tree Algorithm - A Complete Guide*. Analytics Vidhya. Retrieved March 31, 2022, from https://www.analyticsvidhya.com/blog/2021/08/decision-tree-algorithm/

Meyerson, M. (2021, August 27). *Regression analysis to improve Google Ads performance*. Search Engine Land. Retrieved March 31, 2022, from https://searchengineland.com/regression-analysis-to-improve-google-ads-performance-313898

Sánchez, P. (2018, February 7). *Data cleansing & data transformation.* Quantdare. Retrieved March 31, 2022, from https://quantdare.com/data-cleansing-and-transformation/

GraphPad Software, LLC. (n.d.). *GraphPad Prism 9 Curve Fitting Guide - Example: Simple logistic regression.* GraphPad. Retrieved March 31, 2022, from https://www.graphpad.com/guides/prism/latest/curve-fitting/reg_simple_logistic_example.htm

ELIZABETH
CLARKE

Beginner's Guide to Data Visualization

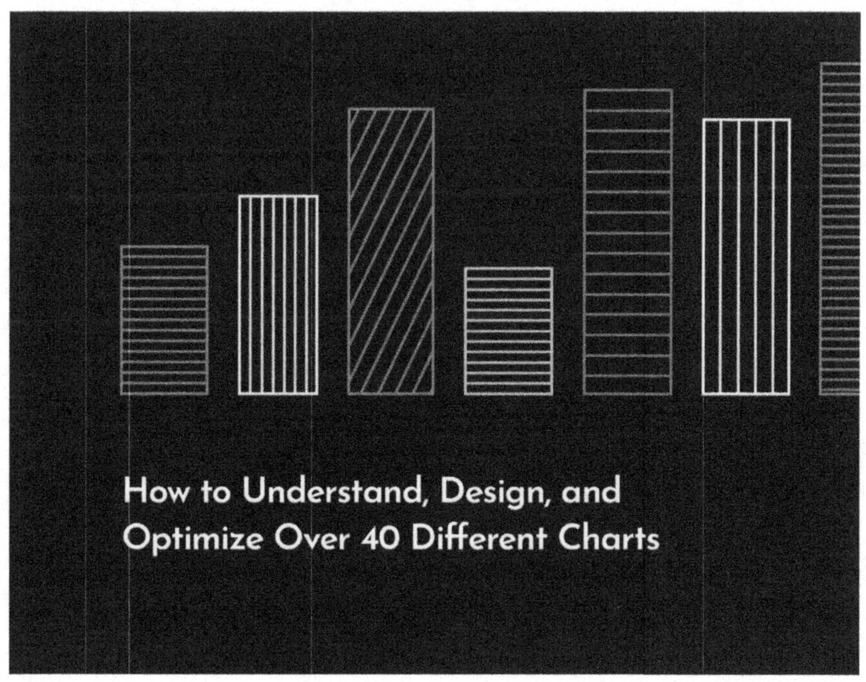

BEGINNERS GUIDE TO DATA VISUALIZATION

HOW TO UNDERSTAND, DESIGN, AND OPTIMIZE OVER 40 DIFFERENT CHARTS

INTRODUCTION

Whether you say it d-*ay*-ta or d-*ah*-ta, data has been around for a long, *long* time. In fact, the history books have records of data collection tools dating back as far as 19,000 BC. This came in the form of an Ishango bone, which was used as a tally stick. The Ishango bone was a primitive brown bone tool consisting of a length of bone with a sharp object like a piece of quartz on one end. Before what we know as modern mathematics or libraries were ever invented, human beings were already interacting with data.

Of course, as humans have evolved, so has how we collect and store data. Naturally, how we display data in visual form has also moved with the times.

Before the Industrial Revolution in the mid-19th century, the main forms of data visualization were maps, which we used as displays of resources, land markers, roads, and cities. But now... Line charts, area charts, histograms, heat maps, pie charts, bar charts... I really can go on and on. There is no shortage of ways that data can be presented in a visual format, and, of course, this variety makes it so that any type of data can be given a visual skin. We really have come a long way in the last 200 years because such formats would have been totally foreign to someone of that time viewing the visualization.

But why was this evolution of data visualization necessary?

The short answer? The sheer amount of data we amass in this modern age makes it necessary to find mediums to present that information in a visual context that is easy for us to understand and gain insight from at a glance. After all, approximately 80 zettabytes (ZB) of data, with 1 ZB totaling 1 billion terabytes, was collected in 2021. Every day, more and more data is being collected and stored on social media, via retail outlets, in small and large businesses... You name it and this entity is collecting data. Even on an individual front, we collect and store data. With the increasing global population and consumption, data volume is exploding. In fact, data volume is expected to more than double the 2021 figure by the time we get around to 2025. Can you imagine the accumulation after that time? It truly boggles my mind to contemplate. Data visualization allows us to easily identify trends, patterns, and outliers from such large data sets. It also makes it so that we can present these data sets to audiences that might not be as knowledgeable as us in a clear, concise, and easily interpretable way.

But data visualization is not just important because it allows us to digest visual information quickly. It allows for faster and more efficient decision-making. It jumpstarts the crucial decisions to improve an organization, such as business productivity, product performance, better services and whatever else pushes a business forward. It increases the probability that people in and out of an organization can share helpful insights and develop solutions to solve whatever problem that makes the need for data collection necessary. It allows for acting on solutions quickly so that success is more likely and fewer mistakes are made. Because of these and more benefits, data visualization can be used in all sectors and niches such as politics, healthcare, sciences, sales, marketing, finance, banking, logistics, and more.

However, despite the many benefits of using data visualization, many people do not understand how to use it to maximum effectiveness. Whether you are a beginner at data visualization or looking for a way to enhance your current data visualization toolkit, this book was written to showcase the many different charts that can be used, what they are good for, and how you can maximize that usage.

Data visualization can seem quite complex and daunting, but I have organized this book in a manner that is simple to understand and utilize. The information has been compiled into four main sections to ensure your toolkit has all it needs to successfully create effective data visualizations. They are:

Section 1: Fundamentals of Data Visualization

Section 2: All about Charts and How to Use them to Your Advantage

Section 3: Fundamentals of Design

Section 4: Case Study and Redesigns

Appendix: Tools for Creating Data Visualizations

To summarize, by the time you read the last word of this book, you will understand the essentials of any data visualization, how to pick the right charts and how to design them for maximum effectiveness.

Project managers, data scientists, marketers, social media analysts, product managers... All these professionals and more would have a far easier time relaying information and insights if they learned the art of telling stories through data visualization. My passion has led me to create a series of books to give you the tools to tell captivating stories with data.

I won't waste any more of your time, lets get right to the good stuff!

1

FUNDAMENTALS OF DATA VISUALIZATION

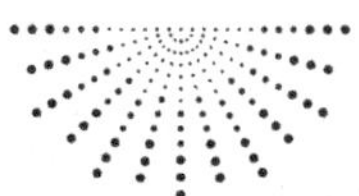

Even though the visualizations that we see as typical, like line graphs and pie charts in this day and age, are relatively new constructs of the late 18th to mid-19th century, data visualization itself is not new. In fact, it has been around for thousands of years in the form of maps. "X marks the spot," is a pirate phrase that has been passed down throughout the ages and is a great example of how we used to visualize information before.

What we know as modern data visualization was created by William Playfair, who was a Scottish political economist. He invented line charts, area charts, and bar charts and shared his invention with the world in 1786 in his publication called *The Commercial and Political Atlas; Representing, by Means of Stained Copper-Plate Charts, the Exports, Imports, and General Trade of England, at a Single View. To which are Added, Charts of the Revenue and Debts of Ireland, Done in the Same Manner by James Correy.*

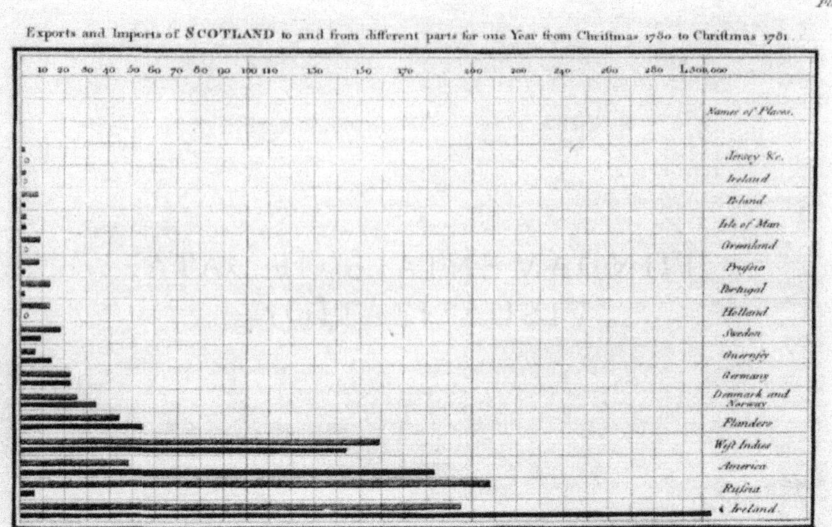

FIGURE 1.1: One of his many charts. Source: The Commercial and Political Atlas, 1786 (3th ed. edition 1801)

He highlighted statistical information in a visual form. Even though the science of how we process information visually had not been anywhere near as advanced as it is today, Playfair understood that this information would be more insightful presented this way compared to it simply being written.

His methodology allowed us to convey and digest important and expanding information. From then, more data visualization tools popped up, but it was with a greater understanding of psychology that these tools were fine-tuned to allow audiences to gain a better understanding of the information that was being presented.

VISUAL PROCESSING

There are several ways that the brain processes the world around us. It does this via our 5 senses (touch, hearing, taste, smell, and sight). The information it receives via our senses is turned into electrical and chemical signals that it uses to make interpretations.

No matter what sense the brain receives this information, most of this process happens outside your conscious awareness. The process whereby the brain subconsciously accumulates information about your environment is known as pre-attentive processing. The brain then filters and processes what it deems important from the received information. Can you imagine if you noticed every single thing, such as how a blade of grass blew in the wind and the lint that landed on your shoe every single second of the day? Your brain would constantly be on the verge of overheating. The brain recognizes this is not a desired state of affairs and therefore, only gives attentiveness to things it deems essential. But how does it make the selection of what is important and discard what is not?

Let's answer this question now. The information received from our senses is given different levels of priority for processing in the brain. As part of our cognitive awareness, taste has the lowest priority. This is followed by hearing and smell and then touch. Finally, the highest priority is given to the information received from sight. You are far more likely to notice something you see compared to what you are tasting under normal circumstances. More than 50% of the information our brains process is gained from what we see around us. This process is called visual processing. It describes how the brain perceives and then processes information gained from what we see. This information may seem boring to some, but whoever masters it will never leave an audience uninspired again.

Cognitive awareness is handled by the part of the brain called the cerebral cortex. This part is responsible for our reasoning. While it is pretty nifty at sifting through the information, it is hindered by the process of evolution. Or rather, evolution has not caught up to it yet because it is a comparatively new structure in the brain. Therefore, it is slower to interpret the information it receives. We would resemble lagging computers at times if we relied on this part of the brain to process the sheer amount of visual input received every minute of the day. However, this part of the brain is quite equipped to handle functions like thinking, understanding language, and perceptions. It also interprets information received from other senses like touch and hearing quite well.

On the other hand, the brain processes the raw visualizations it receives in another part of the brain called the thalamus. It is older than the cerebral cortex on the human evolutionary scale and can process visual information in a few hundred milliseconds. This is much less taxing on the brain and allows pre-attentive processing to occur. As long as your eyes are open, it receives input, but we are unaware of most of this intake. That is not until an element of a visual catches the brain's attention and goes through the cognitive tunnels of the thalamus.

VISUAL VARIABLES

The differences in elements of items received by the human eye for visual processing and analysis are called visual variables or pre-attentive attributes. As you see below, many of these elements you've probably seen in graphs before and they can work wonders when it comes to highlighting insights.

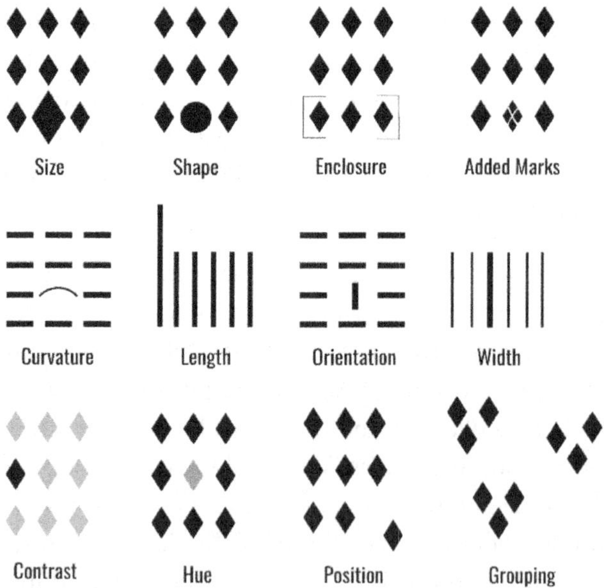

FIGURE 1.2: Pre-attentive attributes

Position

This variable describes the way that the element has been situated relative to other elements. It is where the object is placed in its environment. This also goes by the name location. This can be given in absolute or relative terms

Size

This indicates the dimensions of the objects in sight. The size of a visual variable can affect how other visual variables are seen. For example, a large element can cause another item to seem smaller than it is by comparison.

Shape

This quality describes the parameter of the objects in sight. Examples of shapes include points, lines, and flat and 3-D figures.

Hue

This variable has two dimensions, which are the hue and the lightness. These can also be counted as individual visual variables as well. The hue is often simply referred to as the color. It describes the name of the color, such as blue, green, pink, purple, or red. Lightness, also called value, describes how dark or how light a hue is. So, while shades of blue or green might have the same hue, they can have different values of lightness or darkness. So, sky blue and navy blue have different lightnesses even though they have the same hue, which could then represent high figures and low figures.

Orientation

This describes elements relative to each other or specific positions. Orientation can create perceptions of likeness or groupings.

Curvature

Utilizing curves in your data visualizations can showcase the flow of the data. Often, this is populated automatically in cases such as a line graph.

When a bar chart is necessary, you can add a supporting trend line to show the flow of the data. Another case would be to visualize smaller instead of larger time intervals. Instead of quarters or years, you can show months or days to see a microscopic view of the data and how it trends over time.

Length

People can easily distinguish the length between separate things. This is why bar charts tend to triumph over pie charts. When a bar is noticeably longer than the other, it is perceived as a more significant value very quickly. We will cover this theory more later.

Width

Width can be used to determine the size difference between various categories. This can be done through a Marimekko chart or stacked area chart, as each category's value is showcased by its width. We will, of course, go in-depth on these later as they are great charts to have in your tool belt

Added Marks

A great way to show separate groups within data. For example, data plotted on a scatter plot. This can also be effective when presenting to someone who is colorblind and separating the groups by color won't be as effective.

Enclosure

Enclosure allows you to quickly determine groupings based on borders or enclosed values. Using too many lines or borders can also add clutter, so keep this in mind.

Color saturation

This relates to the intensity of the color of an element. The more saturated a color, the richer it appears. At 100% saturation, a color has no gray added to it. The less intense the color, the paler it appears. At 0% saturation, a color will appear gray no matter the hue.

Grouping

This describes the layout of predetermined elements. It helps establish relationships between elements as well as appearance to achieve an overall visual flow. This means that a particular eye movement will be prescribed to these elements.

Contrast

This variable describes how an element stands out from another—potentially a different tone or lightness than the others or its transparency level. Another example would be hot and cold, where colors over a spectrum gradually change to a different value.

UNDERSTANDING these attributes will allow you to choose, design, and present your charts far more effectively. The key to data visualization is for the audience to understand the significant insights as quickly as possible. Focusing on the science behind how an audience perceives information will form a strong foundation for all your future presentations.

PRINCIPLES FOR EFFECTIVE VISUALIZATIONS

The brain would crash and burn just like an overheated computer if it were just bombarded with visuals and no ordered way of processing that data. Since self-destructing is certainly not the desired option, the brain's structure has evolved into seeing patterns, logic, and structures in the things that we see. If such mechanisms were not in place, we would not make sense of the world. The world would simply be a place of color and shapes with no identity. We would not note patterns, nuances in appearance, and how things related to each other in any one environment. Gestalt principles were developed in the 1920s to help explain how the brain processes the complex images that it receives by subconsciously organizing the individual parts to create full imagery. This happens even if these individual parts do not relate in a collection of items. For example, the brain will note that a mountain is shaped like a triangle even if there are gaps in your vision, like the presence of trees obstructing your view. The brain does this so that there is order and logic to the world around you.

To settle the confusion, pre-attentive attributes or pre-attentive processing are essential to attention and focus. The sorting of visual information to quickly make sense of what we are seeing on a smaller scale. It's a process. While with Gestalt Principles, we see the meaningful result of a purposeful collection of elements.

Pre-Attentive Attributes: Drawing attention

Gestalt Principles: Seeing the overall result

Help bring order and logic to your data visualization by applying these principles. Or, in some cases, the data will do it for you. When working with large data sets, highlight the patterns purposefully. These principles are as follows:

Law of proximity

This law refers to how closely different visual elements are positioned in relation to each other. Items that are close to each other are perceived as a group. This will naturally appear when potting many data points in a scatter plot. From there, you can highlight specific groups and their significance.

FIGURE 1.3: Law of proximity

Law of closure

This law refers to how the brain simplifies complex arrangements of visual elements by organizing those elements into recognizable patterns. The brain will fill in incomplete images to make the visualization makes sense based on this law. As the presenter, you need to be mindful of this law and ensure that your data visualizations are as complete so that your audience grasps as accurate information from the data as possible. Therefore, a broken line in a line chart can unwittingly confuse your audience because the image is incomplete. On the other hand, a continued line displaying the same information on a line chart gives more information so that the brain gets a clearer picture. If you look below you can see the missing value and what the value actually looks like. The missing point is unclear as to what the data was doing in that specific time frame and could be misconstrued.

FIGURE 1.4: Law of closure

Law of similarity

This law describes the brain's tendency to group like things together. Therefore, the brain will perceive things with similar shapes, sizes, colors, orientations, or textures as belonging to the same group. Use this law to help your audience more readily identify patterns based on your data. You can also use this law to ensure that your audience more easily perceives different groups by using dissimilar elements such as color to make that differentiation.

FIGURE 1.5: Law of similarity

Law of enclosure

The brain also identifies visual items as grouped together based on them being enclosed in a particular group. That is the basis of this law, which is also sometimes referred to as the Common Region Gestalt principle.

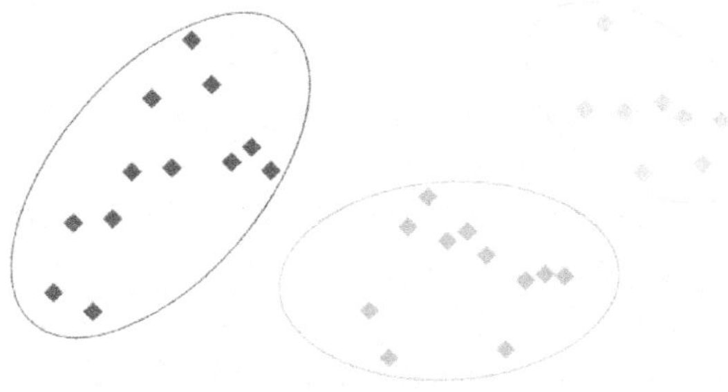

FIGURE 1.6: Law of closure

Law of continuity

This law is based on the fact that the human eye tends to follow lines and perceives direction based on the curvature of that line. Use this law in your data visualization by arranging visual objects in lines to simplify comparisons and create groupings. For example, your audience will more readily digest the data being portrayed in a bar chart that moves figures from highest to lowest or vice versa in a straight line compared to a bar chart that has scattered figures and varying heights of bars.

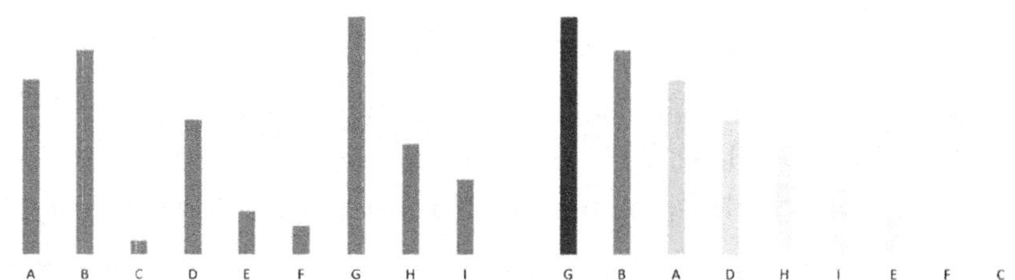

FIGURE 1.7 Law of continuity

Law of figure-ground

The brain places objects either in the background or foreground of your vision without conscious effort. That is the basis of this law. Items placed in the foreground of your vision are moved from pre-attentive processing to visual processing. They are given higher priority compared to those in the background. Foreground elements are noticeable because they contain a visual variable that catches the eye more readily. Make your data visualizations more credible by giving contrast to foreground and background elements. Contrast can be created by using color and contrasts that move your audience along the line of data. On the other hand, using too many colors and too much contrast can overload your audience's senses and thus, create confusion. A good example of this law in action is the use of a color gradient moving from blue to yellow to orange to red to show rising temperatures in a bar chart with a white background. The shift in color variation of the bars brings these to the forefront while the white scale of the chart is in the background.

Law of symmetry

This law states that visual elements with symmetry are perceived as a uniform group by the brain. Symmetry refers to similar parts that face each other or are ordered similarly around an axis. This gives the sense that things are in balance and as they should be. On the other hand, asymmetric (the opposite of symmetric) visual elements give the sense that something is missing or that there are differences between the visual elements. You can use both states in your data visualizations to show similarities with symmetric elements and differences with asymmetric elements.

THE QUESTION REMAINS - how can these laws guide you to creating visualizations that allow your audiences to note patterns and see the insights pertinent to that presentation? To answer that you must keep in mind the goals that must be accomplished every time you create data visualizations:

1. Tell a story in a graphic way.
2. Establish and maintain your credibility at all times.

FOUR BASIC PRINCIPLES TO FOLLOW

There are 4 basic principles of ensuring that your charts always conform to these goals:

Honesty is a must

It is unfortunate that it needs to be said but your charts must portray the truth at all times. But there is a disparity that happens to many who unwittingly deceive their audience with a few common mistakes. Some of those include:

First and foremost, never omit the baseline of your chart. The baseline of any chart is the horizontal line that conveys the basic measurement of the variables of that scale. Most often, the basic measurement is zero (0) but this is data/chart specific and is not always the case. Incorrectly determining your baseline will result in a biased view of the data, making differences seem more significant than they actually are.

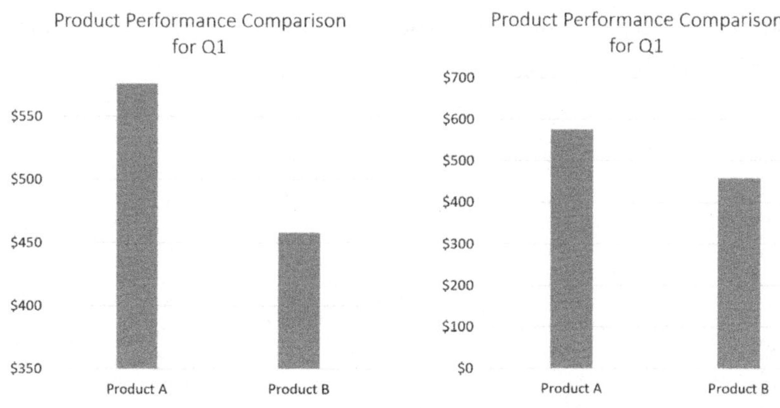

FIGURE 1.8:

The second most common mistake is going against conventions like using larger areas to indicate higher number values. Audiences are typically familiar with conventions and going against that grain can leave them with the wrong impression.

Lastly, do not cherry-pick data to place in your charts. Your audience needs a whole picture of what the data represents to make informed decisions and showing only a few data points can mislead and, thus, deceive your audience. For example, you can present a data set from the last 6 months as an upward trend.

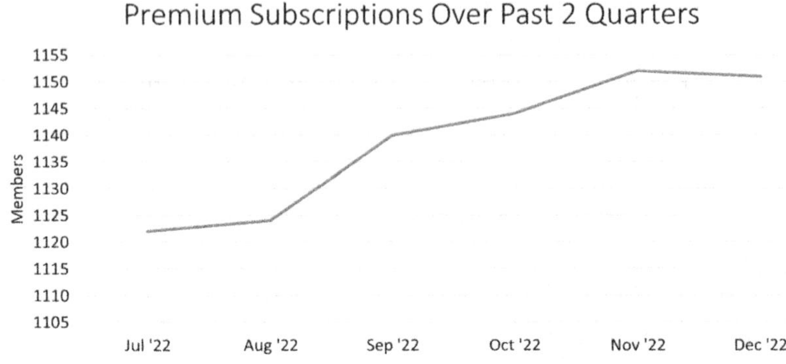

FIGURE 1.9

Although this is true, if you look at the past year, premium subscriptions have been steadily declining.

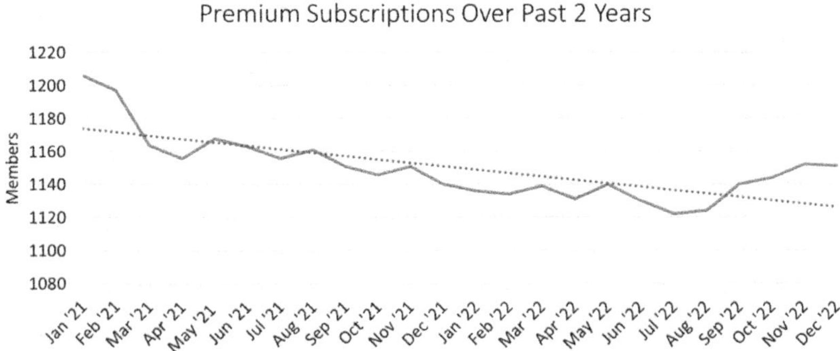

FIGURE 1.10

The more significant insight is why it's on the decline and will it continue even after this minor spike is over. Always showcase the full picture.

Know your audience

We use data visualizations to communicate with others – the audience. Even though the message might be the same, how we communicate with a group is more important than what is said in conveying the right message. You need to create your visualizations in a way that your audience wants to see and can understand. Therefore, before you picture a type of chart or the colors that will be used on that chart, you need to study and understand who you will be presenting to. Based on what your research says about your audience, you can cater to their method of communication. Items that affect the audience's communication style include their job position. Typically, higher levels of management need more of a helicopter view to see what is going on, without as many details. If they are requesting the details, multiple charts will be in order. While department-specific employees will need more details for better and more accurate decision-making. Technical literacy is also a factor that determines how data should be presented. The more knowledgeable the audience is about the statistics and niche-specific items, the more complicated the charts can be without losing insight. The opposite is true for less knowledgeable audiences.

How much background knowledge the audience has on the topic is also important. The more they know, the fewer details that need to be given upfront. On the other hand, if the audience does not have any prior knowledge of the subject matter, then your charts need to include information that will get them up to speed. It's always good to have some extra charts that go into detail on some points just in case a few people need more insight.

Presenting a detailed story to high-level executives is a challenge on its own. Check out my book "How to Win With Your Data Visualizations" if you want a more in depth view of presenting data. Here, I go deeper into understanding your audience and how to present effectively to different people. Scan the QR below to check it out! (or once you've finished this book.)

Make the key insights the feature

Key insights are the most important facts that summarize the data being presented. They are the star of the visualization and as such, it is only fitting that you put the spotlight on them.

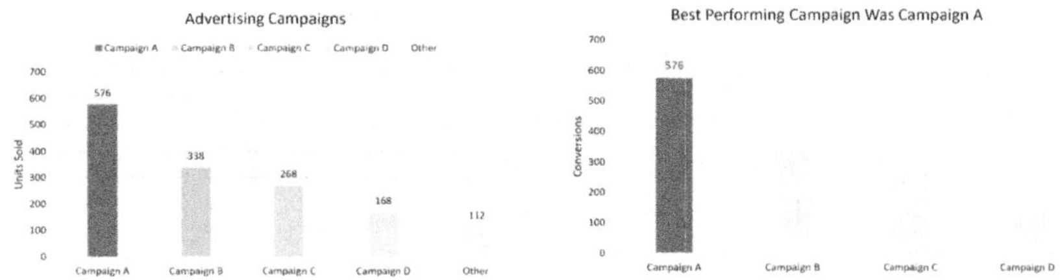

FIGURE 1.11

How to do that? It is no hard feat. Start by eliminating distractions. Of course, choosing the right chart to deliver your key points is a must. But going hand in hand with that is also being strategic about the colors and text that enhance those points. All visual elements must serve a purpose in your charts. Use uniform color schemes and easily readable fonts that ensure your core messages are easily understood.

Next, get rid of any element that is not essential to highlighting the insights of your charts. Examples of elements that might not serve to enhance your message include gridlines, labels, and bright colors. It is a must that you examine each addition to your chart to ensure it belongs and makes your message clearer and better understandable. If it does not? Discard without mercy.

Lastly, use visual variables to highlight significant data points. Such variables can be colors or shades. Use them to draw your audience's eyes to the most important facts.

Insights before aesthetics

The 4th and final principle is insight before aesthetics. How your graphics look is mighty important when you present data but there is something that deserves an even higher priority than that. You must get the point across to the audience. There is, after all a reason why this data visualization's creation was necessary. Do not get caught up in the aesthetics and forget that point. Your visuals (and all these laws and principles that you learned above) will become worthless if you neglect the core message of the data. Your visualizations need to support your information, not detract from it. Incorrect, untruthful, or badly portrayed data certainly do not convey your message accurately. For maximum effect, always keep the goals of creating your visualizations in mind *then* apply the principles described above.

SIGHT IS HOW WE, as a human race, learn most effectively. It is what allowed us to survive the stone age and what allowed us to sail the high sea while still making it safely back to land. So, it only makes sense that we would convey data in such a way to make for an easier understanding of complex and often large volumes of data. That is the basis of using data visualizations. Ever since the modern era of publishing charts to visually present information began in the 1780s, we have not looked back and we continue to fine-tune processes that make it easier and easier to break down complex matters into understandable points through graphics.

However, there is a natural ebb and flow to the way we process what we see. This chapter was written to get in touch with what the brain does with the images that it receives from our eyes and how you can use that psychology to make better visualizations. The visual variables used in your charts allow your audience to visually process the most key insights and levels of perceptions and bring them into states of cognitive awareness. Take advantage of the Gestalt principles so that your audience will subconsciously organize the imagery that you are delivering to them to create a whole picture of the data.

We have taken a brief delve into biology in this chapter but the science gives you a sound foundation of how to approach your data visualization development. You must note though, that no matter how well you learn to apply these principles and laws, always keep sight of what truly matters – telling a data story while establishing your credibility. Know what your audience wants from you and deliver that message truthfully while making the key insights clear.

With that knowledge in your bag, let's get into the fun stuff – the different types of charts at your disposal and when you should use them. Just as plumbers, carpenters, mechanics, and electricians have those specialized tools they only bring out once and a while, we, as data professionals, can benefit from the same strategy. Having an arsenal of chart knowledge allows us to bring out the most in our data when it is absolutely essential. Let's build up our tool belt.

Download the Color PDF!

As a small indie publisher, in order to publish the book at a reasonable price point, printing in B+W was essential. Although not ideal, I hope it doesn't take away from the valuable information.

If you would like the color PDF, you can scan the QR code below and get it for free. Refer back to it in instances where you think seeing the color might be of value.

If you have any issues, please reach out at contact@elizabethsclarke.com. Thank you for understanding!

-Elizabeth

2
CHANGE OVER TIME

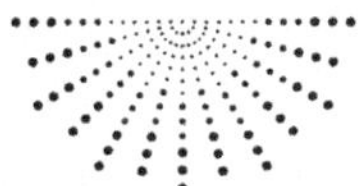

As mentioned before, you can't randomly choose charts to portray data. The basis for your chart selection is based on the type of data you want to display and what insights you want to gain from it. To start your education, we will cover charts showing change over time.

Change over time is a display of how trends in data move across time values. These time values can be as short, like a 24-hour period, or they can be long such as trends over months or even years. Time is displayed on the chart's horizontal axis (Y-axis) and moves from left to right. The variable or trend being studied over that time interval is displayed on the chart's vertical axis (X-axis). Examples of types of data that can be displayed with such charts include:

- A retail store's sales revenue over the last year
- Stock price movements
- A product's launch performance in the first few days
- Website visitors over the 1st quarter of the year

While time is the common denominator that links the types of charts we will discuss in this chapter, it is important to note that the appropriate time must be displayed. Otherwise, you risk confusing your audience. They need to have the proper context of the time movement, so this is one of the first things you need to nail down before developing data visualizations.

There are many options when visualizing change over time. The chart that you choose will depend on 2 factors:

1. The type of data being presented
2. The end goal of presenting this data to your audience.

With these two factors in mind, we will discuss 5 of the most widely used change-over-time charts next.

LINE CHARTS

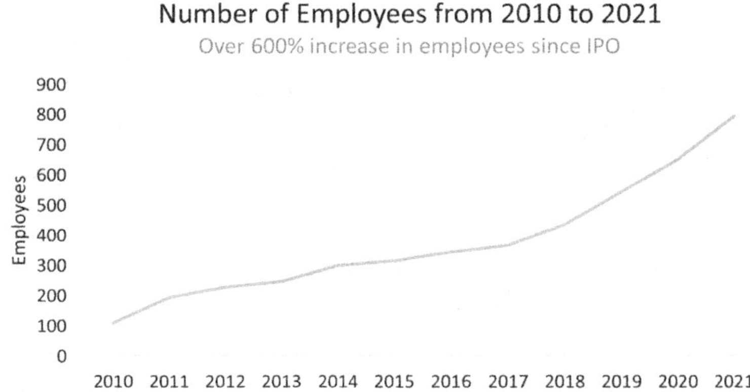

FIGURE 2.1: Basic line chart

A personal favorite. A line chart is one of the first charts that come to mind for most people when they hear data visualization, but what is a line chart exactly? Also called a line graph or a line plot, a line chart is a graphical representation of data that uses points connected by line segments to demonstrate the change in volume. This demonstration moves from left to right. As usual, with charts that illustrate change over time, the horizontal axis represents a continuous progression of time from left to right and the vertical axis reports the values that change along that progression.

The most common use of line charts is to emphasize the change in variable values represented on the vertical axis against the continuous values noted in time intervals like hours, weeks, months, and years plotted on the horizontal axis. The plotted line will allow for changes in patterns and trends as it slopes up or down. Single and multiple lines can be plotted on a line chart. Multiple lines are used to compare trends of different variables and subgroups with a data set.

Even though the components of a line chart are quite simple, here are a few practices that be used to make these devices pop out as your audience and, of course, be effective at bringing your point across:

Use appropriate measurement intervals on the horizontal axis

Using time measurements that are too short can create a rather busy-looking line graph when using time intervals that are too far apart means that it is harder to follow the trend being depicted by the data. You must find a healthy medium between these two extremes for your line chart to be a credible source to your audience. Do so by testing out different intervals to get a feel of one representing the data to its highest potential. This could be made simpler by your knowledge of the data. If you find out the data cannot be accurately represented by one line, it is possible to use a second line. The first can highlight the marginal differences in the time interval and the second line can serve to highlight the overall trend with a rolling window. A rolling window refers to noting trends in a subset of the data. It does not represent the data entirely but rather a sub-series of the full set.

Refrain from plotting too many lines

Technically speaking, you can place as many lines on a single-line chart as you would like. However, not because you can means you should. Too many plotlines can make your line graph harder to interpret. Try to stick to plotting 5 lines or less if multiple trends need to be noted on the visualization. As you can see, too many lines clutter the visual and hide any insights.

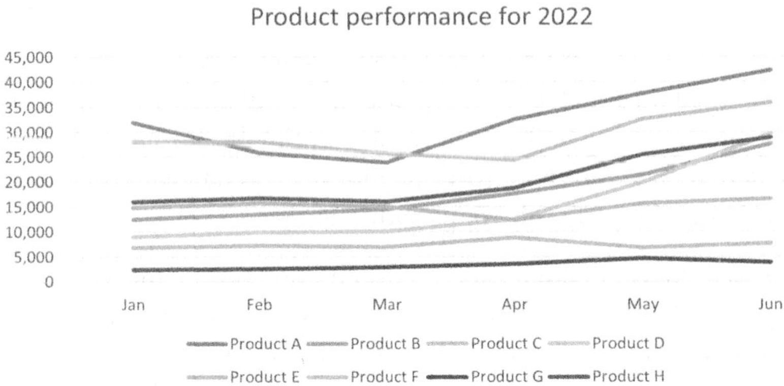

FIGURE 2.2: Cluttered line chart

In instances where more lines need to be used, use attention-grabbing attributes to highlight the important information. Always ensure that the key points are easily identifiable in your visualization and not hidden by noise. Also, ensure that plot lines are well separated so that each change in value is easy to track. A useful strategy when plotting multiple lines is to show the overplotted chart for an overall view of all the data, then show a second chart with only significant points highlighted in color.

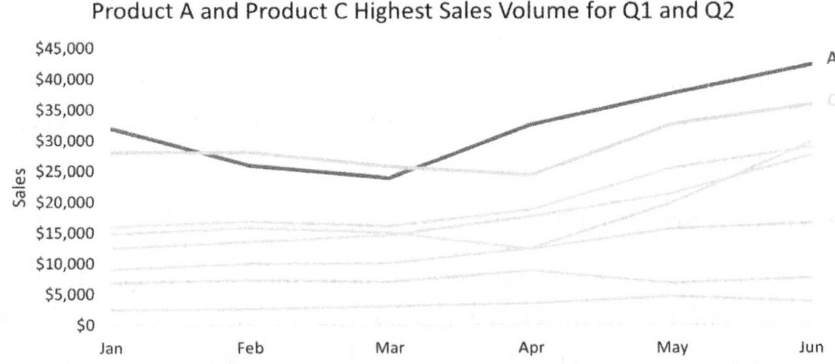

FIGURE 2.3: Highlighting specific information

Ensure gaps between points are identified

In instances where there is missing information between plotted points, ensure these missing values are labeled for easy identification. This can be done using a dotted line or a gap to highlight the absent value. Sometimes a missing value can be of use. Why was it missing? Has it always been missing? Missing values can bring insights of their own.

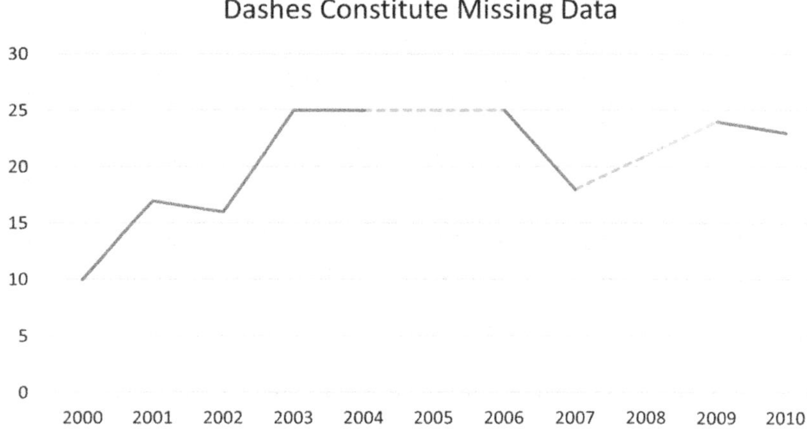

FIGURE 2.4: Always showcase missing data

Use the appropriate baseline

While using zero (0) baselines is necessary for charts like histograms and bar charts, it is not a strict requirement for use in line charts. In visualizations such as bar charts, using a non-zero baseline skews the relative difference between the bar heights and can therefore mislead the audience.

On the other hand, a line chart shows increases and decreases of the variable represented on the vertical axis over time. The rate at which this variable changes is relative to the horizontal axis and therefore, its distance from zero (0) does not skew the audience's perception of what the data represents. There may even be instances where the use of a zero baseline can mislead the audience when used in line charts. This happens in cases where the rate of change from zero to the first instance where the line slopes upward or downward is entirely flat.

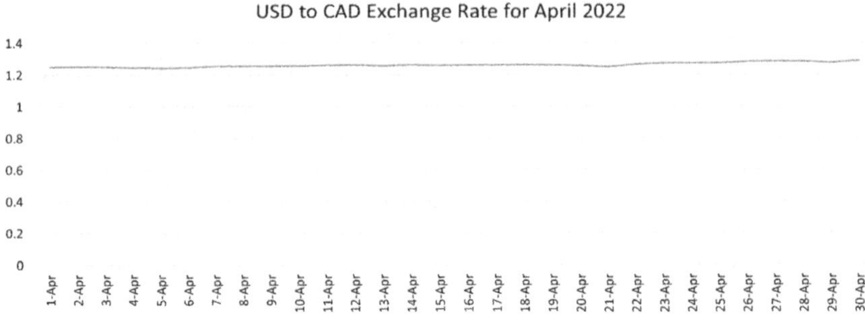

FIGURE 2.5

As you can see, there is a serious issue with the visualization when setting a zero baseline. Let's change the baseline for a better result.

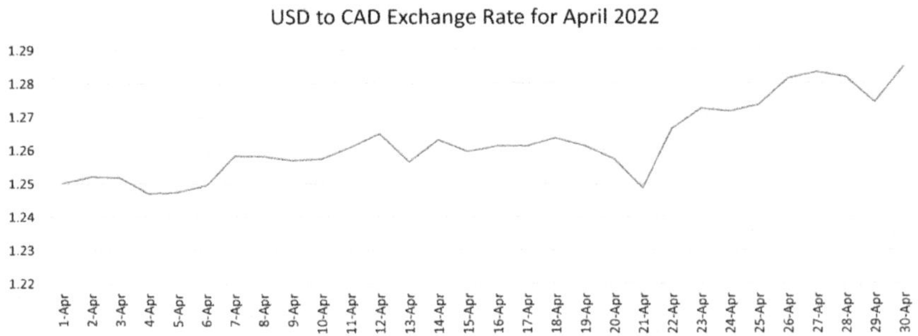

FIGURE 2.6

We now have a better view of how the data changes over time. Normally decimal points don't warrant a significant change and shouldn't be exaggerated. However, when it comes to currency exchange rates, a matter of cents makes a big difference and it's essential to see the fluctuation. Look at the data you're presenting before you determine your axis values.

Whether or not you use a zero baseline or a non-zero baseline in your line chart is dependent on the data at hand. As a rule of thumb, zero baselines are not a strict requirement with statistical summaries for accurate interpretation by the audience.

Avoid a smooth line

On a typical line chart, each plot point is connected with a straight line moving from left to right. Another common mistake to avoid is linking points with a smooth curve rather than a straight line going through each point one by one. Using curved lines distorts the perception of the trends represented in the data. A straight line lets us quickly note drops and spikes and when exactly they took place. Always remember; insights before aesthetics!

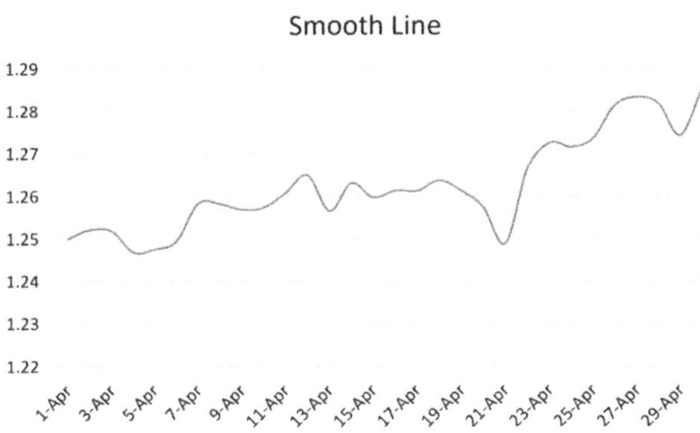

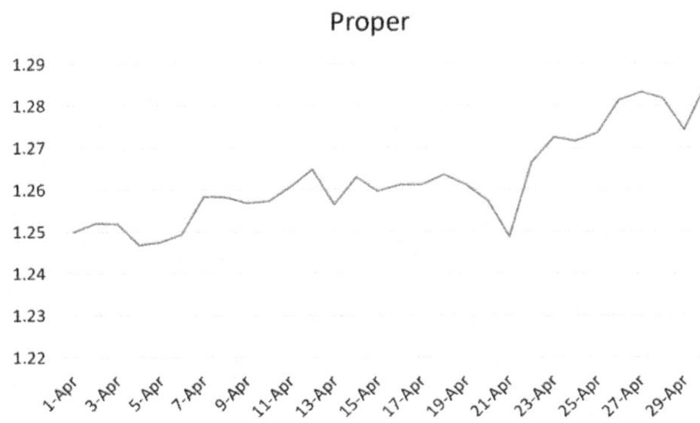

FIGURE 2.7

DUAL-AXIS LINE CHARTS lead to skewed information

While using a dual vertical axis on a line chart can serve to highlight different trends on one chart, this practice can easily lead to misinterpretation depending on how each axis is scaled. The same information can look entirely different with a few changes on each axis. To lessen the chances of this happening, ensure that the lines plotted are separated with appropriate scales on each vertical axis. The audience is less likely to make false comparisons between the variables being noted. As you can see below, this is the same set of data with different axis'. This is just an example. It can be skewed in many ways to make it appear however you want. People who know nothing about the dataset will indeed be misled.

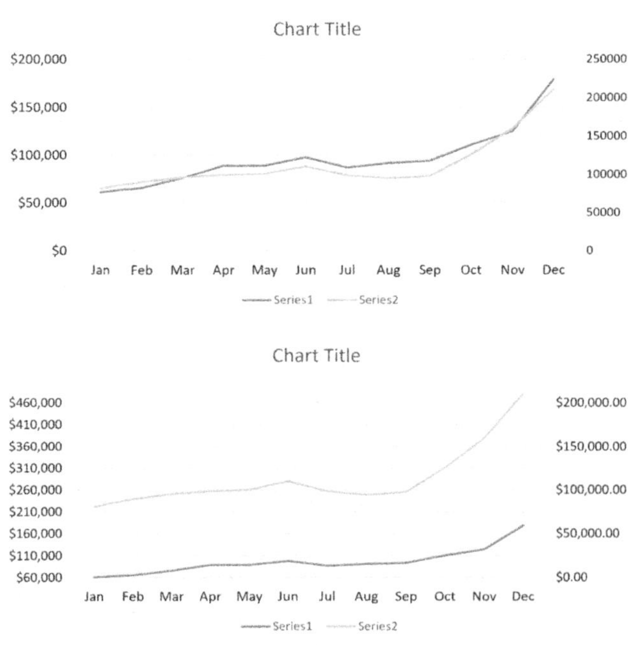

FIGURE 2.8

FAN CHARTS

A relatively uncommon visual is a fan chart. It joins a line graph that observes data from the past with a range area chart that determines future predictions. As forecasts become uncertain, the fan chart fades wider and becomes more transparent. They are often used to predict exchanges tares or inflation but can essentially be used to display any data with an uncertain future value.

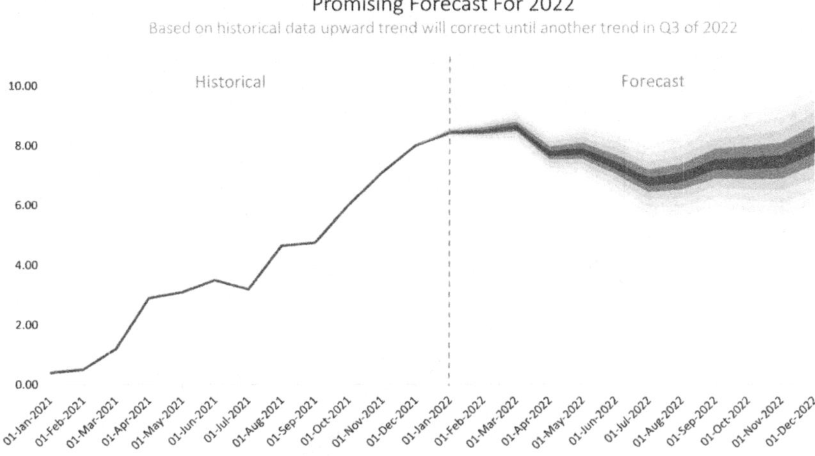

FIGURE 2.9

SLOPE CHARTS

At the risk of sounding obvious, I state this - slope charts are composed of slopes. A slope is a mathematical measurement of how steep a straight line is when plotted against a pair of coordinated axes like time intervals. The steepness is indicative of how that line increases or decreases in value. An increase in the steepness of the slope indicates a positive value change for the variable being displayed, while the opposite is true for a decrease in the steepness of the slope. A zero value in the slope means it aligns with the horizontal axis. Slope charts make use of these conventions to show comparisons between two variables, such as countries, locations, and regions. It also shows how trends develop over time in addition to rankings, transitions, and absolute values. Examples of when to use a slope chart is to display the number of customers who signed up for a monthly subscription between 2010 and 2023, or a comparison in the employment rate between men and women. These simple charts can give an effective picture of before and after scenarios while allowing audiences to visualize changes in variables such as sales, costs, prices, revenues, losses, profits, and any crucial aspect over specific amounts of time. They are often used by upper-level management to gain simple yet powerful insights.

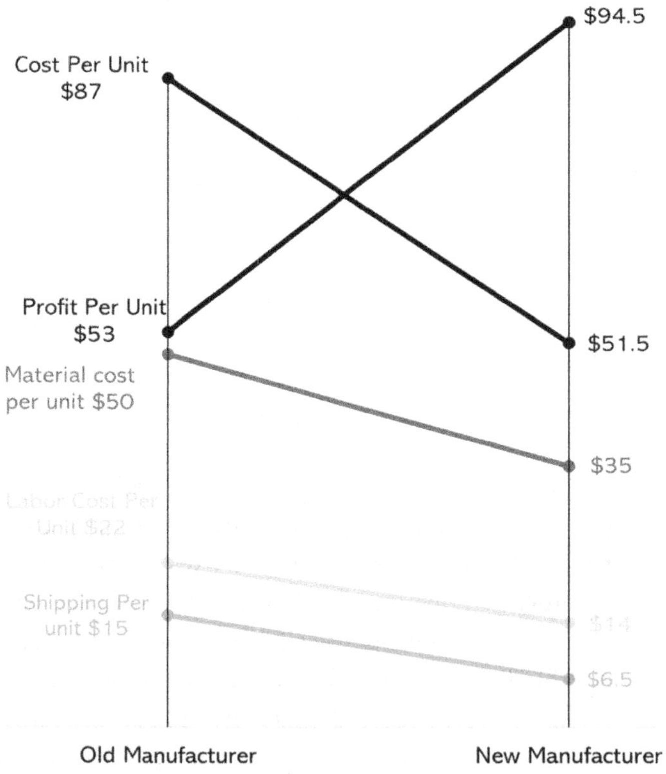

FIGURE 2.10

You can improve the insights gained from a slope chart by including a table alongside it. This is particularly useful in situations where the variable on the vertical axis portrays ranking order. Adding a table will allow the audience to note the values in order in addition to seeing the visual change in the form of the degree of the slope.

Other ways that you can make a slope chart a more effective storytelling device include using specific attributes that grab attention so that the audience better understands the values. For example, you may choose to use blue or green to indicate rising slopes while using orange or red to highlight falling slopes. Additionally, you can also increase the thickness of lines that indicate a great degree of change while making lines that show a lesser degree of change with thinner lines. Both uses of visual variables draw the audience's attention to the important trends indicated by the chart. On the other hand, you must ensure that your slope chart does not become too busy by adding several intersecting lines.

A great alternative to a slope chart is the bump chart. This chart shows the change in ranking over time. In particular, the bump chart helps an audience visualize how different variables change in rank over time. They differ from slope charts in that they can highlight multiple time intervals along the horizontal axis. With slope charts, the goal is to show the change in the value of the slope value. With bump charts, the aim is to highlight how the positions in rank change over time.

FIGURE 2.11

You can also easily highlight specific items for a better view.

FIGURE 2.12

To create a bump chart In Excel, we can use a ranking system based on the categories' values. Lets say between 1 and 4. The lowest figure being 1 and the highest figure being 4. For the example above, we did this for shoe sales from every month throughout the year—an efficient way to see the best performers and the best-performing months per category.

AREA CHARTS

If there ever was a marriage between a bar chart and a line chart, you would get an area chart. This chart displays how at least one set of numeric values changes over time. This progression is indicated by a line that moves from left to right but the difference between a line chart and an area is that the space between the line and the baseline is shaded. Area charts are most commonly used to show how multiple groups of values compare to each other. Therefore, such cases will have multiple lines as part of the makeup of the chart.

There are different types of area charts and each has a specific purpose.

Stacked area chart

This is the type of area chart that is generally implied when the term 'area chart' is used. Unlike the overlapping area chart, stacked area charts use lines that are plotted one on top of the other with the most recently plotted line serving as the baseline for the next line to be plotted.

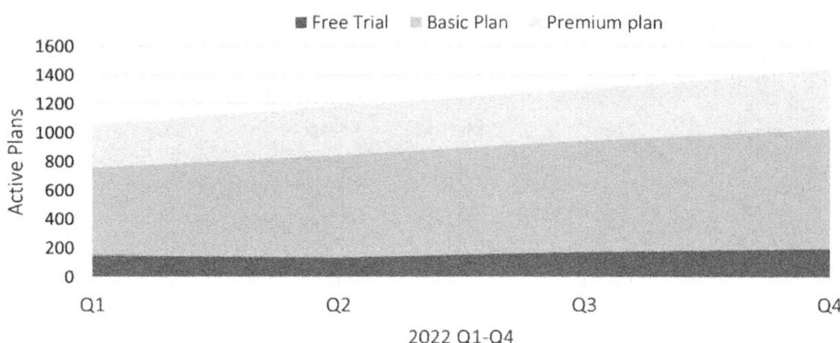

FIGURE 2.13

The highest line serves as the total of the values when they are summed up. As such, providing the total value is one of the functions of this type of chart. It also provides a breakdown of each group of values in addition to allowing for comparison between these groups via each shaded part. To summarize, the audience gets a general idea of how each group of values performs when stacked against each other and how they contribute to the total.

Get the most from your area charts but following the next few guidelines:

Add transparency to better compare

When working with an overlapping area chart, you can add transparency to see how the figures compare to each other a lot easier.

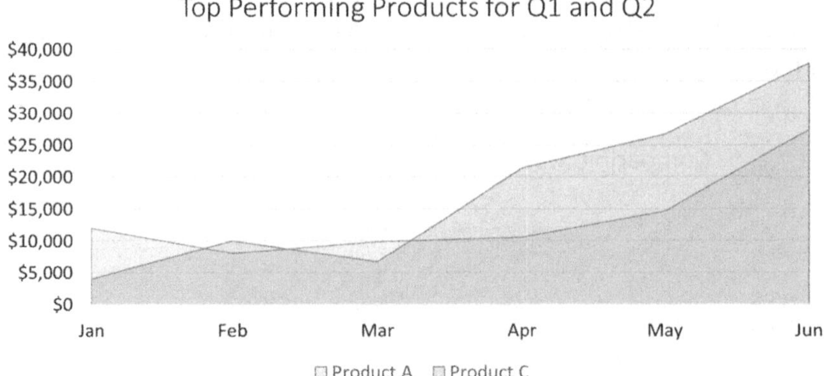

FIGURE 2.14

Use a zero baseline

Because of the shading in this type of chart, a zero baseline becomes a necessary addition. Just like with a bar chart, this ensures that the heights of the shaded areas are not distorted and misleading.

Ponder the number of groups in overlapping area charts

The more groups of values that need to be represented in an overlapping area chart, the more colors are required for shading. This can make the charts busy and difficult for the audience to interpret. As a rule of thumb, limit the number of groups to be portrayed in an overlapping area chart to 3. Any more than that and consider using a line chart instead for an easier comparison of the groups of values.

Consider the order of lines in stacked area charts

The sum of groups will be the same no matter how you stack them, but the order must be strategic to avoid confusion. It is best to put the largest or the least variable groups at the bottom of the stacked area chart. The smallest or more variable groups should be placed at the top of the stack. Unless the data sets need to be in a specific order, this trick can make it a lot more readable and clear.

Avoid using an area chart for a single group of values

As mentioned before, area charts are used to show comparisons between groups of values. Therefore, they are not suitable for displaying single sets of values. In such cases, it is better to use a line chart to show the progression of the values over time.

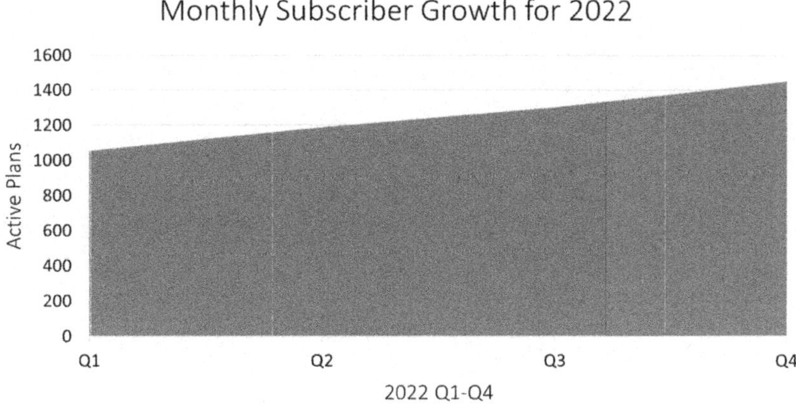

FIGURE 2.15

An area chart in this scenario doesn't add any value. A line chart is essentially the same thing with less visual noise.

FIGURE 2.16

Lets look at another great area chart. In this case, one showing the distribution of Co2 emissions since 1860.

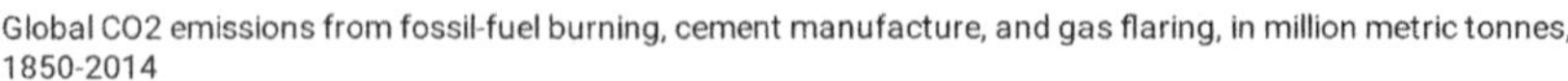

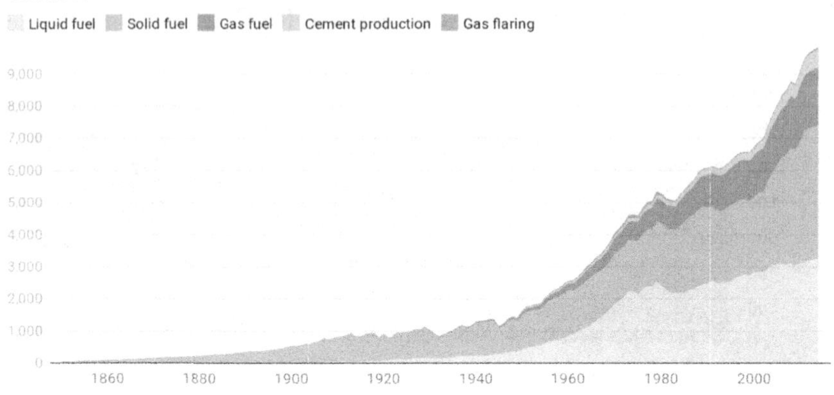

FIGURE 2.17

Consider creating an interactive area chart to showcase individual sections easily. You can run your cursor along and see the data from each point.

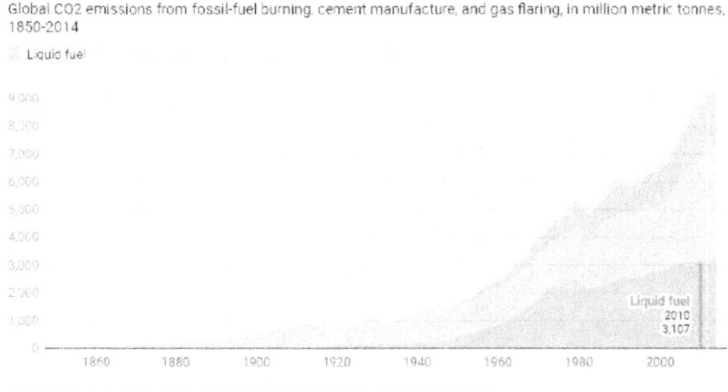

FIGURE 2.18

As an alternative to an area chart, you can use a steam graph. It is most closely related to the stacked area chart, but while the stacked area chart features the baseline at the bottom of the stack of values, the steam graph features the baseline running through the center of the chart. The values are symmetrically assembled around the baseline. As a result, the steam graph is not ideal if you would like to note an overall value or even the precise values of each group, especially in comparison to each other. This chart is, however, great for inviting interactivity from a wide audience. The members can play with the chart to note findings and the level of interplay can serve to make the presentation more memorable and educational to some audiences.

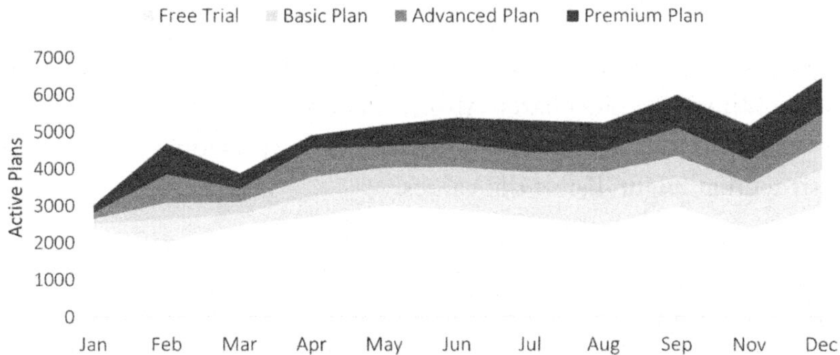

FIGURE 2.9

CONNECTED SCATTERPLOT

This type of chart is one used to display the progressive development of a numeric variable over time. The plotted points are represented by dots and connected by straight-line segments. You can think of connected scatter plots as line charts with highlights to make the individual plotted points more visible. One drawback of using line charts is that it is not always easy to note the breaks in the line of plot points. A connected scatter plot allows you to get around that problem. In particular, connected scatter plots are great for showing the timeline progression of information, such as how stock prices change throughout the day. You can easily hover over each point to highlight the specific value for that time frame.

FIGURE 2.20

To use this type of chart with maximum effectiveness, follow the same advice outlined for line charts. Also, it is not necessary to use a zero baseline with this type of chart due to the lack of shading of any other construct that might distort the values.

GANTT CHART

This type of chart is great for project management as it shows a project's schedule and the task and events that occur in that lifecycle.

FIGURE 2.21

The specific nature of the Gantt chart allows it to be used to:

- Build complex project schedules
- Manage complex project schedules
- Monitor the tasks dependencies of the project
- Keep track of a project's progress

Because of these functionalities, the Gantt chart is great for mapping out marketing campaigns, outlining the deliverables for a client, planning a product launch, and similar items.

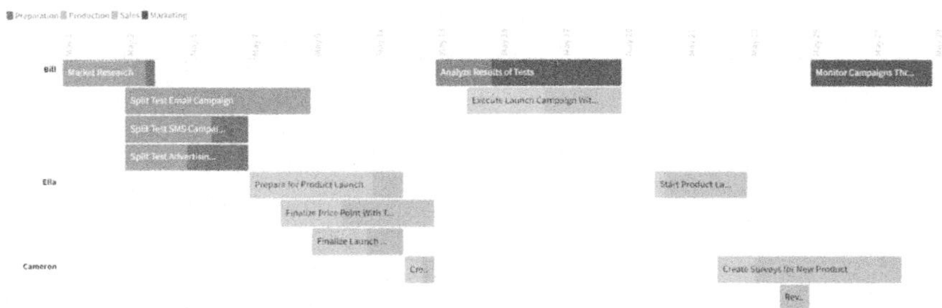

FIGURE 2.22

We often have to look to the past to formulate a plan to achieve our goals in the future. The same holds true for businesses and organizations. Change over time charts allow you to streamline that planning process by noting how past variables have changed as time passes. They educate audiences about trends and thus, invite investigation into why these trends progress in the way they do over time. The findings of such investigation allow for developing solutions to maximize these trends when they are favorable or turning the situation around when they are not.

These charts also allow for noting comparisons and even totals. We have outlined several changes over time charts in this chapter with the aim of showing you which are best used under particular circumstances.

3
COMPARISON

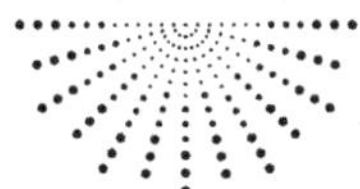

More often, at least two groups of data need to be displayed and compared to each other. Comparison charts are the go-to data visualization tool in these cases. They help highlight the differences and similarities between sets of values.

But do not disregard them as tools that can be used to display single variables. Even in single sets of data, there can be multiple categories and these types of charts come in handy to showcase the differences and similarities between these subsets.

There are many, many types of comparison charts. This chapter highlights several of the most common with definitions of what they are, when to use them, and how to maximize their use.

BAR GRAPHS

You can't study the topic of data visualization without coming across the infamous bar chart. Also called a column chart or a bar graph, the bar chart is used to plot numeric values featuring categories represented by a bar. Each numeric value is represented by one bar and the length of that bar corresponds to one axis while the values of these bars are plotted on a common baseline. This commonality allows for each comparison of values portrayed by the levels of the bars.

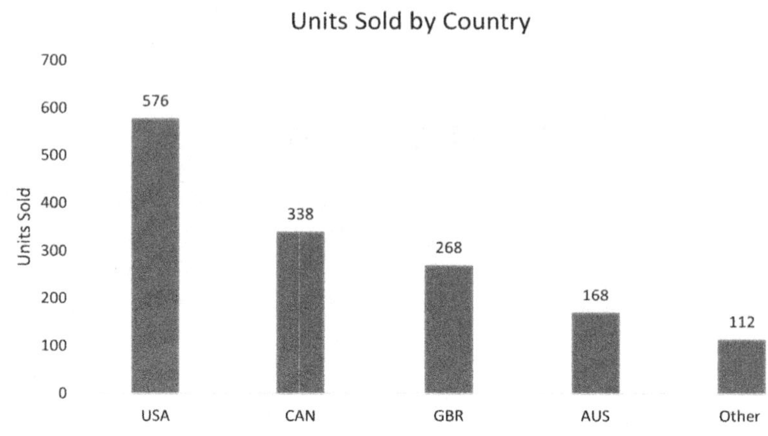

FIGURE 3.1

Bar charts are the go-to when the distribution of data points across multiple categories is being plotted. These categories can be across multiple sets of data of multiple categories within one group of values. The length of the bars gives insight into the most common or highest groups or subgroups and how other groups or subgroups weigh against these.

Get the most out of your bar charts with the following tips:

Avoid 3D

3-D effects can be difficult to align the bar with the baseline and can be a major readability issue. I also stay away from 3D charts as they do more harm than good.

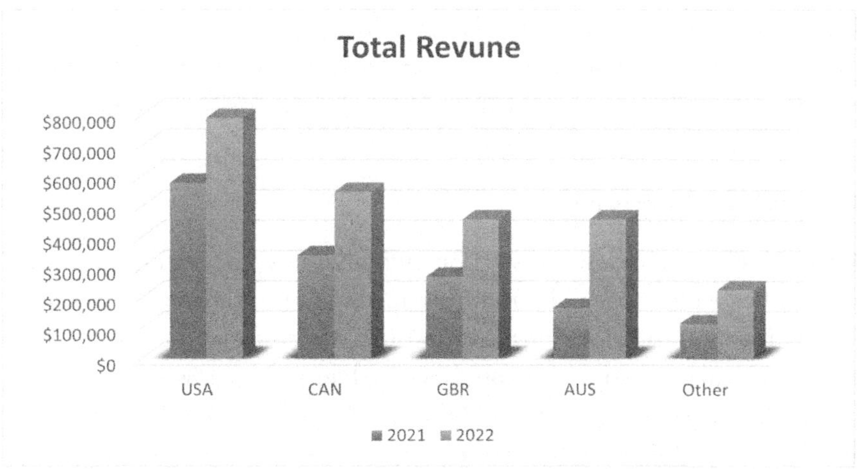

FIGURE 3.2

If you see here, the 3D effect just takes away from the insights and the chart is immediately harder to read.

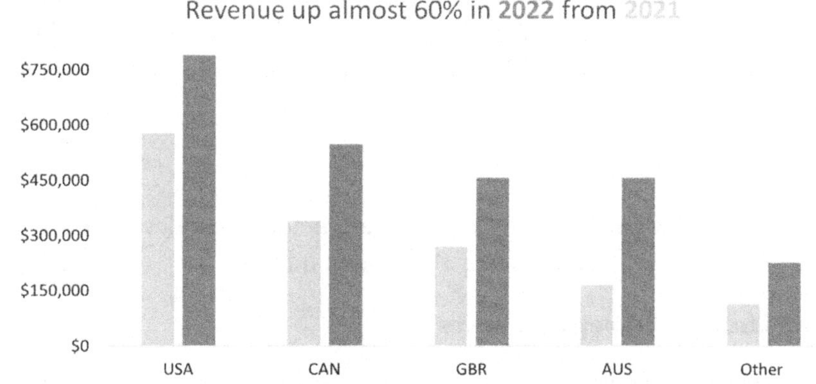

FIGURE 3.3

This rendition is a lot easier on the eyes.

Be mindful of how you order the categories

Ensure good visual flow by first sorting the bars with the largest values first and gradually progressing to the smaller value. This makes the bar length move from longest to shortest. Your audience will appreciate making easy comparisons between the bars. The only time you should deviate from this practice is when categories are labeled in a particular order. This order takes precedence.

Use color effectively

Color can be your friend or your enemy when it comes to designing bar charts. Use color sparingly and only to draw attention to key insights. When it comes to color, don't reinvent the wheel. Keep the overall color usage neutral to ensure unwanted biases, like red for loss and green for gain. I like to start with a bar graph with no color and ask myself what needs to be highlighted. We will cover color in more detail in our design chapter.

Include value annotations as necessary

Annotations, or data labels help explain parts of the chart that might not be immediately clear from a glance. Even though a good bar chart allows the audience to compare the lengths of the bars and make approximations of their values, the exact figures might be unclear. The use of annotations makes values clear when it is important that they be noted. Use these when necessary by adding them in the middle or at the end of the bar.

THERE ARE a few common mistakes that are made when developing bar charts. These mistakes and how to avoid them include:

Using images to replace bars

The aesthetic of such a practice can be tempting but remember that understandability comes before visual appeal when it comes to data visualization. Images can make it hard to derive key insights into the data. Any visual variable that distracts the audience from the core message must be avoided. Stick to using rectangular bars to present the data.

Using dark gridlines

Gridlines are the light gray lines that run across the axes, carrying the value to line up with the plotted data points. They can be placed vertically or horizontally and help the audience differentiate between the specific insights being depicted. The key word here is *light*. You might be tempted to darken the lines for visual appeal, but the practice will likely distract your audience. Always keep visual clutter to a minimum. If gridlines are not a necessary addition to your charts, bar charts, or otherwise, do not use them. In cases where they help educate the audience, keep them faint to maintain a good visual flow of the chart.

Great alternative versions to your standard column chart include:

Horizontal bar graphs

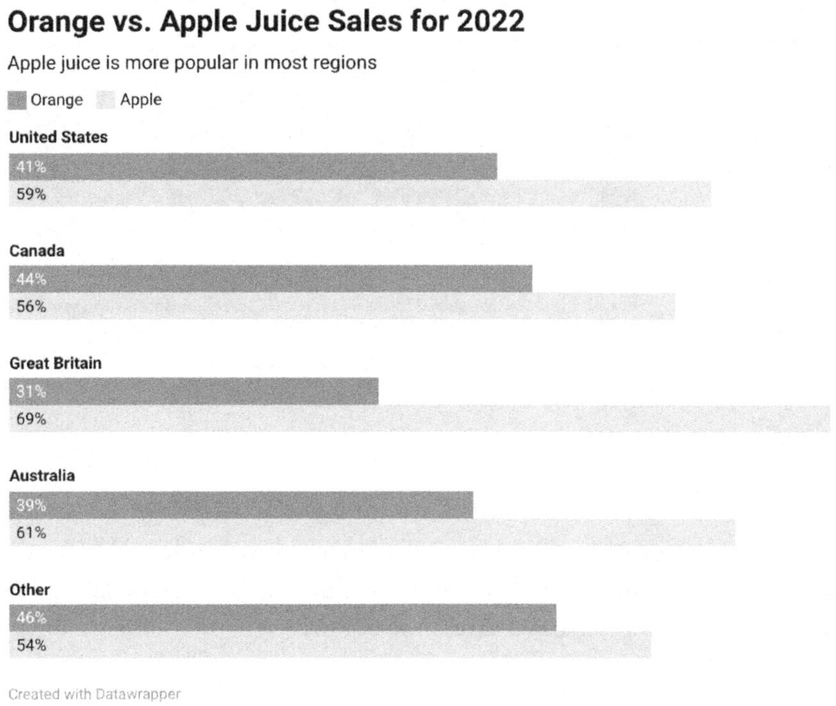

Orange vs. Apple Juice Sales for 2022

Apple juice is more popular in most regions

Orange Apple

United States

41%

59%

Canada

44%

56%

Great Britain

31%

69%

Australia

39%

61%

Other

46%

54%

Created with Datawrapper

FIGURE 3.4

When thinking of a bar chart, we typically think of a vertical column chart, but you can switch things up with horizontal bars instead. Horizontal bars can be particularly useful in situations where the labels are long. The layout makes them easier to read.

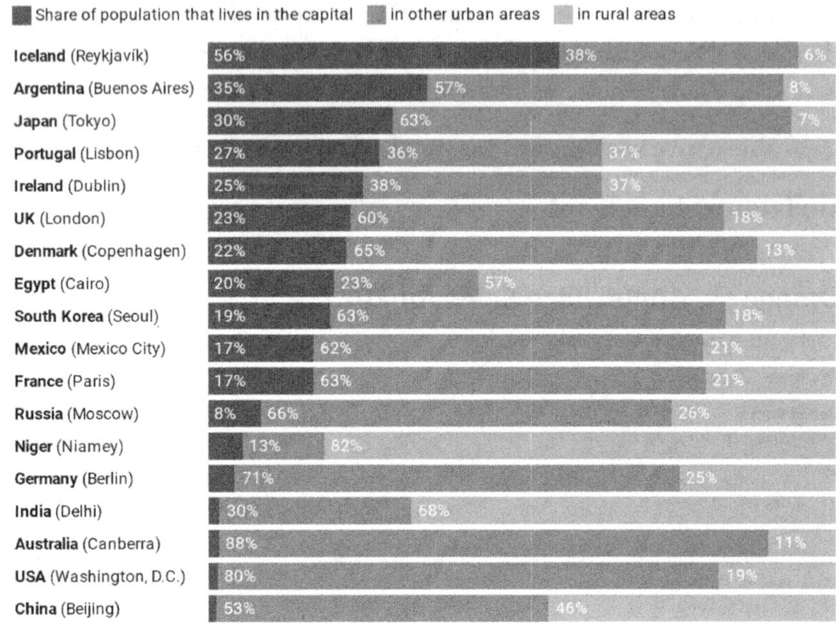

FIGURE 3.5

It also can be organized in more of a hierarchical order. Where the highest figure is on top, and the lowest underneath, which makes for an easy understanding. Like we have done below.

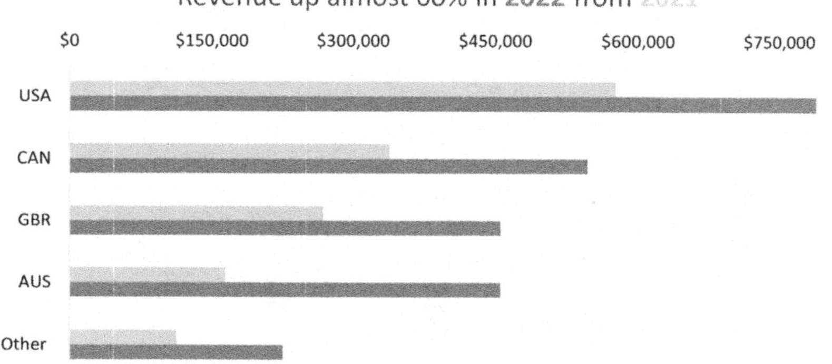

FIGURE 3.6

STACKED bar Chart

Another common variation. Instead of having the bars either horizontal or beside each other, the categories are stacked upward. Although effective in some scenarios, it makes it more challenging to compare specific categories.

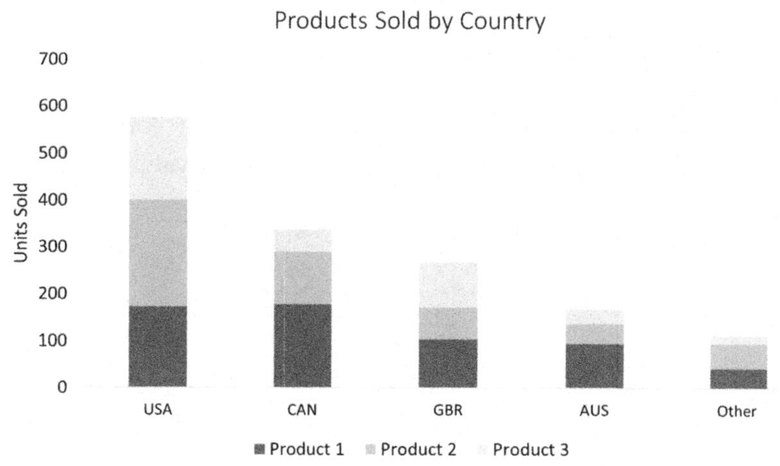

FIGURE 3.7

In this case, a regular column chart might be more effective.

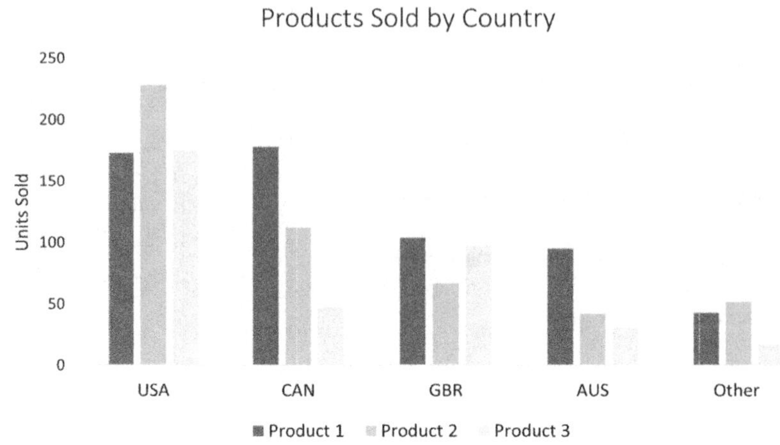

FIGURE 3.8

When creating a stacked bar, I prefer to use it horizontally like the one shown above. It makes it a bit easier to compare insights, and the data labels add key information.

Lollipop chart

These charts use different forms of aesthetics to deliver the same information. Lines topped with dots that resemble lollipops are used instead of bars. These types of charts are useful when lots of categories are close together. It allows the audience to focus on the data values and, thus, increasing readability.

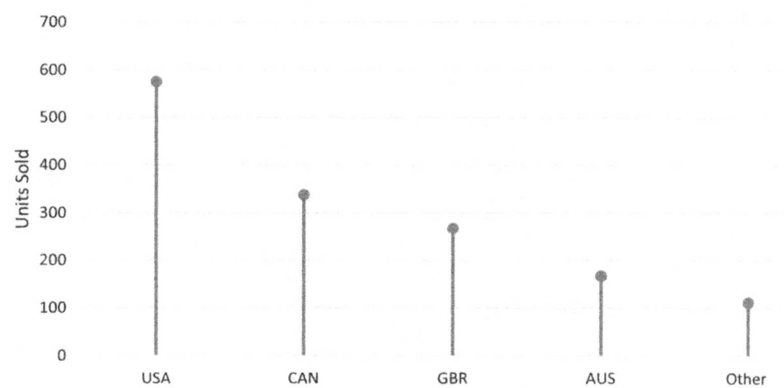

FIGURE 3.9

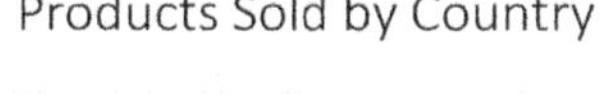

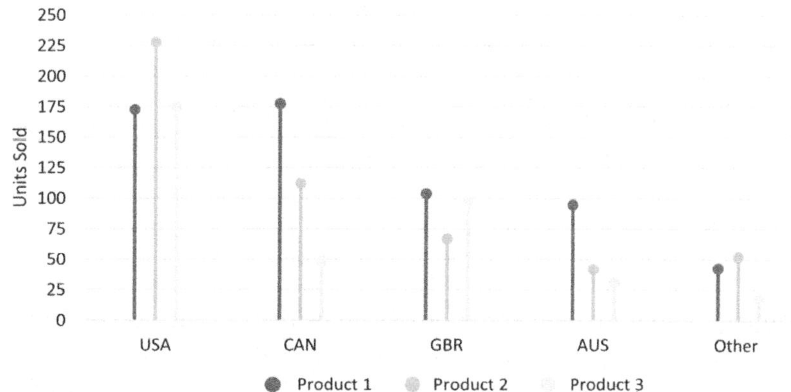

FIGURE 3.10

DIVERGING BAR

To diverge means to move apart or separate. When the data values between groups or subgroups indicate an increasing difference, diverging bars are the appropriate visualization tool to use. As such, they make a great resource to compare two alternatives and display results from surveys and questionnaires. They make it easy to visualize opposing responses and compare them.

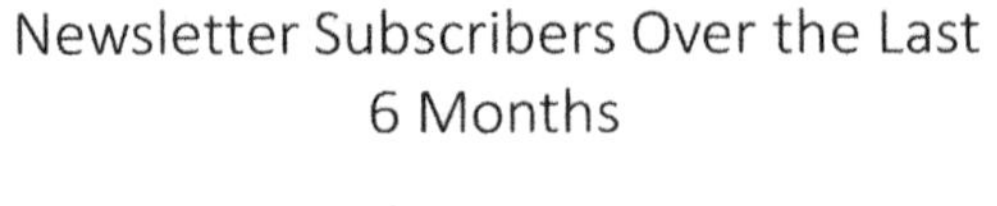

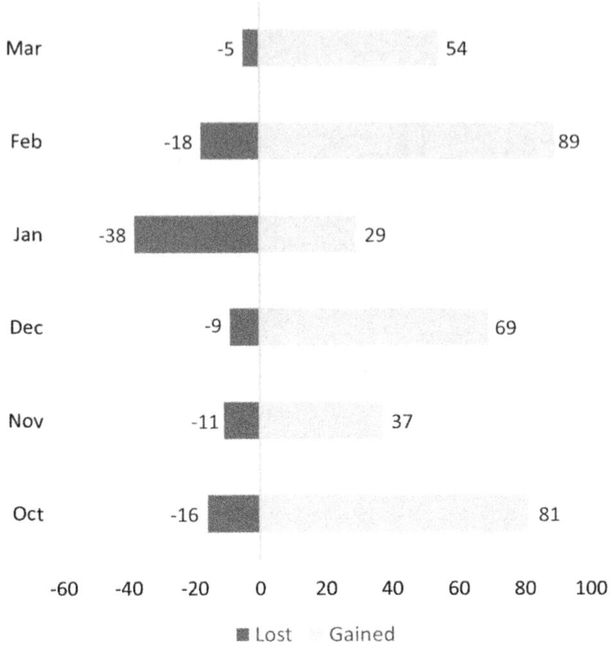

FIGURE 3.11

Diverging bars emphasize variations, one positive (+) and one negative (-) from a fixed reference point. The scale normally starts at 0, but this is not always the case. It can be a target or long-term average. Two horizontal bars are aligned on this scale, with one running to the left and the other to the right, starting at the common vertical baseline. The length of the bars corresponds to their numerical value.

A similar chart that can be used in place of a diverging bar is the diverging stacked bar. It features an additional vertical baseline with horizontal rectangle bars stacked on one to the next. The values these correspond to can be percentages or absolute values.

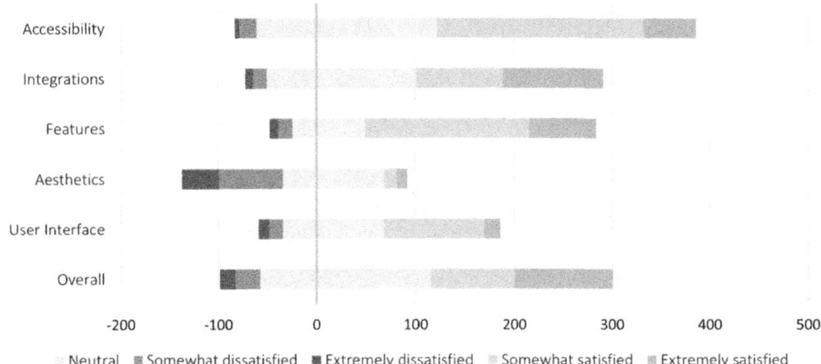

FIGURE 3.12

Maximize the use of diverging bars by:

- Use different colors or color contrasts to distinguish each side of the baseline.
- Place the responses in increasing or decreasing order to ensure a good visual flow.

BUBBLE CHART

Also called a bubble plot, the bubble chart is a relative of the scatter plot, which uses dots to show the values corresponding to three numeric variables. Each dot on the bubble chart represents a single point of data. The value of that point is indicated by the size of the dot as well as its position on both the horizontal and vertical axis. This chart makes it possible for you to combine and compare three groups of data on the same chart and show their relationship through comparison. Examples of points of data that can be displayed on a bubble chart include a sports teams average points per game on the horizontal axis (Y axis), the average points scored by each team on the vertical (X axis), and the number of wins each team has (the size of each bubble). Larger bubbles would show more wins and the opposite would be true for smaller bubbles.

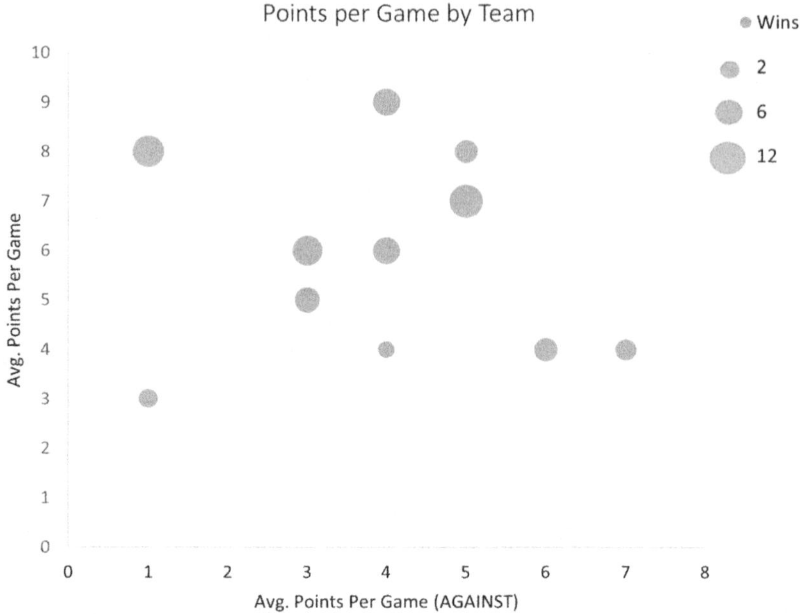

FIGURE 3.13

To afford your audience the most value from your bubble charts, use the following tips to maximize their effectiveness.

- Ensure the bubble sizes are relevant to the value of the data. Therefore, a bubble with a value of 50 should be half the size of a bubble with a value of 100. Do not skew the sizes of the bubbles, as this is misleading. As we covered in chapter 1, your brain subconsciously categorizes items based on size. Accuracy is key.
- Limit the number of data points on your bubble charts. Typically, bubble charts use transparency. As a result, there will be overlapping between the dots. The more overlapping there is, the harder it is to distinguish between values. If you have lots of points to plot, make the points transparent while bolding the outlines of the circles.
- Include a legend. A legend is a key that describes the parts of a chart based on visual variables like color and size. Ensure that

your audience understands what the bubble sizes represent by using a legend.
- Make sure you're showcasing a clear trend. The bubble chart is the tool you are using to help the audience visualize this trend.
- If your data contains negative values, use transparent dots or distinct colors to highlight this characteristic.

If you have a lot of values that need to be displayed, you may consider using a bubble cloud as an alternative to the bubble chart. However, note that while it makes easy to observe relationships, it is hard to determine the exact figure or difference between metrics with this type of chart.

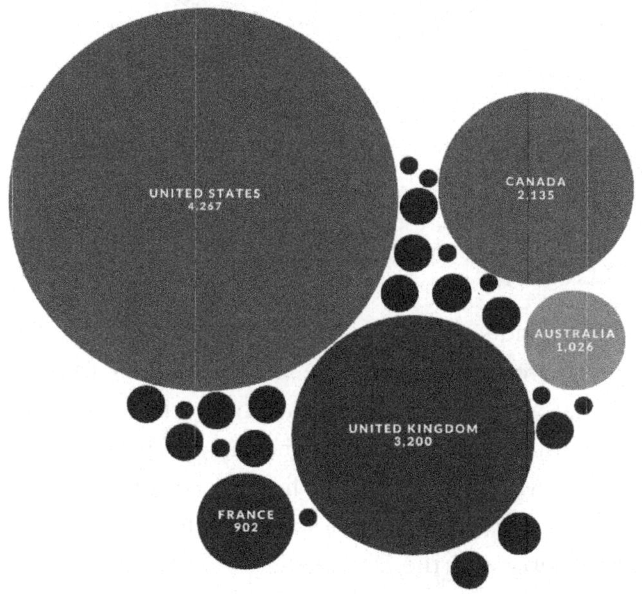

FIGURE 3.14

Another alternative could be a nested bubble to distinguish the largest to smallest categories easily.

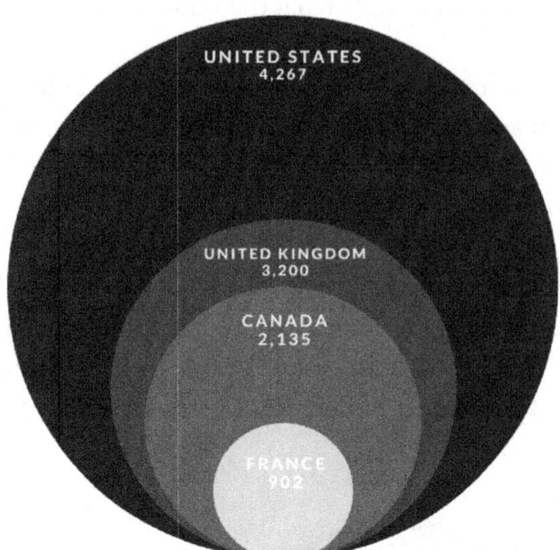

FIGURE 3.15

WATERFALL CHART

Also called a cascade chart or a bridge chart, this chart displays how initial values increase and decrease before leading to a final value. Before this final value is arrived at, the chart will display the intermediate values that raised the initial number up and down. This data visualization tool is widely used in the finance section to show how net values are reached by outlining the starting values and the positive and negative contributions of the intermediate values such as expenses and costs.

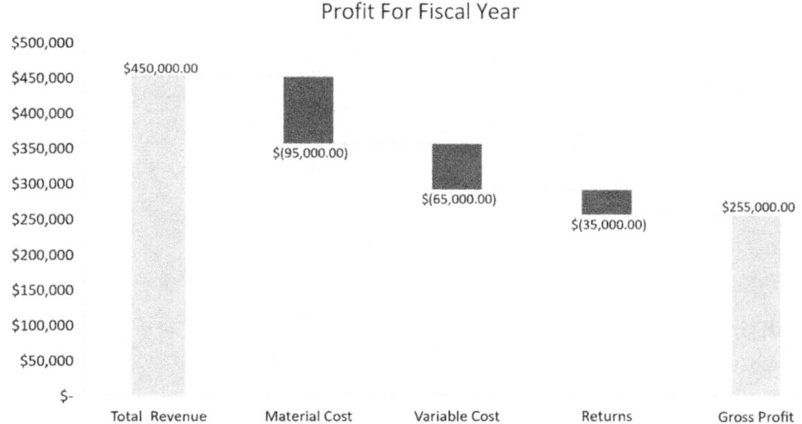

FIGURE 3.16

The waterfall chart can be used for quantitative analysis of:

- Inventory level fluctuations over a period of time
- Sales over a period of time
- Profit and loss statements
- Comparison of product earnings

SANKEY DIAGRAM

This is a chart with a very specific use. It allows for highlighting the flow of assets. Therefore, how a company's sources, the uses of, and even the costs of these resources can be noted by looking at these visualizations. Many organizations use such charts to make decisions on how to expend resources like time, money, and energy because the chart simplifies the complex process that goes into managing that one resource. A bird's eye view can be obtained in addition to getting specific details. As a result, the highest contributors or dominant consumer base stand out, so the areas with largest opportunities can be spotted.

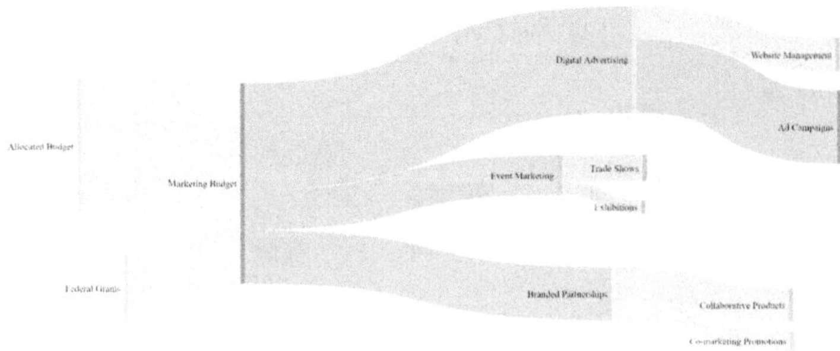

FIGURE 3.17

When we put the same data in a bar chart, it's a lot harder to visualize where our resources are going.

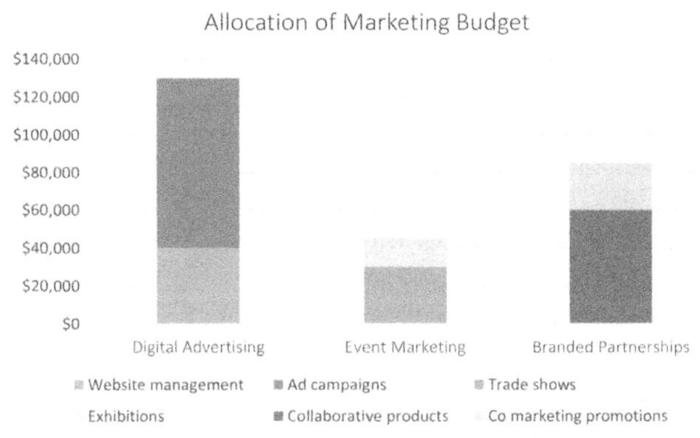

FIGURE 3.18

When developing a Sankey chart there are a few considerations that must be made. You must ask the tough questions like:

- Are you using the chart for exploratory analysis?
- Are you trying to tell a story? Trying to change someone's mind? Perhaps promoting the desire to take a specific action?
- What is your audience's experience level with the data?
- What will your audience be looking for or need to be convinced of to take action? Are they looking for a return on

investments (ROI) to improve effectiveness, gain profitability, make regional comparisons, etc.?

Asking and answering such questions allows you to solidify the purpose of creating this chart and develop the key takeaways it must deliver.

But what does this chart look like? The chart uses rectangular or connector lines with proportional widths to represent the significance of values so that flow quantity can be visualized. These values are highlighted by the flow lines' width, color, saturation, length, and shape. Some flows will have smaller widths than others. Consider cutting them and combing their values in an 'other' category to limit clutter.

A great place to start creating sankey diagrams with no code required is Flourish.

MARIMEKKO CHART

This chart can be considered a stacked bar chart with bars that vary in height and width. Both of this chart's axes are completely stacked in a 2-D effect. The chart is used to showcase 2 numerical values for each category.

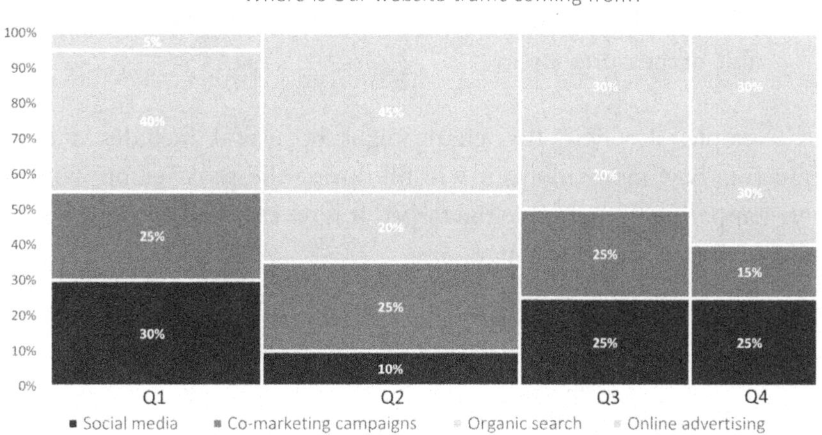

FIGURE 3.19

The nature of this chart makes it great for:

- Highlighting parts of a whole
- Allowing the evaluation of hierarchical data. This is particularly useful for data with parent-child relationships.
- Giving a general overview of data that will be further dissected to give a deeper explanation, whether this is for one or both of the segments used in the chart.
- Showing the interaction between two categories. For example, the relationship between marketing and sales data can be noted with a Marimekko chart.
- Displaying categorical values like products, regions, sectors, and more
- Displaying numerical variables like sales, profits, costs, margins, growth rates, and more

BULLET CHART

Also known as a bullet graph, this chart allows you to perform three activities in one go. These functions are:

- Feature a single value variable
- Compare that value to a target value
- Indicate if the featured value has fallen short of the target value or measured up it.

An example of where this chart might be useful includes a hotel projecting how many rooms it will fill during the peak season months, then comparing the actual to the target. It is an easy and efficient way to indicate the year's performance.

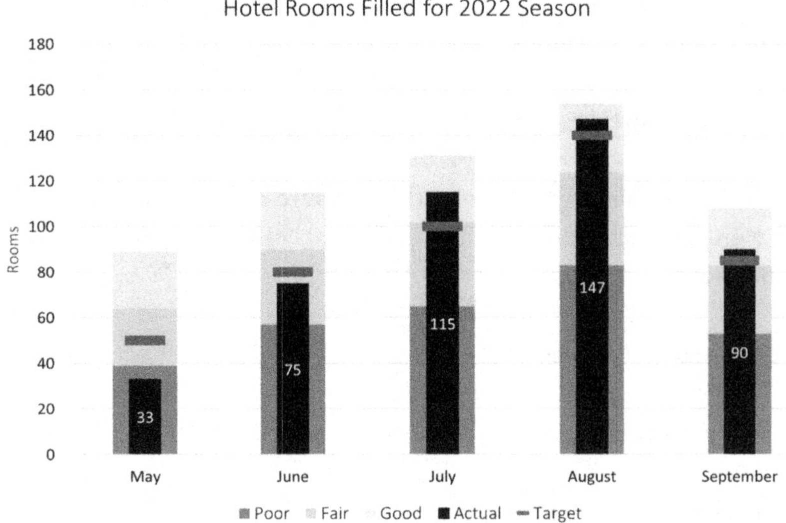

FIGURE 3.20

The bullet chart is a cousin of the bar graph appearance-wise. The featured value is represented by a rectangular bar and a vertical line represents the target value. If the rectangular bar fails to meet the position of the vertical line, then the featured value is less than the target value. The featured value has met or is greater than the target value if the horizontal bar touches or reaches past the vertical line. The chart can be oriented both horizontally and vertically.

While a bullet graph features a primary value for comparison, it also includes other measured values to enhance the visual display and to provide more information for analysis. So, while the primary featured value of a bullet chart might be the end-of-year revenue of a company, the chart can also feature the end-of-year revenue for previous years or projected forecasts for the future. The primary featured value must stand out on the chart though and this is why it has a stronger color and bold lines to differentiate from the other values.

A good bullet features 5 main characteristics:

1. **Text labels**

These are captions that state what the chart is displaying and the unit of measurement for the values.

1. **A quantitative scale**

This shows the linear progress of the measure of the metric values. In other words, it shows the start and end points of the featured and target measurements.

1. **A featured measure**

This is a measure of the actual performance of the variable.

1. **A comparative measure**

This highlights the target metric that the featured value is being compared to.

1. **A qualitative scale**

This is a background fill that shows ranges like good, satisfactory, and bad to define how the featured value compares to the target value.

When designing bullet charts for maximum effectiveness, use a color coding system. In addition to using a strong, clear color for the featured value, you should further highlight its measure by using softer colors for the comparative values. Also, use a scale from dark to light to show the qualitative scales. The darker colors will represent the lower, less favorable values, while lighter hues will showcase the higher, more favorable values.

Limit the number of variables added as well. Because so much is going on in one chart, the sight can be confusing at the initial glance to a new viewer. Make sure to explain further so they understand the chart and limit the number of values displayed as much as possible.

Additional tips for maximizing the use of bullet chart include:

- Redesign the chart for values that require low numbers, like costs and expenses.
- Ensure qualitative scale (background fill) is in sync with values being displayed.
- When reversing the qualitative scale, keep your audience in mind. Will they quickly glance at the chart and determine the low results? Consider reversing the direction of the quantitative scale if not.

Bullet graphs have a wide range of useful applications like:

- Allowing marketers to note the performance of their campaigns compared to others
- Showing charities how they are progressing toward a fundraising goal
- Depicting business analysis to allow departments or teams to see if they are meeting their goals
- Allowing manufacturers to note production levels and the if output is on par

You should not fall into the trap of using them for the following applications:

- Comparing the performance of the several categories. So while a bullet chart might show the production levels of a manufacturer in one country, it should not be used to compare the performance of production across regions.
- Using sets of data that are not measured using the same length of time. Therefore, one value type cannot be measured in months while the other is measured in years.

DUMBBELL PLOTS

Also called connected dot plots, gap plots, range plots or arrow plots, dumbbell plots showcase 2 or more related series of data on the same axis through the use of connected dots linked by straight lines. These charts are great for showing the range between the minimum and maximum values of categorical data. They are called dumbbell charts because they imitate their namesake with dots at either end of a straight-line.

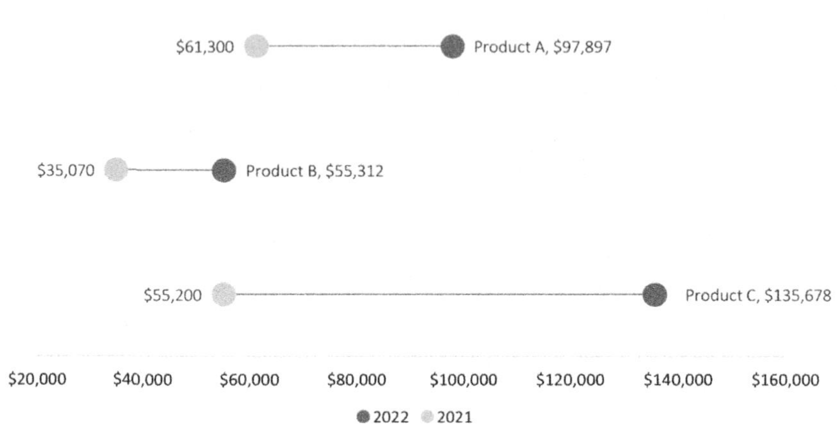

FIGURE 3.21

All these 'dumbbells' are plotted on the same charts, making efficient use of the graph space designed with multiple data variables being highlighted. One axis of the chart shows the range of values or the categories that the data points have been grouped. The second axis highlights the number of data points in each category. The chart can be plotted either vertically and horizontally, whichever works best for readability in the particular instance of the data set.

The values are normally quantitative in nature. They are a great alternative to using line charts or grouped bar charts. They can be used to represent up to 1000 data points but note that the chart can get cluttered the more data points that are added.

FIGURE 3.22

While dumbbell plots should not be used to plot large data set due to this possible clutter, advantages to using these charts include:

- They allow for representing proportions and frequencies easily.
- They allow for showcasing outlets and density distribution easily.
- They allow for plotting small to medium-sized data sets.

Dumbbell plots are such a great comparison chart because, at a glance, the audience can note the trend that the data is taking as well as any skewness suggesting anomalies. They are used often by financial institutions in instances like expressing interest rate projections and in scientific research to highlight the similarities and differences between variables.

Comparison charts allow audiences to note and analyze the progress of different groups of data and how these progressions relate to each other. Are they similar or different? Which group of data is most prominent and how does it stand out against the rest? What measures of action should be implemented because of these notations? All of these questions and more can be answered by using such charts.

While the data they present is complex, the insights do not have to be. Comparison charts give a helicopter view of these findings for easier analysis and thus, more informed decision-making.

4
DISTRIBUTION

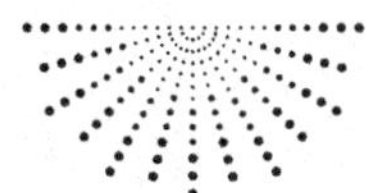

The name says it all. Distribution charts allow for visualizing how data values are distributed or spread out on a grid. They let the audience know how frequently these values occur and how uniformly or disbursed they occur. Several groups of data can be compared in such charts as a result.

Let's get right into noting the different types of charts that fall under this bracket and when and how you should use them for maximum effectiveness.

HISTOGRAM

This is a common chart that most people are familiar with. It is most frequently used to show statistical distributions as it plots the dispersion of a numeric variable's values as a series of bars. The numeric values are grouped into classes that occur in equal-sized intervals. Classes are also called bins. This feature allows the audience to understand the approximate probability of the quantity occurring. The bars can adopt either a horizontal or vertical orientation. Each bar normally covers a class. Thus, a bar's height indicates the rate at which data points occur within the corresponding bin.

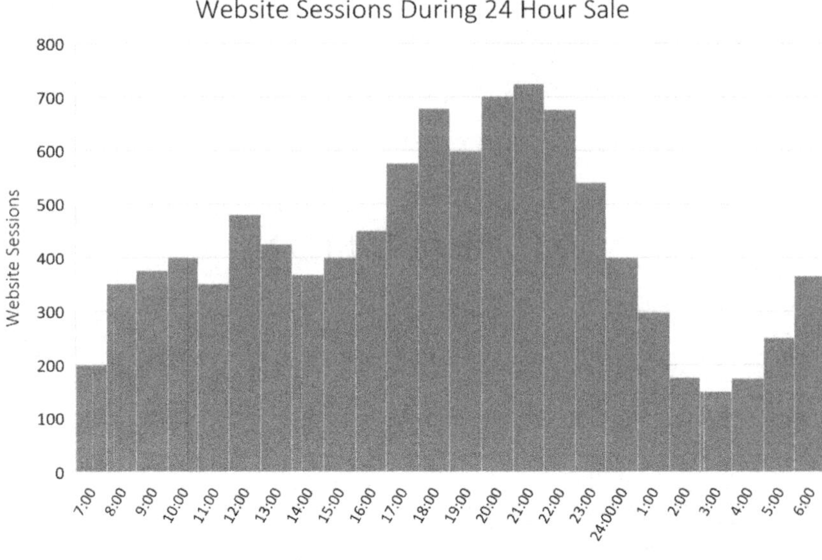

FIGURE 4.1

Because of the structure of the histogram, it can be noted if the distribution is spread out, the peaks of distribution, if the data is skewed in one direction with extremes or symmetrical, or if there are outliers. Outliers represent data points that are not typical for the dataset. They are either much bigger or smaller than the nearest data point. There is 6 main outcomes of a histogram to look out for, they are:

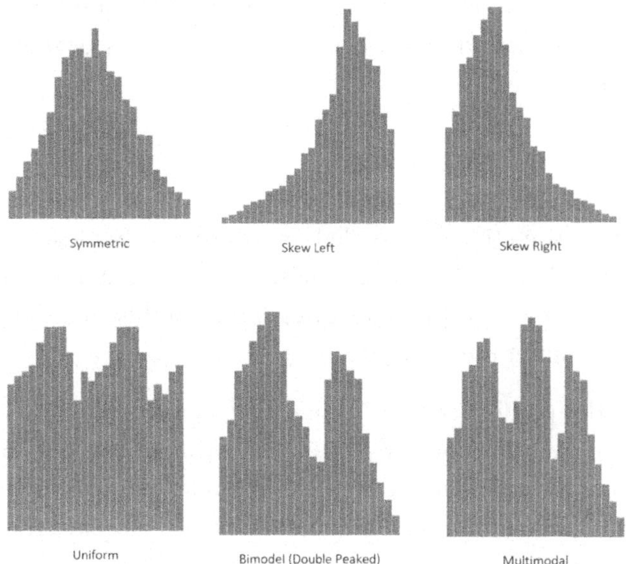

FIGURE 4.2

While the appearance of the histogram is reminiscent of a bar chart, do not confuse the two charts. They have different functions in the data visualization community. The bar chart compares values of categorical data. On the other hand, the histogram notes how many times continuous values that are grouped into ranges occur. Visually, they are also different as there are typically larger spaces between the bars of a bar chart, while histograms are more crammed together as the separate bars make up one dataset. Additionally, while the bar chart consists of bars of equal widths, in some cases, the bars in a histogram are not.

To maximize the effectiveness of your histogram:

- Use a zero-baseline to ensure the visual is not skewed
- Select an appropriate number of bins. The larger the bins, the fewer bins that will occur over the range of data being displayed. The opposite is true for smaller bin sizes. If there are too many bins, the data will be hard to read. If there are too few bins, the histogram will seem to lack enough detail. Choose a healthy medium between these two extremes.

- Select bin boundaries that are easy to interpret. Add labels to define these boundaries to best inform the audience where it is applicable.

DOT PLOT

This chart is sometimes shrouded in confusion because it is often mistaken for others like icon bars, scatter plots, dumbbell charts, and beeswarms. But we will list the features and what this chart is used for to ensure you do suffer the same fate.

A standard dot plot is a statistical chart that shows at least one quantitative value for each category by plotting one or more dots on a numerical axis. This data is represented by filled-in circles. Unlike the histogram that displays distribution on a range, the dot plot displays the distribution of individual values along the X axis. The dots show the frequency at which these individual values occur along the Y axis. As a result, dot plots are particularly useful for showing specific values and how they compare to different categories with similar values. Such a comparison may be hard to note on a bar chart since the end of the bars are difficult to compare to each other.

FIGURE 4.3

Color is an instrumental part of this chart. You can use color in various ways to maximize the chart's effectiveness. Such techniques include:

- Highlighting the numeric value of dots with darker and lighter hues to emphasize that value.
- Color coordinating dots according to their category. This should be a consideration when there are multiple categories with the same values. Color coordination makes it easy to distinguish these categories.
- Symbolizing time periods to show the past and present through chronological values.
- Changing the opacity of the dots if there are slight overlaps to make it easier to read or highlight higher or lower values.

RIDGELINE PLOT

Also goes by joy plot, a ridgeline plot is a chart highlighting how numeric values across several data groups that overlap are distributed. The chart's name comes from the fact that it resembles an overlapping range of mountains. As a rule of thumb, use this chart when you need to highlight the distribution of at least 6 groups of data. You will find many cases with large volumes of data featuring time displayed in such a chart. An example would be a measure of the rainfall in a particular region over the last 20 years. The chart would give insight into the values of each year and allow for noting the trends that have developed in that timeframe. Comparing temperature averages between separate years is also a common dataset for this chart.

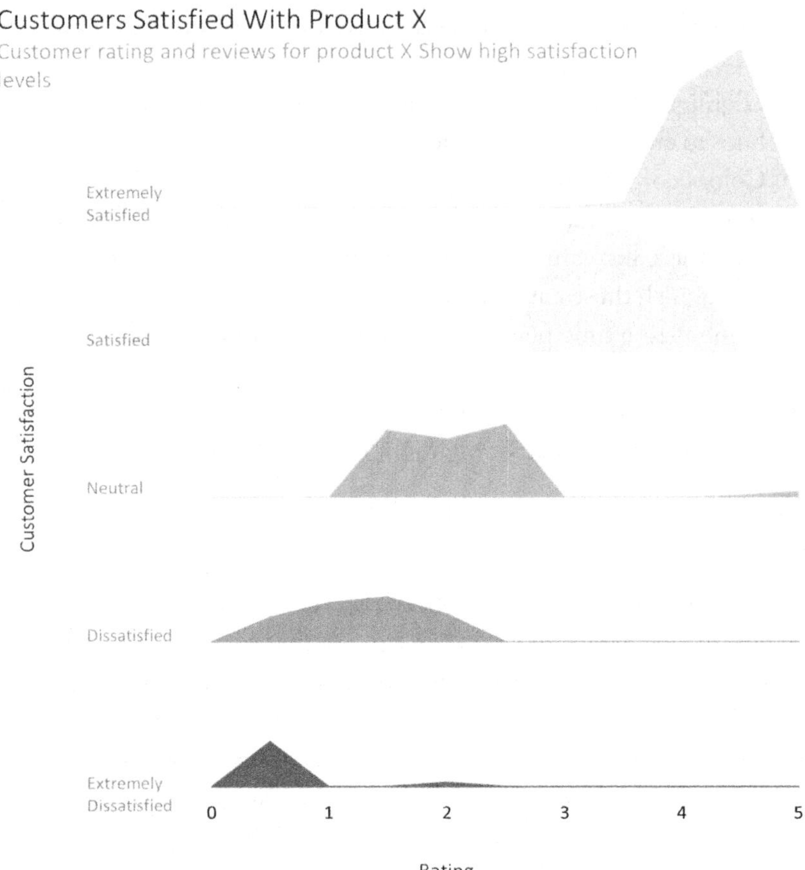

FIGURE 4.4

Ridgeline plots are great when you want to quickly see data distribution over a specified period. This allows you to easily see where the spikes and dips are and compare them to different categories. They are a creative chart you don't always see used, but they're worth experimenting with to create a memorable visual.

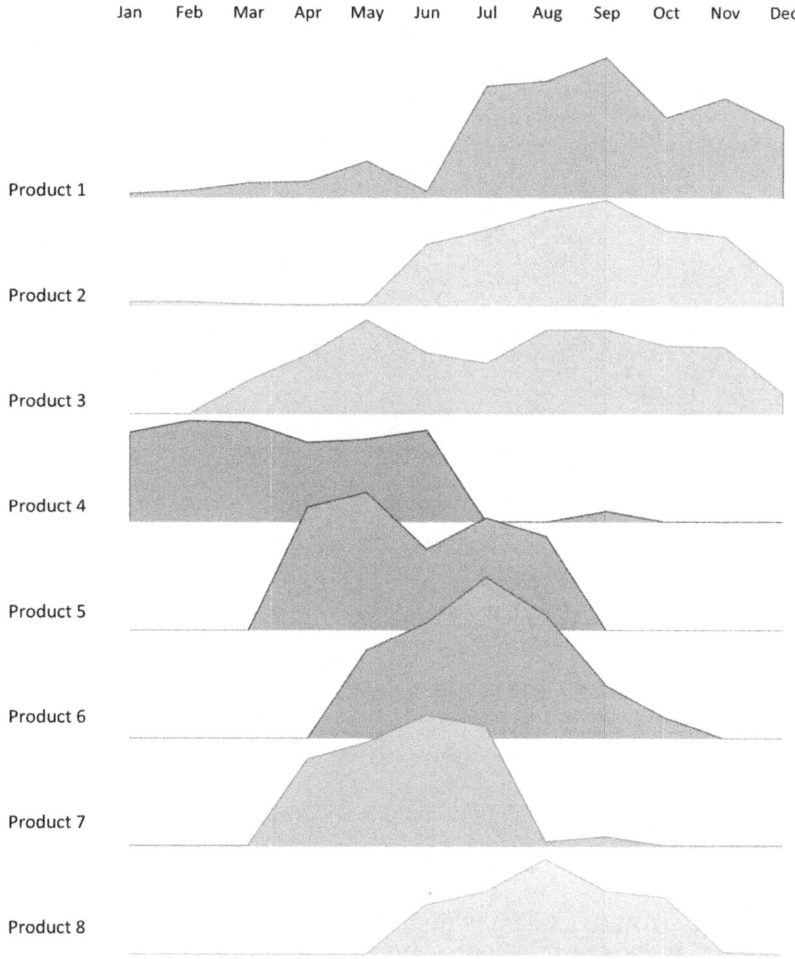

FIGURE 4.5

BOX PLOT

This chart utilizes lines and boxes to show the distribution of values of at least one dataset.

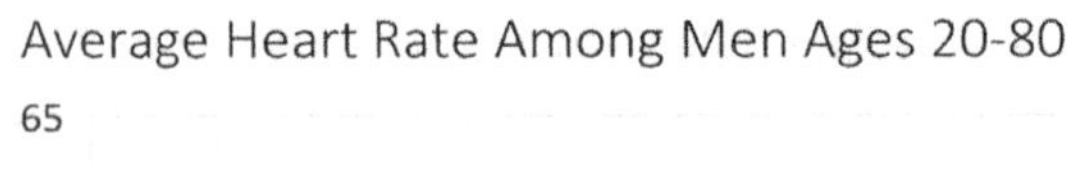

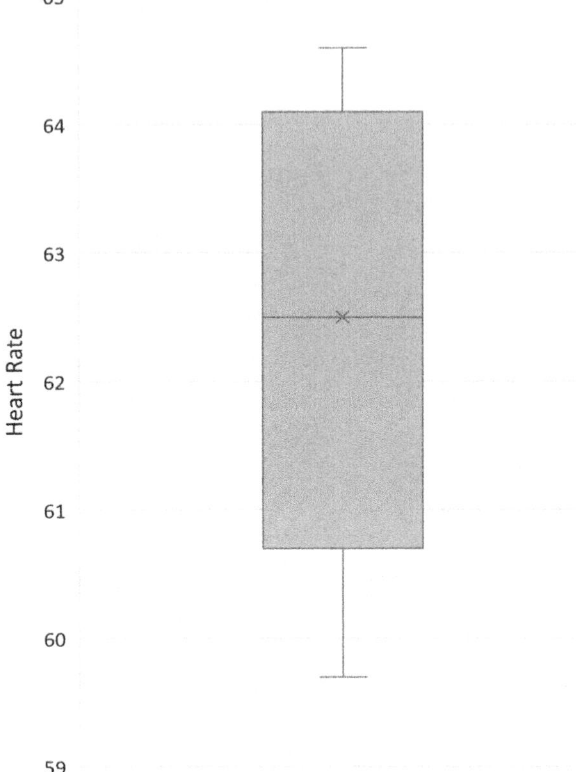

FIGURE 4.6

Box plots showcase data in quartiles. This means that the values of a dataset are divided into equal fourths. Jutting from either side of the box are lines representing the dataset's min and maximum values. The left side (or bottom) of the box represents the lower quartile (Q1) and the right side (or top) represents the upper quartile (Q3), with the median line marking the center point of the data. The first quartile is greater than 25% of the data but less than the other 75% of the data. The third quartile is larger than 75% of the data but smaller than the remaining 25%. The range between Q1 and Q3 is called the interquartile range (IQR).

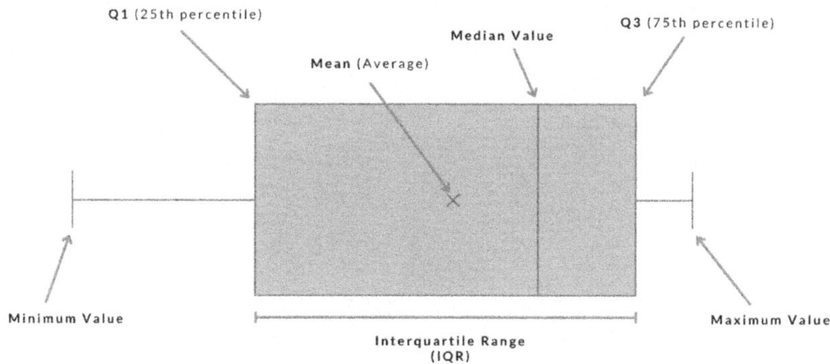

FIGURE 4.7

The IQR determines how long the lines extend on either end of the box. The most that either line can extend is 1.5 times the IQR. If the extension exceeds that, this is marked by dots representing outliers. Box plots can be effective when you're looking for outliers in your data, as you can set the parameters and they will appear as a separate dot outside the plot.

Use this type of chart when comparing the distribution of the values between multiple groups of data as they provide several details at a glance. Such details include:

- Data symmetry
- The level of skewness
- Any variance
- Outliers

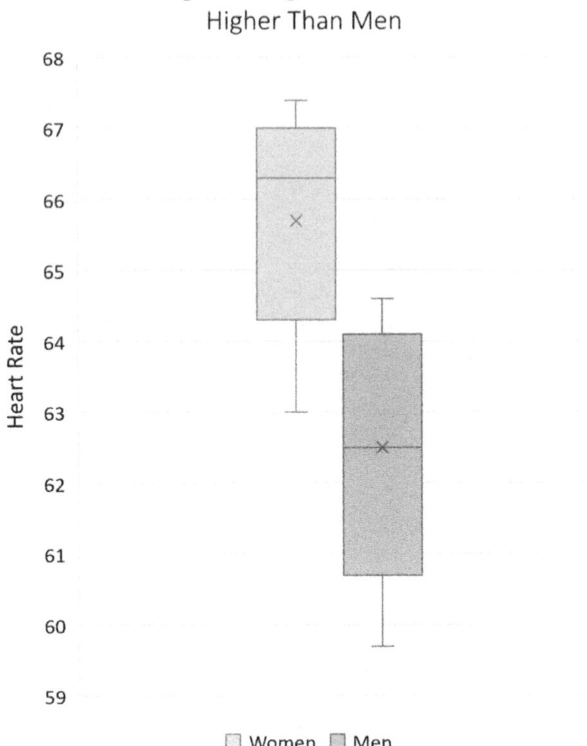

FIGURE 4.8

The data is summarized effectively and shows the difference in the positions of values. This chart also allows for visually noting high and low values, unlike a histogram.

Make the most out of box plots by arranging the values in an order that highlights the specific patterns. This makes insights clearer.

FIGURE 4.9

CANDLESTICK PLOT

Stock, derivatives, currency, cryptocurrency, bonds, commodities... If you plan to or already invest in or trade any of these assets (and others), you will use and analyze candlestick plots. Invented in Japan over 100 years ago by a man called Munehisa Homma, they are used to analyze the price movements of assets over time. While the invention was made to show the link between the price of rice and its supply and demand, in this day and age, their use is being applied to a wider variety of resources and their price variations.

FIGURE 4.10

Let's start with what this chart looks like. It gets its name because it features multiple bars with lines that look like wicks on both ends that look like candlesticks. These candlesticks give a visual representation of how the asset's price changed over a given amount of time. This time period can be as little as a few minutes or as long as years.

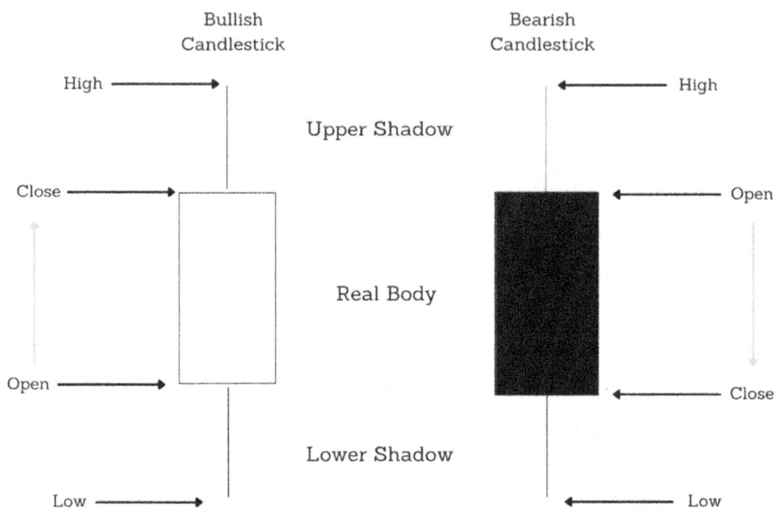

FIGURE 4.11

Each "candlestick" on the chart provides traders and investors with several sets of important information. First, the bar's color indicates the price increases or decreases. An increase in an asset's price is represented by green or white. This candle is referred to as bullish and shows that the asset's value closed for that period of time at a higher price than it opened with. The opening price is at the bottom of the bar while the closing price is at the top.

A decrease in an asset's price is represented by red or black. This candle is deemed a bearish one and shows that the asset's value closed at a lower price than it opened during that time frame. The opening price is indicated at the top of the bar, while the closing price is at the bottom. Opposite of the bullish candlestick.

The difference between the price the asset closed with and opened with is represented by the length of the bar between the wicks. Longer lengths indicate a larger change in price. Shorter lengths indicate smaller price changes.

The wicks also serve a purpose. The upper wick shows the highest price of the assets traded during the specified time, while the lower wick shows the lowest price.

Candlestick plots are useful for quickly determining whether an asset's value went up or down and if this movement is peculiar or part of a trend. Time is money for traders and investors. Waiting too long can mean they miss out on potential buying opportunities. Therefore, this fast analysis is key to staying ahead of the game with quick decision-making.

VIOLIN PLOT

Similar to a box plot, the violin plot highlights the distribution of the numeric data for at least one group using density curves. The box plot and violin charts are so closely related that they typically accompany each other when presenting to provide supplementary information. A violin plot includes all the features found on a box plot, such as the median, outliers, quartiles, and the spread, but the difference is that the violin plot also shows the probability of data occurring at different values.

Incme Level Determines Life Expectancy in Most Cases
Countries with higher avg. income have a higher life expectancy

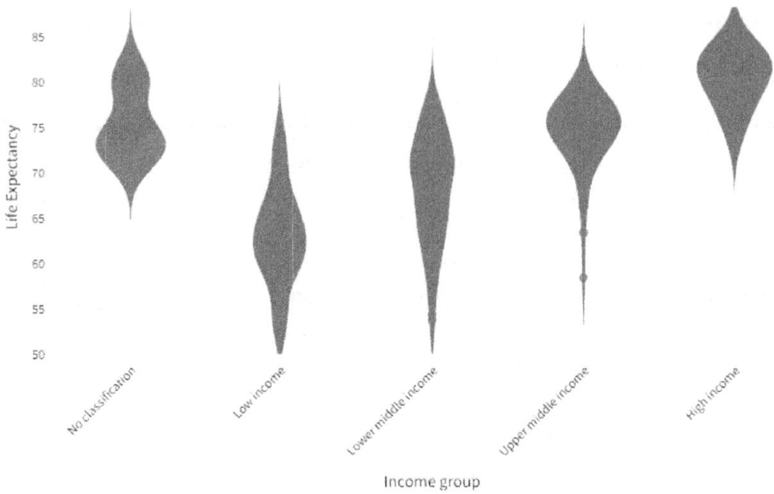

FIGURE 4.12

Each density curve is made up of peaks, valleys, and tails. The density curve also goes by the name kernel density estimator (KDE). Each data point of the KDE contributes a small area to the true, overall value of the data. The distribution of these points determines the shape of the curve. This shape is called the kernel function and can vary from triangular to bell-shaped. The final shape of the density curve is determined by stacking all the data points together to form a whole. Density curves are developed around a center line instead of a baseline but follow the same convention of construct and interpretation.

Violin plots are especially useful for showing the distribution of value between multiple data groups so that comparisons can be made by noting the differences and similarities between each group's peaks, valleys, and tails.

POPULATION PYRAMID

The alias of this chart gives away what it is used for. Also called the age-sex pyramid, this chart displays how age and sex are distributed within a stated population. This information is highlighted with the use of horizontal bars stacked one on top of the other. If the final look of stacked bars is that of a triangle with equal sides, this is an indication that the population is distributed with more young people than older people. The opposite is true if the shape is reminiscent of an inverted triangle. If the stacked bars are square-shaped, the age groups of the population are about the same size. Short bars indicate that an age group forms a smaller part of the population, while bars that jut out mean that this age group forms a larger part of the population.

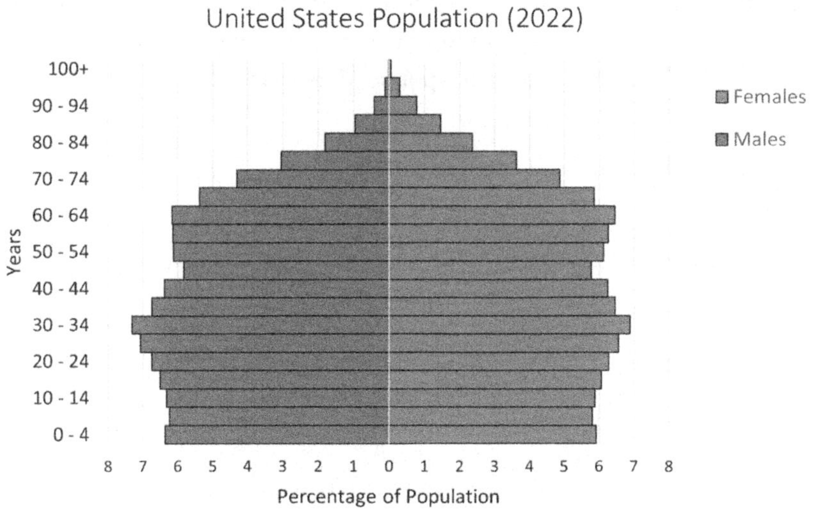

FIGURE 4.13

Apart from measuring the spread of a specified population by age and gender, population charts are great for visualizing a region's projected growth and encouraging the exploration of factors that determine populations' economic outlook by working-age distribution. They also allow for noting life expectancy and birth rates.

You must adjust your expectations to get the most out of your population pyramids. Data involving populations are not perfect. Therefore, you will not get perfect data. It is better to focus on the averages in that data set. Organize these by age ranges and sort them by descending value to make an easy-to-interpret appearance. Also, ensure that your age groups are consistent. For example, using the age ranges 0-5, 6-10, 11-15, 16-20, and 21-25 works to ensure that the chart's appearance is straightforward. On the other hand, using age ranges like 0-5 and 6-25 will distort the shape of the pyramid. Consistency is key.

STRIP PLOT

This chart is similar to a scatter plot but is used to express the value of 1 variable per column. Strip plots can be effective when raw data is important because they simply show the data with no added trend lines or design features. Wherever the data points fall, you can easily analyze them. This also makes it easy to spot outliers in the data.

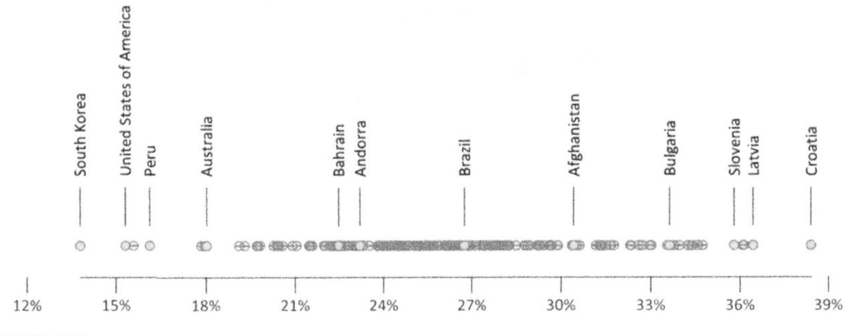

FIGURE 4.14

A strip plot features dots stacked in a row either vertically or horizontally. With this orientation, the dots tend to overlap. To increase readability, Adding transparency to the dots and bolding the borders can be effective. This makes the chart more legible as the individual dots are more easily distinguished.

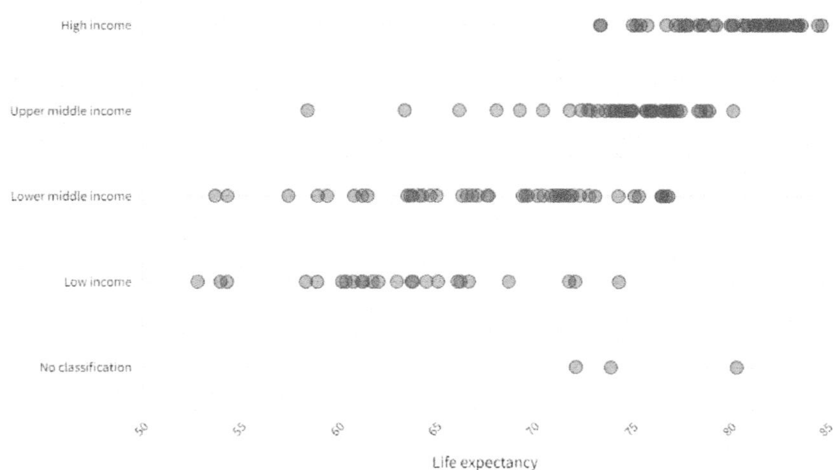

FIGURE 4.15

Due to the high concentration of the dots that is possible with this type of chart, legibility decreases with increasing dot numbers. Don't trash your strip plot if that happens. Instead, use a technique called jittering. All you have to do is disperse the data points across the X-axis to increase readability. You can also convert to a beeswarm plot, essentially the same concept.

BEESWARM PLOT

Think of this chart as a strip plot thats easier to read. A beeswarm plot has the same functionality as a strip plot, simply showing the data exactly where it lies. It has a slight advantage as the points are spread apart by improving on the jittering effect, which reduces overlap. Because of this, beeswarm plots are great for displaying the distribution of dense data sets.

FIGURE 4.16

THE NAME COMES from the fact that the slightly spread-out nature of the dots looks like bees buzzing around a hive. Improve the chart's readability by adding labels to make outliers clearer to identify. A good data analyst visualizes data beautifully. A great one does the same thing, except highlights the key insights.

Income Level Determines Life Expectancy in Most Cases
Countries with a higher avg. income have a higher life expectancy

No classification
High income
Lower middle income
Upper middle income
Low income

Hong Kong
Life expectancy 84.69
Income group High income

50 55 60 65 70 75 80 85
Life expectancy

FIGURE 4.17

Distribution charts allow for noting when trends develop and when unusual values (outliers) occur over a given period. To select the right distribution chart for your audience, you need to ask yourself a few questions:

- How many sets of data need to be expressed?
- What is the nature of the values that will be expressed? Is it categorical? Is it statistical? Is it numeric?
- How many data points need to be plotted?

Answering these answers will give you a clear picture of what you are trying to accomplish by developing distribution data visualizations. The list of charts outlined above is by no means all that can be used to show the spread of values in data sets but they are a good foundation that allows you to express the disbursement of several types of data.

5
PART-TO-WHOLE

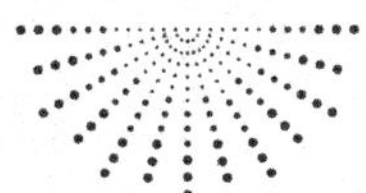

Often in business, we run into scenarios where we need to compare a value to its significance to the whole. Whether the regions our customers are coming from or which products perform the best, Part-to-a-whole charts are the go-to in such cases. They show how a variable is divided and how those divisions relate and are totaled.

This chapter delves into such charts and the more specific circumstances where each of them can be applied.

PIE CHART

Pie charts are the data visualizations that typically come to mind when talking about part-to-whole comparisons. Therefore, it is only fitting that we start our exploration of these chart types here. Just as the name suggests, a pie chart takes on the form of a circle and even if you are not hungry, it is quite reminiscent of a pie. The entire 'pie' represents the total value of the data set (100%). The 'pie' is sliced into radial portions that present the categorical variables of the subsets that make up the total. The sizes (AKA the arc length and area) of those portions showcase the proportion of the whole they take up.

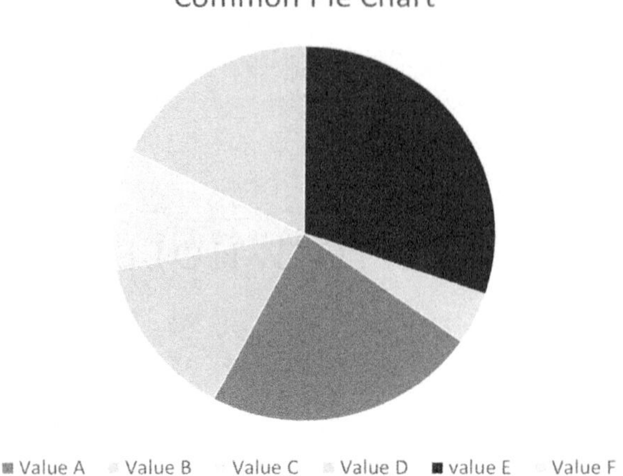

FIGURE 5.1

The use of pie charts is quite effective in certain situations. In scenario 1, it shows a simple part to whole analysis with few values that are easily interpreted. In scenario 2, it allows for emphasizing 1 or 2 values that make up a majority of the whole. Such instances are highlighted in the definition of what a pie chart is. The primary objective is to compare a category's distribution to the total value instead of each other. To use pie charts effectively, you must know the whole value of the data set.For example, you may use a pie chart to show which product performs better or which advertising campaign converts more.

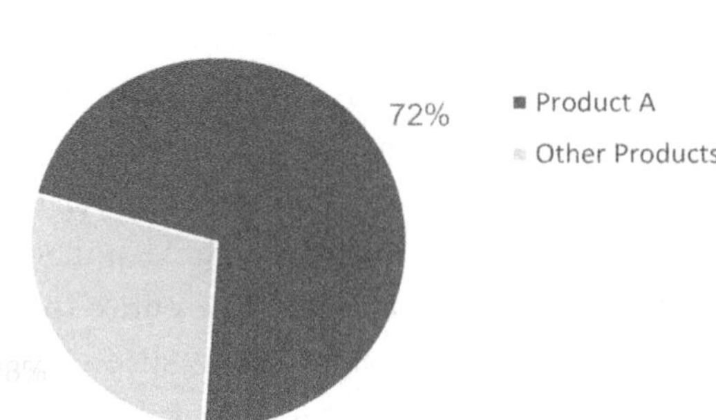

FIGURE 5.2

But using a pie chart correctly is crucial, otherwise, you're doing more harm than good. Would I use a pie chart to showcase a neck-and-neck race between 5+ political parties? Absolutely not. There will be no significance or uniqueness to the information. I would use it to compare the top two parties, so you can easily see who has the majority of the whole. A quick but effective way to visualize this type of data. A pie chart with too many slices shouldn't be a pie chart to begin with.

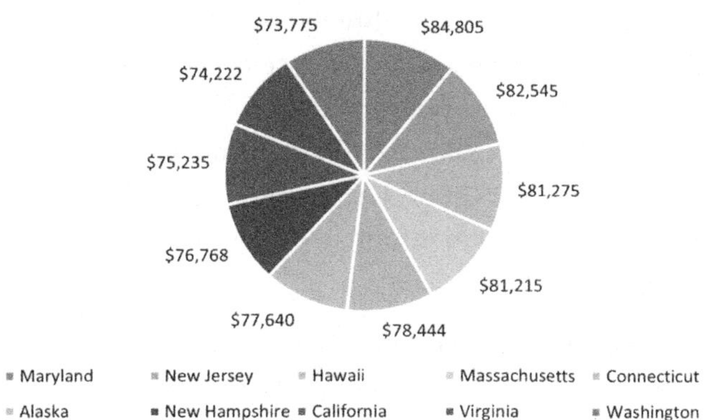

FIGURE 5.3

In this case, you could use a bar chart or lollipop chart since the values are very similar.

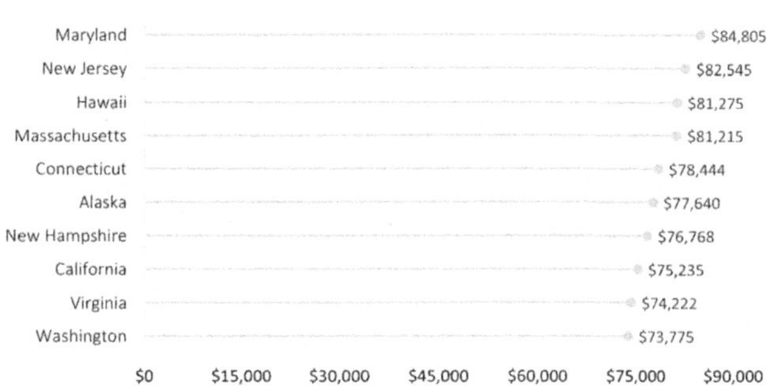

FIGURE 5.4

To GET the most value from a pie chart, only use it to highlight a few values that can easily be distinguished. A pie chart filled with lots of figures with similar values will essentially not show you anything. You need to be able to easily distinguish the contribution of each value. noting the highest and lowest from a glance. Or any significance in the data.

A great practice that will maximize the use of pie charts includes using color appropriately. Do not use highly distracting colors, and keep those colors consistent throughout the presentation. Ensure that these colors reflect the theme of the data. You can be sparse with your use of color by only adding color to the main insights that are being showcased and leaving the rest of the slices gray. This is a great practice as it allows the audience to decipher the important parts and can be effective if you have many categories.

Since exact proportions can be difficult to interpret by looking at a pie chart, you can consider using annotations to the chart. In fact, the addition of annotations to pie charts is standard. They can be in the form of fractions or percentages with the category name started.

An alternative to using a pie chart is the use of a donut chart. Also known as a donut plot, visualize this as a pie chart with the center removed. There is no significant difference in its readability.

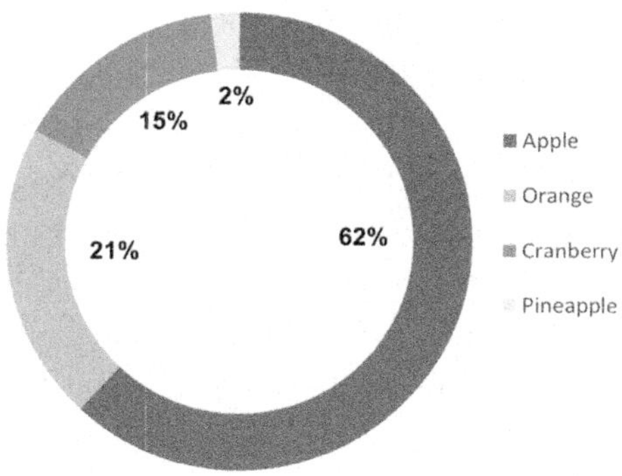

FIGURE 5.5

TREE MAP

Pie charts are the go-to when it comes to comparing the different elements of a single entity. However, they can be difficult to use effectively. That is why there are other options such as this one, the tree map, that can be alot more effective.

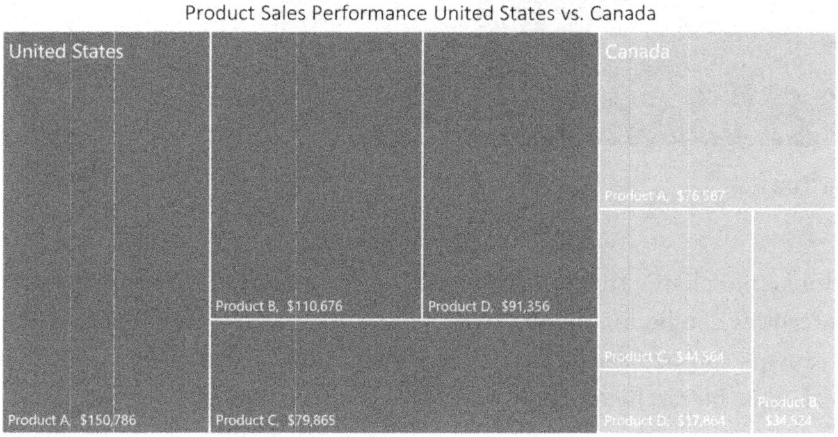

FIGURE 5.6

The tree map, in many ways, is thought to be a better version of a pie chart by data visualization experts. It represents hierarchical data in a tree-like structure with sub-branches of the data being represented using rectangles called nodes. Each node allows for the showcase of 2 quantitative values. This structure makes it easier to spot trends like the best-selling items bought by new customers in the current year and the growth rate from the previous year. Even better is that data can be drilled down into an infinite number of levels while still maintaining the distinguishability of the categories at a glance. They are often populated in a hierarchical order, showing the highest value first and down the ladder to the lowest. They can even be made interactive with certain software so the reader can take their time and go through each point if all of the data is significant.

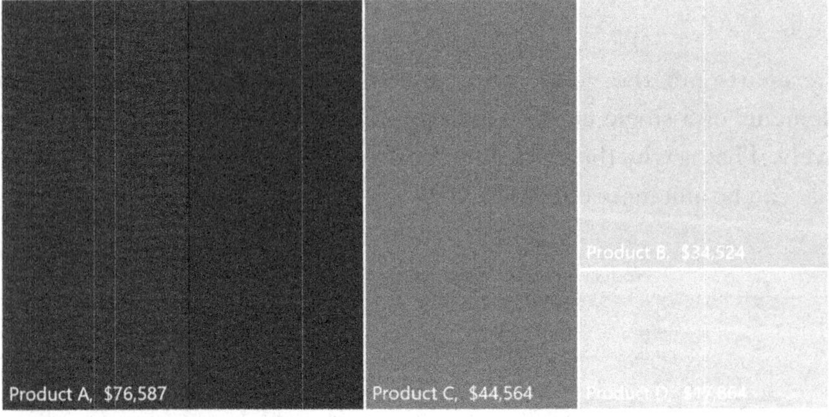

FIGURE 5.7

Unlike pie charts, tree maps allow a larger amount of data input. More categories can be highlighted within a smaller space. To be more exact, treemaps can be used to plot tens of thousands of data points! So, why pick this hierarchical chart over others like a multi-level pie chart? Treemaps have the advantage of allowing the plotting of these many, many data points in limited space. Even a multi-level pie chart is circular, so the space available is limited to the diameter of that space. Only so many data points can be added to the structure.

On the other hand, treemaps are plotted in a linear fashion. This space offers far more possibilities. Do note that the deeper we delve into the level of a tree map readability decreases. Therefore, this advantage can turn against you if you are not careful with its use. In some cases removing data points to create a smaller dataset will remove critical insights. In this case, It can be an effective practice to make the chart interactive and send it out to the team, so they can easily zoom in on details and categories no matter how big or small the chart is.

The structure of tree maps also allows for easy identification of trends and patterns as the nodes are proportional to the amount of data they represent. The similarities can be summarized within a category and its components or between multiple categories. This functionality is allowed because the different datasets are assigned different colors. Anomalies can be sighted as well because of this feature. This is allowed through the use of node dimensions and colors of the nodes. These are derived from the numerical values of the nodes.

Use a data set with a distinct hierarchy to get the most out of your tree map. Ensure that the highest level of the hierarchy is obvious. Also, ensure this data set has distinct numerical values. They can also be useful when a quick presentation isn't necessary and the executives want to take their time reviewing the data in an interactive way like we stated above..

This chart is not appropriate to use if you have similar values as the nodes will be similar in size and hard to distinguish. In such a case, the better alternative would be using a bar chart with the data arranged from the highest to the smallest value.

SUNBURST CHART

This chart goes by other names, including radial tree map and ring chart. It is also used to visualize hierarchical data sets. Unlike the tree map, which uses a linear structure, the sunburst chart uses a series of concentric rings to highlight hierarchy. Every ring coincides with a level within the hierarchy. The details of that data set are recorded with the segmented rings. The part-to-whole relationship between the subsets of data that is noted within each ring respective to its parent ring.

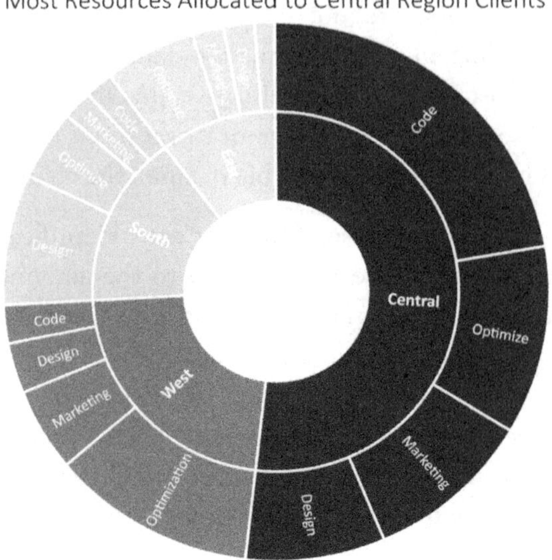

FIGURE 5.8

The radial layout on the sunburst chart gives an immersive experience and is easy for the eye to follow. The center of the charts is the first level of the hierarchy. The parent rings are found there. From there, rings representing subcategories within the parent rings are plotted from the categories that contain the highest value within that hierarchy to the lowest value. This must be applied at every level of the hierarchy. Moving away from the center of the chart means moving down the hierarchy.

FIGURE 5.9

This chart is often compared to a tree map but this chart has an advantage over the tree map. The categories are noted in an outwardly expanding circle, so noting the plotted categories as we go down the hierarchy becomes easier because of that expansion. If you have a lot of space to work with, this chart can trump a tree map to get a full picture of hierarchical data.

Another advantage to using a sunburst chart is that because it is visually similar to a pie chart, most audiences can more readily follow the flow of information it offers.

The disadvantages to using a sunburst chart include the limitation of the level that can be plotted based on its structure. Just like a pie chart, the number of categories that can be included in the circle space is fewer than in a linear structure. Also, angular recordings and smaller proportional segments might be difficult for the audience to read.

Circumstances, where you can play on the advantages while minimizing the disadvantages, include:

- In website development to outline the landing and navigation paths of a website.
- To provide a visual aid of the file sizes within the different modules contained within software packages.
- To break down the revenue sources of a business.
- To break down the expenses of a business.
- So that the world population can be broken down into categories such as continent, country, region, state, and cities.

NIGHTINGALE ROSE CHART

This chart was made famous by Florence Nightingale, the English statistician, social reformer and the founder of nursing training and theory as we know it today. Born in 1820, she used the Nightingale Rose chart to highlight how many soldiers died on hospital beds during the Crimean war, which was waged from 1853 to 1856. She broke down these deaths based on battle wounds, disease and other causes. The chart was divided into 12 segments that highlight the months of the year from April 1854 and March 1855.

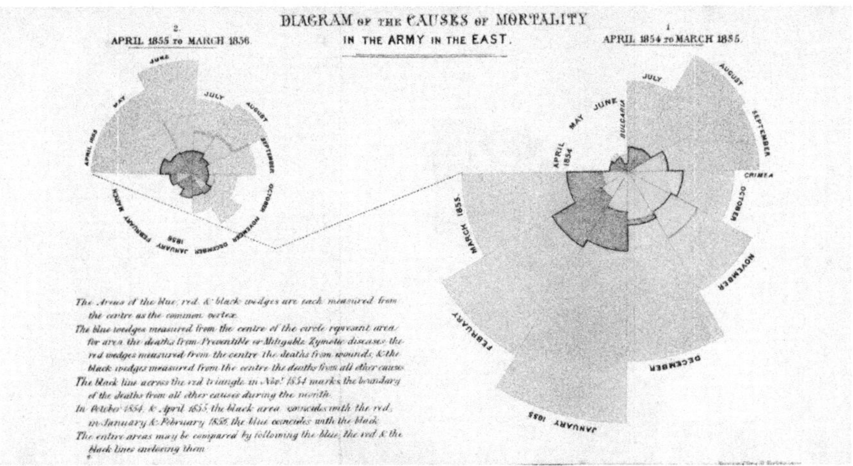

FIGURE 5.10: Source: Florence Nightingale, Public domain, via Wikimedia Commons

Also called the coxcomb chart or the polar area diagram, this chart gave her this ability by combining components of a column chart and those of a radar chart and so, this chart was presented to the world in 1858. Plotting occurs in proportional areas in a polar coordinate grid system. These areas (categories) are equally divided into segments with the same angle.

The funny thing about the dataset she visualized is other chart options probably would've been better for the data. But this rendition stuck within the data community until today and will for years to come. When you want a memorable visual to enhance your story is exactly when you would use a nightingale rose chart.

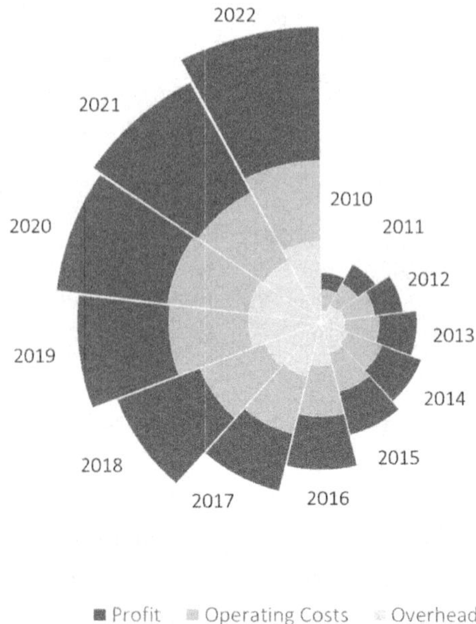

FIGURE 5.11

The most notable features of the Nightingale Rose chart include it is used to plot multiple data series. They are represented by rings that radiate from the center of the chart, hence why this chart looks similar to a pie chart. They represent the cardinal points North, East, South, West and the points in between or the degrees of a circle. The data values are recorded on these circles and divided into proportional slices representing the quantity. The value is highlighted by how far the segment extends from the center.

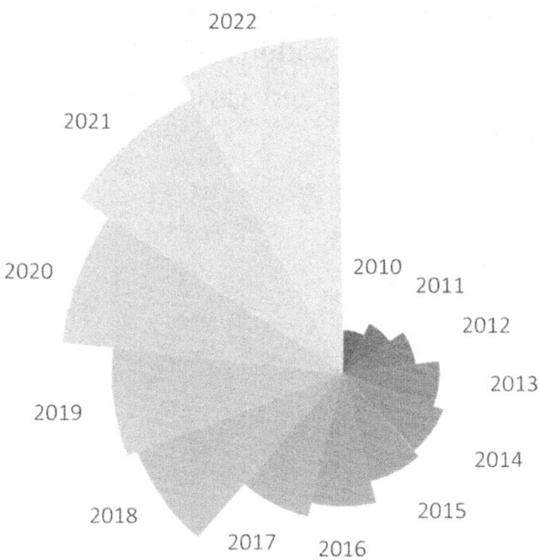

FIGURE 5.12

This chart is highly used in the scientific field to highlight statistics. For example, they are used by meteorologists to note and thus analyze quantities and direction for items such as wind direction, strength and frequency. That is why the chart is referred to as the wind rose in the field. It is used as a reference to discern the cardinal and ordinate direction of winds.

As great of a statistical tool this chart is, it has a major disadvantage. The other chart segments are larger, so their size draws more attention. This disproportionately represents an increase in value when this is not the case. The value is represented by the area and not the segment's radius. This can be unintentionally misleading to audiences.

. . .

THE FREQUENCY with which we work with different data sets makes it easy to forget that we also need to understand the interconnectivity and differences between the subgroups within individual data sets. This chapter highlighted that importance and gave you a variety of chart options to act on that understanding.

6
RELATIONSHIP

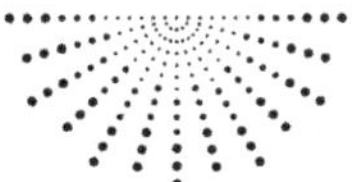

Also called correlation charts, relationship charts are visual representations of how different sets or subsets of data are connected or affiliated with each other. Relationship charts use links on the chart structure and other visual elements like color and size to highlight the connection between different variables. Audiences from all businesses can use such charts to note the complexity of such links for better decision-making.

There is quite a range of charts that allow you to pick on the links that connect these data variables. This chapter highlights several situations where they are best used.

SCATTER PLOT

Scatter plots use dots to represent the value of 2 numeric variables. These values are highlighted by where the dots are positioned on the horizontal and vertical axis. An example of where you might use a scatter plot is to showcase housing prices based on square footage. The vertical axis displays the price while the horizontal axis indicates the home's square footage. Each dot plotted on this chart will represent a house for sale or that has been sold.

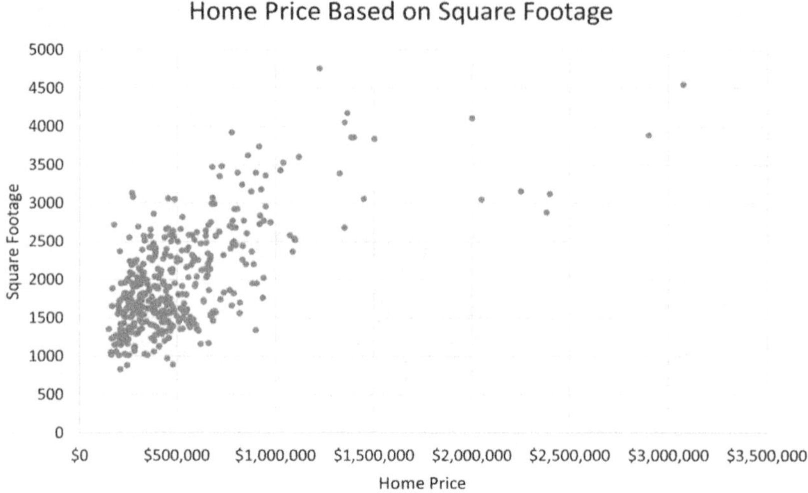

FIGURE 6.1

As seen with the example above, scatter plots are used primarily to note relationships between 2 quantitative variables. They note not only data points but the patterns of the data as a whole as well. For example, the chart explained above may show a concentration of dots representing the majority of home sales based on size. By looking at how the dots are concentrated, you can determine how the relationship between the variables can be described. Is the relationship weak or strong? Is it positive or negative? Is it linear or nonlinear? You will make this determination by examination of how the axes affect each other.

Additionally, scatter plots can be used to identify unexpected gaps or outliers in the data. These will stand out quite a bit when they are removed from the concentration of the other dots.

While a scatter plot is quite useful in showing the relationships between 2 data variables, that functionality will be lost if they are not used correctly. The don'ts of scatter plots include:

Overplotting

As with other charts that utilize dots as the visual representation of data, too many plotted items can lead to overlapping. The high density of data points occurs when there are many dots in one location. The chart becomes hard to understand as the points are hard to distinguish. As a result, the relationships these points signify will also be hard to distinguish.

Luckily, if you find yourself in such a situation with your scatter plot, there are 2 easy ways to resolve this. They are:

1. Sampling only a subset of data points. Do this by selecting a random set of points that showcase the general idea of the trends in the full data.
2. Change the visual format of dots by making them transparent. Transparency allows overlaps to be visible. Alternatively, you may reduce the size of the points so that fewer overlaps occur.

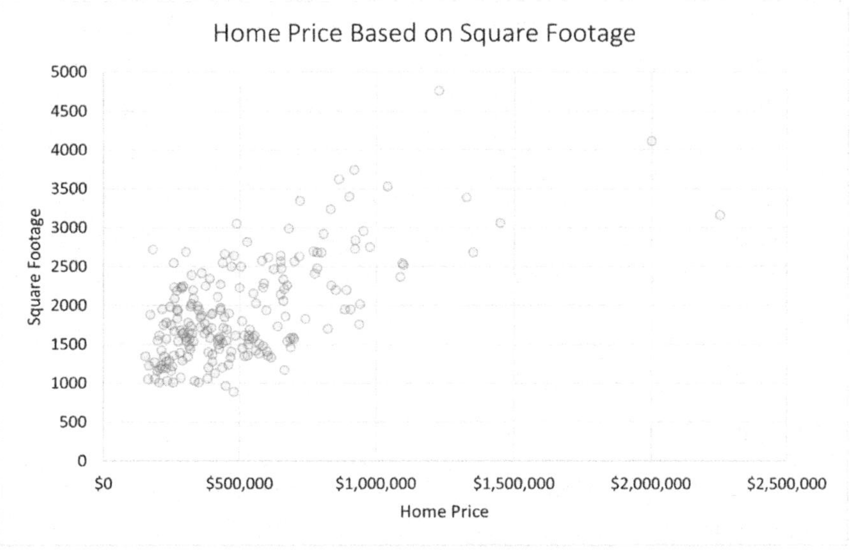

FIGURE 6.2

Although overplotting can be redundant in scatter plots, it can also be their strength. Scatter plots can be effective when working with very large sets of data. It allows you to easily see the trend or trajectory of the data and look at it as a whole instead of individual points. Adjust your scatter plot accordingly based on your needs.

Interpret correlation as causation

Noting the relationship between 2 variables of data does not mean that the causation is understood. This serves as a lesson in real life and when using scatter plots. While this point is more geared toward the issue regarding observation and not the creation of a scatter plot, you as the designer must understand this. You may need to also include data that supports highlighting the causation of trends noted in these charts. Always remember that a change in one variable is not necessarily responsible for or linked to changes in another. The observed relationship between these 2 variables can be driven by a third variable affecting both plotted variables. With the housing price example above, there is no way to know if square footage and price affect each other unless data is noted outside the chart to support this. The pattern can be purely coincidental. Looking at other factors like location and the year the house was built might bring a lot of insights to light. A newer home closer to downtown might have much less square footage but be at a much higher price than one further from downtown and potentially built some time ago.

Properly observing the data is a must when it comes to scatter plots. Some data sets may be harder to understand than others. It's important to consider all factors before drastic changes are made based on the insights.

To maximize the use of scatter plots, you can:

Add a trend line

A trend line or regression line is a line added to a chart to indicate the general trajectory the data takes. This can help your audience better understand what is going on. Remember, you've been staring at these spreadsheets and creating this visual for quite some time. Your audience has been looking at it for 5 minutes. Don't assume they know what you know. In fact, it is a common practice for this addition to be made to show the strength of the relationship between the two variables. The presence of this line also makes it more apparent if there are outliers. They may affect the trend indicated by the line.

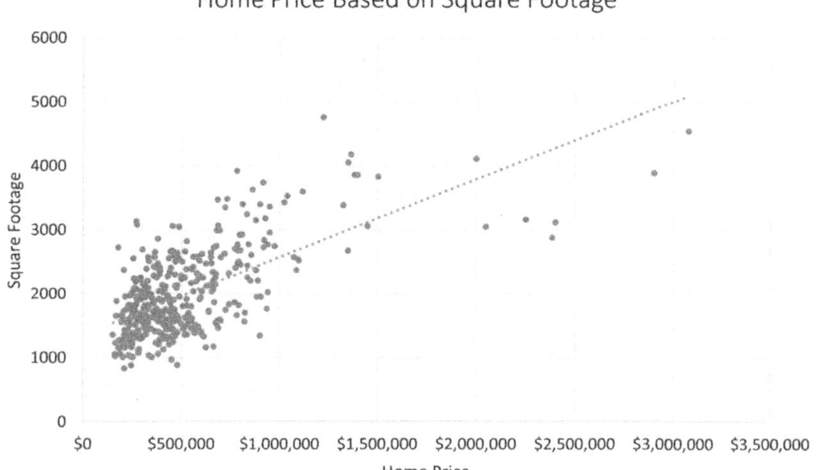

FIGURE 6.3

Add a third categorical variable

You are not limited to plotting just two variables on a scatter plot. A third variable may be added. In this case, the addition is categorical rather than numeric. Examples of such categories include gender or region. This addition is done using different colored dots. The addition may also be done using different shapes as this might make distinguishing data variables easier. For example, separate dots representing apartment sales can be added to compare to home sales and see if the same patterns exist based on the square footage.

RADAR CHART

Also called a spider chart, web chart, or radial chart, a radar chart displays quantitative multiple data variables. This is plotted starting from the same center point. The general shape of the final layout of data resembles that of a web.

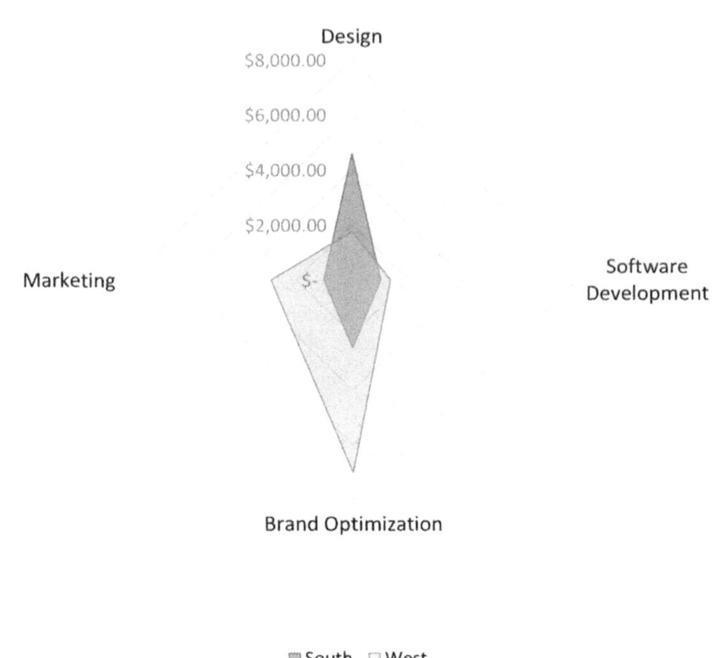

FIGURE 6.4

Radar charts are used when there are large numbers of variables. These can be plotted on a bar chart but such a situation tends to make a bar chart look cluttered and the data is hard to understand. Radar charts also make it easier to review multiple performance metrics of a single subject area.

One niche where radar charts are commonly used is in employee performance reviews. You may have seen it labeled as an Employee Chart outlining the employee's ratings in different skillset areas like punctuality and technical knowledge. This is useful in such an arena because radar charts make commonalities and outliers strikingly obvious.

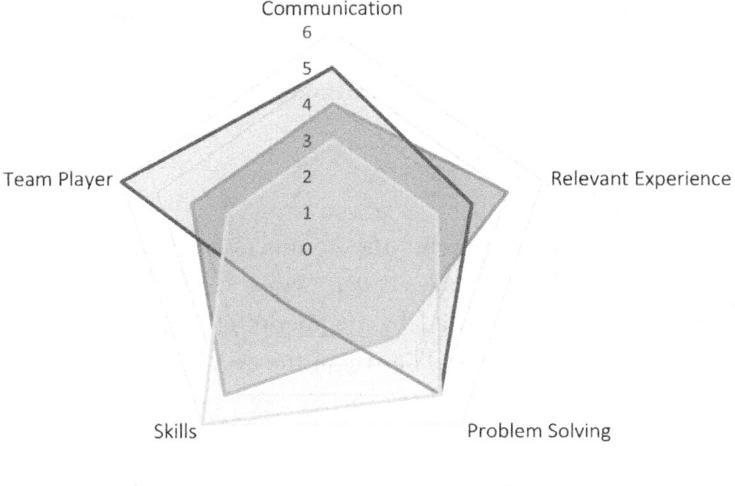

FIGURE 6.5

You can maximize the use of radar charts with a few practices that include:

- Limiting the data groups plotted to no more than 4.
- Limiting the data variables plotted to less than 15.
- Using different colors to represent different variables. Make these variable representations as visible as possible by adding transparency.

You may find that your radar charts become cluttered when more data groups and variables are added. You can take the small multiple approaches to rectify this. Make this work for you by segregating information based on quantity and plotting these on multiple radar charts that highly the data for individual variables. The actual value is compared to the average value. This is easier for the audience to mentally digest as they can note the relative variables compared to an average instead of being confronted by an overly cluttered graph. This can be done in the employee skillset chart. Have each employee have their own radar chart. A lot easier to analyze each individual person.

CHORD DIAGRAM

This type of chart highlights the connections or flow of information between several data variables called nodes. With chord diagrams, these connections are represented by fragments of a larger circle. Arcs are used to connect the nodes. The size of the arcs highlights the strength of the connections.

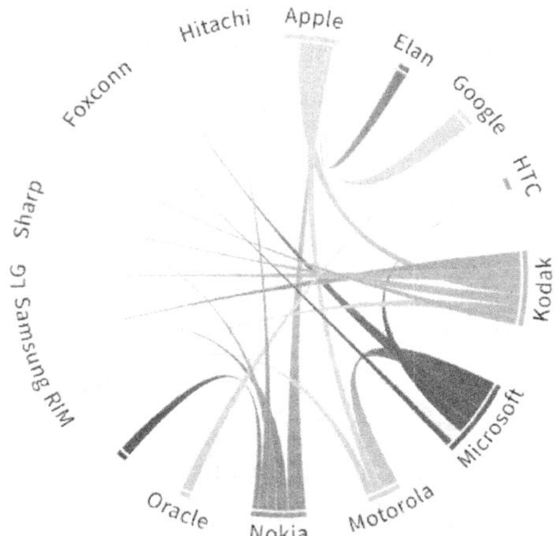

FIGURE 6.6

Such charts are used in circumstances where:

- There is a need to visualize weighted relationships between data variables.

- Simple representation to highlight interconnections between large sets of data.
- There is a need to quickly identify dominating categories.
- The flow of resources between departments or places is necessary to visualize.

This chart is particularly useful when the visual appeal of the data presented is important. Therefore, you might find information like immigration flow from one country to the next represented by a chord diagram.

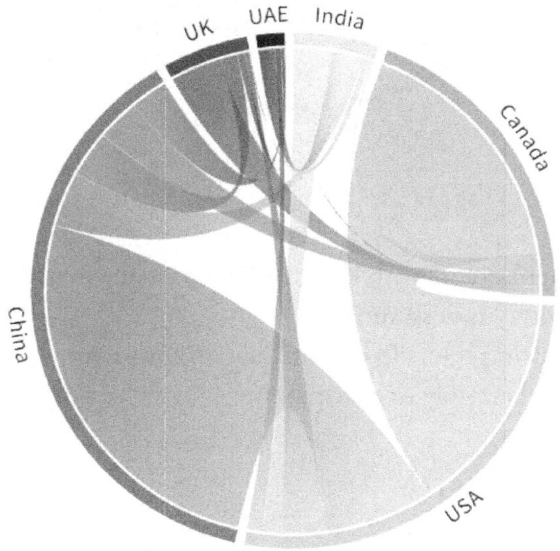

FIGURE 6.7

To maximize your use of chord diagrams, note the following practices:

- Consider adding a second visual and highlighting specific points if many arcs are needed. A broad overview and a highlighted insight work well together as two charts.

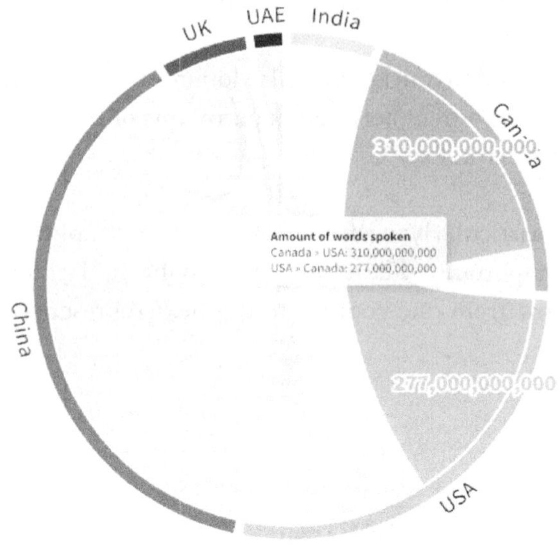

FIGURE 6.8

- Use aesthetic colors with levels of transparency to make the arcs clearer to understand.
- Consider using colors to identify key insights while keeping the rest of the chart gray or transparent.

NETWORK DIAGRAM

Like a chord diagram, network diagrams show interconnections between data variables with nodes representing each entity and connections between these nodes with links.

FIGURE 6.9

Network diagrams are typically used with larger, more complex sets of data and most data analysts will rarely see one in their career. It shows a broad overview with the ability to zoom in and view specific relationships.

Lawsuits in the Mobile Industry

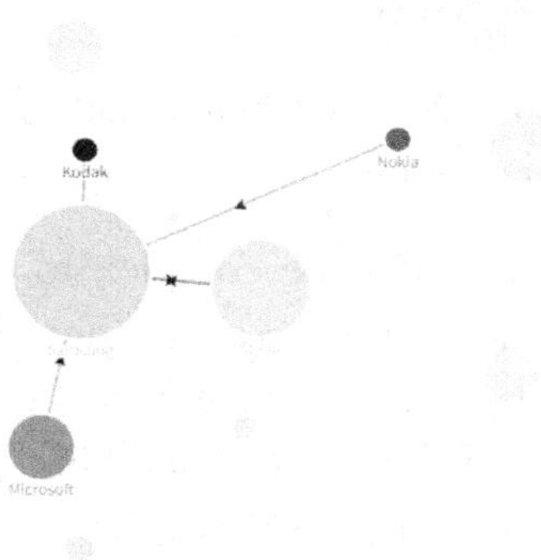

FIGURE 6.10

There are 4 types of network diagrams to choose from. Which one you choose to use depends on the method of data input. Let's highlight the specifics for each input method:

Undirected and unweighted

This input type shows that the entities are connected but there is no direction and no weight. An example would be to plot the data points that show Jim, Linda, and Lauren live in the same house.

Undirected and weighted

With this input type, the data points are connected and give information based on the weight of the relationship. To illustrate, let's say that these people above are connected if they published a blog together. The weight of the line is the number of blogs they have published together. The more pieces of work they have published together will determine the strength of the relationship.

Directed and unweighted

Let's say Josh reads Amanda's, Ella's, and Isabella's blogs. But only Isabella reads Josh's blogs. Ella and Amanda read each other's blogs, and Amanda reads Isabella's blogs. The connections are unweighted. They are either connected or not.

Directed and Weighted

People migrate from one country to another. The weight of the line determines the number of immigrants. Direction is the destination.

Network diagrams can be quite complex to develop, so we use more advanced platforms and software to create them. For the advanced analysts, Depending on the algorithm you use, your network diagram will take a specific form based on the built-in layouts. This form is important as finding an optimal position for each node highly impacts the output your audience will view. Network diagrams also have the ability to be interactive, and you can select a node and drag it around to better view the relationships. Several algorithms have been developed for different scenarios, including:

- Circle
- Sphere
- Fruchterman
- Reingold
- Random

Whatever scenario is relevant to your data output, ensure that your links overlap as little as possible and that there is minimum crossing at the edges. You can choose to make the lengths of the edges uniform or not. Depending on your data, you don't always have the freedom to change the overlap. The data does what it does, but smaller sets showcased in different visuals can help simplify large data sets.

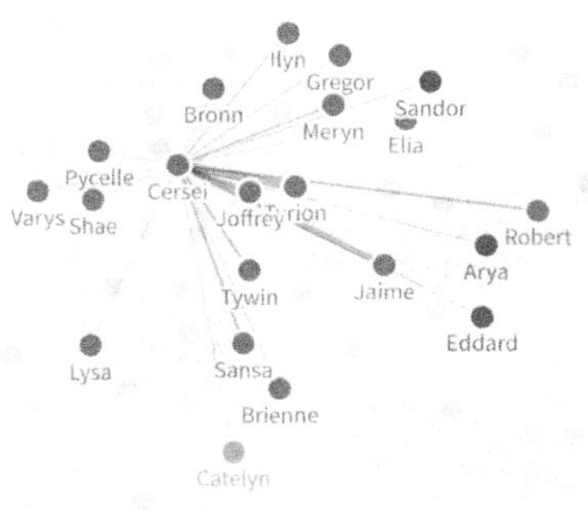

FIGURE 6.11

These algorithms can be customized via the shape and color specifications of each node to add more insights to the data. You can also customize these charts by creating a series of network diagrams over a long time span so values that have changed over time can be compared. We will keep network diagrams brief in this book, but if it is something you're interested in, I would recommend expanding your knowledge on them.

TREE DIAGRAM

This chart also goes by the names linkage tree and organizational chart. It helps audiences note data hierarchy in a tree-like structure. This structure consists of the following elements:

- Root node, which is a member that has no superior or parent.
- Nodes. They are linked with line connections. These connections are called branches. They represent the relationships between the variables.
- Leaf nodes. These are also called end nodes. They are components with no children or child nodes.

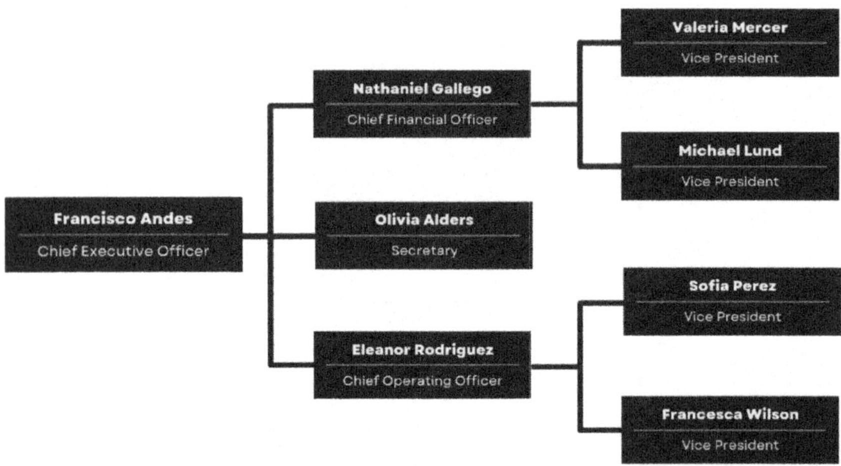

FIGURE 6.12

Tree diagrams are used to make strategic decisions for calculating probabilities and making market valuations. As a result, tree diagrams are used to:

- Show family connections and descent.
- Categorize data such as breaking down the world into continents, then countries, and then regions.
- Showcase supply chain breakdown
- Highlight evolutionary science like classification.
- Show managerial purposes in business and organizations.

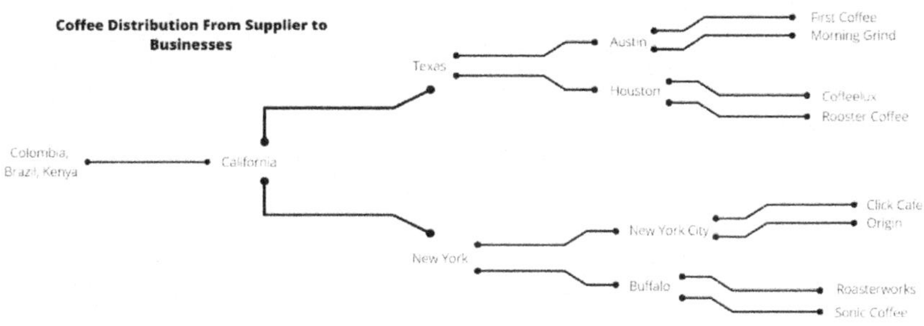

FIGURE 6.13

PARALLEL COORDINATES PLOT

This chart shows the relationships between multiple numerical data variables indicated by lines. In other words, several individual observations are compared on a set of numeric variables. Each variable is given its own axis. All the axes are parallel to each other. Each axis can have its own scale. As the plotted line moves across the chart, it highlights changes based on the axis and the value to indicate that variable. Because several lines are plotted on the same chart, parallel coordinates allow the comparison of many quantitative variables on one screen. It also allows for easily identifying relationships between these variables.

One of the best features of this type of chart is that the variables can have different ranges and different units. A parallel coordinates plot may be developed to show the anatomy of certain flower species. Each species is mapped as a line and each variable (sepal length, sepal width, etc.) is represented by a point on the line.

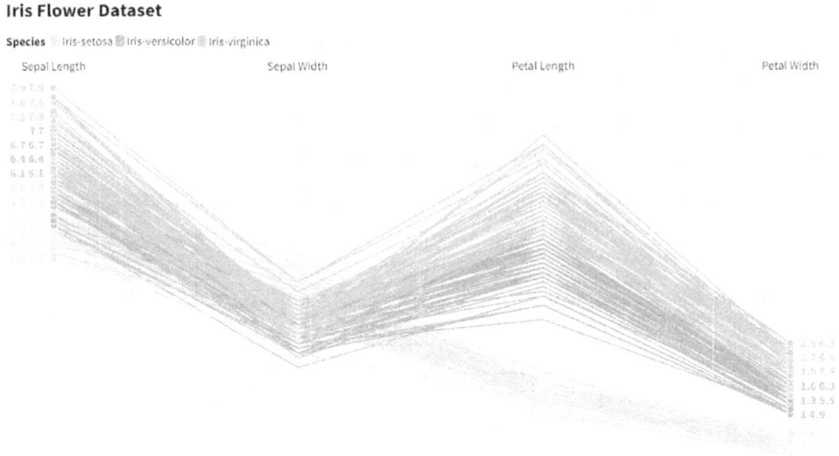

FIGURE 6.14

It can also effectively showcase sales throughout the year and determine the item's overall sales volume. Usually, you would use a line chart or a bar chart, but a parallel coordinates plot adds a refreshing spin to the data. It also allows you to add an extra variable to categorizing the data, in this case, determining if the sales volume was average, high, or low.

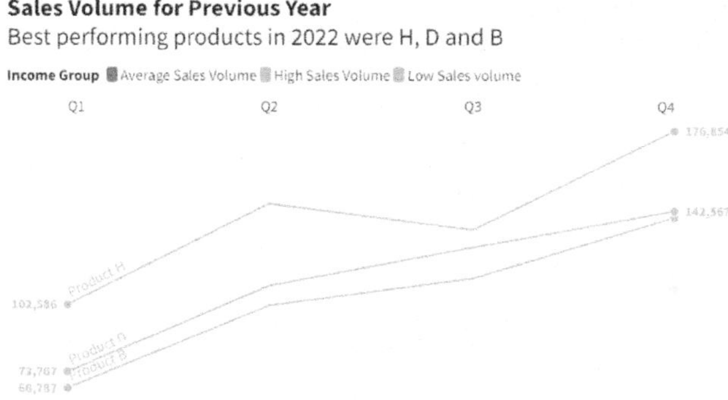

FIGURE 6.15

ON THE OTHER HAND, something like the scale of different attributes of emerald jewels can be plotted. The attributes (variables) can be the prices, hardness, refractive index and more can be plotted. The scale for these may be good, great, premium and ideal. The scale allows for comparing the different variables.

To get the most of these charts, here are a few tips:

- The order of the variables determines any trend line. Make these trends clear by ordering variables accordingly to showcase certain insights. Try different scaling to note which works best to suit your data.
- Parallel coordinates plots can become cluttered and even illegible quickly since so many variables can be compared on one chart. You can avoid this clutter and keep insights clear by using the technique called brushing. The technique highlights and isolates a selected line/s and fades out the others. This makes for easy interpretation of specific data. This can also be done interactively as you present, selecting separate lines showcasing their insights.

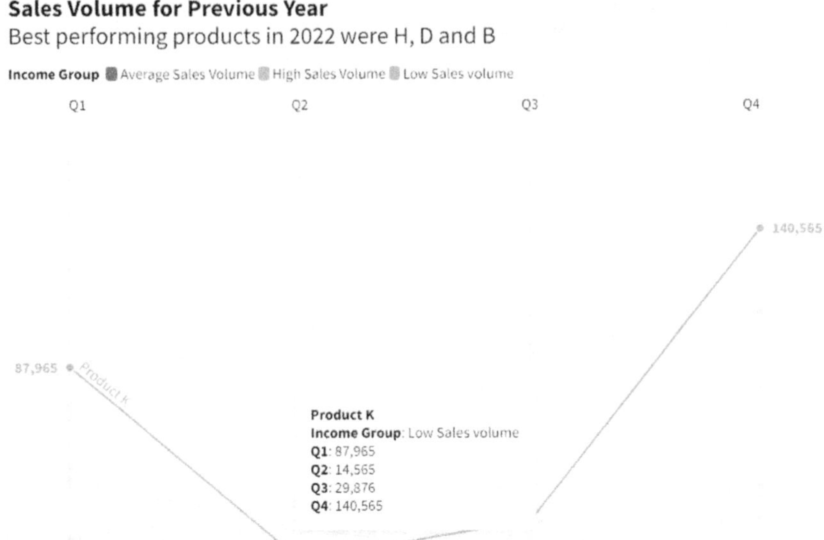

FIGURE 6.16

- Further, decrease possible clutter with axis order. Moving just one variable position on an axis can minimize the number of times lines cross. Do not sort variables on the X axis as it causes line crosses.

DATA SETS OFTEN OVERLAP and mingle with each other. So do subsets in groups of data. We need to highlight how these variables interact with each other as they can and do sometimes affect each other. Relationship charts allow us to dissect those connections.

7
GEOGRAPHICAL

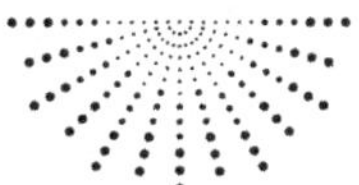

Quite a number of us have trouble giving and following verbal directions. The availability of a map makes things much easier because we now have a visual aid. However, think of geographical charts as serving the same function on a more advanced level. To be more precise, geographical data visualization allows the representation of location data in a visual format so that trends, patterns and relationships can be deduced. Note that they also go by the names geo charts and map charts so do not be surprised if you come across such terminologies in reference to them.

Location is a tricky data matrix to communicate to an audience in a tabular or textual format. Giving such data even poses a challenge for most data graphics. For example, where you might be able to use a bar chart to convey not only comparison but also relationships, geographical charts are unique in that no other chart can replace the precision with which they convey that specific type of data.

Let's have a look at some export data on a horizontal bar graph.

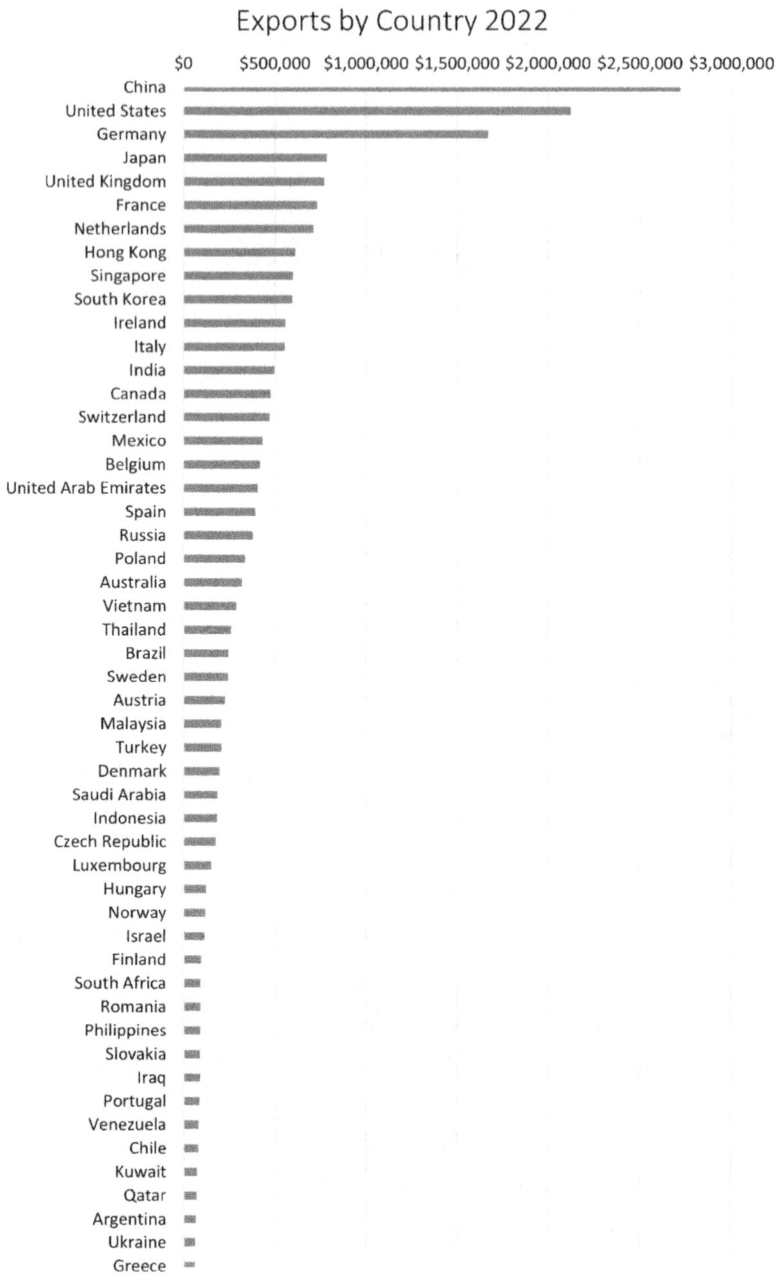
Exports by Country 2022
$0
$500,000
$1,000,000
$1,500,000
$2,000,000
$2,500,000
$3,000,000
China
United States
Germany
Japan
United Kingdom
France
Netherlands
Hong Kong
Singapore
South Korea
Ireland
Italy
India
Canada
Switzerland
Mexico
Belgium
United Arab Emirates
Spain
Russia
Poland
Australia
Vietnam
Thailand
Brazil
Sweden
Austria
Malaysia
Turkey
Denmark
Saudi Arabia
Indonesia
Czech Republic
Luxembourg
Hungary
Norway
Israel
Finland
South Africa
Romania
Philippines
Slovakia
Iraq
Portugal
Venezuela
Chile
Kuwait
Qatar
Argentina
Ukraine
Greece

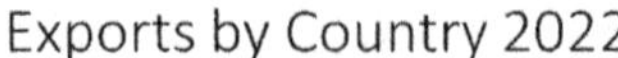

FIGURE 7.1

The audience is left without a visual aid. Geographical charts come to the rescue and provide a better understanding of location-based data. The best geographical charts allow information to be understood without the need for further explanation. However, this does not mean that your audience needs some geographical skills to understand the patterns, trends and correlations that are needed to draw educated conclusions. Let's see the same data but on a map.

FIGURE 7.2

It might be worth showcasing the two charts together. The geographical chart gives them a visual representation they would understand, and the bar chart can go into detail regarding values. Geographical charts provide context to data that highlights the function of population or of regional statistics. For example, the population of the United States by state can be displayed in such a chart with densely populated areas highlighted in darker colors and more sparsely populated areas highlighted in lighter shades. Highlighting the population for 50 states can become difficult and hard to interpret through other mediums such as a bar chart.

Geographical charts can also be used to display data such as the number of facilities like parks and schools in an area, the changing wildlife population in a region over time, the rate at which the forest is being depleted in certain areas and so much more. These charts are even useful in the business arena. For example, a coffee company can analyze which regions enjoy specific blends or consume the most coffee.

Let's get into some different types of maps.

CHOROPLETH

This type of geographical map displays divided geographical areas or regions. This display is facilitated by shaded or colored sections based on the numeric value. Choropleths are great for showing clear regional patterns in data. For example, unusually high crime rates in a particular neighborhood in contrast to its adjacent city could be illustrated using a choropleth.

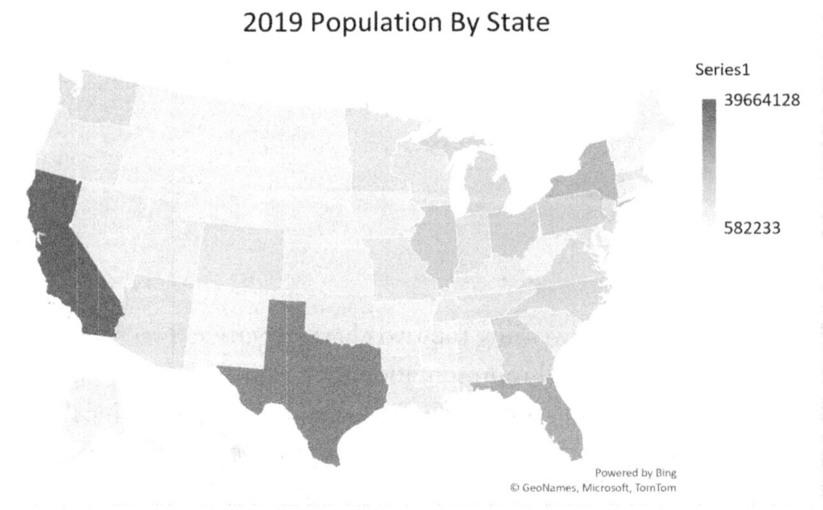

FIGURE 7.3

These types of maps allow you to see the big picture but they are not great at allowing your audience to see the subtle differences. Using chloropleths as a birds-eye view and then another chart for a zoomed-in insight can be an effective strategy to get the visual representation from a map and a memorable insight from a more detailed view.

Another downside is that intervals between colors do not equate to the same interval between your data values. While these charts are great for highlighting patterns, they do not make a great tool for comparing exact values between regions. If exact values are needed for decision-making, using a zoomed-in view or another chart in collaboration with this chart can be effective.

With Choropleth maps, color is your best friend and worst enemy. Being strategic is important for the effective representation of the data. Some things you can do to maximize your color are:

Use the right color scheme

Use lightness to highlight the difference in sequential and diverging color schemes. Color gradients from light to dark to help the audience spot high, low and mid values because that is the natural inclination of the brain. That is the practice for sequential color schemes. On the other hand, with diverging color schemes, the extremes need to have the darkest colors and the lightest colors should be in the center.

Use fewer colors in qualitative color schemes

The more colors on your map, the harder it will be to note their various meanings. Make it easy for your audience to make that recollection by limiting it to 3 colors when using qualitative color schemes. This will ensure that your audience does not have to constantly refer to the key to familiarize themselves with what these colors represent.

Ensure the audience sees the difference in data

Show the difference in data values with different colors. Use the brightest and darkest colors to show extremes. Make use of stops. These are equally sized parts of the color palette. These can initiate low and high values. Using stops highlights the contrast between these extreme values. Do not use stops too much as this will cause too much contrast.

Consider using a continuous color scheme over a discrete color scheme

This ensures a smooth visual gradient or eye flow. Continuous color schemes allow for comparing neighboring regions with one color used in different shades. On the other hand, discrete color schemes assign distinct colors to different values. Subtle differences are not very noticeable with such a scheme, even though these do allow the audience to note the range that these values fall in quickly.

Create an accurate color legend

Ensure that your key is immediately readable to your audience. With a sequential color scheme, layer the scheme from lowest to highest value with the 2 to 4 other values in between. These are placed in equally spaced intervals like 50, 100 and 150. With divergent color schemes follow the same logic with a display of the center values.

Use labels for relevant insights

Highlight pertinent information with the use of labels.

PROPORTIONAL SYMBOL MAP

Typically making use of circles and squares, this chart proportionally scales the size of simple symbols so that data volume based on location can be visualized. The premise supporting the development of such a chart is simple: the larger the size of the symbol, the larger the data of volume that exists in that particular location and vice versa. The smaller the size of the symbol, the smaller the data volume recorded for that particular location. This is because the symbols are scaled directly proportionate to the data. So, if the data volume for Florida is twice as large as New York's, then the symbols (mainly circles) highlighting that volume will be twice as large.

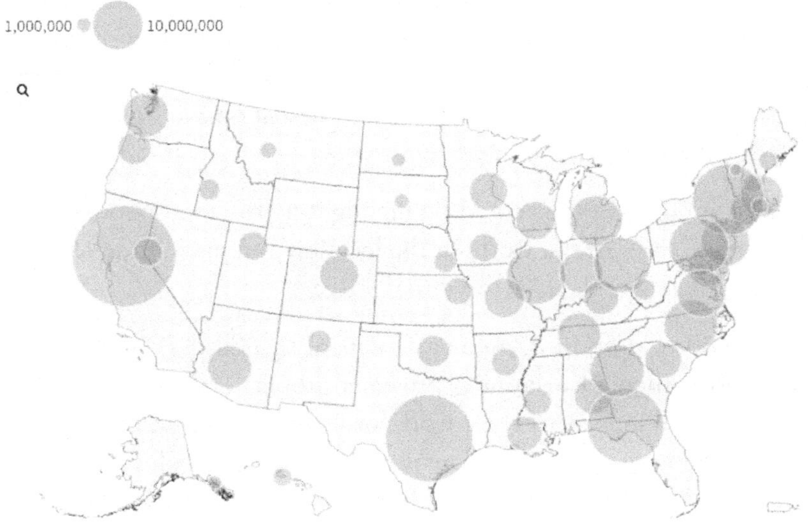

FIGURE 7.4

This data can be grouped into categories or numerical ranges. From this, graduated symbol maps can be created. This allows you to reduce clutter by reducing the number of symbol sizes corresponding to different categories.

Proportional symbol maps are useful in a variety of circumstances. First, they allow for showcasing or comparing the relevance of data value based on a region. The audience is given a clear insight into the significance of a region's data. There may be times when smaller regions have more significant data. They can quickly get lost in the sea of larger regions in other types of charts but not with this one. The more significant the data noted in a region, no matter its size compared to others, the bigger the symbol overtop. Data will not go unnoticed no matter the location.

Proportional symbol maps are also great for highlighting the risks or chances of something happening in or to a geographical area.

Proportional symbol maps allow great flexibility because they can represent numerical data like age but also ordered categorical data like low, medium or high data variables. That flexibility also extends into these charts having the function to highlight geographical points such as exact locations as well as geographical areas such as countries over a world map. Large circles will be easily noticeable and can be immediately understood as a country with a high value. A great option for a birds-eye view to see the best performing regions.

Examples of effective uses could be highlighting the total population of the 10 largest cities in the world or the location and magnitude of earthquakes in Japan over the last 100 years.

Symbols tend to overlap if large variations or several data locations are near to each other. Overlapping prevents proper analysis of the data. But you can still make this chart work for its intended purpose by using various elements such as size, transparency and exact color to improve the audience's ability to interpret different values of the map. These visual elements allow for separating the symbols.

Another way to bypass this problem is to move the symbols so that they have a bit more room to breathe and thus, be clearer to the audience. Be careful with this practice, though, as you risk removing the symbol from its factual location. This can lead to misinterpretation of data.

More ways to maximize the use of proportional symbol maps include:

- Ensure the size of symbols are relevant to data. If one continent has double the population of another, its circle or square should be exactly double the size of the other continent.
- Provide context of the scale in a legend so the audience understands the rough difference between a small and big symbol.
- Highlight specific points that are relevant to your presentation.

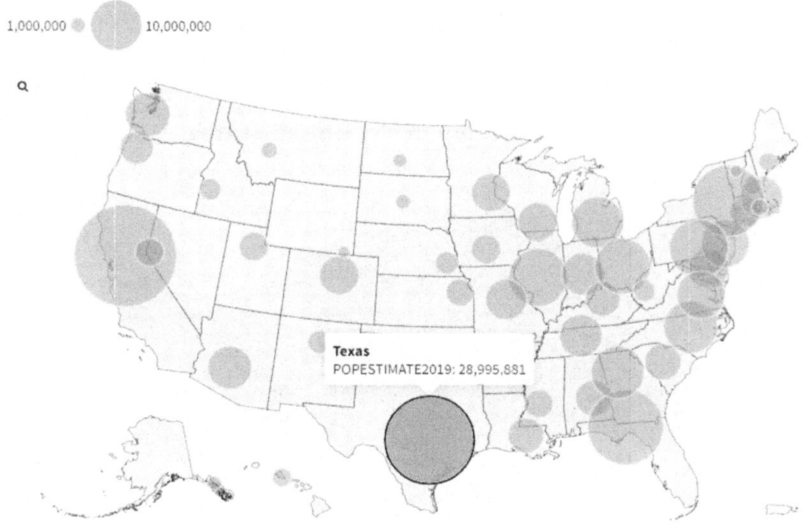

FIGURE 7.5

FLOW MAP

This type of geographical chart shows the movement of information or objects from one location to another. This chart also highlights the value of these motions. Think of flow maps as a combination of a map and a flow diagram. The most common use of flow maps is to show the amount and magnitude of the migrations of items like people, animals, or products in a single line. Even the flow of money and vehicular traffic can be highlighted in this way. This relative amount is showcased in the thickness of the lines in some cases. As a result, flow maps help highlight the distribution of these data variables geographically. To sum it up, flow maps have four functions. They show distribution, volume, movement and location.

Flow maps have unique anatomy. The lines start at the point of origin on the map and branch out in flow lines. The movement is indicated by an arrow. The arrowhead lands on the destination. These parts come together to show the contrasts in the qualities that make up the spread over territories of the items illustrated.

There are three categories of flow maps:

RADIAL FLOW MAPS

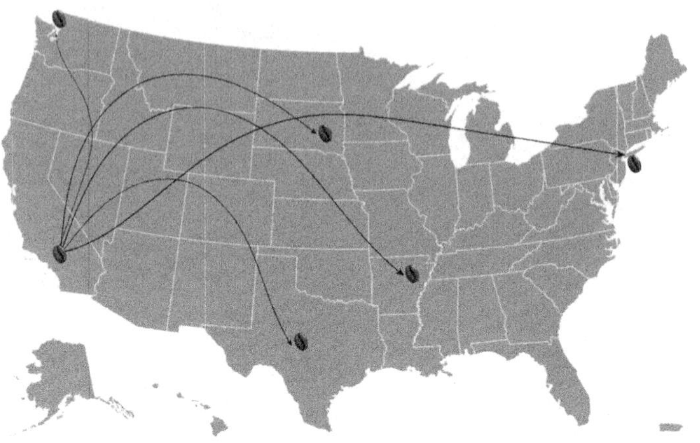

FIGURE 7.6

These types of flow maps showcase the relationship between one source of an item and its many destinations and uses. This is highlighted by several lines coming from the origin and radiating out to show the movement. The accuracy of the route is not the main focus. Rather, the general direction is. Radial flow maps are commonly used to show the volume of goods being traded on a global scale. Getting products delivered to your home from across the sea is facilitated by charts such as these.

NETWORK FLOW MAPS

These are used to highlight the flow of quantities over existing networks such as supplier to the distributor, and distributor to customers.

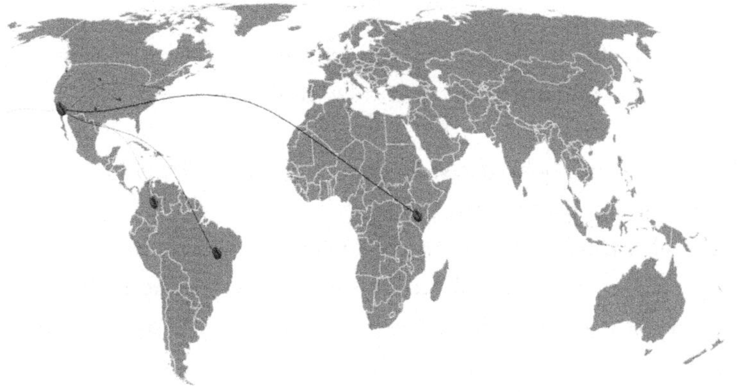

FIGURE 7.7

DISTRIBUTIVE FLOW MAPS

This type of flow map operates much like a radial or network flow map but instead shows a schematic path from one origin to many destinations with thicker single lines. The size of the lines determines the number of goods. They also have smaller flow lines with diversions from the destination points. This is often used for the spread of disease, worldwide trade, and in this case, coffee suppliers.

Coffee Supply Chain Operations

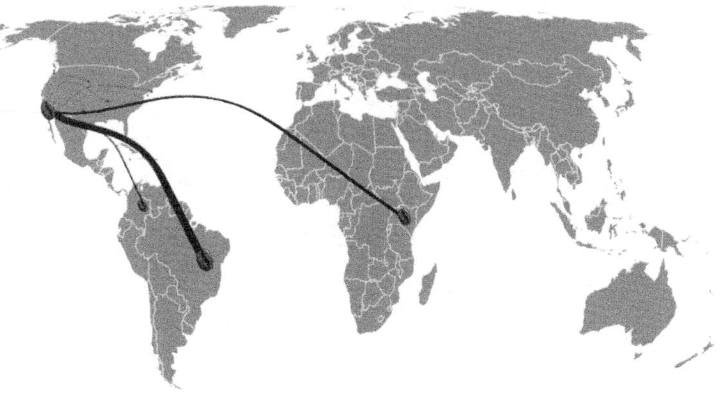

FIGURE 7.8

No matter the type of flow map you used, there are a few universal strategies that can be used to maximize their function:

- If many lines go to the same location, merge the edges to reduce the visual clutter.
- Employ intelligent routing by ensuring flows do not cut directly across other objects. Route arrows aesthetically so every flow is visible. Do this by creating a wide route along the edge of the map or curving lines.
- Choose the correct width of flow to best showcase the data if this becomes necessary.

Geographical charts are in a class of their own. There are often times when we might work with data covering regions or even worldwide. In many cases, the amount of categories that make up this data far exceeds the comfortable amount for your standard chart. Geographical maps are an excellent way to visualize regional or national data with many categories and make it easy to interpret.

8
TABLES AND PICTOGRAMS

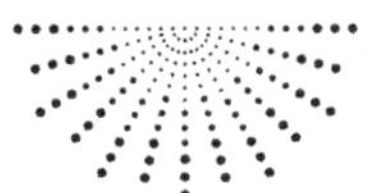

Charts are wonderful for many reasons. These pictorial depictions of information help simplify complicated data so that it can be understood at a glance. This is particularly helpful for visual learners and allows the presenter to waylay the need to provide much explanation. Charts help streamline meetings and business gatherings so that the audience gets a helicopter view of the data and the problems that need addressing. Charts make it easy to identify trends.

However, another side to the scale is the possible disadvantages of using charts. One such downside is that charts may oversimplify data, thus unintentionally misleading the audience as critical issues are missed. You may try to fix this issue but this can lead to them overcomplicating the view. Also, with the many options available for picturizing data, it can be difficult to choose the right one, especially if inexperienced in the world of data. Although I do hope by this point in the book, you will have a better understanding of chart selection. Adding too many charts can either bore the audience or, worse, confuse them, especially if irrelevant information is added or there is a lack of clarity.

So, how do you offset these disadvantages of using charts in some scenarios? The use of charts is not the only way that data can be presented to an audience. This chapter explores alternative methods, namely the use of tables and pictograms, that allow you to offset the possible drawbacks and showcase pure data in its true form.

TABLES - WHEN AND HOW TO USE THEM

Tables are databases that maintain information in categorized rows and columns. Every row is a unique data record and each column stands for a field of similar records. To be clear, tables do not allow data to be visualized. An audience will not be able to look at a table and gain a clear view of the big picture of what is represented in an instance like a data visualization would. The audience needs to study the data and be familiar with the context for that to happen. But if done correctly, tables can be extremely effective for showcasing data and highlighting insights and trends.

Product	**Q1**	**Q2**	**Q3**	**Q4**	**Total**
Product A	$12,654	$17,675	$13,789	$26,876	**$70,994**
Product B	$4,986	$5,768	$14,876	$9,876	**$35,506**
Product C	$27,876	$35,647	$21,897	$41,987	**$127,407**
Product D	$9,786	$14,786	$17,758	$25,879	**$68,209**
Total	**$55,302**	**$73,876**	**$68,320**	**$104,618**	**$302,116**

FIGURE 8.1

Tables are a powerful tool for communication when used correctly and under the right circumstances. They fight that under simplified view of some charts as they convey a significant amount of information. They are best used when highlighting data relating to benefits versus risks to the audiences. This is possible because of the simple yet flexible nature of the table structure. They can be easily adapted to allow the audience to gain fast yet efficient readability across rows and columns. Tables can provide consistency and clarity, both features needed for informed decision-making. An appropriately designed table allows the audience to quickly extract the required information, decreasing the cognitive burden placed on the audience.

When to Use Tables

Instances where using tables makes sense include to:

Allow the audience to look up particular points of information

Often, an audience will not find it pertinent to peruse all the data in a table, especially since tables tend to be jam-packed with a high volume of data. The audience will only seek out the data that is relevant to them and the problem that they are trying to solve. We are naturally attuned to sifting through data to only focus on what is applicable to the situation.

Most Visited Museums Worldwide

Search in table

Page 1 of 8 >

	Name	City	Visitors 2018
1	Musée du Louvre	Paris	10.2M
2	National Museum of China	Beijing	8.6M
3	Metropolitan Museum of Art	New York City	7M
4	Vatican Museums	Vatican City	6.8M
5	Tate Modern	London	5.9M
6	British Museum	London	5.8M
7	National Gallery	London	5.7M
8	National Gallery of Art	Washington, D.C.	4.4M
9	State Hermitage Museum	Saint Petersburg	4.2M
10	Victoria and Albert Museum	London	4M

Source: Wikipedia • Created with Datawrapper

FIGURE 8.2

Take advantage of this tendency to look up only what is relevant by structuring your table in such a way that the information of interest to your audience is not embedded in a block of data. Instead, make the data visible by laying it out in a way that is natural for the eye to follow and ordered appropriately. We will cover more of this in the "create better tables" section

Highlight precise numbers if they apply to the data presentation

Tables and charts can be used in tandem. It may be hard for the audience to note figures of interest in charts because they focus on the relationship between data sets and categories within data variables. But using tables along with charts allows for more clarity of specific figures such as the best price to list a product or the best interest rate for the highest rate of return 10 years down the line.

Country	2020 Exports	% of Global Exports 2018	Main Export 2019
China	$2.72 Tril	10.78%	Broadcast Equipment
United States	$2.12 Tril	10.26%	Refined Petroleum
Germany	$1.67 Tril	7.62%	Cars
Japan	$785 Bil	3.73%	Cars
United Kingdom	$770 Bil	3.58%	Cars
France	$733 Bil	3.59%	Planes, Helicopters, and/or Spacecraft
Netherlands	$711 Bil	3.14%	Refined Petroleum
Hong Kong	$612 Bil	2.77%	Gold
Singapore	$599 Bil	2.70%	Integrated Circuits
South Korea	$596 Bil	2.92%	Integrated Circuits

FIGURE 8.3

Highlighting numbers with tables is particularly useful to audiences that intend to act urgently using the data presented. They want the information to initiate effective decision-making.

Allow the audience to compare data variables going in two directions

Let's consider that a data presenter needs to highlight the sales for the stores of a particular region for the last 12 months and not just the last month. This is a case where the audience's decision-making process after that presentation is influenced by data that moves in more than one direction. In such a case, visualization could be confused compared to simply being presented with the data in table format. Be sure to make the comparison of values moving in these different directions easy for the audience with the table's structure.

Creating Better Tables - What You Need to Know

To ensure the readability of tables, here are a few tips:

- Emphasize the desired reading direction by adding shading (color) that does not overshadow the information. Vertical shading of columns emphasizes reading from top to bottom, while horizontal shading emphasizes reading from left to right.

- Further, help the audience navigate your table with the use of color by considering using different colors for different categories or coloring highest to lowest values within columns. Do not overwhelm the audience with this use of color. Be strategic. Use bright colors when coloring text so that they stand out against white space. However, use a pastel background when highlighting entire rows, columns, or cells.
- Ensure that information is aligned within columns. Be mindful that different types of alignment can be used in one table. For example, text in one column can be left justified while numbers in other columns can be centered or right aligned to keep higher readability levels.
- Keep the typeface and numbering styles consistent.
- Sort your table based on what information is most relevant rather than the first inclination of doing so alphabetically (Unless Necessary). Always sort your data to bring the most interesting information to the top.
- Consider making your table sortable and searchable so that different readers can more easily access the information that is relevant to them.
- Keep the table as simple as possible by using a condensed font to keep the data compact. This also ensures that the table is easy to scan. More ways to keep the structure of the table simple include not using hyphenation, icons, shorter number formats and abbreviating details when it is possible. Simplify information so the audience is not confronted with a screen full of text and numbers.
- Narrow down the number of columns used to what is vital. Consider which categories can be combined to form one column rather than multiple. You might also consider swapping rows and columns so the audience can visually scan through the information vertically rather than horizontally.
- If you cannot scale down the number of columns in the table, consider using light gray shading every second row to increase the readability. This is called zebra shading.

- Consider structuring your data so that your table has more rows than columns. This is easier to read with the human tendency to read from left to right. Consider adjusting the row height to the number of rows. More rows might mean lowering the row height so more information is condensed within view, allowing the audience to peruse more data quicker. The opposite might be a consideration with fewer rows.
- Consider using pagination when using long tables where all the data will not fit onto the screen. This will allow the audience to realize that the data continues below what has been presented currently and thus, pursue that information.
- Consider adding an element of visualization to your tables with the use of heatmaps. Make the background of higher numbers darker or saturated compared to their counterparts. Use more than one color gradient for columns that have the same measurement. Also, use different color gradients to separate different heat maps used in a singular table.

Product	Q1	Q2	Q3	Q4
Product A	$12,654.00	$17,675.00	$13,789.00	$26,876.00
Product B	$4,986.00	$5,768.00	$14,876.00	$9,876.00
Product C	$27,876.00	$35,647.00	$21,897.00	$41,987.00
Product D	$9,786.00	$14,786.00	$17,758.00	$25,879.00

FIGURE 8.4

- Another way of adding a dimension of visualization to your table is to show development over time. This is facilitated by a tool known as sparklines. These are mini-line charts at the end of a row that show the development between the time points. The general trend is highlighted by each sparkline. It is an easy way to make your char more visual and insightful.

Product	Q1	Q2	Q3	Q4	Total
Product A	$12,654.00	$17,675.00	$13,789.00	$26,876.00	**$70,994.00**
Product B	$4,986.00	$5,768.00	$14,876.00	$9,876.00	**$35,506.00**
Product C	$27,876.00	$35,647.00	$21,897.00	$41,987.00	**$127,407.00**
Product D	$9,786.00	$14,786.00	$17,758.00	$25,879.00	**$68,209.00**
Total	**$55,302.00**	**$73,876.00**	**$68,320.00**	**$104,618.00**	**$302,116.00**

FIGURE 8.5

We have addressed how to use tables for the best communication with your audience. Experiment and try out new techniques. Tables can be more effective than you think.

Next, let's discuss the appropriate circumstances for using pictograms and how you can optimize them.

ALL ABOUT PICTOGRAMS

If you want your data to be memorable, easy to internalize and look great, pictograms are the medium of choice. Pictograms are simple to develop and simple in how they translate visually, yet their use is wildly popular in data visualization. They use a series of repeated icons and images to visualize data. The icons or images are arranged in a grid or a single line, with each icon or image standing for a particular unit. So, 1 icon might stand for a unit of 10, 100, 1000, or any other number. In other words, pictograms show the frequency at which a data point occurs in a set. They showcase one specific insight through bold text or a guage.

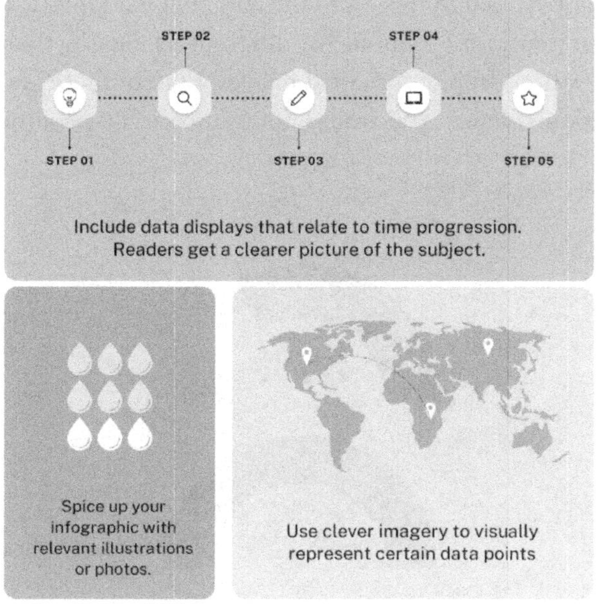

FIGURE 8.6

Advantages of pictograms include:

- Allowing large data sets to be expressed in a simple form or insight.
- Being easy to read as all the information is expressed in a format meant to be digested at a glance.
- Not requiring an explanation as pictograms are a universal tool for simple data expression

Creating a pictogram is not complicated. Here is the outline of a simple process for doing so:

Gather the data

The relevant data is collected and compiled into a list or table.

Select the icons or images

Pick a relevant symbol to represent the data. For example, if you want to represent data outlining rainfall for different islands in the Caribbean, you may use water droplets or cloud images. Both of these are relevant to the information at hand. You would not use something completely unrelated like cat icons.

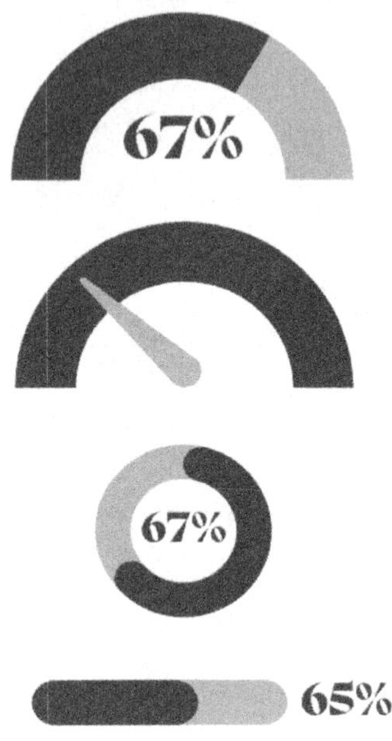

FIGURE 8.7

Create a key

The key is a tool that highlights the values assigned to each icon or image used in the pictogram. To illustrate, you may use dog icons to show the number of stray canines roaming a particular city and in need of a good home. You may denote a value of 100 for each icon. Another use would be many small human icons representing 100% of your customer base, and a percentage of them are filled in with color signifying said percentage are returning customers.

FIGURE 8.8

Create the pictogram

Two columns that represent the data and categories will be created. The icons or images will be added to show the frequency of the data. If the frequency is not a whole number, fractions of icons or images can be used.

When to Use Pictograms

Pictograms also go by other names such as icon charts, picture charts, pictographs and pictorial unit charts. They are used to transform data into a simple and clear insight for quick consumption. The specific instances where the use of pictograms are applicable include:

Show ratings, scores, or changes over time

We see examples of pictograms being used in this way all the time. The 5-star ratings of products and services on websites like Amazon and eBay. These ratings show proportions and percentages of simple data. Presenting such figures in tables or charts can add unnecessary complications. As a result, pictograms are a good medium for their expression.

Indicate progress to a goal in a project status report

We see pictographs used in items like product roadmaps, project status reports and project plans. Anyone can use pictograms to highlight the progress of any project visually. However, on a higher scale, pictograms allow businesses and organizations to note the status and progress of items like budgets, schedules and scopes of multiple items relating to the different aspects of a project.

Color is the most common visual element used to show progress in this way. Darker colors are used to show the progress thus far. Lighter colors are used to indicate the work in progress and what remains undone or unfinished. This can also be done through a gauge that is full or empty. An easy visual everyone understands.

Large Sets of Data

An effective pictogram can be in the form of a word map. When using regional or worldwide data, a word map can easily express which regions make up the majority of the data. This is also good when you have many rows of data as it can be paired with a table, so the audience gets a visual representation but can easily look deeper within the data.

Source: Gapminder, United Nations Population Division

FIGURE 8.9

Elaborate on a simple chart for extra impact

If your data can be compiled into a simple chart like a bar chart or a pie chart, use a pictogram to make the presentation of this data more compelling with the visual interest that these tools generate.

Visually tally and summarize survey results

This is supremely useful in presenting the results of surveys. You can simply show the compilation of these results in spreadsheets and tables but you risk boring your audience or making them feel intimidated by large amounts of data. Since we always want to avoid these situations, using pictographs to tally results, give a summary and highlight key insights is a better choice.

How to Maximize the Use of Pictograms

We expect pictographs to be simple to understand but many beginners make them overly complicated and thus, they give up the advantage of using them. This section describes how you can make the most effective use of pictographs by creating them in the proper way. Here are these useful tips:

- Use straightforward icons to make information clear. Remember to make these icons relevant and related to the topic at hand.
- Avoid contrasting colors for proportions and percentages. Do not use too many colors in one pictograph at one time. Doing so defeats the purpose of simple yet effective information. Too much detail distracts the audience from the information that needs to be in the spotlight.
- Before using color combinations like red and green or blue and yellow, be mindful of color-blind audiences. More on color blindness relating to data visualization in the next chapter.
- Do not be afraid of negative space in your pictograph. Use an appropriate denoted value for each icon so that the space becomes filled with them.

INFOGRAPHICS

Infographics are information packages that compile a collection of data visualizations, images and a few texts. The aim of infographics is to give audiences an easy-to-comprehend overview of a subject matter. They serve as a visual tool to facilitate communication and decision-making. Pictograms are often used as a feature in infographics. Why? Because they turn otherwise boring information or data points like statistics into attractive, eye-catching items. Other items that utilize pictograms to catch and hold attention include resumes, reports and presentations.

IT'S ALL ABOUT THE

Data Infographic

Infographic makes it easier for readers to absorb chunks of information. Shortly explain here what will this infographic cover.

DATA 1

Include data displays that relate to time progression. Readers get a clearer picture of the subject.

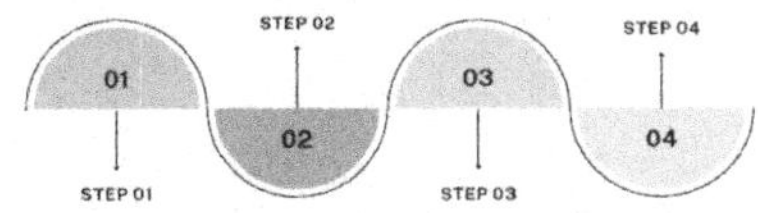

DATA 2

Spice up your infographic with relevant illustrations or photos.

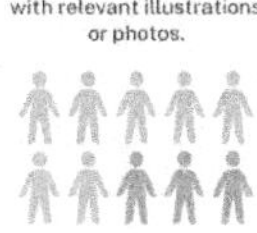

DATA 3

Use this space to highlight essential data that readers need to take note.

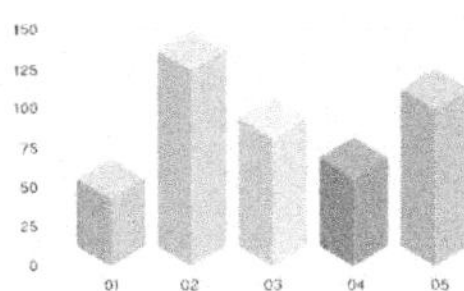

DATA 4

Include data like percentages and average. It helps the reader get insight about the topic.

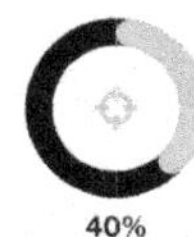

40% 65% 80%

DATA 6

The organizational structure determines how activities such as task allocation, coordination, and supervision are directed toward achieving organizational goals.

DATA 5

Provide data displays that show step-by-step progression. Readers get a clearer picture of the subject.

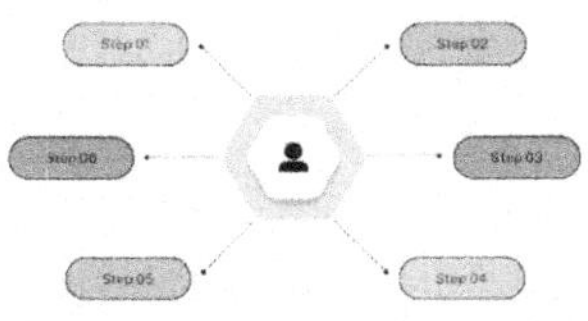

reallygreatsite.com

FIGURE 8.10

FIGURE 8.11

Relaying insights doesn't have to be intricate and interactive. Often something as simple as showing a single figure with a visual to represent it is all you need to get your point across. The most important thing when visualizing data is understanding and interpreting the insights. Don't overcomplicate it if you don't have to. Tables and pictograms are an excellent way to showcase the data in its purest form.

9
FUNDAMENTALS OF DESIGN

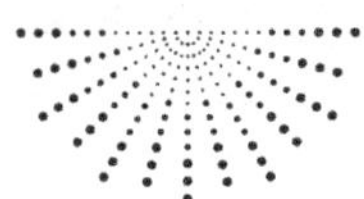

You have chosen the right medium to express the story that you have developed to relay the information to your audience. But your job is not done. You need to be able to sell your story to your audience. Doing so is not based on luck and chase. It is based on you combining the right elements in the right order to grab their attention and keep them engaged enough to wonder what's next. This chapter outlines these elements and how you can use them most effectively.

7 PRINCIPLES FOR TRANSFORMING DATA INTO STUNNING, INFORMATIVE VISUALS

Creating stunning data visuals is certainly an art. However, science can guide the flow of information with 7 principles:

- **Balance of Design**

Balance refers to the designed elements of your data visualization being distributed equally across your charts. These elements can be the colors used, the negative space, which is the unused spaces around and between objects like the unused spaces between bars on a bar chart, shapes and texture.

There's no formula for perfectly balancing each visualization. Simply look at your data, and determine how the chart represents it. Is there a smooth visual flow? Clean color theory? Minimal elements? You should naturally create a balanced design after going through the remaining 7 principles and optimizing your chart elements, which will come later in the chapter. Asking yourself if your design is balanced is the first and last thing you should always consider in the design phase.

- **The Emphasis of Key Insights**

You need to draw your audience's eyes to the key data points by using color contrast, different colors, negative space, size and shapes. Because we read from left to right, naturally, viewers' attention tends to fall on the top left corner of a plot first. It is a good practice to make use of that space for important insights or, often the title. With this, of course, having some information to back it up is necessary.

"As you can see, we have been steadily declining in our premium memberships. However, We have recently released the next version of our software, which has many improvements such as bug fixes and user experience upgrades. With this release, we have run multiple marketing campaigns and seem to have brought in many new customers."

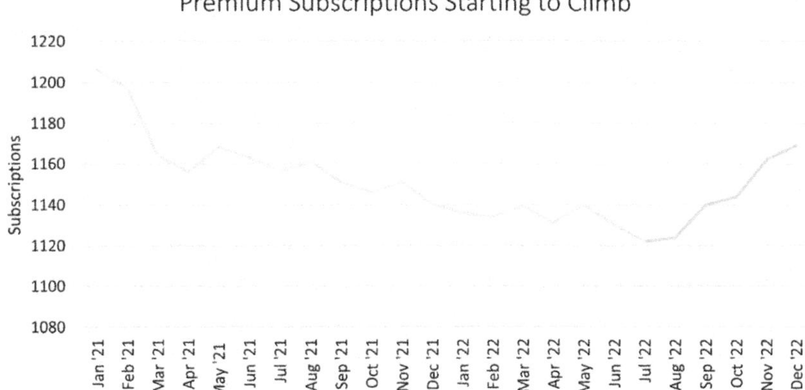

FIGURE 9.1

THIS CAN ALSO BE DONE by showcasing specific data points of relevance based on what your needs were.

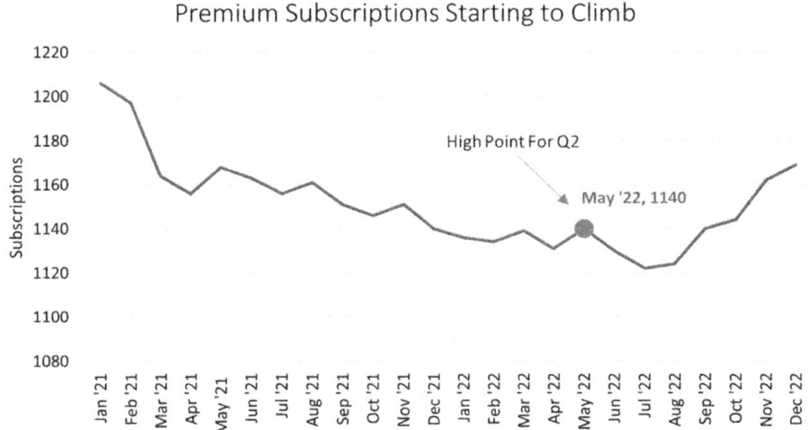

FIGURE 9.2

- **Show Clear Movement**

A cluttered design will have your audience's eyes darting all over your plot with no clear spot where they should land or how they should move to create cohesive absorption of information. Avoid this confusion by creating a clear flow of information. Another tendency we, as human beings illustrate, is that we read in an 'F' pattern. First, our eyes move from left to right, then gradually down a page. You can use this tendency to create movement from key insights to supporting points in your data visualizations.

You can also create this smooth movement using colors to direct the audience's eyes across your plot if your visualization is static. Movement is implied if your visualization uses interactive and animated tools or light to dark hue.

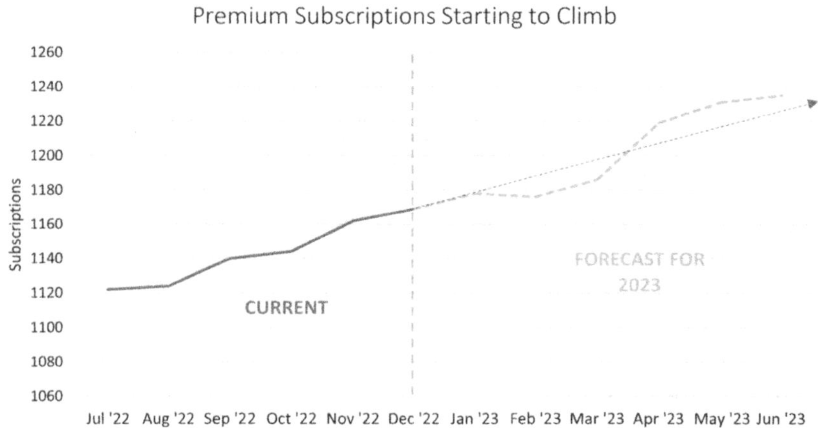

FIGURE 9.3

A simple trend line visually shows the audience where the data could go without needing any information. With this, you can add extra visuals, a table, or insights about why this is happening or how you can make it happen.

- **Utilize Patterns to Highlight Insights**

Patterns are developed when design elements are repeated. Use this repetition to your advantage to display similar types of information across your plots. This repetition can come in the form of colors, types of charts and the elements used on these charts.

Showing patterns not only highlights similar relationships between different data groups but also shows anomalies and differentiations when elements break from the trend of repetition.

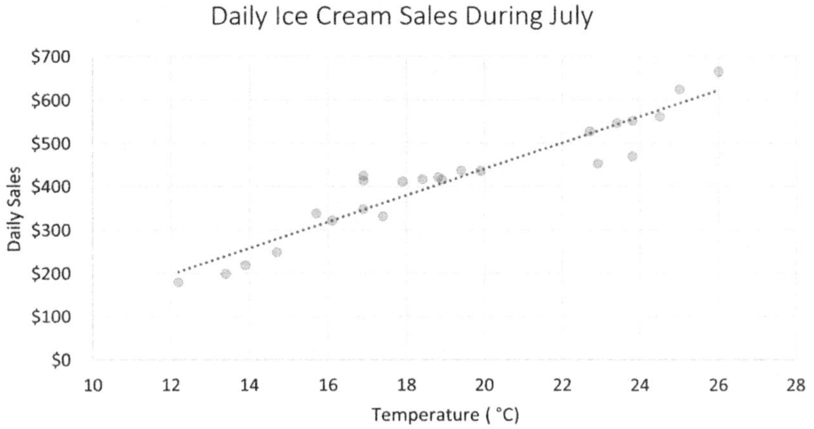

FIGURE 9.4

In the case of the ice cream sales, we added a trend line to reveal the pattern of the data and its trajectory.

- **Use Proportion**

Proportion refers to the size of the elements plotted on your data visualizations. Use these relative sizes to indicate the weight of significance of different data sets and the relationship between the values of these different data sets. Make key insights bigger than the rest of the information plotted to visually convey their importance.

Also, ensure that charts reflect the interdependent relationships between different values accurately.

- **Give your Audience Variety**

Watching the same ole thing over and over again creates boredom. As much as you want to create coherence in your visualizations, you need to also spice things up. Use different, interesting, relevant design elements to break the repetition trend. Instead of falling asleep, your audience becomes more engaged with you and the visualization presented. In this case, we can view ice cream sales with a regression line showing the upward trend.

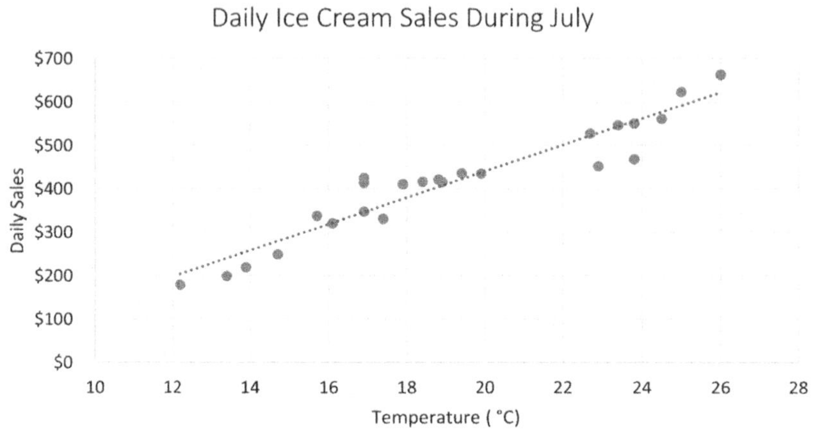

FIGURE 9.5

Additionally, you can use multiple visuals to stress important points. Adding a simple bar chart comparing the previous year to confirm that trend adds more context and helps the audience better understand the insight.

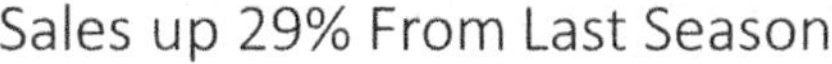

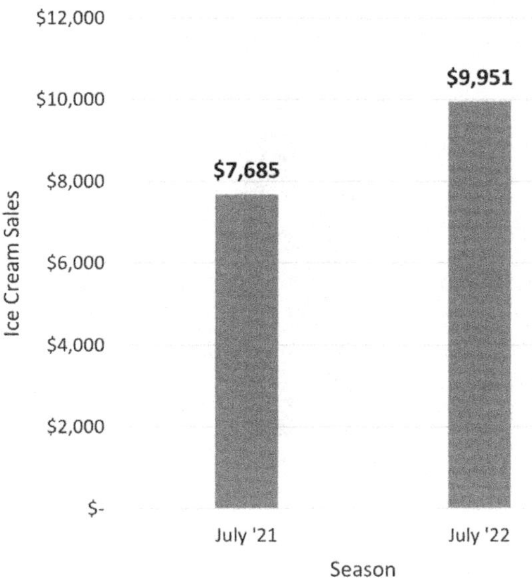

FIGURE 9.6

By having two visuals to look at, you better understand the overall trend and performance of the data.

- **State your Theme**

The theme of your presentation is the dominant idea that unifies all the elements of the data visualizations. Make this idea clear to your audiences with consistency and a clear standard. Developing your theme is not a difficult task. In fact, this would have been developed while you studied your audiences and while you developed the key insights to be presented.

How you state your theme to your audience depends on the niche of the data and on the culture of the audience. Find that core element that links all your insights to show a prevailing objective and concept. Colors tend to tell someone how to feel. Keep this in mind when figuring out what the goal of your presentation is.

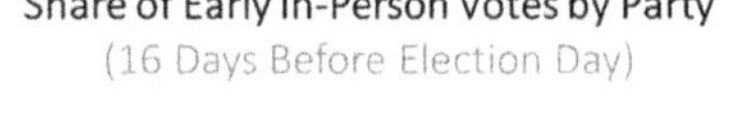

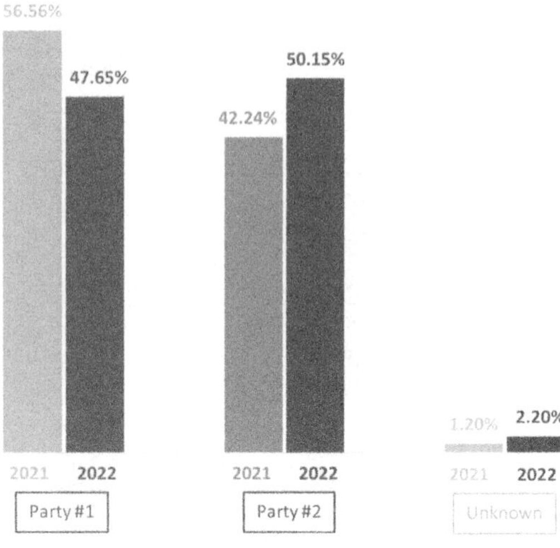

FIGURE 9.7

In this case, we based the theme of the parties so people can easily distinguish which is which.

OPTIMIZING CHART ELEMENTS

The presence of, or lack thereof, certain chart elements can either compromise the understanding or help your audience grasp the information that you are portraying. How these elements are used if they are present also plays a significant role. Here are a few of these elements and how you can use them effectively if they help your visualization be more impactful.

Axes

An axis is a line drawn on charts. It gives the audience a point of reference regarding the values the points plotted represent. Ensure that you provide the audience with a clear description of what each axis on your chart represents. Also, add units of measurement.

Tick Marks

Tick marks indicate a reference value at given points on a chart. Think of them like the lines on a ruler. They are not all labeled but they established a continual flow that shows intervals between values. When using tick marks, keep the labels to a minimum. Avoid labeling each one.

Use smaller tick marks for non-labeled lines and longer tick marks for labeled increments to avoid visual clutter. Only show what is relevant to getting your point across to your audience.

Grid Lines

Grid lines are lines plotted to show the divisions along each axis of a chart. They allow the audience to see the value represented by unlabeled data points. They are not necessarily for inclusion in every data visualization. In fact, you should avoid the use of them if possible. Only use them when they are helpful to your audience. When used, ensure they are colored light gray to minimize visual distraction.

Lets take our chart from above.

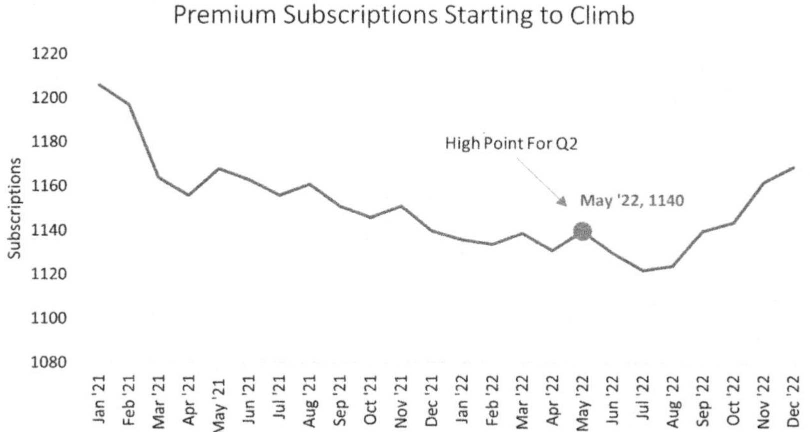

FIGURE 9.8

Removal of gridlines creates a smoother visual flow and adding a data label with the key insight ensures they won't be missed. The visuals look a lot smoother, in my opinion. This can also be done with our accompanying visual aswell.

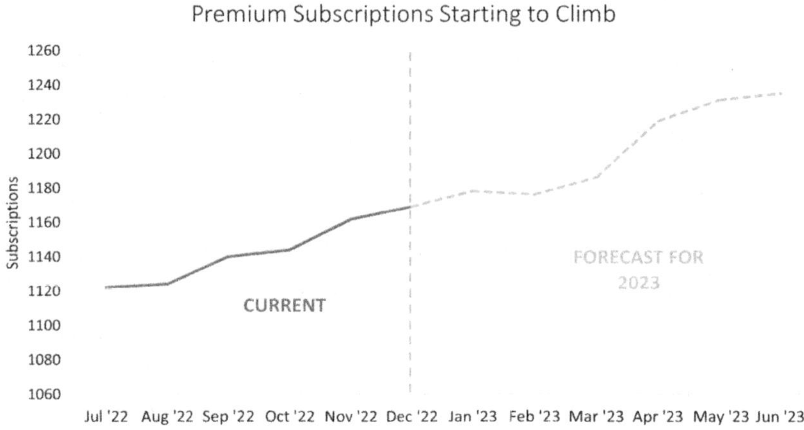

FIGURE 9.9

The goal of the visual is to show an overall trend, not each specific value. The gridlines were not adding any significance and the removal made a cleaner visual.

Data Labels

Labels give your audience context as to what is being presented visually. However, when they are used incorrectly, they can cause confusion rather than aid.

Number of Employees from 2010 to 2021

Over 600% increase in employees since IPO

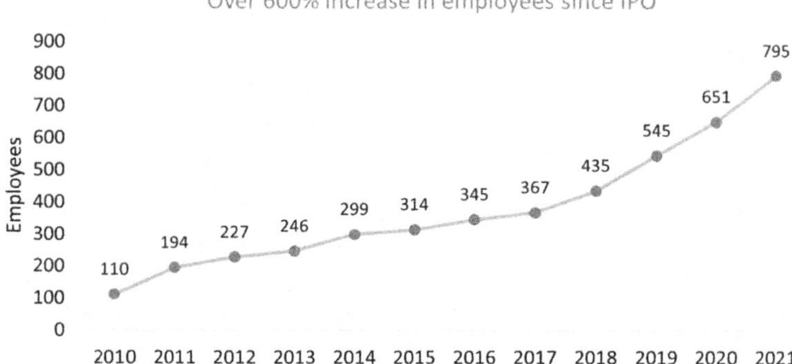

FIGURE 9.10

This is a great way to add confusion to your visual. Be meticulous when adding data labels and ask yourself, "What insight is worth highlighting."

Number of Employees from 2010 to 2021

Over 600% increase in employees since IPO

FIGURE 9.11

This is a lot better and gives the reader a great understanding of the data.

Typography

Don't use typography that is too loud as this will distract from your insights. Not only does your font matter but so too does the title case.

Ensure that capitalization is used correctly. This depends on the exact nature of your labels.

Map Labels

When labeling maps, be consistent with abbreviations. Use the USPS abbreviation preferably (or the relevant labels for countries other than the US). For example, AZ should be used for Arizona in place of A.Z., Arizona. Whatever you decide, keep it consistent throughout.

Also, customize map labels to represent the country. This easily distinguishes them so that confusion is avoided.

Legends

Legends are visual representations of data series on charts. They are used when displaying multiple series data or combinations of charts. They use color to show the correlation between the data points plotted.

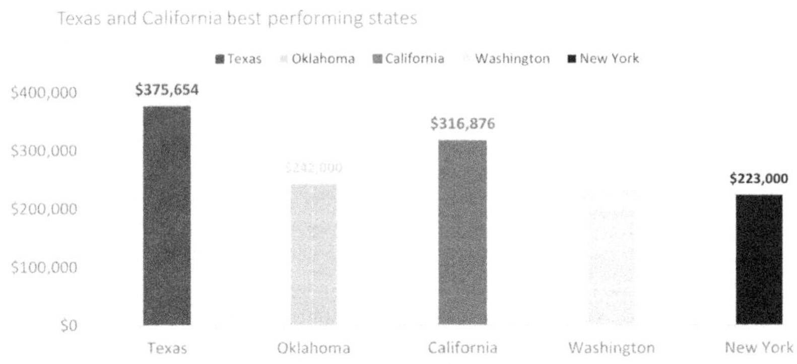

FIGURE 9.12

Integrating them with your titles is an excellent way to enhance a legend's effectiveness.

An example of this would be *Texas and California are our best performing states.* Instead of a legend, you can color the state names as they would appear in the chart itself. This eliminates the need for unnecessary glancing and can be a unique creative approach.

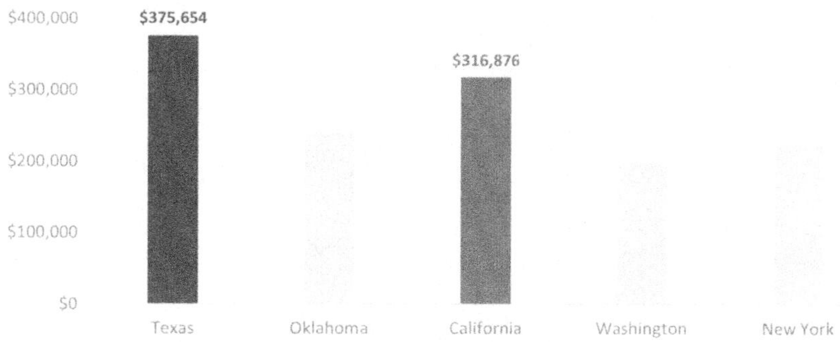

FIGURE 9.13

How legend elements are ordered is also important. When working with sequential data, always have the highest number at top of the legend in descending order. A vertical legend with the most extreme values at opposite ends works best with diverging data.

Placement also plays a significant role. Always place elements below or beside (parallel to) the visualization so as not to obstruct the audience's view of values related to that data. Legends should not add technicality to the visual, just an easy way to understand the symbols or colors the reader is looking at.

Titles

This is a line of text that broadly describes what the visualization represents without identifying trends. Ensure this is not long-winded with no more than 2 lines of text or 8 words. Always place the title directly at the top of the chart in the center or to the left.

A title can be accompanied by a subtitle if necessary. Subtitles are a more detailed explanation of data trends and highlights that will be spotted in the chart.

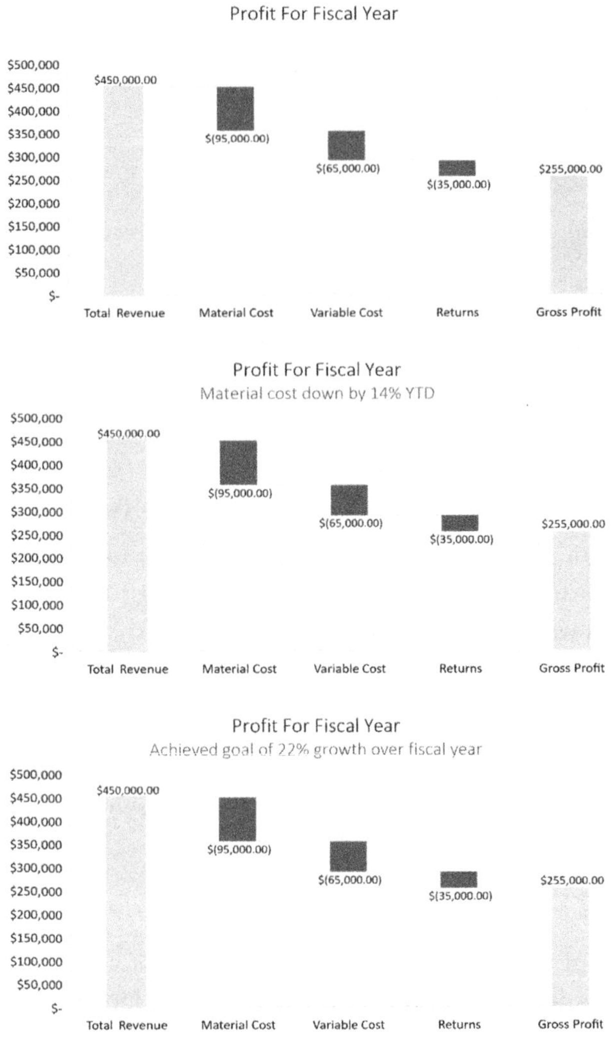

FIGURE 9.14

They also serve the purpose of indicating the unit of measurement used. An effective title paired with a subtitle looks like this: *World Population For 2023: World population is expected to cross 8 billion by the end of 2023*. Depending on the main parts of your analysis, curate the title accordingly to direct the audience to the key outcomes you found.

An excellent format to remember is Title: A general overview of the data in front of them. Subtitle: Detailed explanation of the critical insight.

A GUIDE TO COLOR

Color theory might seem like a concept that graphic designers and those in similar posts should know. However, understanding color theory is a necessary component of developing visually attractive and informative charts. Color theory combines art and science to explain how human beings perceive and interpret colors. By understanding color theory, you develop the mastery of communicating messages effectively by mixing, matching and contrasting colors on your visuals. How colors are combined is called a color scheme.

Picking a Color Scheme

Picking the right color scheme for your chart depends on grasping the anatomy of color. Just like human anatomy describes the different parts that come together to create a whole being, color harmony refers to the different aspects that make up color so that we can perceive it. I would highly recommend you check out Paletton.com. It is an excellent tool for creating color schemes that go together naturally.

FIGURE 9.15

Color anatomy is made up of the following parts and are processed in the following ways by your audience:

Hue

Hue is just another name for color. It describes the specific name or shade of a color. In data visualization, different hues refer to different values or categories. It shows relationships: whether or not the values or categories are related.

Saturation

This part of color anatomy refers to a chart element's brightness relative to the area it occupies. Highly saturated elements have vibrant colors in comparison to their environment and other elements, while less saturated elements produce duller, more washed-out colors. Both ends of the spectrum are useful in chart design as too much saturation can make elements overwhelm your graph while too little saturation can make it difficult to identify visual elements.

Lightness

This feature of color anatomy is closely related to saturation but instead of the brightness of a color, it refers to the shades and tints (degrees of black and white) that make up a color. It should be noted that playing both lightness and saturation leaves you with striking variations in colors' scale of intensity. These degrees highlight the differences in chart elements.

For example, changing the lightness of a color can showcase different values within a given category while still insinuating they are of the same category. The reader can then easily compare the metrics across regions.

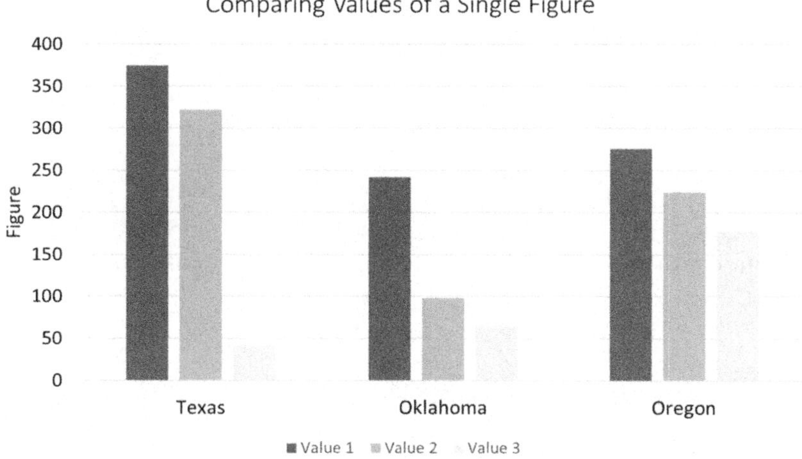

FIGURE 9.16

Color Harmony

Certain color combinations are easier on the eyes and thus, easier for the brain to perceive. They create contrast and cohesion so that multiple levels of perception are derived. Diverging from that causes confusion. To ensure that you use color combinations to your advantage, you need to become acquainted with the color wheel. The color wheel is an abstract illustration of colors organized around a circle. These colors are not randomly situated. Instead, they are placed to show the relationships being primary colors (red, blue and yellow), secondary colors, which are the mixture of two primary colors (orange, purple and green), tertiary colors, which are a variety of primary and secondary colors being mixed (for example blue-green), and more variations.

Color harmony is achieved when designers pick colors from the color wheel and arrange them in such a way so that data visualizations gain depth by virtue of the contrast and cohesiveness those colors allow. Consider color harmony when creating your theme to represent the data and tell a story in the most effective way possible.

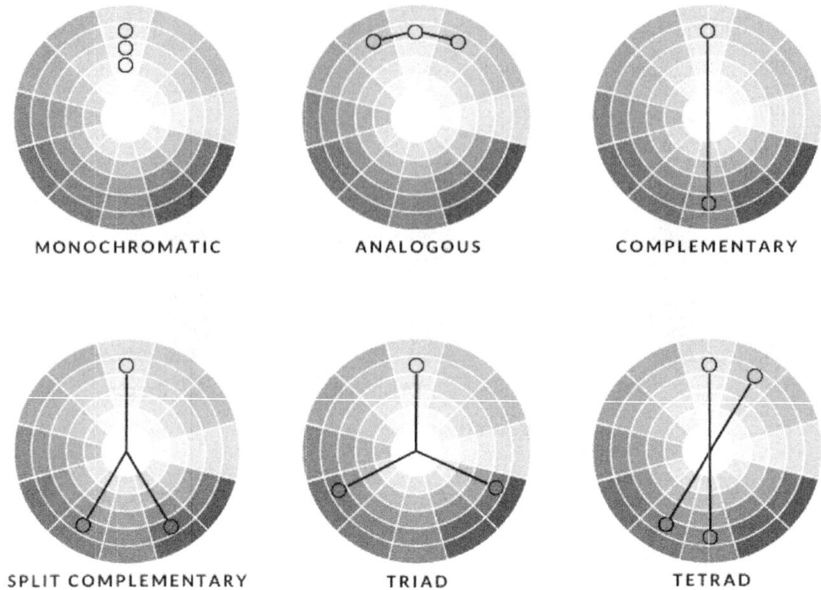

FIGURE 9.17

Monochromatic

This color arrangement consists of a single color being used in different shades (the addition of black) and tints (the addition of white). Therefore, you use light and dark versions of that one color.

FIGURE 9.18

Analogous

Three colors situated next to each other on the color wheel are used in this arrangement. For example, orange-yellow and orange-red can be used to develop a data visual with such an arrangement.

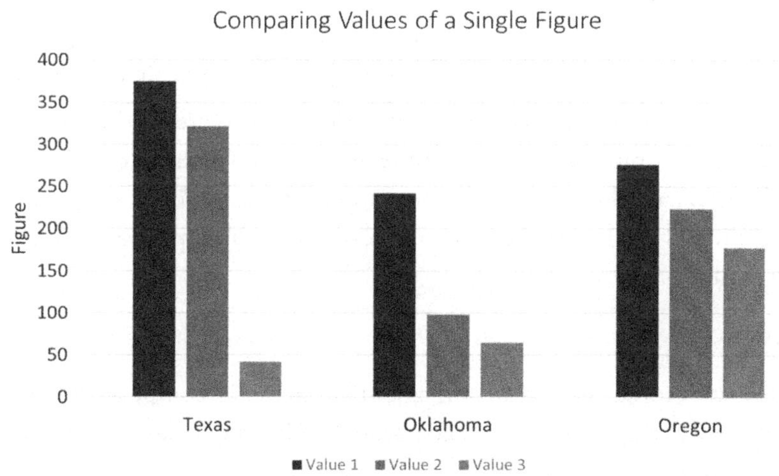

FIGURE 9.19

Complementary

This arrangement makes use of colors that are on opposite sides of the color wheel. This can be expanded into shades and tints of these two colors. Green and red are examples of complementary colors.

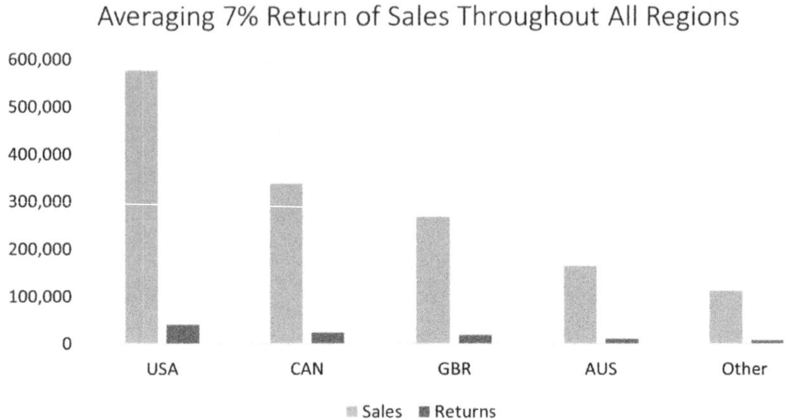

FIGURE 9.20

Split complementary

This is a variation of the complementary color scheme. However, instead of using two colors, three colors are used. One of the complementary colors is split into the two adjacent colors to create the trio. The use of orange, blue-purple and blue-green is an example of a split complementary color scheme. Orange and blue are opposite on the color wheel. Blue is split into the two adjacent colors blue-purple and blue-green to make the trio.

Triad

Triad means three, so this arrangement of colors is composed of three colors evenly spaced on the color wheel. The most basic triad color schemes are composed of:

- The primary colors, which are red, blue and yellow.

- The secondary colors, which are orange, green and purple.

Tetradic

This arrangement of colors comes with four colors from the color wheel, as indicated by the prefix 'tetra'. The colors are picked for a rectangular shape and are evenly spaced on the color wheel with no color being dominant over the others. This color arrangement is also called double complementary.

A GUIDE TO USING COLOR PALETTES ON DIFFERENT TYPES OF CHARTS

The type of data being expressed determines the best-used color palette. As such, color palettes that are largely used for creating data visualizations are:

Qualitative

FIGURE 9.21

This type of palette is used when the data variables are categorical. These variables do not have a distinct order. Tips for making the best use of such a color palette include:

- Each category must be assigned a specific color.
- If you are working with more than 10 variables, consider grouping small
- values into an 'Other' category to limit the use of colors and keep your charts from becoming too busy.
- Create additional variation by using lightness or saturation strategically. This can serve to highlight the importance of

specific values.
- Use the same color in varying saturations to separate values if they are related.

Sequential

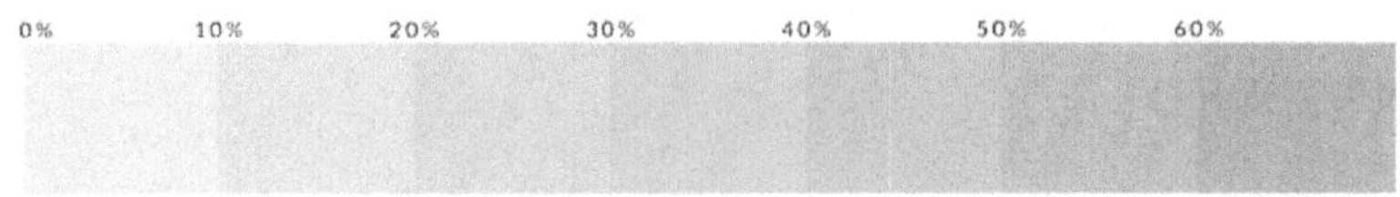

FIGURE 9.22

The sequential color palette is used when the values plotted for one subject are numerically ordered. The colors assigned must exist in a continuum. For example, if your data is presented in percentages (0-100), lower numbers should be lighter while higher values should be a darker shade. The same color is used. The difference is the changing lightness.

Alternatively, you can use transitions with different hues. Use light or cool colors like blue for lower values and transition into darker or warm colors for higher values.

Diverging

FIGURE 9.23

A diverging color palette should be used if your data contains a central value such as zero (0). A diverging color palette is essentially a combination of two sequential palettes that share an endpoint as the central value. Highlight this feature with a distinct hue used for each side, such as with positive versus negative values. The central value should be a light hue that darkens at the sides.

The Best Practices for Effective Use of Color

To end this chapter, I leave you with a few more tips to make color work for you and not against you for data visualizations.

Where to put color

A trick I like to use is to create your entire chart and make everything gray. From there, with nothing grabbing your attention, you can focus on what information needs to be in color. And only add it where necessary.

Consider color blindness among your audience

About 4% of the human population and 10% of men has a form of color blindness. In some cases, there is confusion when viewing red and green, or yellow and blue. Make your data visualizations accessible and interpretable for everyone by using color selection tools to assess how our visuals look for people with color perception difficulties. A quick Google search will place a plethora of color selection tools at your disposal.

Lets see how we can improve some charts for color blindness.

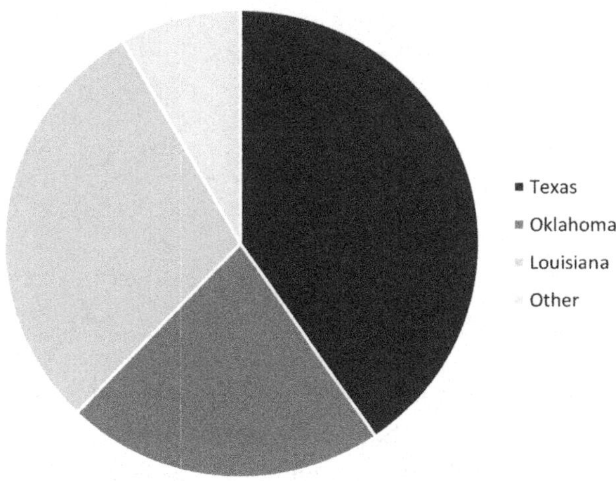

FIGURE 9.24

A more effective approach would be to use a horizontal bar graph. It eliminates the need for color to distinguish the categories.

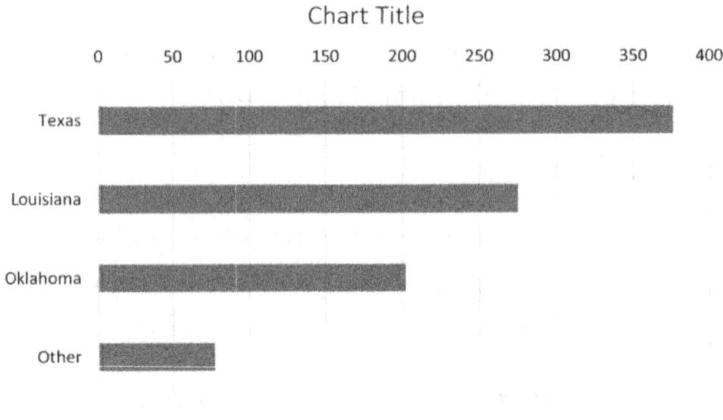

FIGURE 9.25

Another effective approach is to use different patterns to categorize the elements to make them unique.

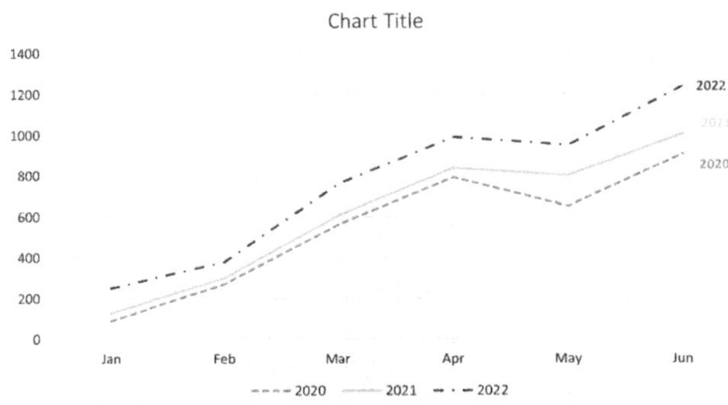

FIGURE 9.26

Be consistent

You might be tempted to play around with color palettes as there is such a vast array to choose from but you must remember to stay consistent with colors throughout the development of your visuals. If your presentation contains different charts highlighting different insights, then, of course, you can use different palettes, but if you use, for example, green and red to show positive and negative values in your sequential palette, make sure this stays consistent for future visualizations. Do not change the association of color to mean something different in different charts.

Don't always rely on color

Color is not the only tool at your disposal in data visualization. In some instances, you can even use other visual elements to magnify the emphasis you are trying to place with color. For example, you can add indicators like an up arrow to show positive or strengthen the insight's meaning. The brain will naturally associate seeing green and an arrow pointing up as a gain of some sort. The opposite applies to using a down arrow along with red to show negativity or loss.

Avoid color clutter

Do not use too much color when creating your visuals. In fact, the first color you should add is gray. Then consider which insights are worth using color to highlight. In some cases, you can give each category a distinct color to signify their difference. The chart might solidify one key point with supporting points in other cases. In that instance, it might be worth highlighting the specific insight with color and keeping the rest of the chart neutral.

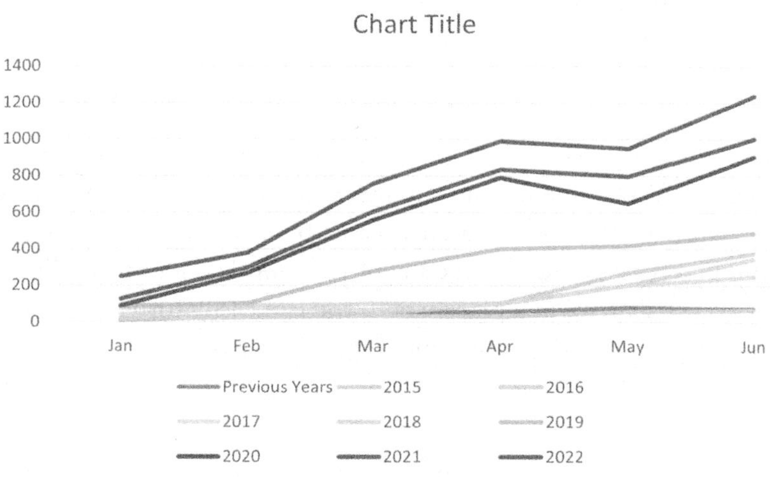

FIGURE 9.27

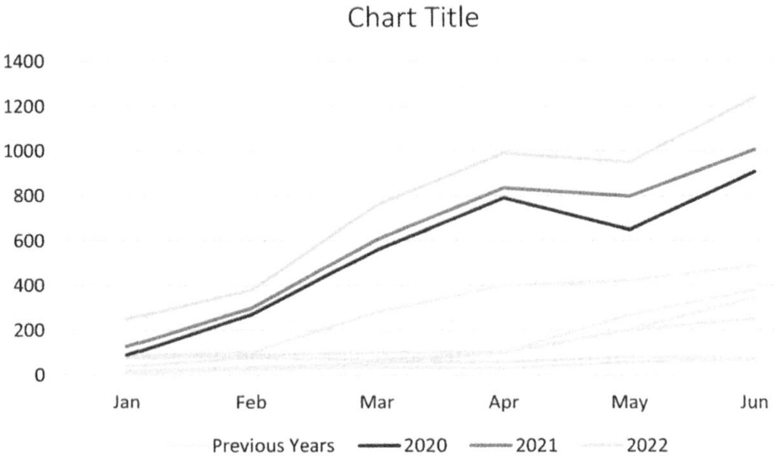

FIGURE 9.28

Color is not solely an aesthetic element. It's a tool that tells your audience how to feel and where to look. I like to think of it as music in a film. It sets the tone for what's happening. A properly selected color palette should convey the data accurately and add to the story. Using color simply to distinguish categories should be the bare minimum. You can get everything wrong on data visualization, but nail the color composition, and you'll get your point across.

When designing your visuals, many factors come into play. Knowing the fundamentals and adding your own flair is the key to creating winning data visualizations. Over time it is good practice to slowly build a style guide and document what worked and what didn't. Eventually, you'll arrive at a place where you can easily turn any dataset into a beautifully crafted and presented story with ease.

10
CHART REDESIGNS

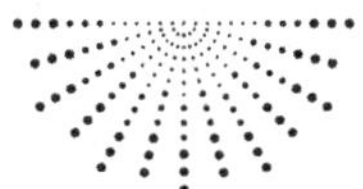

Data visualization is a skill you will constantly improve throughout your career. I hope I have helped you create a baseline that sets the stage for all your future visualizations and gives you valuable information to work off of and expand upon. Although we covered a lot of stuff, I think it's important to see some real-life examples and some redesigned visuals to understand better what it requires of us as data professionals. Let's go through an example and then look at some redesigned visuals.

Let's say our company is one of the top suppliers of above-ground pools, pool accessories and parts. We are tracking our website traffic over the year based on our primary sources to determine where to allocate our resources to grow our business in the coming years. Let's throw the numbers on a typical chart people use in this scenario.

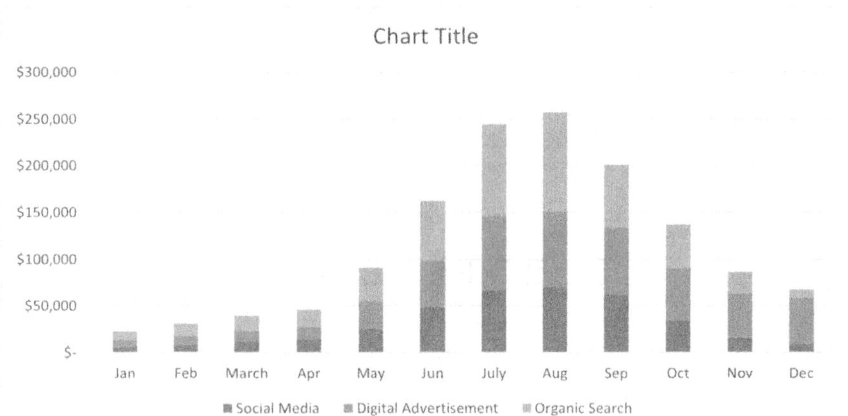

FIGURE 10.1

I DON'T LIKE A STACKED bar chart because it's difficult to compare the categories over time or even compare specific metrics within one month. Readability is essential for your audience and this falls short. You've missed the mark if you have to tell the reader what they should be seeing before they see it. Your narrative should support what the chart already shows. I'm sure there are ways to make it work, but I would rather scrap it altogether. A line chart is more effective when showcasing trends over time.

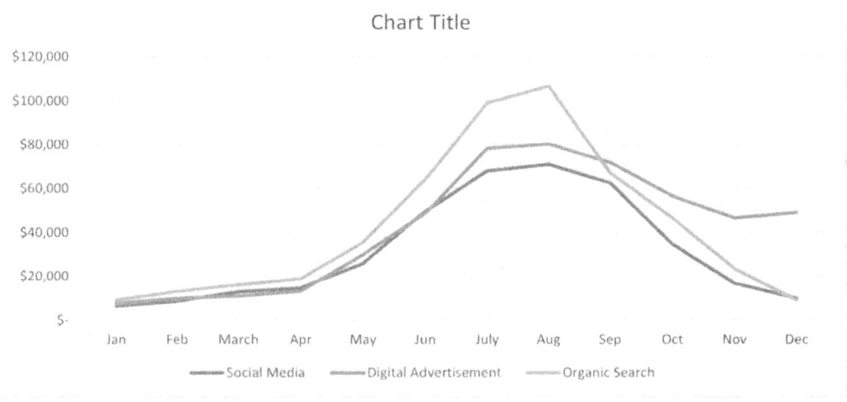

FIGURE 10.2

Now it's important to ask yourself specific questions to ensure the success of your visual. The first thing I always Like to ask is

What does my audience see first?

So, what do you see first? Besides the apparent spike in the summer months, no real insight is showcased. We need to dig deeper so the audience has some valuable insights and potential action steps based on the data. That leads us to the second question we need to ask,

Can we remove anything?

This happens to be one of our best years for organic traffic and sales. Since it is 2020 and everyone is forced to stay home, many families brought their summer fun to their houses.

Let's focus our chart more on the specific insights that stand out and lead our audience to some action steps to benefit from this spike. We can remove the traffic from social media and advertising and start by comparing the previous year's organic search sales to this year's.

This is the first chart we will present to our audience, but not before a few tweaks.

FIGURE 10.3

LET'S get into our next important question, which is

AM I USING COLOR, labels, and aesthetics effectively

Color does a great job of emphasizing key metrics; you can use it to tell the audience where to look. In this case, fading the previous year and enhancing the new data seems like a good option. Still easy to compare but focuses on what's important.

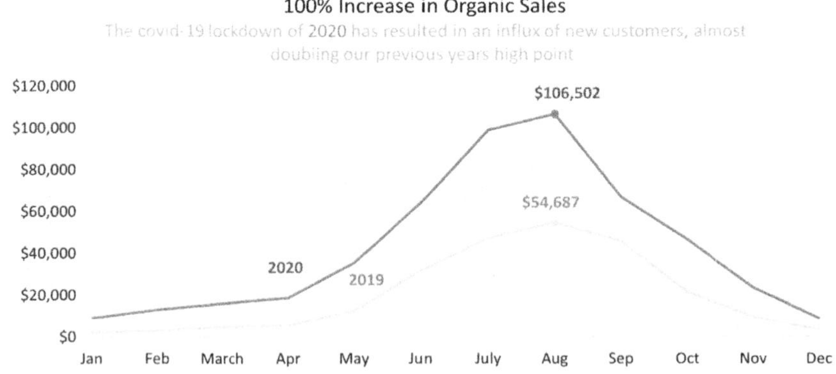

FIGURE 10.4

In terms of labels, we will remove the legend and add the years onto the chart to avoid unnecessary glancing back and forth. It's common practice to place data labels at the end of the lines, but given this specific chart and how close the ends are, putting them at the beginning might be more effective. This can also be effective because people read left to right, so they will see the year and its corresponding income in the same color, resulting in a quick understanding of the key points.

We can also remove the gridlines and chart border for a smooth visual flow and update the title to be more detailed and clear.

Now the chart looks quite presentable. But we can't forget our most important task as data professionals, guiding them to the proper insights that lead to better business decisions.

This leads us to our next question.

What action does my audience need to take, and do they have the tools to see this?

Covid-19 has been an anomaly for our business regarding sales and new customers. But trying to surpass an anomaly year is not feasible.

Considering we have gained a substantial number of new customers, the most effective thing to do is to ensure those customers continue to purchase for years to come, even after the pandemic.

. . .

With insights from our organic search, we can now allocate a considerable amount of our marketing budget to retargeting in the following season, so they continue to return for the things they need, whether another pool, pump, chemicals, or anything else. This can be done through our promotional emails, digital advertising campaigns and social posts.

To help the audience reach this conclusion, we can pair our new line graph with a simple metric, Showing that in the previous years, around 50-64% of our sales were from returning customers. They continually bought the supplies they needed year after year. With the influx of new customers, 2020 resulted in only 35% of our sales from returning buyers.

FIGURE 10.5

Although we will have more data after the next peak season, we can use the most recent insights to focus our budget on retargeting and keeping those customers, so when lockdowns lift and our sales return to normal, we have gained, and kept many reliable customers. If we spend our resources trying to continue to gain more and surpass our anomaly year, we are setting ourselves up for disappointment.

. . .

This is just a taste of telling a compelling story with data. If you want to dive deeper into the presentation process, check out my first book, *How to Win With Your Data Visualizations*. It is all about presenting data effectively captivating your audience.

Let's have a look at some more chart redesigns.

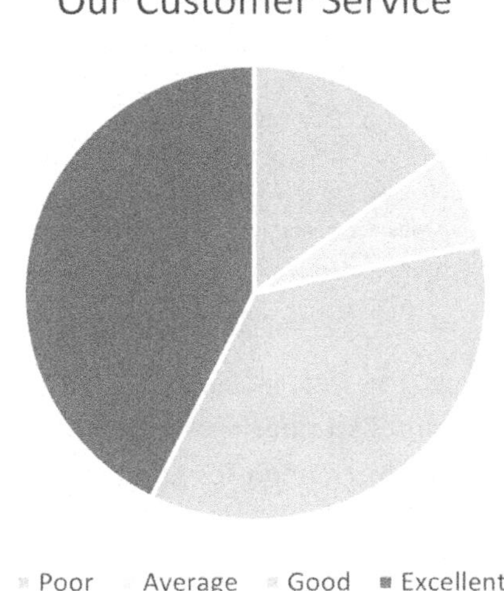

FIGURE 10.6

Here is a basic pie chart. Although it falls under the parameters of an effective pie chart, with this specific dataset, I think a simple bar pictogram is a lot more effective and showcases the insights in a clear way.

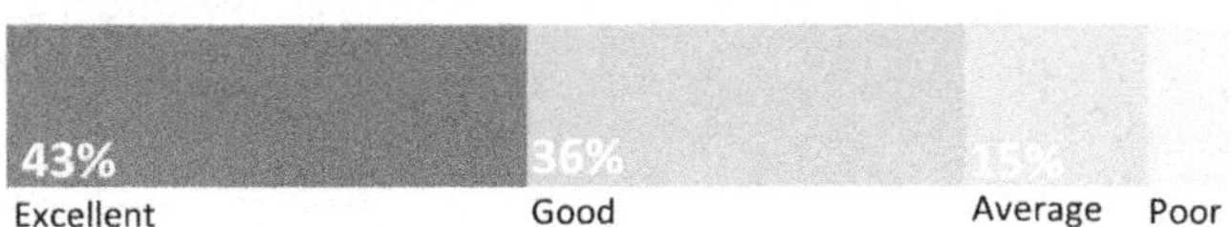

FIGURE 10.7

Comparing categories within categories with different sets of values is always a challenge. People often fall on some sort of bar chart variation, but they aren't the most effective way to view such data.

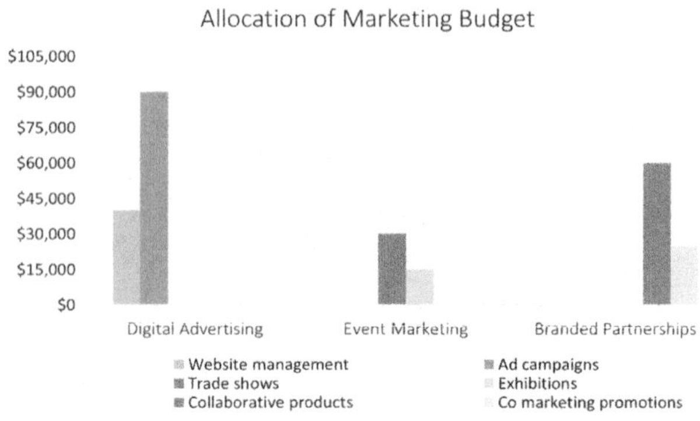

FIGURE 10.8

In these scenarios, Marimekko charts can be highly effective. You can compare the categories within categories and the main categories to each other with ease. Let's look at the same data but in a Marimekko chart. Whatever metrics you choose to compare, a Marimekko makes it easy to isolate and compare specific information.

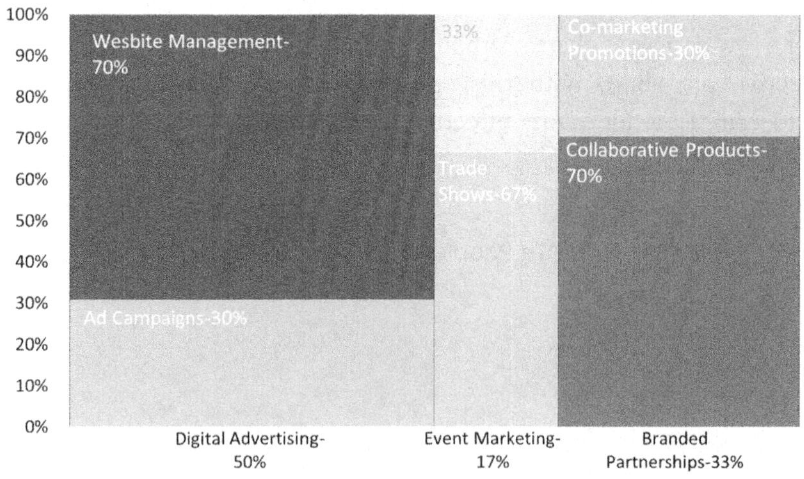

FIGURE 10.9

IT ALSO INCORPORATES the legend into the chart so that you don't find yourself glancing back and forth, trying to piece together the visual. (Which is what I found myself doing in the original bar chart).

Although line charts are a fan favorite, they can still be done incorrectly.

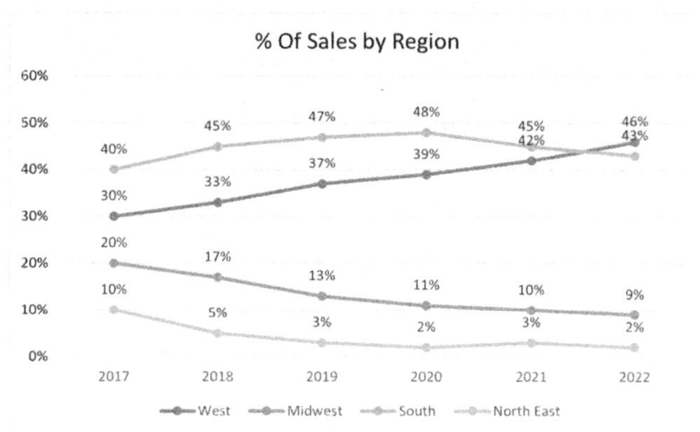

FIGURE 10.10

As you can see, there is an awful lot of clutter. Although it shows all the information, I think it's possible to make it much more exciting and effective.

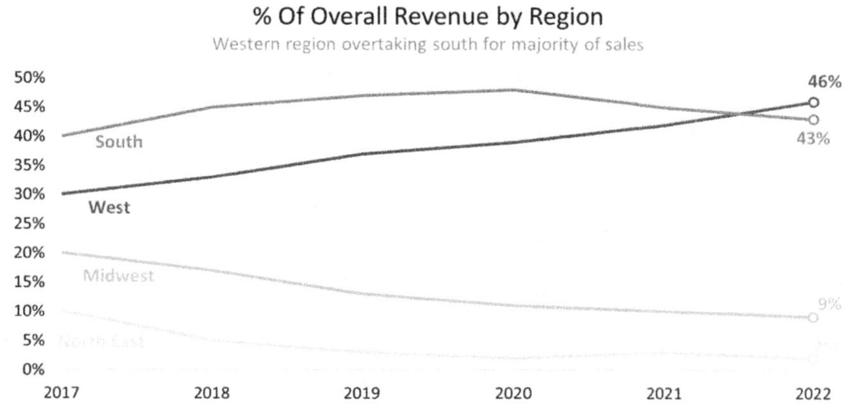

FIGURE 10.11

By only highlighting the essential metrics, the audience can see where we were in 2017, the trend over the years, and finally, where we are now. The extra values seemed irrelevant. This way, they can see the sales trajectory and where more resources need to be allocated. The readability goes way up by adding the locations onto the chart and changing the color scheme. By adding insight to the subtitle, we can better focus our audience's attention while still having all the necessary metrics clearly visible. Highlighting one specific line wouldn't be effective here as the performance of all the regions is essential to see.

Many people naturally gravitate to bar charts. Although this isn't necessarily negative, let's see how we can make them more effective based on the data.

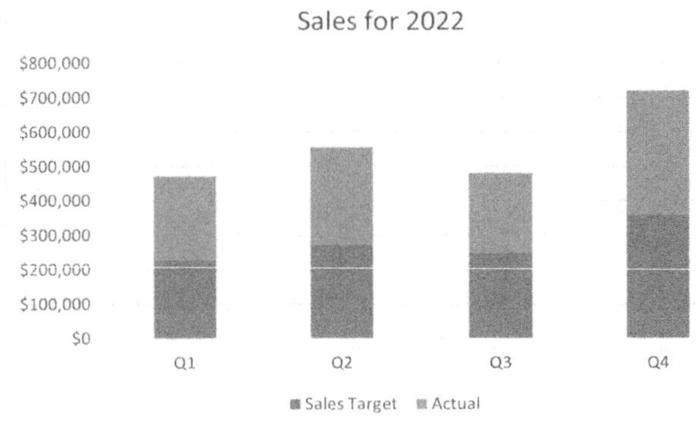

FIGURE 10.12

In my opinion, it really doesn't do much for the data.

FIGURE 10.13

This regular bar chart seems to be better. However, When comparing actual to targets, there is a better way to do it. You can either go the route of a bullet chart or, in this case, we can take the elements of a bullet chart and execute them in a simple yet effective way.

FIGURE 10.14

The horizontal bar works great in this scenario. By adding the target as lines, the viewer will naturally check to see if the bars are below or above them, even if they dont know what they mean. A great way to compare sales to targets. We can add the actual values as data labels to get more insight out of the chart.

FIGURE 10.15

This makes it easy to see the numbers without guessing.

From there, we can potentially highlight any important insights that we gained from our analysis. In this case, we can highlight Q3 as we did not hit our target.

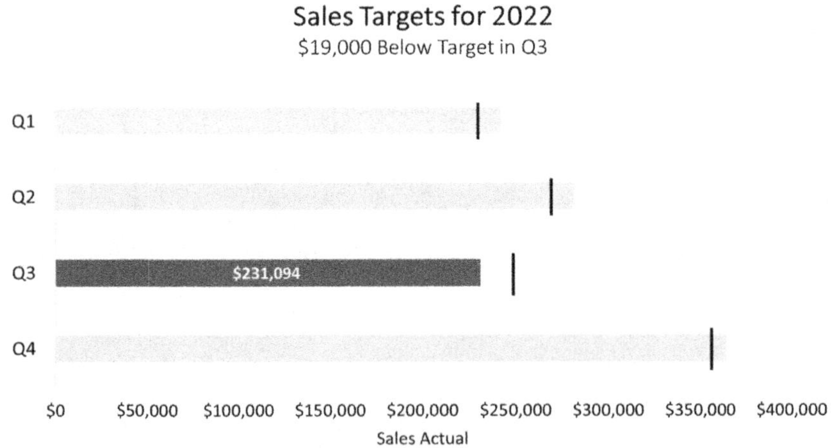

FIGURE 10.16

If required, we can further dive into the metrics from Q3 and see where we fell short.

There are many ways to redesign and visualize the information above to be effective. Don't take these rules as set in stone, be creative and present the information most memorably. Data visualization is an art in itself. Create your style and continue to expand upon it with new insights and knowledge. With the number of new people in the world of data, standing above the rest is crucial to making yourself known. Harnessing your data visualization skills will allow you to stand above the rest.

CONCLUSION

Data. It seems to pour like raindrops during a storm but unlike those passing clouds, it never stops. Data is constantly being generated during every microsecond of the day. Gone is the time when our economy and many social constructs were driven by manufacturing. We have entered the information age and there is no end in sight for this time period. Also gone is the time when the world's most valuable resource is oil. The intangible components that make up this age, data points, have become the most valuable thing on this planet. People are willing to pay big bucks for data but that would not be the case if there was no way of translating data from its raw state into a medium that is easy to interpret.

Data visualization is the translation of data into a visual context such as a chart or a map. Data visualization is that bridge that makes data the value item for which people are willing to write big checks. The human brain is hardwired to pick information received through the sense of sight far faster and easier than information derived from any other sense. That's the power of visual processing. That is the power you can harness to bring your point across to audiences. You can show patterns, showcase trends and highlight outliers without saying a word, even when working with large data sets.

You might be an academic. You might be an intern. You might be an entry-level employee. You might be a manager. You might be a business owner. No matter your job title, understanding the value of data visualization and using it effectively goes across the board. It all starts with a plan. This plan will tell you which is the right chart to pick for your particular presentation and which design elements will enhance that chart visually and make it the most informative for the audience. The "right" chart is dependent on what you want to tell your audience. This is the overall theme of the chart development. The themes stated in this book, along with a brief outline of what they are and some of the graphs that fall in this category, include:

Change Over Time

These charts show the changing trends of data set over both short time frames like 24 hours and over longer periods of time like years. Charts that show change over time include:

- Line charts
- Slope charts
- Area charts
- Connected Scatter plots
- Gantt charts

Comparison

Such charts show the differences or similarities between multiple variables in data sets or multiple categories within a single variable. Charts that show comparison include:

- Bar graphs
- Diverging bars
- Bubble charts
- Waterfall charts
- Sankey diagrams
- Marimekko charts
- Bullet charts

- Dumbbell plots

Distribution

This theme of data visualization expresses the frequency of data to show uniformity or a lack thereof. In other words, such charts highlight how data is spread out. Charts in this group include:

- Histograms
- Dot plots
- Ridgeline plots
- Box plots
- Candlestick plots
- Violin plots
- Population pyramids
- Strip plots
- Beeswarm plots

Part-to-the-Whole

These charts highlight how a single entity compares to its elements' distribution. The common function of these charts is to show how something is divided up. Such charts include:

- Pie charts
- Treemaps
- Sunburst charts
- Nightingale Rose charts

Relationship

This group of charts aims to show the relationships or connections between two or more data variables. Examples of such charts include:

- Scatter plots
- Radar charts
- Chord diagrams

- Network diagrams
- Tree diagrams
- Parallel coordinates plots

Geographical

These charts are used to highlight data sets when precise locations are important to note. Such charts include:

- Choropleths
- Proportional symbol maps
- Flow maps

It is not enough to simply pick the right chart. You must also walk your audience through a story that captivates and engages them. That story needs to have a beginning, a middle and an end. Using the right visual elements helps you do just that. The principles of design that make your chart visually appealing include:

- Making the design balanced
- Emphasis of key insights
- Showing clear movement
- Creating smooth flow
- Using patterns to highlight insights
- Using proportion
- Giving your audience variety to prevent boredom
- Stating the theme of your design

The use of charts helps simplify complicated data to be easily understood. However, this advantage can become a disadvantage as data can become overly simplified, leading to an audience misunderstanding the message being delivered. In such a case, using tables and pictograms instead of and in conjunction with charts is an option. Tables allow audiences to:

- Easily look up specific data points

- Note the precise numbers that are applicable to the data presentation
- Note ranks
- Compare data variables going in two directions

Tables are particularly useful when the audience is used to reading certain types of information rather than seeing it in a visual format.

You have reached this book's end and are now equipped to use charts like a pro. Enhancing your ability to communicate data will slingshot you far in this day and age and lead you to success in your role and a pat on the back from your superiors (Hopefully, that comes with a raise.) I hope I have shined a light on an essential skill and I wish you luck on your journey of telling better stories, communicating more insights, and driving better business decisions.

APPENDIX - TOOLS FOR DATA VISUALIZATION

I'm sure you've asked yourself, "How on earth do I create these charts?!". Considering that could be a topic for an entire book, We won't go through it step by step this time. But I can assure you not to panic. There are many programs to create stunning visualizations regardless of your expertise. Let's go through some of them so you can start getting your feet wet.

Best options for beginners

Excel

Being the industry standard, I'm sure you've heard of Excel and its many capabilities. Excel is an easy way to take a spreadsheet of data and immediately turn it into a chart without any complex processes or code. With many design possibilities, it is a great way to visualize data quickly and effectively. Many of the data visualizations in this book are made through Excel.

Pros: Easy to generate charts directly from your data.

Cons: It lacks advanced chart types and you must customize your visuals, so they are up to speed. Auto-populated charts aren't the most stunning.

Flourish

Flourish is another great option for data visualizations. Where excel lacks, flourish picks up the slack. More uncommon charts such as beeswarm plots and network diagrams are made easy with Flourish as they come pre-built, just waiting for your data. There is a free version as well as a paid version that comes with different visualizations and features.

Pros: Lots of advanced charts that are easy to set up.

Cons: It can sometimes be difficult to populate charts if you arent data-savvy. The data needs to be formatted correctly.

Datawrapper

Datawrapper is an online tool with one of the least barriers to entry. From the homepage, you can simply click *Start Creating*, which will walk you through the process to a finished data visualization. It also has pre-made colorblindness palette options, which change the color accordingly. Go use one of their sample data sets and try it out.

Pros: Creates professional-looking charts quickly and walks you through the process.

Cons: It doesn't have as many detailed design features.

Infogram

Infogram offers interactive charts, infographics, maps, and many free templates to tell compelling data stories. It supports data uploads from google sheets, dropbox, MySQL and more. Infogram is known for its interactive features to enhance your visualizations and allow for movement such as zoom, bounce, fade, rotate, and slide objects into your work. Infogram is often used by marketers, media companies, and whoever wants their visualizations to stand out and be different.

Pro: Easy to create interactive and engaging visualizations

Con: You must upgrade to the paid version to remove the watermark if embedding your visualizations.

Mid-level options

PowerBI

PowerBI is another great data visualization tool. It has the extra processing power to work with larger sets of data. Their dashboards can also be more customizable than Excel. It's essentially a more powerful Excel. It's used prevalently in business intelligence.

Pro: Can connect with many different file data sources, including Excel and CSV, as well as database sources like Oracle, SQL Server, IBM and much more.

Con: Although capable, can sometimes have trouble processing large sets of data

Tableau

Tableau is one of the most used programs in the business world. Tableau excels at visualizing even the most extensive data sets without limitations on the number of data points or rows.

Pros: Fast, with many extensive features for creating intricate visualizations.

Cons: With the free version (Tableau Public) Your dashboards can be viewed publicly, which can cause problems with confidential data.

Advanced Options

Python

Python is a programming language with many built-in libraries that make it possible to visualize data. Libraries such as Matplitlib, Pandas visualization, Seaborn, and Plotly make it possible to curate your data into a wide array of dashboards and visuals. Although effective, it takes experience with Python programming. Creating these visualizations requires you to write lines of code for your desired output.

R

R is another statistical language used for the analysis and visualization of data. It connects with various libraries that, with some coding, you can turn your data into visual insights. It can be very effective and professional yet has a higher barrier of entry.

As your career in data evolves, so will the software you use. Inevitably, if you can effectively visualize data, it doesn't matter which program you use. Find one you like or that fits your business needs. Whether you need access to large databases or quick insights on the fly, there should be a tool for you.

REFERENCES

(PDF) Emotional storytelling. (2005, January 1). Retrieved from https://www.researchgate.net/publication/228941237_Emotional_storytelling

Axes. (n.d.). Retrieved from https://xdgov.github.io/data-design-standards/components/axes

Effective data visualisation | 8 design principles | PromptCloud blog. (2022, June 20). Retrieved from https://www.promptcloud.com/blog/design-principles-for-effective-data-visualisation/

How to choose colors for data visualizations. (2019, November 11). Retrieved from https://chartio.com/learn/charts/how-to-choose-colors-data-visualization/

In defence of the humble pie chart. (2017, April 9). Retrieved from https://briancort.com/in-defence-of-the-humble-pie-chart/

Kazakova, E. V. (2021, May 5). The psychology behind data visualization techniques. Retrieved from https://towardsdatascience.com/the-psychology-behind-data-visualization-techniques-68ef12865720

Kazakova, E. V. (2021, May 5). The psychology behind data visualization techniques. Retrieved from https://towardsdatascience.com/the-psychology-behind-data-visualization-techniques-68ef12865720

Presenting data in tables and charts. (2014, March). Retrieved from https://www.ncbi.nlm.nih.gov/pmc/articles/PMC4008059/

The role of color theory in data visualization. (2022, 3). Retrieved from https://www.revunit.com/post/the-role-of-color-theory-in-data-visualization

Roxanne. (2020, December 3). The history of data. Retrieved from https://www.thinkautomation.com/histories/the-history-of-data/

Wang, M. (2022, February 26). 6 examples of beautiful Marimekko charts (a.k.a. mosaic plots) & 2 examples with D3 code! Medium. Retrieved August 23, 2022, from https://medium.com/visual-analytics-field-notes/6-examples-of-beautiful-marimekko-charts-a-k-a-mosaic-plots-2-examples-with-d3-code-34b73f2396c7

C. (2021, December 12). 7 Key Principles of Effective Data Visualization - GoBeyond.AI: E-commerce Magazine. Medium. Retrieved August 23, 2022, from https://medium.com/gobeyond-ai/7-key-princi ples-of-effective-data-visualization-b854b0b81946#:%7E:text=Some% 20of%20the%20key%20aspects,comparing%20parameters%2C% 20and%20creating%20interactivity.

D. (2020, December 21). 31 July 2020: About Dumbbell or Connected Dot Plots. Observable. Retrieved August 23, 2022, from https://observ ablehq.com/@didoesdigital/31-july-2020-about-dumbbell-or-connected-dot-plots

Yi, M. (2019, September 16). A Complete Guide to Area Charts. Chartio. Retrieved August 23, 2022, from https://chartio.com/learn/charts/ area-chart-complete-guide/#:%7E:text=An%20area%20chart%20com bines%20the,like%20in%20a%20bar%20chart.

Yi, M. (2019a, August 23). A Complete Guide to Bar Charts. Chartio. Retrieved August 23, 2022, from https://chartio.com/learn/charts/bar-chart-complete-guide/

Yi, M. (2019c, October 23). A Complete Guide to Bubble Charts. Chartio. Retrieved August 23, 2022, from https://chartio.com/learn/charts/ bubble-chart-complete-guide/

Yi, M. (2019b, September 6). A Complete Guide to Histograms. Chartio. Retrieved August 23, 2022, from https://chartio.com/learn/charts/ histogram-complete-guide/#:%7E:text=A%20histogram%20is%20a% 20chart,value%20within%20the%20corresponding%20bin.

Yi, M. (2019b, August 29). A Complete Guide to Pie Charts. Chartio. Retrieved August 23, 2022, from https://chartio.com/learn/charts/pie-chart-complete-guide/

Yi, M. (2019f, November 15). A Complete Guide to Violin Plots. Chartio. Retrieved August 23, 2022, from https://chartio.com/learn/charts/violin-plot-complete-guide/

Success, C. O. H. P. S. S.-, & Success, C. O. H. P. S. S.-. (2021, August 3). A deep dive into. . . dot plots | Blog | Datylon. Datylon. Retrieved August 23, 2022, from https://www.datylon.com/blog/dot-plot-deep-dive

Axes | Data Visualization Standards. (n.d.). Data Visualization Standards. Retrieved August 23, 2022, from https://xdgov.github.io/data-design-standards/components/axes

Kędzia, Ł. (n.d.). How to Make Ranking Bump Chart. Best Excel Tutorial. Retrieved August 23, 2022, from https://best-excel-tutorial.com/56-charts/306-bump-chart

Yahoo is part of the Yahoo family of brands. (n.d.). Yahoo Finance. Retrieved August 23, 2022, from https://finance.yahoo.com/quote/BTC-USD/history/

Bullet Chart - A Complete Guide | FusionCharts. (n.d.). Fusioncharts.-Com. Retrieved August 23, 2022, from https://www.fusioncharts.com/resources/chart-primers/bullet-graph

Candlestick Chart - Learn about this chart and tools to create it. (n.d.). The Data Visualization Catalogue. Retrieved August 23, 2022, from https://datavizcatalogue.com/methods/candlestick_chart.html

Healy, Y. H. A. C. (n.d.). Chord diagram. From Data to Viz. Retrieved August 23, 2022, from https://www.data-to-viz.com/graph/chord.html

Chord Diagram. (2021, December 7). Think Design. Retrieved August 23, 2022, from https://think.design/services/data-visualization-data-design/chord-diagram/

Healy, Y. H. A. C. (n.d.-b). Connected Scatterplot. From Data to Viz. Retrieved August 23, 2022, from https://www.data-to-viz.com/graph/connectedscatter.html#:%7E:text=A%20connected%20scatterplot%20displays%20the,of%20time%3A%20a%20time%20series.

Grid, E. O. T. (2022, February 3). Create a fan chart in Excel. Excel Off The Grid. Retrieved August 23, 2022, from https://exceloffthegrid.com/create-uncertainty-chart-fan-chart/

Weitz, D. (2021, December 16). Diverging Bars, Why & How - Towards Data Science. Medium. Retrieved August 23, 2022, from https://towardsdatascience.com/diverging-bars-why-how-3e3ecc066dce

A. (2022, August 1). Use the Right Design Principles for Effective Data Visaulization. PromptCloud. Retrieved August 23, 2022, from https://www.promptcloud.com/blog/design-principles-for-effective-data-visualisation/

Exports by Country 2022. (n.d.). World Population Review. Retrieved August 23, 2022, from https://worldpopulationreview.com/country-rankings/exports-by-country

Fitbit's 100+ Billion Hours of Resting Heart Rate User Data Reveals Resting Heart Rate Decreases After Age 40. (2018, February 14). Business Wire. Retrieved August 23, 2022, from https://www.businesswire.com/news/home/20180214005548/en/Fitbit%E2%80%99s-100-Billion-Hours-of-Resting-Heart-Rate%C2%A0User-Data%C2%A0Reveals-Resting-Heart-Rate-Decreases-After-Age-40

Deep, M. (2022, April 17). Five Free Data Visualization Tools for Beginners - Nightingale. Medium. Retrieved August 23, 2022, from https://medium.com/nightingale/five-free-data-visualization-tools-for-beginners-fb3645d3b110

Flow Map - Learn about this chart and tools to create it. (n.d.). Data Viz Catalogue. Retrieved August 23, 2022, from https://datavizcatalogue.com/methods/flow_map.html

A. (2022a, January 31). Gantt Chart 101: A Complete Guide •. Asana. Retrieved August 23, 2022, from https://asana.com/resources/gantt-chart-basics

Priyanka, N. (2021, December 14). Geospatial Data Visualization - Dr Neena Priyanka. Medium. Retrieved August 23, 2022, from https://neenapriyanka.medium.com/geospatial-data-visualization-b81f6e18f8fd#:%7E:text=Geospatial%20Data%20Visualization%20is%20an%20effort%20to%20represent%20the%20importance,correlations%20to%20help%20draw%20conclusions.

Yi, M. (2019f, November 11). How to Choose Colors for Data Visualizations. Chartio. Retrieved August 23, 2022, from https://chartio.com/learn/charts/how-to-choose-colors-data-visualization/

Yi, M. (2021, December 12). How to Choose Colors for Your Data Visualizations - Nightingale. Medium. Retrieved August 23, 2022, from https://medium.com/nightingale/how-to-choose-the-colors-for-your-data-visualizations-50b2557fa335

How to Create a Bullet Graph in Excel –. (2020, October 7). Automate Excel. Retrieved August 23, 2022, from https://www.automateexcel.com/charts/bullet-template/

C. (2019, April 7). How To Create A Diverging Stacked Bar Chart In Excel. Christopher Vasquez. Retrieved August 23, 2022, from https://www.christophervasquez.net/post/how-to-create-a-diverging-stacked-bar-chart-in-excel

How to create a Strip Plot in Excel. (n.d.). SimplexCT. Retrieved August 23, 2022, from https://simplexct.com/how-to-create-a-strip-plot-in-excel

Y, J. A. (2022, June 18). Dot Plots in Excel. WallStreetMojo. Retrieved August 23, 2022, from https://www.wallstreetmojo.com/dot-plots-in-excel/

Muth, L. C. (2022, May 19). How to pick more beautiful colors for your data visualizations. Datawrapper Blog. Retrieved August 23, 2022, from https://blog.datawrapper.de/beautifulcolors/

A. (2022b, March 28). How to Visualize Ranking Data? An Easy Guide to Follow. PPCexpo. Retrieved August 23, 2022, from https://ppcexpo.com/blog/how-to-visualize-ranking-data

Payne, L. (2020, December 21). I Swarm, You Swarm, We All Swarm for Beeswarm (Plots). Rho. Retrieved August 23, 2022, from https://www.rhoworld.com/i-swarm-you-swarm-we-all-swarm-for-beeswarm-plots-0/

International Database. (2022). United States Census Bureau. Retrieved August 23, 2022, from https://www.census.gov/data-tools/demo/idb/#/country?COUNTRY_YEAR=2022&COUNTRY_YR_ANIM=2022&FIPS_SINGLE=US

Weitz, D. (2021a, December 15). Mekko Charts - Towards Data Science. Medium. Retrieved August 23, 2022, from https://towardsdatascience.com/mekko-charts-f38311c576e2

A. (n.d.). Mosaic Chart | Chartopedia. AnyChart. Retrieved August 23, 2022, from https://www.anychart.com/chartopedia/chart-type/mosaic-chart/

Healy, Y. H. A. C. (n.d.-c). Network diagram. From Data to Viz. Retrieved August 23, 2022, from https://www.data-to-viz.com/graph/network.html

A. (n.d.-b). Nightingale Rose Chart | Chartopedia. AnyChart. Retrieved August 23, 2022, from https://www.anychart.com/chartopedia/chart-type/nightingale-rose-chart/#:%7E:text=Nightingale%20Rose%20Chart%20(also%20known,%2C%20seasons%2C%20etc.).

Nightingale Rose Chart - Learn about this chart and tools. (n.d.). The Data Visualisation Catalogue. Retrieved August 23, 2022, from https://datavizcatalogue.com/methods/nightingale_rose_chart.html

Briney, A. (2021, December 23). Overview of Flow Mapping. GIS Lounge. Retrieved August 23, 2022, from https://www.gislounge.com/overview-flow-mapping/

Healy, Y. H. A. C. (n.d.-d). Parallel coordinates plot. From Data to Viz. Retrieved August 23, 2022, from https://www.data-to-viz.com/graph/parallel.html

Proportional Symbols. (n.d.). Axis Maps. Retrieved August 23, 2022, from https://www.axismaps.com/guide/proportional-symbols

Radar Chart - A Complete Guide | FusionCharts. (n.d.). Fusioncharts.-Com. Retrieved August 23, 2022, from https://www.fusioncharts.com/resources/chart-primers/radar-chart

Healy, Y. H. A. C. (n.d.-e). Ridgeline plot. From Data to Viz. Retrieved August 23, 2022, from https://www.data-to-viz.com/graph/ridgeline.html

Yi, M. (2019e, October 16). A Complete Guide to Scatter Plots. Chartio. Retrieved August 23, 2022, from https://chartio.com/learn/charts/what-is-a-scatter-plot/

Weitz, D. (2021c, December 16). Slope Charts, Why & How - Towards Data Science. Medium. Retrieved August 23, 2022, from https://towardsdatascience.com/slope-charts-why-how-11c2a0bc28be

Kokenes, S. (n.d.). Strip Plots. Axis. Retrieved August 23, 2022, from https://www.axisgroup.com/data-industry-insights-blog/strip-plots#:%7E:text=Strip%20plots%20are%20a%20form,discovering%20outliers%20in%20the%20data

Sunburst chart. (n.d.). Fusioncharts.Com. Retrieved August 23, 2022, from https://www.fusioncharts.com/resources/chart-primers/sunburst-chart

Healy, Y. H. A. C. (n.d.-f). The Boxplot and its pitfalls. From Data to Viz. Retrieved August 23, 2022, from https://www.data-to-viz.com/caveat/boxplot.html

Kazakova, E. V. (2022, January 7). The Psychology behind Data Visualization Techniques. Medium. Retrieved August 23, 2022, from https://towardsdatascience.com/the-psychology-behind-data-visualization-techniques-68ef12865720

RevUnit. (2022, August 17). The Role of Color Theory in Data Visualization. Retrieved August 23, 2022, from https://www.revunit.com/post/the-role-of-color-theory-in-data-visualization

Stafford, A. (2021, December 11). The What, Why, and How of Sankey Diagrams - Towards Data Science. Medium. Retrieved August 23, 2022, from https://towardsdatascience.com/the-what-why-and-how-of-sankey-diagrams-430cbd4980b5

What Is a Tree Diagram? (2022, February 28). Investopedia. Retrieved August 23, 2022, from https://www.investopedia.com/terms/t/tree_diagram.asp#:%7E:text=In%20addition%20to%20mathematics%2C%20tree,and%20provide%20a%20strategic%20answer.

Treemap chart-A Complete Guide | FusionCharts. (n.d.). Fusioncharts.-Com. Retrieved August 23, 2022, from https://www.fusioncharts.com/resources/chart-primers/treemap-chart

Understanding and using Symbol Maps. (n.d.). Tableau. Retrieved August 23, 2022, from https://www.tableau.com/data-insights/reference-library/visual-analytics/geospatial/symbol-maps

US Dollar to Canadian Dollar Exchange Rate Chart | Xe. (n.d.). Xe. Retrieved August 23, 2022, from https://www.xe.com/currencycharts/?from=USD&to=CAD&view=1M

Scher, E. (n.d.). Using a chord diagram | Data Visualizations | Documentation | Learning. Dundas BI. Retrieved August 23, 2022, from https://www.dundas.com/support/learning/documentation/data-visualizations/using-a-chord-diagram

Waterfall Chart - A Complete Guide | FusionCharts. (n.d.). Fusioncharts.Com. Retrieved August 23, 2022, from https://www.fusioncharts.com/resources/chart-primers/waterfall-chart

What is a Pictogram and When Should I Use It? (2021, August 19). Venngage. Retrieved August 23, 2022, from https://venngage.com/blog/pictogram/

Muth, L. C. (2021, January 4). What to consider when creating choropleth maps. Datawrapper Blog. Retrieved August 23, 2022, from https://blog.datawrapper.de/choroplethmaps/

Muth, L. C. (2021b, January 11). What to consider when creating tables. Datawrapper Blog. Retrieved August 23, 2022, from https://blog.datawrapper.de/guide-what-to-consider-when-creating-tables/

Muth, L. C. (2022b, August 16). What to consider when visualizing data for colorblind readers. Datawrapper Blog. Retrieved August 23, 2022, from https://blog.datawrapper.de/colorblindness-part2/

Enjoying the series so far? Consider leaving your feedback!

I greatly appreciate you taking the time to read my series. As a small indie publisher, it means a lot and I hope I am making a difference in your career.

If you have 60 seconds, it would mean the world to me if you could leave a short review on Amazon. It does wonders for the book and I love hearing how you benefited from it.
You can also wait till you've finished!

To leave your feedback:

1. Open your camera app
2. Point your mobile device at the QR code below
3. The review page will appear in your web browser

Or

Visit Reviewbundle.elizabethsclarke.com

Thank you!

How to Win with your Data Visualizations

ELIZABETH CLARKE

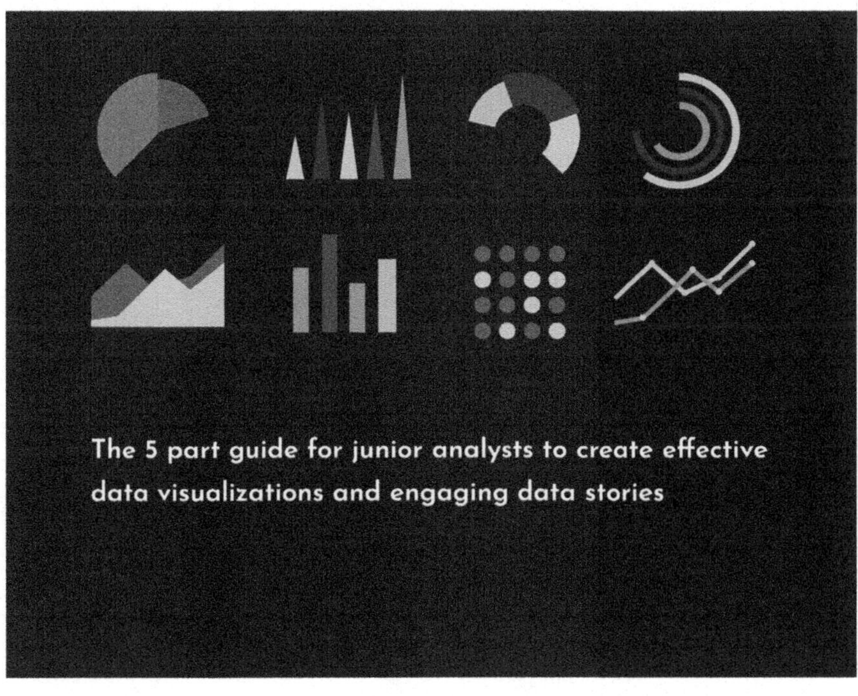

HOW TO WIN WITH YOUR DATA VISUALIZATIONS

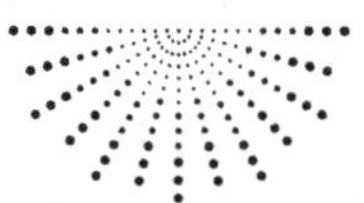

THE 5 PART GUIDE FOR JUNIOR ANALYSTS TO CREATE EFFECTIVE DATA VISUALIZATIONS AND ENGAGING DATA STORIES

INTRODUCTION

"Data are just summaries of thousands of stories – tell a few of those stories to help make the data meaningful."

— CHIP AND DAN HEATH, NEW YORK TIMES BESTSELLING AUTHORS.

Data volume reached 79 zettabytes (ZB) by the end of 2021. By the end of 2025, that figure is expected to more than double to 181 ZB. To be clear, 1 ZB is 1 billion terabytes!

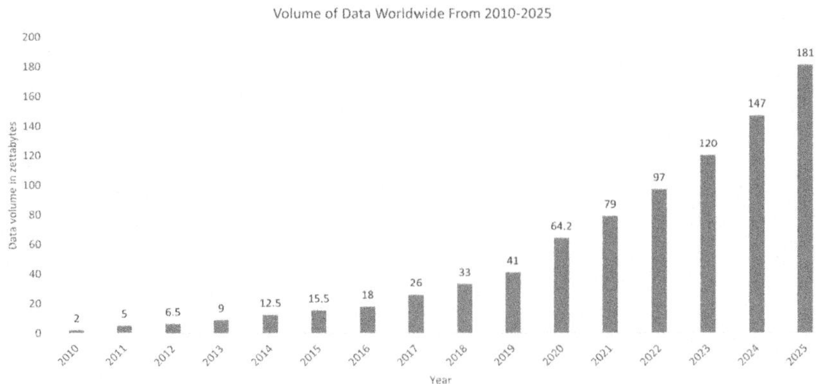

FIGURE 0.1

As impressive as those numbers are, none of those bytes would amount to much if they were not translated into an easily digestible format.

Enter left stage... More specifically, data storytelling.

For decades, the traditional way of presenting data was to pull out the old faithful pie or bar chart and spit out facts like a robot reciting the numbers on a spreadsheet. In such scenarios, most often, the listeners needed clothes pins to keep their eyes open. There was often the request to have the same information sent over through email or another method for "review" - a cleverly disguised way of gaining the information that was not digested during the boring presentation.

Ensure that is not the reality that you face when presenting data by tossing tradition out the window. Basic charts and numbers just do not cut it anymore. When most people have the attention span of a squirrel hopped up on caffeine, there needs to be a more compelling, more enticing way of delivering this data. And this is what data storytelling is all about – remixing the quantitative and qualitative nature of data and bringing the point across in a way that makes other people want to listen and learn more.

Over the last few years, the data industry has exploded in growth because this secret is out of the bag. Politicians use data storytelling to persuade voters to place the tick on their side of the ballot with touching commercials highlighting their contributions to the community. Marketing departments use it so that their brands touch your heart, and thus, you fork over some of your hard-earned cash before you make a conscious decision to do so. Data storytelling drives innovation and product development and adds to the zeros on the bottom line of major corporations like Coca-Cola, Mercedes Benz, and Amazon.

The examples of effective data storytelling in action are almost endless because it has been realized that there needs to be a change in the way we present data to conferences, seminars, potential and existing clients, customers, business executives, and more.

Through this change, others can happen. Without this change, most of these many bytes of information would go unnoticed.

This change does not have to just happen on a big business level.

This change can start with you.

As an established marketer with a repertoire of scaled brands, I have met many people in my line of work. I have met people new to the industry who want to leave a mark when making their first few presentations. I have met people who have made presentations in the past but failed to drive the message home to their bosses, board members, and other listeners. I have met small business owners who are stumped about how to win over new clients and customers when telling their brand stories. I have met people who simply want to have the know-how of crafting a captivating and engaging presentation in their back pocket so that they can pull it out whenever they need it.

All these people had one thing in common even though they came from a vast array of industries – They were struggling to present data in an effective, straightforward way that gets to the heart of the message they were trying to convey. These people had figured out that pulling out the old presentation board and pointing at charts and numbers does not make an impact and were seeking a better way.

If you can relate to how these people feel, this book was created specifically to help you get ahead of the curve and discover how to develop storytelling expertise that will give your presentations the panache they need to hit hard and hit home.

Data storytelling and visualization are quite hefty words for the tongue to lift, but they are not as complicated as they sound. They do not always have to involve learning to code or sweating over complex charts, as many assume. They are simply methods of clearing the clutter that zettabytes of data can produce to reveal a clean, concise goal around which a story can be created to drive change. This book helps you clear the clutter and create that path with ease.

You, too, can impress your boss and other executives with your presentation and data visualization skills. You can also win over new clients and customers and convince the existing ones to recommend you to their peers. You can convert data to dollar signs for your company and be on the fast track to your next promotion. The things that you can do by supporting data with a story are only limited by your imagination. You have the power to drive change and be part of this evolution of how data is presented and consumed.

You can do all of this and more by learning the five parts of crafting an effective and engaging data story. This book was broken down into five parts to make it easy for you to understand the strategies and knowledge outlined in the pages to come. You'll also have a guideline to follow when creating visuals and presentations. Let me give you a brief breakdown so that you get the gist of the exciting things to come:

THE FOUNDATION, THE NARRATIVE

You need to be able to quiet the noise of all the bytes of data and focus on what is truly important – the goal of your presentation. The goal is what allows for the proper development of the narrative of your data story. Your narrative defines the sequences of events and how you will layer your data for the best appeal. The narrative structures the whole story and holds everything together. Call it your data story glue, if you will. Without this glue, everything will inevitably fall apart. Without a solid narrative, not even the best visuals will salvage the wreck that the presentation is bound to be.

This part of the book focuses on helping you drill down on your presentation goal and how to sequence your data story around it for an easy, natural flow that resonates with your audience and solves the right solution.

CAPTIVATING YOUR AUDIENCE

A good data story is effective not just because of what you say but *how* you say it. To deliver your message most effectively, you need to understand your audience and speak their language. Captivating your audience with an engaging story is what plants the seed to significant change and growth.

CHOOSING THE RIGHT CHART

Now, do not get me wrong. I am not knocking the tremendous contribution that a good chart or well-dressed set of numbers can have to a presentation. The problem is that too many people focus solely on this and forget the narrative to support these data visualizations.

The correct chart presented at the right time can take a simple analysis and give it a visual form that people can use to develop a mental image of what you are presenting. This will help your presentation stick in their minds. It will make *you* memorable.

Data visualization is another crucial component of the data storytelling process that you must nail on the head. You will surely learn all you need to know about presenting effective data visualizations in this part of the book.

A WINNING DESIGN

Sight is the most used of all the human senses. Use that knowledge to your benefit. Do not just drop bland, tasteless charts and graphs on your audience's laps and call it a day. That will only leave a bad taste in their mouths and make you look less than the competent business person you are.

The face of any data visualization is the design. Having clean, concise, clutter-free designs is crucial to keeping your audience informed *and* engaged. As they say – presentation is everything. When it comes to data storytelling, you need to take the saying literally and figuratively.

CRAFTING A WINNING DATA STORY

The parts discussed above are essential, but none of them will give your presentation the edge it needs alone. You have to bring them all together to amaze, astound, educate, and convince your audience. This last part of the book shows you how to do just that, painlessly and cohesively.

I run into large amounts of data every day during my career in product marketing and social analytics. If you are anything like me, you find yourself fascinated with the components that make up company growth statistics, consumer and social analytics, sales figures, expenditure reports, and all the other numbers that show a company's performance. While these figures excite the senses of the data science nerd in me, I also realized that they could look like a foreign language to someone else. I have a few failed presentation stories of my own that I can tell.

When I was new to my career, I struggled to translate these figures. I would present basic, uninspiring charts with little information—stuttering at even the simplest questions. I always knew there had to be a more effective way to present data. Many failed presentations have taught me the best ways to transform any form of data into a language that everyone can understand. Translation through storytelling is a method that cannot be beaten.

Data storytelling is a vital part of any company's growth and management. Big businesses need it and so do small ones. Executives that have proved their mettle need it no matter how much they advance in their careers, and so too does the intern just starting in a field. My passion is to help as many people and businesses across the board take raw data and translate those bytes into stories that encourage change that allows meeting goals and targets. Call me quirky, but I always love when people reach out to me with stories about how the words I have written have helped inspire the change they need to take their professional lives to the next level.

I hope to hear a similar story from you. A data story of how much you have achieved using the words in this book, perhaps.

I suggest you get out a highlighter and mark anything you find valuable and worthy of remembering. One of my favourite tricks for revisiting valuable information with ease.

The data shows that anyone who reads past this page to the first chapter dramatically increases their chances of becoming a data storytelling superstar. So, what are you waiting for? Turn the page!

1

THE FOUNDATION OF DATA STORYTELLING - DEVELOPING THE NARRATIVE

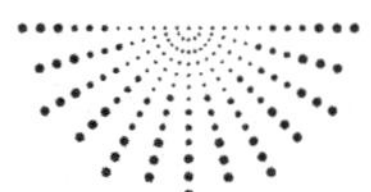

"The goal is to turn data into information and information into insight."

— *CARLY FIORINA, FORMER CEO, HEWLETT PACKARD*

With the many, many bytes of information available for relating to other people, how do you decide which ones deserve precedence and should be added to your slides? That is a fundamental question when approaching data storytelling. If this question has come to your mind, you have set yourself up with the right mindset to present data in the most digestible way to your audience.

The answer of which bytes of information you will relate to your audience depends on your final goal in the presentation. Too many business professionals get stuck on the visual aspects of the presentation and leave the information that needs to be relayed as an afterthought. But it is truly the other way around. The visuals do not matter if your audience cannot follow a defined path from the initial insight to a solution.

A narrative is about developing a language that allows for augmenting data in the most effective way to deliver to an audience so that the people in the audience are not left confused and trying to piece together these bytes of information. The narrative is the vehicle that conveys insights on the data that has been collected to the audience.

There are 3 main components of a great narrative. The *what,* The *who,* and the *how.*

The *What:* *What* is the goal of your presentation? What insights do you need to convey? What solutions do you need to guide your audience toward? *The "what"* is arguably the most important part of any data story. Without having a goal in mind, you will not know what insights to bring forward and how you will effectively present them.

The *Who:* Who are you presenting to? Knowing this is essential when presenting data because you need to know what they already know, and what they don't. What you present to your product manager vs. the CEO is very different. Finding out *who* you're presenting to will allow you to determine what you need to present and how you will present it. This will be covered more in-depth in chapter 2.

The *How:* Now that you know what you're presenting and who you're presenting it to, how you will do it should come naturally. Based on what you've already learned, you can select specific insights with supporting information and transmit them through beautifully crafted data visualizations in a favorable sequence. Of course, the bulk of the book shows you exactly how to do this, so I will not go any more in-depth here. Keep reading!

STRUCTURE

How will you structure all this information and present it effectively?

When relaying information, an effective structure I like to follow is the hook, the aha moment, and the solution.

The hook comes at the beginning of your data story. It is what captures the attention of your audience. The hook can be a question or stating a problem that this audience shares as a commonality, supported with a simple insight. It gets the audience thinking and engaged.

The "aha" moment is your audience coming to a favorable conclusion on their own, based on your strategic delivery of insights. Simply telling someone what they should do rarely works. Strategically delivering information so that your solution seems like the only option is crucial for a successful data story. (Of course, this is only if you've done the proper analysis and believe it is the right course of action. Ensure you don't leave any crucial data out. In more complex situations, having multiple solutions can also work in your favor, so your company comes to the best conclusion possible.)

The solution, is the reiteration of your end goal and call to action. This is where valuable business change happens. Getting your audience to come to this conclusion on their own and simply reiterating it to validate their realization is the best-case scenario.

Understanding the hook, aha moment, and solution gives you a great structure to base your narrative off. What information should be delivered as the hook, what will be the central insight of the presentation, and what is the goal of it all.

Let's run through an example.

Your company's primary goal is to gain new customers for maximum growth. However, your analysis leads to discovering there are few returning customers, leading to losses over time. You've discovered not enough attention has been targeted toward giving new customers an incentive to come back a second time and become recurring customers.

Simply stating this might not be enough. The audience of executives might just see consistent customer growth and want to stick with the strategy. However, constantly acquiring new customers means a lot is spent on advertising. We need to change our focus and build a robust and reliable customer base instead of a large volume of customers. How would you hook this to the reader? What are some possible solutions to the problem? How can you layout the information gradually, so the audience concludes on their own? In this case, a straightforward narrative could be:

Hook:

"It is extremely costly to acquire new customers at the rate we do so, and it is not a sustainable strategy. Our advertising costs are growing faster than our profits." (Show them that something has to change without relaying the details)

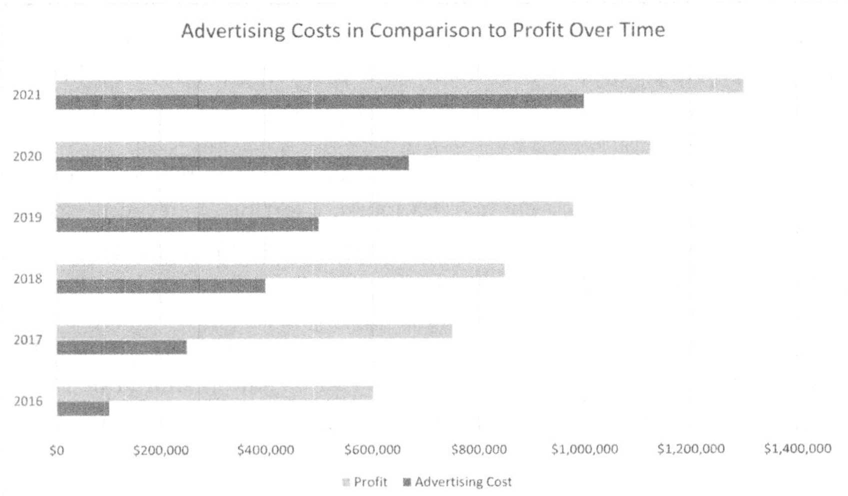

FIGURE 0.2 Horizontal bar graph comparing advertising costs to profits from 2016-2021.

Aha moment:

"While our focus is on acquiring new customers, few become consistent or even return. Our initial growth strategy was effective, but it is now becoming an issue in the business's long-term growth. We are spending a dollar to get a dime, over and over. As you can see, only 7% of our customers are returning customers, yet they make up 38% of the revenue. "(They realize what they are doing isn't sustainable, and they should be focusing on keeping customers, not just acquiring new ones)

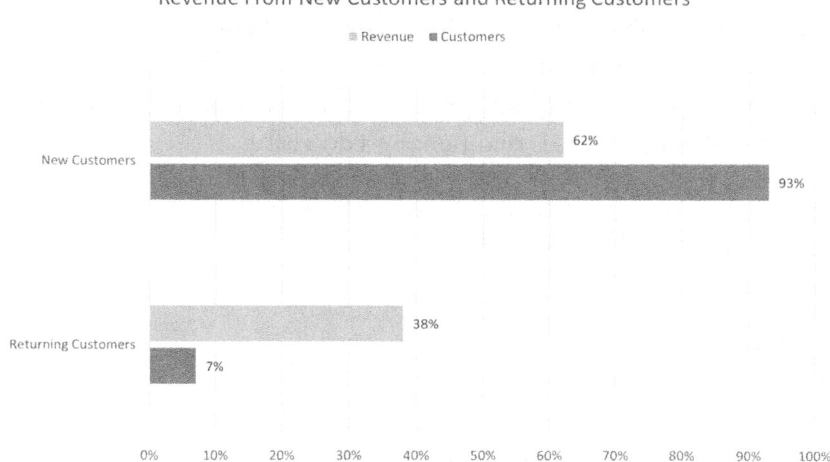

FIGURE 0.3 Comparing revenue of returning customers vs one time customers.

Solution:

"We can create long-term success and a better customer base by incentivizing customers to return. Allocating more budget to retargeting campaigns can also create many loyal customers." (*A good solution is one that an audience comes to independently. Your main points should guide them where they need to go. In some cases, the solution is a reiteration of what they concluded on their own*)

TYPES OF DATA

When compiling a presentation, an important thing to note is what you need to showcase. The type of data you're presenting determines the visualizations you use and the timeline in which you present it. Let's look at some common data types.

Trends

Presenting trends focuses on how figures rise and fall over a given amount of time and how these patterns of number behavior affect the audience. For example, a business analyst may present data to the executives that show sales figures rise towards the end and beginning of the year but dip around the middle of the year. Using this data, the narrative can be focused on why these figures are so and what can be done to increase sales when there is traditionally a decrease.

FIGURE 0.4 Scatter plot showcasing data trend throughout the year.

Comparisons

Showcasing comparisons builds on trends and shows how data changes over time in relation to specific periods. For example, let's say the revenue from a product launched in 2017 was on a steady incline until 2020, where it started to trend downward. We can look at other metrics from 2017 and 2020 to see if any significant changes in our business strategy or our market could've caused this. Catching a potential downward trend early on is critical for correcting it. We can also compare it to the performance of other products.

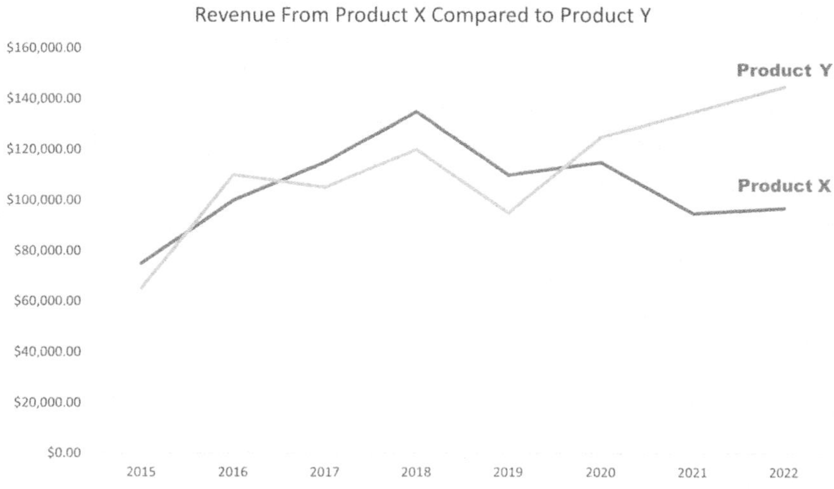

FIGURE 0.5 Comparison of two products of time

Rank Order

Communicating a hierarchy of factors to make a large amount of detail easier for the audience to digest. For example, the business analyst may present a table highlighting the best performing and worst performing campaigns. With this data, the executives can reallocate the budget and focus on their top converting revenue streams. Also, the marketing team can focus on promotions that showcase their best-selling softwares.

	Q1	Q2	Q3	Q4
Campaign 1	$50,000	$85,000	$75,000	$98,000
Campaign 2	$75,000	$79,000	$65,000	$86,000
Campaign 3	$100,000	$110,000	$90,000	$125,000
Campaign4	$56,000	$59,000	$50,000	$67,000
Campaign 5	$43,000	$69,000	$60,000	$65,000
Campaign 6	$78,000	$70,000	$77,000	$82,000
Campaign 7	$68,000	$67,000	$60,000	$77,000
Campaign 8	$55,000	$50,000	$56,000	$62,000

FIGURE 0.6 Table highlighting campaign performance.

Statistical Relationships

Statistical relationships allow the audience to know the relationship between different data types and how a change in one variable will cause an increase in the other. As an example, a business could be monitoring website traffic throughout the day to find the busiest times.

FIGURE 0.7 Line graph showcasing website visitors over a 12 hour period.

---

*"**Quick tip** - A Quarter is a three-month period on a company's fiscal year that acts as a basis for periodic financial reports and the paying of dividends. A quarter refers to one-fourth of a year and is referred to as Q1 (January, February, March) Q2 (April, May June) Q3 (July, August, September), and Q4 (October, November, December). You will be seeing these terms used throughout the book."*

Counterintuitive Data

This narrative shows surprising data that contradicts what the norm is. The counterintuitive nature of data invites further exploration, especially in instances where it has an adverse or alternatively, favorable impact on the business. Perhaps you have a spike in sales in January and July, which are normally two of the slower months. This unexpected data needs further exploration as to why this happened to determine if more sales can be derived from the revealed answer.

FIGURE 0.8

IMPORTANT THINGS TO CONSIDER

A good narrative gives you direction and purpose. It is essential for giving meaning to random bytes of information. Some baseline knowledge to have when presenting data are:

Only Present Relevant Data:

For example, let's say we're using our example from before, comparing new customers to recurring customers. It would be beneficial to compare sales between new customers and returning customers over the last year or more, but presenting these figures on a month-by-month basis doesn't tell the audience enough and is irrelevant based on this situation.

However, you cannot throw all of this data at your audience, expecting them to understand it even if you do. This will only serve to make your audience feel like a leaf in a thunderstorm - with no sense of direction of which byte of data to grasp first.

Cite only Credible Data

From the tons of available data, you need to remember that not all data sources are relevant or credible when presenting your data story. Understanding this allows you to specify what types of data you will present and where you cite this data.

Your audience needs to trust that the information you are sharing with them is credible. It needs to ensure people look at you as a credible source of information, and when they relay that information forward, it is accurate.

All the data that you need while creating your presentation might not be available immediately. Because the narrative of your data story helps guide the purpose of your presentation, you can then reason what information should be included in your presentation and approach the suitable sources for that missing data.

Develops A Clear Path

Building your narrative beforehand is essential for your presentation to be effective. It allows you to format the correct information in the appropriate sequence to lead your audience to the desired outcome, avoiding mid-presentation fumbles and confusion.

This is because a narrative helps define the events that must be touched on to reach your goal. Those events can then be broken down into plain language for a straightforward presentation. Like all good stories, the narrative must have a beginning, a middle, and an end.

Development of Proper Visualizations to Best Match the Context

Graphs, charts, photos, text, maps, tables. All of these charts and more can be used to create an effective and engaging presentation. However, just because they can be used doesn't mean you should use them.

Building a narrative allows you to select the proper chart for the data and any extra visuals required by your audience. If you were presenting last quarter's numbers to the project manager, you could keep it simple and straight to the point, as they are familiar with the campaign and its details. However, if you have to showcase this quarter's figures at an executive level, they might need more insight. Potentially a comparison between quarters throughout the year and some projections for the new year. We will dive deeper into presenting to your audience in chapter 2.

Using visuals that are not effective for your data story can confuse your audience far more than enlightening them. Therefore, it is imperative that you choose the proper visualization to enhance your details. We will go deeper into selecting and designing visualizations in chapters 3 and 4.

DEVELOPING THE NARRATIVE OF YOUR DATA STORY

Step 1 - Identify the Goal of your Data Story

To set up the goal for your data story and subsequently, set up the foundation for the narrative, there are a few questions that you need to ask yourself before you do anything else. These questions include:

- What is the problem that will be presented in your data story?
- What is the possible solution or solutions for solving that problem?
- What would you like to achieve by the end of your data story?
- What call-to-action can you strategically place in your presentation that will likely cause your audience to react in the way you would like?
- What takeaways would you like your audience to live with by the end of your data story?

Answering these questions thoroughly will allow you to set up the plot for your data story. You will know the beginning, middle, and end of that story so that you can extract data in alignment with that vision.

The important thing to remember when answering these questions is to let the data guide the narrative. Sometimes we believe that data is driving us in a particular direction, but picking out only irrelevant information will misguide us. To make sure you have the correct data and it is guiding you in the proper direction involves doing a few activities. Such activities include:

- Making comparisons of different sets of data. This will allow you to form correlations to see how these datasets relate to each other.
- Look for trends. Trends allow you to note how different aspects of the business are developing, changing, or remaining stagnant.
- Noting anomalies. Anomalies are sets of data that do not align with what you expect or are outside the norm. Noting anomalies will prompt you to look at *why* this is happening and whether this is in favor of your business or detrimental to its activities.
- Noting counterintuitive data. Counterintuitive data is surprising or not what you would expect out of evaluating specific trends or making comparisons. Like anomalies, such information needs to be analyzed to determine whether or not they are favorable to the runnings of the business or detrimental to it.

It is essential that you take this time initially to do this analysis so that you realize the true goal of telling your data story rather than what you believe it to be. Analyzing data is quite an adventure as it can bring up unexpected twists and turns.

Step 2 - Align Your Data Story Goal with Your Audience

This step aligns with creating the setting, like in a fictional novel or a movie. It sets up the who and when of your data story. The "Who" is your audience. To tell a data story relevant to your audience, you need to take the time to learn about them. You need to understand factors such as their:

- Demographic
- Age
- Knowledge of the subject matter that will be prominent in your presentation
- Careers and educational background

Knowing these details and more allows you to develop your data story in a way that is most relatable to your listener. This will allow you to see if you can add more specific jargon to your data story or if you need to simplify the language for clearer takeaways while you are presenting. More importantly, knowing your audience allows you to understand why they care about the problem and the most specific solutions.

Knowing your audience allows you to develop the *when* of your data story. The "when" describes how far back the information needs to be provided and what current analysis and future predictions are specific and relevant to that group. These are the specific types of information that will be included in your data story to have the most impact on this group.

Step 3 - Develop the Structure of Your Data Story

With your audience and goal in mind, you can start developing the structure of your narrative. This structure will include the following elements:

1. The context of your data story. This speaks to why the story is relevant and worth telling to your audience. Knowing the context of your story allows you to develop a hook that engages your audience and makes them invested in it from the get-go.
2. The key players that are related to the context of that data story. Like in a book or movie, some characters are significant to the advancement of that story. These players could be executives, customers, clients, and more.
3. The problem that needs solving. The problem stated in your story is the whole reason this presentation was necessary in the first place. There is a conflict that your audience is invested in,

and you need to state this clearly so that this group knows why they are being presented with this data.

4. The solution to the problem. Of course, if there is a problem, you cannot leave it unsolved. So, the follow-up to letting your audience know what the problem is to provide them with possible solutions. These solutions need to be broken down into clear action steps that can be taken to solve this problem. You also need to provide your audience with this solution in a relatable way that allows them to know what value they are gaining by following the action solutions you have provided instead of other solutions.

It is best to tell your data story linearly. Following the structure from context to key players, and then problems and solutions. Just like you would not tell a story in a book or movie by starting with the middle or the end, you also need to deliver your data story in a way that makes sense to your audience.

Step 4 - Consider Your Visualizations

This is the climax of your data story. When you get to this point in your data story, you should be able to tick off your ultimate goal in having created that story in the first place. Your data visualizations bring all the previous elements together in a small flow that engages your audience and allows you to retain their attention so that you can deliver the climax of your data story, which is the solution to the problem.

Data storytelling is not just about *telling* your audience. You need to *show* your audience, and that is the role of creating visualizations. Visualizations enhance the story you are telling and help simplify the information so that the most important parts are highlighted clearly and immediately.

Remember that the visuals that you choose need to be relevant and engaging to your particular audience and be relevant to the insights being presented. These visuals need to capture their attention immediately *and* hold onto it for the duration of your presentation.

Infographics vs. Data Visualization

On the topic of data visualizations, it is pertinent that we take the time to address a point where many people feel confused. The fact is whether or not data visualizations and infographics are the same. The answer to that is they are not one and the same even though they are similar types of visual content.

Data visualizations are translations of datasets through individual charts that make that data easy to understand in a visual format. Whereas looking at massive spreadsheets with figures upon figures can be confusing, using data visualizations like a bar chart or a scatter plot allows you to digest that information in a much easier, faster way.

The purpose of infographics is to allow persons to note a large amount of information through the combination of text, icons, data visualizations, and illustrations to make an informed decision. As you can note from this definition, infographics include the use of data visualizations. Whereas data visualizations are typically brief visual content that communicates a certain point, infographics allow more information to be condensed in an organized flow. It is typical to note the use of infographics in areas such as the homepages of websites, landing pages for marketing campaigns, brochures, and social media.

Both of these types of visual content can have quite an impact when presenting data. However, which one you use depends on the purpose of the presentation. Infographics are typically used in marketing campaigns. Data visualizations are more prominently used for data storytelling.

You CAN SEE how crucial it is to present the right information in the right way. That is why developing your narrative is the first and, frankly, one of the most important elements of presenting data.

Now that we have developed our narrative let's move on to identifying, and captivating our audience.

2
CAPTIVATING YOUR AUDIENCE

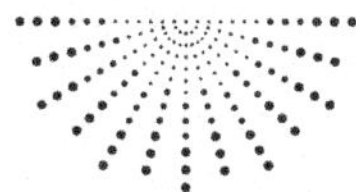

"Presentations aren't about the presenter; they're about the audience and what the audience needs."

— *SIMON RAYBOULD*

By now, you would have realized that your data story presentation's success depends on the depth of knowledge that you have about your audience. You need to have a profile of these people before you take even the first step in putting your information together and certainly before you start designing that presentation. Doing otherwise is like hunting in the dark and hoping to hit the target - a nearly impossible task.

Ensure that you hit the mark as close to the bullseye by putting in that preliminary groundwork about the people you will be presenting to. Ensure that you captivate these people to have the highest chance of eliciting the change you want from making that presentation.

The question that has many business professionals abandoning this vital task is the *how* of it. How exactly do you go about finding what you need to know about your audience so that you cater your data story to touch their emotions and better get your point across?

Luckily, this is not a matter of guesswork. You can implement proven methods to gather the information you need to know about this group. This chapter focuses on the "how" of getting this information and using it to maximum effect.

IDENTIFYING YOUR AUDIENCE

There are many questions that you can ask and, therefore, develop answers about your audience. However, just as you can get bogged down by the many bytes of data you want to convey to your audience, you can also get overwhelmed by the sheer number of questions you can ask about them. That does not have to be your reality. The solution here is to keep things as straightforward as possible.

Some important factors to consider are:

Job title. Knowing this will help determine what information they have access to frequently and the most important tasks they're involved in on a day-to-day basis. Knowing your audience's baseline knowledge can make or break your presentation.

Literacy level: Knowing your audience's literacy levels will greatly determine how you convey the information. Some common literacy levels are:

Analytical: Loves the fine details and data-driven solutions. Great at making sense of the data on their own. Show them as much valuable information as possible.

Competitive: Very fast-paced, motivated individual. Usually wants valuable insights they can act on, and they want them quick—no room for fluff.

Amicable: Very patient individuals. They love to discuss different avenues of action and the best possible solution to optimize the business's trajectory. It's worth having multiple possible solutions and lots of extra insights, showcasing different courses of action.

Don't ignore the importance of a simple personality type when presenting data.

Although all this background work can be rather tedious ill leave you with a quote to shift your perspective:

> "Give me six hours to chop down a tree and i will spend the first four sharpening the axe"
>
> — ABRAHAM LINCOLN

Who Is Your Audience?

The answer to this gives your audience a face. It makes you feel like you are talking to real people while compiling your data and preparing the visuals to support your message. This will undoubtedly help you build a better presentation compared to having an obscure image in your mind of what this group of people looks like.

With the power of knowing what your audience "looks" like, you are better able to shape a message that will be received by that audience.

There are five main categories of audiences that you will encounter as a data storyteller. They are:

The Novice

This is the type of audience's first exposure to the subject matter. In such a case, you want to simplify the information so that it is easy to understand. Therefore, jargon and technical terms should be avoided.

Be very clear, concise, and informative. Focus on guiding them from knowing very minimal to understanding the entire sequence of events regarding the data.

The Generalist

This type of audience is more aware of the topic of discussion but still lacks understanding in certain areas. As the data storyteller, it is your job to fill in these gaps and provide this audience with knowledge on the major themes connected to the data being conveyed.

The Manager

Such an audience has an in-depth, actionable understanding of intricacies and interrelationships about the data due to their experience and access to details. As a data storyteller, you do not have as much to do concerning explanations, but that still does not take away the importance of conveying your message to this group in an efficient and effective manner. The manager will want straight to the point, yet valuable insights.

The Executive

This audience understands the importance and probable outcomes of certain situations but still needs the details. It is your job as the data storytelling to build the bridge between the data and those possible outcomes.

The Expert

This audience has the most in-depth knowledge about the data and does not rely as heavily on your presentation to be informed. This group is more interested in gaining more information compiled in a cohesive way to generate faster conclusions about the data.

IDENTIFYING your audience's job title and the depth of their knowledge of the data allows you to develop a strategy for how specific you need to be when explaining terms and designing your visuals. For example, a novice audience to the marketing strategy might need a rundown on the marketing budget allocation before they can understand why advertising performance is dropping. At the same time, a group of marketing managers or media buyers do not require such an explanation as they most likely will be familiar with the marketing budget. Knowing what your audience already knows determines how your data story will play out for the most effective communication. Keep in mind, being a novice doesn't mean it's their first day on the job. A higher-level executive might be unfamiliar with the new advertising strategy and needs a simple explanation to understand your point entirely.

Knowledge of your audience and understanding of the data also allows you to know what the listener is trying to gain from your data story.

Let's have a look at an example together and see how we would present to a specific audience.

In this case, we are presenting a product pricing recommendation for our new product launch. We had to consult the product manager for a potential price point change. They have very versatile knowledge of the product and were very motivated to launch, making them a competitive and analytical audience. The product manager and product team briefly determined the price point based on the average pricing of similar product launches in the industry. with further research, the product's initial pricing has changed over time and come to a new average price point. Our launch price needs to be corrected to be competitive. In this case, our audience knows many small details, so we want to be very straightforward with our data. Visualize the data in an easy-to-understand way that shows where we initially were pricing, where the competitors ended up, and our new recommended price point.

Before you compile your visual, we determined:

- Who: Product Manager ("The Manager, The Expert")
- What: Product launch price change

Now let's create this in visual form and present it.

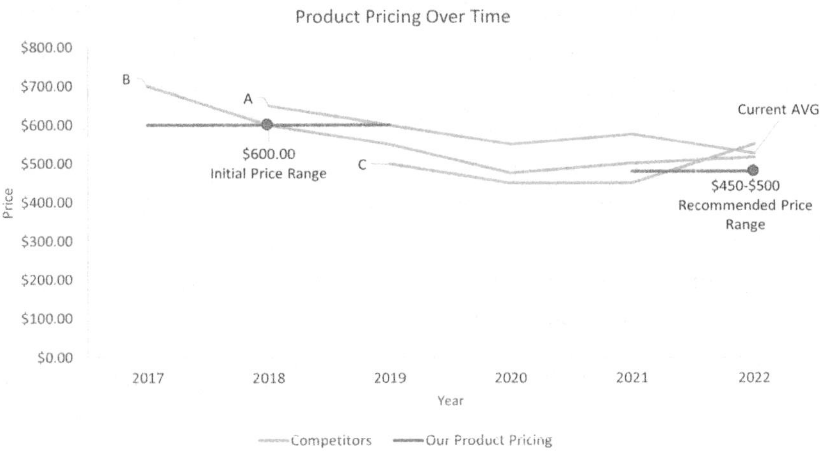

FIGURE 0.9- If you would like to follow along with a full color PDF, please join my email list at ElizabethSClarke.com and respond to the first email. I will happily send you the PDF version of the book.

"OUR FURTHER RESEARCH showed a trend in many companies initially pricing the product at an average of $600 (which was our initial price range) but reducing overtime to reach the industry sweet spot of $520, which is where we should be closer to. As you can see, At a price range of $450-$500, we fall just under the industry average to be competitive yet still in our desired gross profit margin of 50-60%."

This audience already knew the fine details, and all they needed was a quick and clear recommendation followed by some data to back it up. They can see the validity of this on their own.

(We will be dissecting this chart in chapter 4 and showcasing how we designed it for success)

Now, let's try this example again but for a different audience. We are the product manager, explaining why we selected this price point to the executives. They are busy with the big picture tasks within the overall company but aren't as in tune with individual product launches and details. This makes them an "executive" audience type. They needed to be filled in about how we got to this point.

Let's go over the questions to ask ourself:

- Who: CEO and executives ("The Executive")
- Literacy Level: Analytical
- What: Why we landed on the specific price point, and will it hit our desired targets.

The chart we used above will be valuable and effective. But with the audience having less knowledge of the details, they want to know why you landed on such a price point. We will need a few more slides to get them there.

When it comes to executives, their main focus is money. So let's show them why this price point will be effective and profitable. In this instance, A horizontal bar graph showing the profit % value can be effective. This way, the executives see what they want right away.

We can show how the costs and gross profit make up the overall price point. We can also compare it to our other products and their profit margins. Our company strives for a 60% gross profit margin for each product. Let's say our product is priced right in the middle of our price range at $475, with our cost at $204. We are left with $271, 57% gross profit. Which is right where we want it to be.

Let's visualize it!

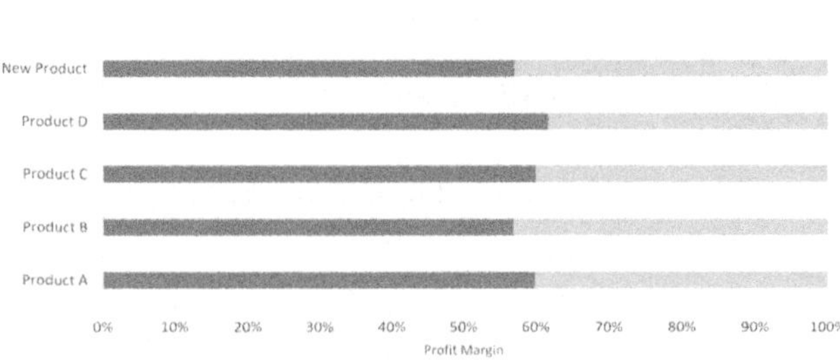

FIGURE 0.10

"Here is an overview of the gross profit margins for our top 4 products compared to our new product about to be launched."

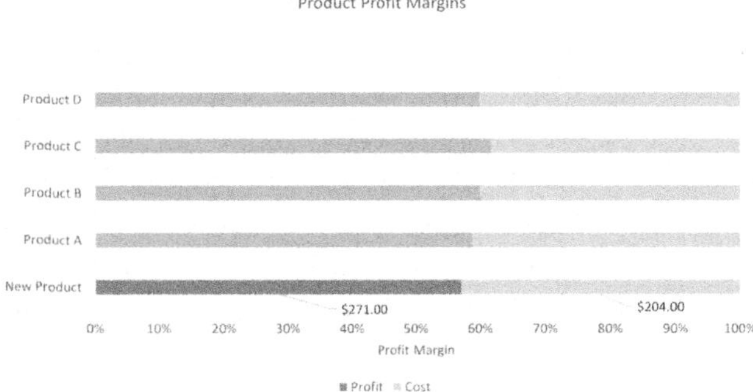

FIGURE 0.11

"As you can see, with our cost at $204, and a price point of $475, we are left with $271 (57%) profit which is right where we want to be."

"Let's have a look at how we ended up here."

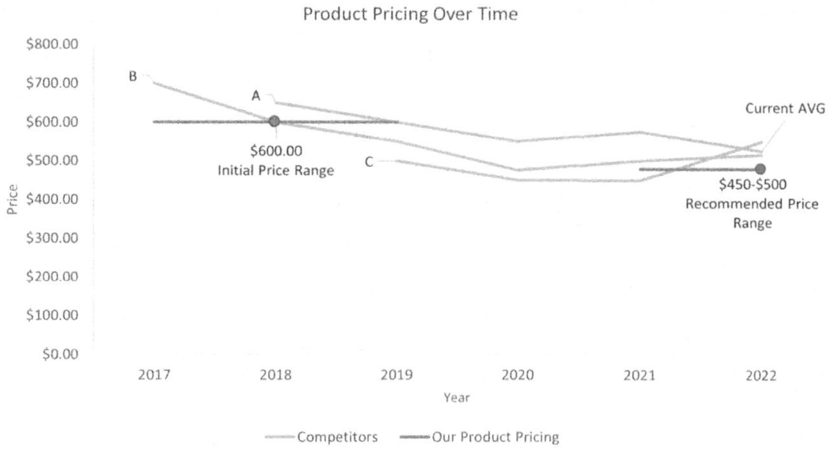

FIGURE 0.12

"As you can see on the chart, Our initial price range was $600. The price was determined by the launch pricing average of our competitors. We discovered that the price points fluctuated over the last few years and landed at an average of $520. If we go with the $475 price point, we can sustain our desired profit margins while being the most competitive option."

By guiding the executives through the whole story and using attentive attributes to place their attention (We will talk more about attentive attributes later in the book), they can easily understand the reasoning behind your decisions and fully support your solution.

THE IMPORTANCE OF LANGUAGE

Judging how well your audience relates to the data that you will represent is very much related to the language you use. For example, if you are presenting to IT professionals about an IT-related subject, then this audience's literacy and numeracy literacy concerning IT-related subjects will be one where you do not have as much explaining to do. On the other hand, you may be presenting IT data to an audience made up primarily of HR representatives, and even if this group of people has excellent overall literacy and numeracy literacy aptitude, this group may find it challenging to understand the particular language, both literature, and numeral, relating to that subject matter. Similarly, if you are telling a data story about HR metrics, IT professionals may not have as high of a literacy and numeracy level to understand that particular language. In either case, you need to break the data down into manageable bite-sized pieces that are easy for the audience to digest.

Many business professionals are wary of approaching an audience with a lower literacy in that particular subject area, but this is instead an opportunity in disguise. See, the thing is, the actual mettle of a data storyteller is not made by how aesthetically pleasing their visualizations are or how well they put all the data together. Instead, this mettle is proven by how well this person can get the audience to follow their train of thought. Suppose you can get an audience with no prior knowledge of a subject area to understand that subject area. In that case, you deserve the title of a true professional data storyteller. Do not worry if you do not quite live up to that title yet, as this is a learned skill rather than one that some people are born with.

Some of the techniques that you can use to better improve the understanding of an audience that might have a lower literacy or number literacy levels include:

Avoid Using Technical Jargon as Much as Possible

All industries and niches have a unique language with acronyms and technical terminologies that will confuse outsiders who are not as familiar with the happenings of that setting. This particular language is called jargon. The last thing you want to do is leave your audience confused when they exit your presentation. Therefore, the best practice is to avoid using unique languages unless your audience is made up of people familiar with that industry or niche.

When it is necessary to use technical jargon with a novice audience, ensure that you take the time to explain what the terms mean and how they relate to the context of the presentation.

Be Humble and Use Humor

One of the best ways to break down jargon is to use humor. A good joke to break the ice is a great way to make everyone feel comfortable, yourself included. Humor is also an excellent tool for ensuring that your audience sees you as a person just like them and not someone talking down to them because of your superior knowledge of the data.

Be sure to convey through language and body language that you are willing to explain things that are unclear to your audience. When presenting a data story, the aim is not to impress your audience with how smart or informed you are. Instead, it is to inform your audience to make a sound decision about how to act thereafter. That means using language that the audience understands.

Pay Attention to Your Audience's Cues

There may be times when your presentation does not immediately resonate with your audience. This does not automatically mean a failed data story. Instead, you can learn to read the non-verbal cues that your audience expresses to adjust your language for effective communication to take place. Simply use a conversational tone to explain whatever information that you just imparted.

Reading the room is a skill that you *must* develop, as data storytelling is fluid and requires you to change and adjust on the spot to reach your audience no matter the circumstances.

Use the Power of Storytelling to Invoke an Emotional Response

Human beings love stories. It is why we read fiction novels and watch movies. It is why we cannot help but be engrossed by the dilemmas going on in other people's lives. It will also help many audiences, especially those composed of amicable and expressive audience members, feel more connected with you and, by extension, your data story. Relating your data to stories can give the audience a better mental visualization of the information you are trying to get across.

Allow Your Data Visualizations to Help Explain Technical Information

Of course, your verbal communication needs to be top-notch to reach your audience effectively. Any written paraphernalia you hand to your audience must also be relayed as professional, easy-to-understand content. However, you need to keep in mind that the human brain more easily deciphers visual content. Therefore, you need to take full advantage of the potential that your data visualizations afford you. This extends across the board and allows you to break down technical language into concise communication.

Focus on the Information That Is Relevant to Your Audience

All the parts of the data involved in your presentation might be fascinating to you. However, you have to remember that your audience is here for a particular reason, and things that you find fascinating might fail to capture the attention of your audience when that information ranges out of that scope.

Therefore, it is best that you highlight the things that your audience finds informative and relates to. For example, you might be presenting to an audience of marketing specialists who want to understand more about media buying. Such a presentation should focus on the process rather than its history or old tactics media buyers previously used.

HOW TO CAPTIVATE YOUR AUDIENCE

No matter how well of a package you have put together to develop your data story, if your audience does not get on board with your vision by finding that data helpful or fascinating, your call-to-action will be left unanswered. Luckily, there are a few techniques that you can use to up your chances of making that vital connection to keep your audience informed and decisive about the following steps to take.

The rest of this part includes nine key strategies for engaging your audience so that your data story is a fruitful one.

Focus on Connection Rather Than Making an Impression

Of course, you want to be seen as knowledgeable and authoritative as you deliver your data story to your audience. You want to make a great first and lasting impression. You want to wow these people. You want to be memorable. There is nothing wrong with such wants. However, they should not be your first priority.

Focusing on making a good impression with your audience makes your data story about you, when first and foremost, it should be about your audience and what they need to gain out of the presentation. Your audience needs to be changed in some way that is valuable to them by the time you say the last word of your data story. That change may be that they are now informed in a way that they were not before. It may be that they now understand the process of making a more informed decision in the future. It may be that they now understand data they did not previously. Any of these positive changes are aided by your hand, and so, your audience will develop a positive connection with you and your data story.

That should be your focus - building a positive connection rather than making a good impression. The best thing is that by prioritizing that connection, you up your chances of making that good impression.

Have a Strategic Plan

With all the bytes of data that you need to wade through to develop clear key points to deliver to your audience, sharing all that you know can seem more straightforward. That urge will be especially strong if your focus is to impress your audience with your knowledge. Your audience will not be impressed by data dumping. Instead, they are more inclined to feel overwhelmed and confused.

Avoid this by developing a strategy for turning all that data into key insights that develop the message you need to give to your audience. Think of the one thing that you want your audience to take away from your data story and develop a story and visuals to support that. Be as clear and as concise as possible as you do this. Everything that goes into your presentation needs to add to this core message. If it does not, remove it from your data story.

Bring Life to Your Data Story With Your Excitement

The first person who needs to feel enthused about your data story is you. If you are bored while thinking about it or while preparing the story, then the chances are that boredom will extend to your audience. You need to get fired up about your presentation to transfer that energy to your audience.

This excitement should not be faked, however. Your audience will feel that energy right away, and the effect will be the same. They will not be excited about your presentation any more than you are. Instead, add life to your story by infusing some of your personality through the use of your natural body language, facial expressions, changes in intonation and pace in your voice, and eye contact. Just remember to not go overboard with this. The personality type of your audience will dictate just how much of your personality you add to your data story. For example, a dry joke here and there will suffice with an analytical audience, while full-blown jokes may get to the heart of an expressive audience.

No matter the audience type, though, if you are rigidly delivering your presentation in a monotone voice and standing in the exact same position the entire time, you will lack the upbeat energy necessary for transferring excitement to your audience.

Use Stories to Make Your Data Story Unique

One sure way to add excitement to your data stories is to use your storytelling skills. The use of stories makes numbers and figures relatable. There is a time and place for hitting people with hard facts and figures. It is even appropriate at times during your data story. However, continually hitting your audience between the eyes with figures and hard facts will leave them lost. Soften the blow with stories. Not only do stories soften the blow, but they also make the data relatable, memorable, and more digestible to the audience.

Stories can come from anywhere that is appropriate to your data. They can be your personal experiences. They can be real-life examples that marry well with the data. Even jokes can be used to tell stories. Just remember to make these stories relevant to the data. An effective approach is to craft a story related to the data and convey it throughout the presentation to give context. People remember stories a lot better than they do numbers.

Use the Sandwich Approach to Highlight Key Insights

There will be a few key insights that support the main point of your data story. These insights are then supported by data points. Using such a structure allows you to know what is relevant to present to your audience.

A strategy called the Sandwich Approach promotes the stating of insight followed by delivering relevant data to support the insight. The insight is then repeated to reinforce that information. Think of the insight as the pieces of bread on the top and bottom of the sandwich and the data as the filling to complete the sandwich. The intended effect is to show the audience how the data is relevant to the keep points that they will be taking away from the data story.

I'll use an example to explain further how to utilize this tactic. Let's say you have some metrics you need to present that look like this:

- According to our metrics, our company's data growth will be 300% higher in 2022 than in 2018.
- Our data collection spending is expected to reach $50,000 in 2021.
- Only 2% of our companies data is being analyzed.
- Only 27% of our data projects have been labeled as "successful."
- 61% percent of our executives admit that we have a long way to go to use company data properly.

A clear insight would be:

Insight: We know that our data is growing rapidly, but the fact of the matter is we are not using it effectively.

Data: Data growth will be 300% higher in 2022 compared to 2018, reaching an estimated spend of $50,000 this year.

This being said, only 2% of our data is being analyzed, and that which is being analyzed is not necessarily helping our organization: Only 27% of our data projects have been labeled as "successful." while 61% percent of executives admit that we have a long way to go in using company data properly.

Insight: So, even though our data is growing, figuring out how to use it effectively will help us have the cutting edge in our industry.

Structuring your insights this way helps the audience to better understand what they need to know. The initial problem, some data to back up that point, and reiterating the initial takeaway/solution. Hence, "sandwiching" the data between two insights, so the data has an introduction and conclusion instead of an open end. The clarity of this method is far superior than a list of information.

Avoid Vague Generalizations

You need to be specific and concise when delivering figures and hard facts about your data. As mentioned earlier, there is a time and place to soften the impact of numbers and facts, but when you do indeed deliver them, do not be wishy-washy about the act. Deliver them so that impact is immediate and deliberate.

You might be worried about overwhelming your audience when you make these deliveries, but the way to avoid this is to ensure that you are not delivering fluff. Any information that you make part of your data story needs to earn its place there. It needs to contribute to the insights and ultimately to the core message of the presentation. Trim the data down to the minimum and deliver it comprehensively.

Spreadsheets... Don't Use Them in Your Data Story

Spreadsheets are beautiful things that help us compile, calculate, and track data. They are a necessary tool for making sense of the many many bytes of data created every day. As useful as spreadsheets are to you as a data analyst, they are not something you should deliver to your audience. Think of it as being the director of a movie. You do not show your audience the script or any of the other raw products used to make that movie. Rather, you present the final product, which will educate or entertain. The same analogy needs to apply to data storytelling.

Your job as the data storyteller is to use that information to design a final product that allows the audience to easily comprehend the relevant data which has already been compiled, calculated, and tracked.

Use Trends and Patterns

Imagine having thousands of small balls of all different colors sent at you simultaneously and being told to catch only blue ones in less than 1 minute. An overwhelming and impossible task, correct? This is essentially the situation that some data storytellers present their audience with.

Being presented with many small pieces to a whole and then being asked to put the pieces together is a formidable task, especially when they are millions of pieces. Your audience is coming to you to avoid this overwhelm, and the best way to facilitate that path of easy understanding is by compiling relevant pieces of data into trends and patterns. In essence, you will be putting all the blue balls together, all the green balls together, and so on.

Trends and patterns allow the audience to grasp how the data is developing over time and what predictions can be made for the future from the present and past data. This facilitates more informed decision-making.

Leave Your Audience With Practical Advice and Takeaways

As I said earlier, the mark of a good data storyteller is leaving the audience with a positive change by the end of a presentation. Do not leave this up to chance, though. Make it easy for your audience to know what you want them to take away from the data story so that they can start acting immediately to make good on your call to action. Give them a detailed outline of how they can use the information they gather from you to pave a better way forward.

HOW TO KNOW IF YOU HAVE GOT IT RIGHT WITH YOUR AUDIENCE

Unfortunately, there is no way of knowing whether or not you have hit the nail on the head with your audience until you are in the thick of things while presenting. This is why it is so important that you do the preliminary work necessary for gathering information about this audience and how best to approach them with your data. We've analyzed the data, we know what it means. It's now our job to persuade and guide our listeners to the proper business decisions.

Do not despair if you do not quite get it right with your audience. There is no such thing as a failed presentation. What there is are business professionals who fail to learn lessons when things do not go quite their way. Analyze how every presentation goes. Gather data about it. As much as I would love to tell you all there is to know about getting it right with your audience, a lot of it boils down to experience. You have to act and note the results from each experience. The more knowledge you gather under your belt, the more you will be able to fine-tune your skills to connect with your audience the next time and the time after that.

Now that we have identified our audience, we will know what information needs to be presented, and with that information, we can select the proper charts. Let's move on to that now.

3
REFINING YOUR VISUALS - CHOOSING THE RIGHT CHART

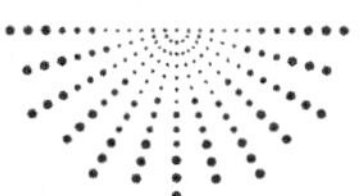

"Data visualization is the language of decision making. Good charts effectively convey information. Great charts enable, inform, and improve decision making."

— *DANTE VITAGLIANO*

So, you have done it. You have taken the time to develop your narrative and find out who exactly you're presenting to. With those two crucial steps out of the way, you now know what information must be presented.

However, no matter how grand your narrative is, there needs to be something that attracts your audience to the data that you have to present. Think of it like this, many people say that we should not judge a book by its cover. But guess what? Most of us do, as we rightly should because first impressions are often correct.

The charts that you choose represent what your audience's first impression will be. Those visuals will draw your audience in for a further examination of what this represents or what will turn them away. Your visualizations need to correlate with the type of data that you are presenting to that audience. It is what will make that data understandable and, therefore, engaging to your audience.

Because data visualizations are such a massive part of making the most impact on your audience, it only fits that those visuals have the spotlight in this chapter. Therefore, the coming pages will focus on the importance of balanced visuals that genuinely represent the narrative of your data story and why it is vital to choose the correct chart, and how to do so.

THE IMPORTANCE OF VISUAL REPRESENTATION

The sense of sight. It is one that we often take for granted, even though it is what we most heavily rely on—approximately 90% of the information that our brains process daily is provided via sight. Most of how we interpret and interact with the world around us results from what we see.

The process that happens from the time we see something to the brain processing what this visual means is called visual perception. It describes the process of the brain analyzing and then interpreting the information it gains from our sight. This process happens so quickly - in an average of only 13 milliseconds - that it is easy for us to discredit the importance that it plays in our daily lives.

Of course, visual perception is a vital process that has allowed the continuation of the human species. Still, it is also essential that you understand how this process can enhance your data story. The human brain processes visual information far faster than textual images - 60,000 times faster, in fact.

I am not just providing these statistics to enhance your mental muscles. I am providing these small tidbits of data to show you that the visual aspect of your data story can be processed far faster than any bit of text that you think to provide to your audience. The human brain is better acclimated to seek out and process visuals, so the many bytes of data can be conveyed to your audience better in this way.

Often pictures speak louder than words. When giving your presentation, you need a powerful visual representation that supports the strong narrative you should have developed beforehand. If you take the time and use the resources available to you to create appropriate and visually impactful charts, your visualizations should allow for:

More Information in Less Space

Here is a comparison for you. It takes an average of almost 2 minutes to read one page of a book. Your brain can visually perceive the same information in that text format in mere milliseconds if presented as a chart.

Higher Engagement Rates

Creating good data visualizations is the one aspect of a data story that you can use to ensure that you not only capture your human audience's attention but also hold onto it for more than 8 seconds. However, you do not only want to capture and hold your audience's attention. You want to also make them feel invested in that data story. This will increase the chances of the audience engaging you for more context to the information being shared. Good visualizations have the power to gain you that objective.

A Higher Rate of the Audience Performing the Call-To-Action Delivered at the End of Your Presentation

With the increased engagement rate that good visuals provide, there is a higher probability that the audience will act in a way that aligns with the call-to-action that you will provide in the climax to your data story. The fact is that the more visually stimulated we are by something, the more emotionally attached we will become to that thing. From that comes the higher likelihood we are to act on these emotions. Therefore, translating your data into appropriate visuals allows your audience to respond quicker to the action steps that you provide in your data story.

Allows for a More Everlasting Effect

It will do you no good if your story is forgotten the minute your audience steps outside the room. You need to ensure that your presentation was impactful enough to stick in their memory. Your data story needs to have a lasting effect that encourages your audience to follow through with the call-to-action and perhaps convince others to participate in fulfilling their call-to-action.

Attractive and informative data visualizations give you the power to stick in your audience's memory and thus, increase engagement.

CHOOSING THE RIGHT CHART

So we have established the value of having attractive, engaging charts in your data story. However, the question remains - how do you choose the correct chart to align with your narrative and allow the natural progression from the problem to be solved? The anxiety that this problem can induce is only compounded when this data story requires multiple charts. How do you keep your message from being lost in the noise of using the wrong charts? How do you use data visualizations to enhance the content you are presenting rather than take away from its value?

Luckily, you can avoid the anxiety of these questions by following the advice provided in this section.

Choosing the correct chart starts with examining the narrative you have developed and then asking yourself what type of data is being represented. You will most likely be dealing with data falling in one of these four categories:

- Comparison
- Composition
- Relationship
- Distribution

Each of these types of data is best showcased by certain types of charts. Therefore, we will break down what each data type means and the charts typically best suited to make that representation.

Comparison

This data type shows how one set of data compares to at least one other group of data. With this type of data, there may be multiple variables from different sets of data or various categories within one data set. For example, if the data you are presenting focuses on salary comparisons, diverse datasets may show salaries within different science communities. On the other hand, a college may show salary variables in the various departments.

Data comparison is often used in data stories because it is simple in concept and application yet allows powerful results. Data comparison provides for:

- Tracking how data changes over time
- Showing the differences and similarities between different sets of data
- Showing the differences between past and current data
- Showing the results before and after solutions and applications have been applied

When making comparisons about particular items in relation to different sets of data, some of the best charts to use include:

- Column charts
- Bar charts
- Tables

When comparison data shows the movement over time, some of the best charts to use include:

- Line charts
- Column charts
- Circular area charts

Composition

This type of data allows noting how part of a data set can compare to the whole data set. Data stories that show composition can be static or show change over time. Also, composition data may be expressed in absolute numbers or in relative forms such as percentages to show the variations of parts of the whole. Just like comparison data, composition data is a widely used type of data.

Examples of visualizations that can be used to show static composition include:

- Pie charts
- Waterfall charts
- Column charts

In the case of composition data that changes over time, commonly used charts include

- Column charts
- Area charts

Relationship

This type of data shows the connection between at least two variables in a given set of data. An example of a relationship with only two variables may be children's height relative to their age. Another data set exploring relationships with multiple variables includes website conversions from specific demographics such as age, gender, etc.

If someone just dumped a bunch of numbers on you, there is no way of finding the correlation between these numbers until they are grouped to show relationships. Good visualizations help determine these relationships.

Scatter plots and bubble charts are typically used to show relationships in presentations. Scatter plots are more commonly used when there are only two variables, while bubble charts are more commonly used when there are more than two variables.

Distribution

Useful in developing trends, this type of data shows how variables in a set of data or multiple steps of data are distributed over time. With trends, probabilities can be developed to offer predictions of possible outcomes based on historical information. For example, data from a swim club may show that swimmers in different height categories swim at different paces. This data can be used to make future predictions as to who might be the top competitors based on different swim categories. Column charts, line histograms, scatter plots, and 3D area charts commonly show distribution data.

WHILE THESE FOUR types of data are considered the pillars of data visualization, there are more techniques that you can use to determine what is the right visuals appropriate for your particular data story. This, of course, involves asking yourself a few questions. One of the commonalities that you might have noticed mentioned in the types of data outlined above is the number of variables in datasets. Therefore, one of the first questions you need to ask yourself is how many datasets are represented and how many variables are outlined in each data set.

Once that has been determined, you also need to question how many data points will be displayed for each variable chosen to be outlined in that chart, as well as you need to determine whether or not these data points will be plotted over a period of time or another variable that shows progression or grouping.

Once you have adequately established the data type and answered the questions above, you can determine the best visualizations for that data story.

TYPES OF CHARTS AND WHEN AND WHY TO USE THEM

There are tons and tons of different types of charts that can enhance the narrative of data stories. There is no way that we can delve into all of them, but we can look at those that are more widely used. You must understand the basics of charts and how and when you can use them before you dive into the use of more complex visuals.

While there was nothing wrong with leaning on more complex charts when it is warranted (remember that balance between problem complexity and visual complexity), there is no disputing the fact that clean, simply-put-together charts can most often get your point across more efficiently and effectively when supported by a good narrative compared to more complex visuals. Again, this is subjective to the data story that you are presenting. Still, you need to know what the foundational charts are, and how, why, and when to use them before you go onto the use of complex graphs.

Some of the foundational charts that every good data storytelling need to know how to use include:

BAR GRAPHS

This type of chart has a lot of aliases. It also goes by the name of a column chart. It is so named because it allows data visualizations where numeric values are featured in the form of bars. The levels of these bars are plotted on one axis while the values are plotted on the other axis. Each category of data is highlighted on one axis, and the length of that bar corresponds to the value on the other axis. Bar charts can make use of either vertical or horizontal bars. The categories are placed on the horizontal axis when vertical bars are used, and the opposite is true when horizontal bars are used. Vertical bars are the norm, but horizontal bars are good practice when working with long category labels. Whether you use vertical bars or horizontal bars, the thing you need to ensure is that you accurately label each axis.

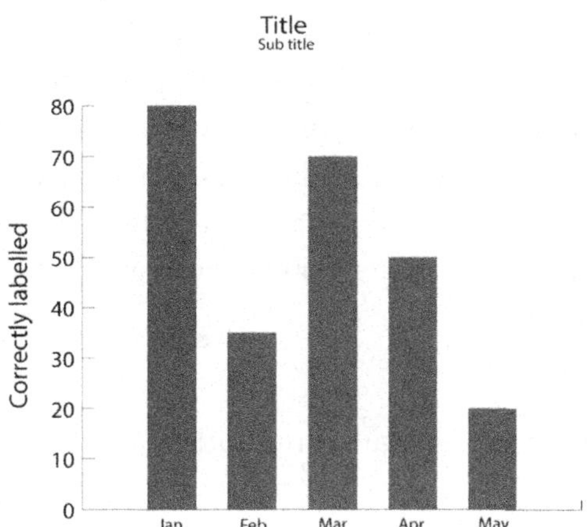

FIGURE 1 Bar graph

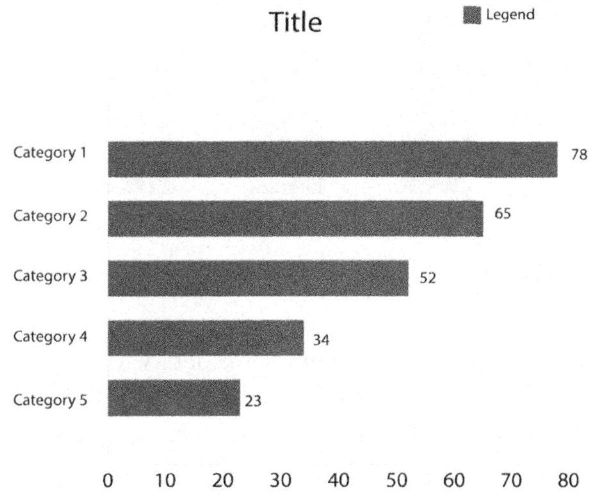

FIGURE 1.1 Horizontal bar graph

Another common type of bar chart is called the stacked bar chart. The name comes from the fact that individual bars are divided into sub-bars stacked on top of each other to show the correlation between different categories. For example, a marketing team may use a bar chart to compare their marketing budget from 2018-2020. The team will further break down each year in a stacked bar chart to show the budget allocation. The height of the bar will establish the total budget, and the bar will be divided into different sections showcasing the portion of the budget for that year.

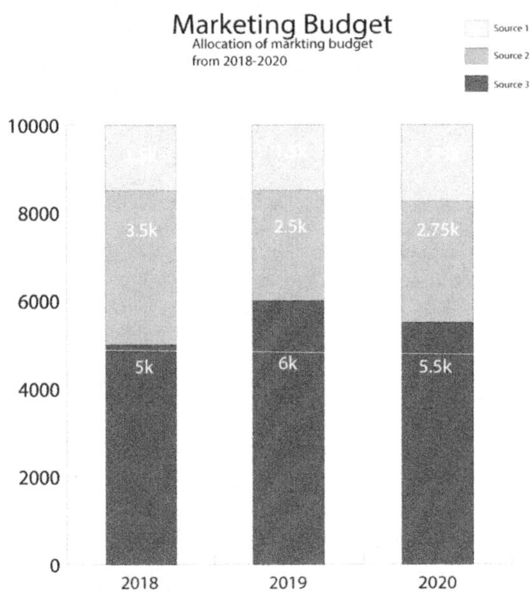

FIGURE 1.2 Stacked bar graph

Bar charts allow for the easy comparison of data variables, so bar charts are commonly used when comparing data types featured in a data story. However, bar charts are not just limited to show comparison data. They are also used to indicate the distribution of data points. So many data stories that showcase groups of highest or lowest, or most common to least common variables showcase bar charts.

To have the most impact when using bar charts in your presentation, there are a few rules that you should stick to. These rules include:

Consider Order of Values

Bar charts are commonly used to show comparisons and trends, and the standard conventionally is to place bar categories from longest to shortest. This allows the audience to interpret comparisons easily and to realize trends.

This rule is not hard set. If categories are inherently ordered in a specific way to serve a particular purpose, then that takes precedence over the longest to shortest ordering convention.

Use Rectangular Shapes

You might be tempted to get fancy when you are doing your bar charts but resist this temptation. Ensure that the shapes of your bar fit a rectangular form with straight edges. You might see rounded bar shapes used in some bar charts, but these types of bar charts can easily be misinterpreted as the audience will find it difficult to tell where the bar indicates the value on the axis.

Also, avoid using 3D bars, even if you might see these being more commonly used. Again, they make it difficult for the audience to interpret the bar's actual value and add unnecessary visual noise.

We will focus more on design in chapter 4.

PIE CHARTS

Pie charts are so commonly used in data visualization that some people might say that they are overused. We will delve into when it is appropriate to use pie charts and times when it is inappropriate. Also, we will look at how to determine what is proper and improper related to pie chart usage. However, before we get to that, let's look at pie charts and their value to data visualization.

Circular in nature, pie charts are data visualization tools that use slice sizes to depict parts of a whole or highlight the relationship between multiple datasets. Investors share percentage, for example.

The primary use of the pie charts is to compare the groups contained within one set of data. Suppose we reuse our investor share example from above. In that case, we can either develop one pie chart showcasing what percentage each investor owns. Or, we can create three separate pie charts to show each investors shares in relation to the whole. In this case, creating three different pie charts doesn't make all that much sense, and those two types of data cannot be compiled into the same pie chart as these data points would confuse your audience. Compilation is best done using bar charts.

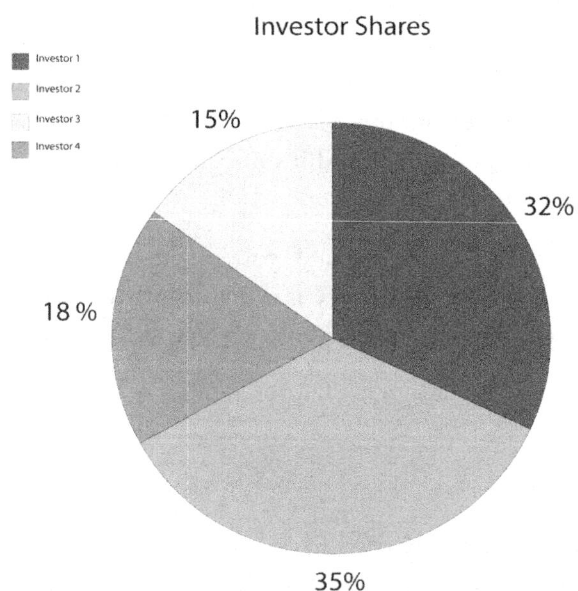

FIGURE 1.3 Non effective chart - Not the best option for this set of values as it is doesn't visually represent the data effectively or draw an easy conclusion.

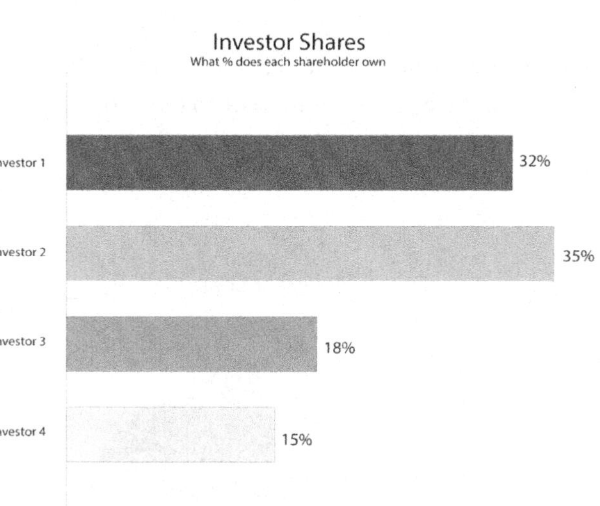

FIGURE 1.4 The more effective choice- A better option for this set of values as you can immediately distinguish who owns what % of shares in relation to each other.

Just as there are rules for creating the best bar charts possible when doing presentations, that also applies to the development of pie charts. Some of these rules include:

Use Annotations

It is often difficult to determine the exact proportion of each pie slice by sight alone. Do not burden your audience with the task of trying to make these determinations but using annotations. These annotations can take up the form of fractions, percentages, or whole numbers.

Use a Limited Number of Pie Slices

Can you imagine if you used a pie chart to present the budget allocation for an entire company? You would need a magnifying glass and lots of time on your hands to go over all that data. That is certainly not a task you want to give to your audience. Therefore, limiting the number of pie slices that make up your pie chart is essential. The use of five categories or less is the standard practice with pie charts. Creating a pie chart with more slices makes the visual look cluttered and hard to decipher. Coming back to our earlier example, if the values have a noticeable difference then it might work in your favor to use a pie chart. As you can easily distinguish who owns how much of the whole at a glance.

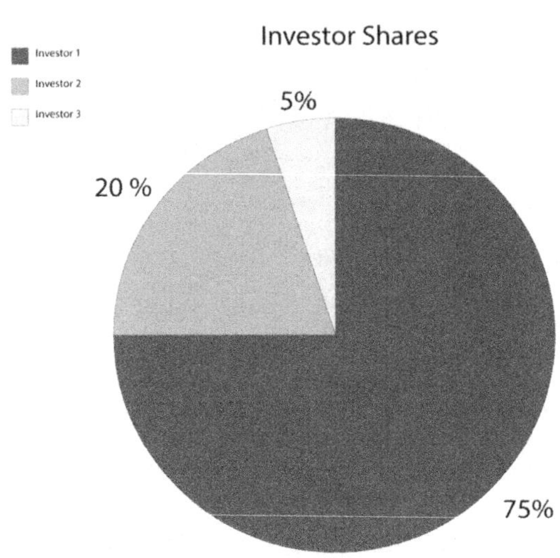

FIGURE 1.5 When to use a pie chart - If you have minimal values and can easily distinguish the parts of the whole, a pie chart may be an effective option.

Personally, if I need more than three or four categories, I'll switch to a bar chart. Pie charts are best used for a simple part of the whole analysis, nothing more. Even very few slices can aid confusion if the figures are similar to each other.

Order Your Pie Slice for Easy Reference

Like with bar charts, the order you choose to deliver your data can enhance the experience for your audience or detract from it. The standard practice is to order the slices from biggest to smallest. Also, just like with bar charts, that regular convention takes a backseat to inherent orders that allow for a better viewing experience.

Use Flat Shapes to Represent Pie Charts

The use of 3D shapes is becoming more and more popular in data visualization with the popularity of 3d modeling, but they leave too much room for misinterpretation. Avoid using anything apart from flat shapes that best show the proportion of data represented by a pie slice.

LINE GRAPHS

Also called a line chart or a line plot, a line graph is just what it sounds like. It is a type of data visualization that shows continuous progression using lines from left to right to show changes in value. This constant progress is shown on the chart's horizontal axis, while the vertical axis shows the value metrics that highlight that change. For example, a marketing agency might use a line chart to show how the website traffic from their top advertising campaigns for one of their clients has been distributed over the first 3 quarters going into Q4. The line will show the progression from January to September on the horizontal axis, while the vertical axis will show the metric value, which is the number of website visitors and how it differs throughout the first 3 quarter's. With this information they can see how their campaign performance is and note some possible projections going into Q4.

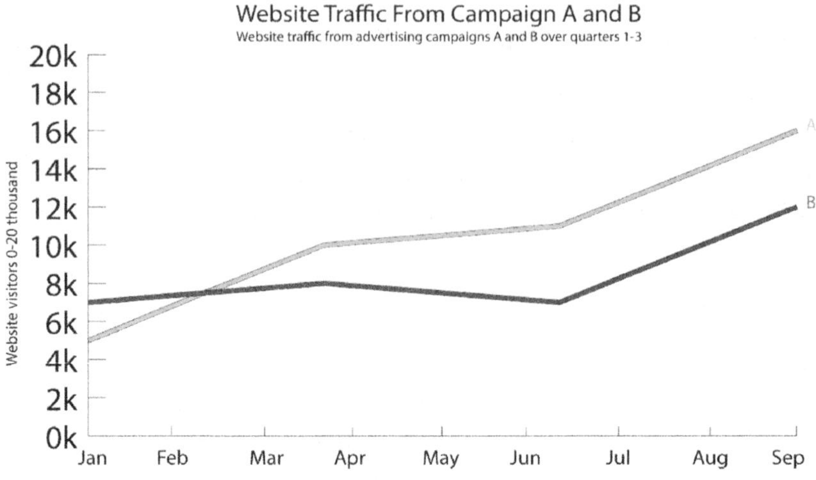

FIGURE 1.6 Comparison - An effective use of a line graph comparing the performance between campaign A and campaign B over the first three quarters.

Because of this structure, line charts are great for showing trends and distribution. To make the most out of the use of line charts, here are a few rules that you can stick to when creating them:

Choose Appropriate Measurement Intervals for Both the Horizontal and Vertical Axis

Also called a bin size, the proper interval between measurements plotted on both axes of a line chart is important for a quick and accurate interpretation of data. There is no strict science on how to choose an appropriate interval. Instead, this relies on your knowledge of the data and how best to translate it to the audience.

For example, if we go back to showing the website traffic for May, a daily interval on the horizontal axis is likely appropriate. On the other hand, this would be inappropriate for visitors over a year. Instead, a monthly interval would be more appropriate because it will be less tedious for your audience to read - 12 intervals rather than 365.

Limit the Use of Lines

More than one line can be used to show the progression on a line chart. For example, a marketing agency might have individual lines to show website visits, add to carts, or purchases over a year to track the conversions rates.

However, while multiple lines are great at highlighting certain pieces of data, too many lines can confuse your audience and lead to misinterpretation. As a rule of thumb, limit the number of lines used to 5 or less.

Limit the Use of Dual Axises

There are times when you will come across line charts with dual horizontal axes. For example, they may be used to show negative and positive values with the line progression. A company can use this to show an audience the periods when it makes a profit compared to when a loss was made over each month of one year.

While a dual-axis can enhance the understanding of your audience, this is typical in a point of confusion. Therefore, where it is possible to communicate the data without a dual-axis, do so even if it means using another chart type.

AREA CHARTS

A slightly more complicated chart is the area chat. What makes the area chart special is that it combines a bar chart and a line chart to show the progression of a variable compared to another set of data. This progression is usually demonstrated over intervals of time. The difference between a line chart and an area chart is the shading notable between the lines and the horizontal axis.

Area charts are typically used to show comparisons between multiple variables or how one set of data is divided into different proportions. Because of this, there are two main types of area charts.

The first one is called an overlapping area chart. This type of area chart shows the comparison between variables and different sets of data. This type of chart offers the standard line, but each point plotted on the vertical axis indicates the value for every variable in the different datasets. Each plot point has shading between the line and the horizontal axis. Of course, this shading can add a little panache to an area chart, but it shows the greatest value in each variable and differentiates each variable from the others. As a result, such a chart will typically be distinct as it has figures that look like mountain peaks. An example of an overlapping area chart could be monitoring website traffic during a product launch throughout the day from different sources.

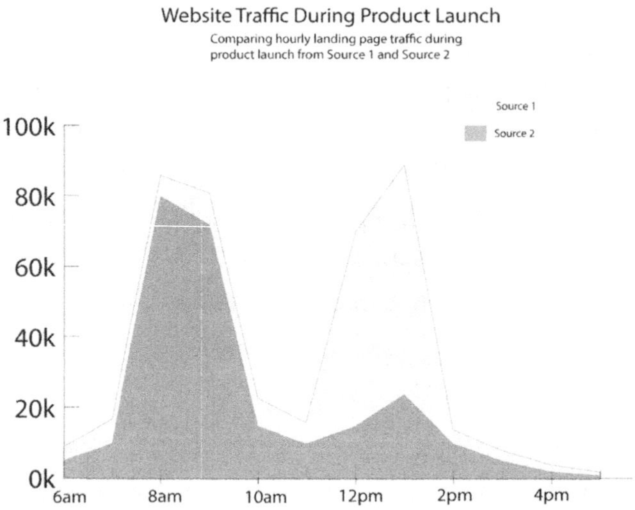

FIGURE 1.7 Comparing landing page traffic - Comparing website traffic from separate sources during a product launch. Can easily distinguish the better performing funnel to focus advertising on that specific source in the future.

While overlapping area charts are great for showing how different datasets correlate and are differentiated from each other, you should limit the number of data groups placed in one such chart. As a rule of thumb, limit the variables to three or less.

The second type of area chart is a stacked area chart, and it is used to show how individual categories of one set of data progress. Such a chart helps track a total value and break that one set of data down into separate categories. Such charts make use of multiple lines, and just like a stacked bar chart makes use of different colors to show subcategories, so does a stacked area chart.

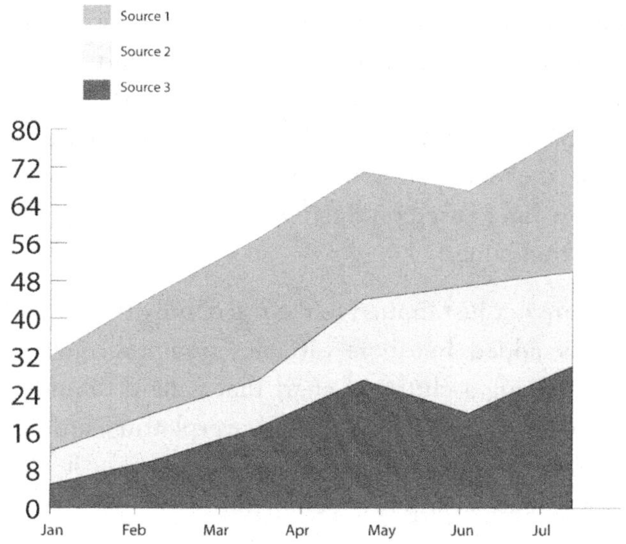

FIGURE 1.8 Stacked area chart - comparing trends over time while easily understanding each value amount.

An example of a stacked area chart would be an airport noting the number of persons entering the country and where each visitor is arriving from for the year.

SCATTER PLOTS

Mainly used to show the relationship between at least two variables, scatter plots use dots to represent values based on these variables and how they correlate in relation to one another. These points allow for reporting the relationship between two variables and show patterns in the distribution of that data.

The relationship between the plotted points can show various positive, linear, and strong patterns. Such a pattern shows the distribution of these dots in a line that has an upward trend. On the other hand, the distribution of dots may indicate no clear relationship between the two variables as these dots are plotted all over the chart. Of course, other relationships can be shown between these two extremes, such as one that is non-linear but still strong. To make the general trends that are developed by the plot points in this type of chart easy to spot, it is helpful to draw lines based on the distribution of those points. This line is known as a trend line.

Scatter plots are not just limited to the use of only two variables. A third variable can be added, but more variables are not recommended as this will lead to creating a cluttered chart that is hard to understand. The plotting of too many variables is called overplotting, and it is so-called because having too many variables and dots makes it challenging to understand the relationship between them.

As great as scatter plots are, there is one possible problem that you may run into when using them. While you can note the relationship between two variables, you cannot determine what causes this relationship based on the points plotted on a scatter plot. The counter to this limitation with this type of chart is that it invites further investigation.

Here are some examples of possible scatter plot outcomes:

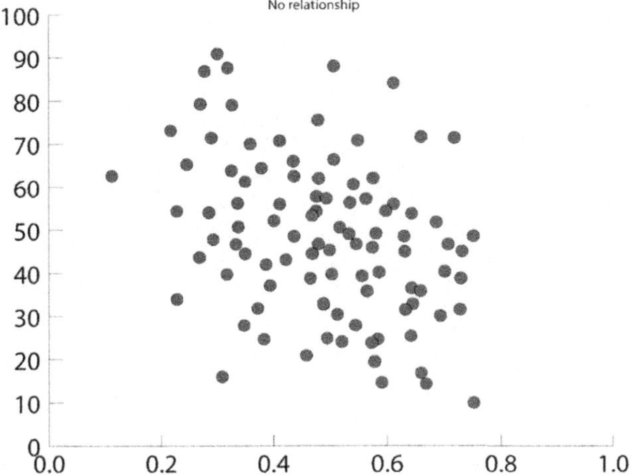

FIGURE 1.9 No relationship known.

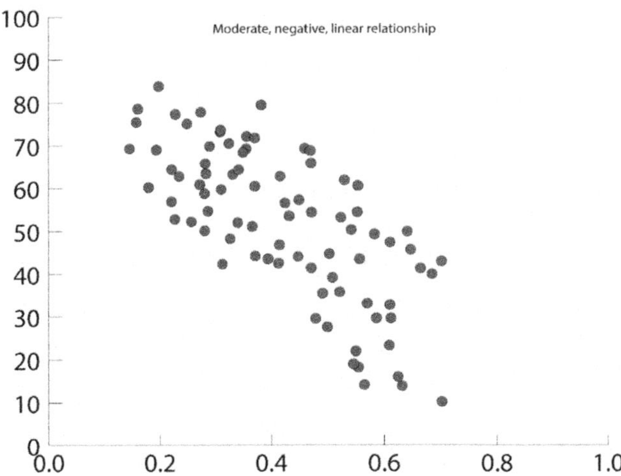

FIGURE 1.10 Moderate, negative, linear relationship.

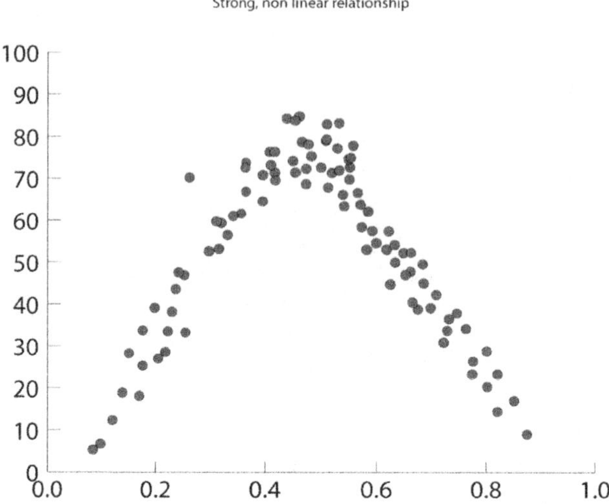

FIGURE 1.11 Strong, non linear relationship.

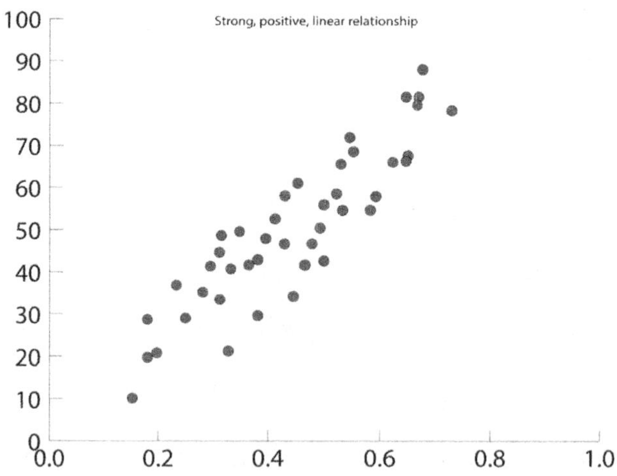

FIGURE 1.12 Strong, positive, linear relationship.

USING TABLES

At this point, I am sure that you might be wondering one thing - so, what about tables? Don't worry. I have not forgotten about them.

Tables are often the source of the data you will develop into visualizations throughout your career developing data stories. You might even find that they make good data visualizations when showcasing comparison, composition, and relationship data types. Especially when there are few variables or data points to be outlined to your audience.

Other times when it would be appropriate to use tables include:

- When the data cannot be easily represented in a visual format.
- When you need to showcase precise values to your audience or bring the audience's attention to unique datasets.
- When the data that needs to be communicated does not involve trends but is instead of a quantitative informative nature
- When the data involved has multiple units of measurement
- When making comparisons
- When you need to showcase individual values to your audience.
- When highlighting causes of the patterns shown in the data presented.
- When specific parameters need to be shown to highlight particular datasets.

Apart from that, charts are the best data visualizations to impress upon your audience the message contained within the data or when you want to highlight the relationship between datasets or groups within a dataset.

Of course, you are not limited to just the use of tables or just the use of charts. As long as the narrative of your story remains concise, use whatever visual properties you think will enhance your message.

WATERFALL CHART

A waterfall chart can be a great option for analytical purposes, especially for explaining and understanding the gradual transition in the value of something subjected to increment or decrement. A good example would be changing revenue or profit between two time periods. It essentially visualizes a running total as values are added or subtracted.

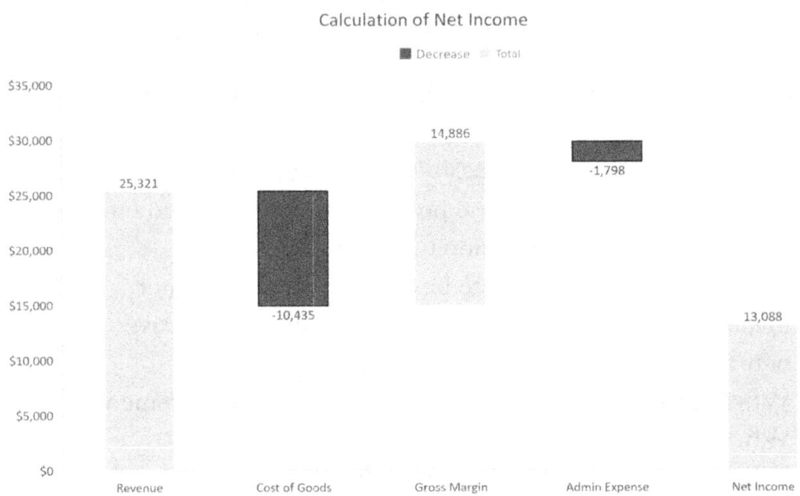

FIGURE 1.13- Waterfall chart calculating net income.

TREEMAP

Treemaps can be used when you want to visualize a part-to-whole relationship amongst a large number of categories. They are mainly used when direct comparisons between categories are not necessary. They allow for the quick perception of the items that are large contributors to each category.

Although treemaps are visually appealing, they can often be used when a different visualization might serve the data better. When encoding data with a large area and intensity of color, it can be hard for the audience to decipher minor differences. We should never make our audience do more work than necessary to understand a graph! Keep this in mind when using a treemap.

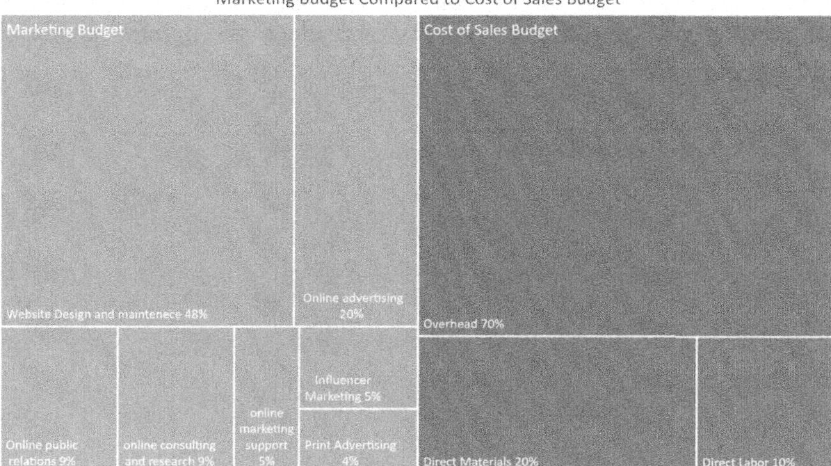

FIGURE 1.14- Treemap showcasing allocation of certain budgets.

FIGURE 1.15- Treemap showing parts of an operational budget.

HISTOGRAMS

Use histograms when you have continuous measurements and want to understand the distribution of values and look for outliers. These graphs take your continuous measurements and place them into ranges of values known as bins.

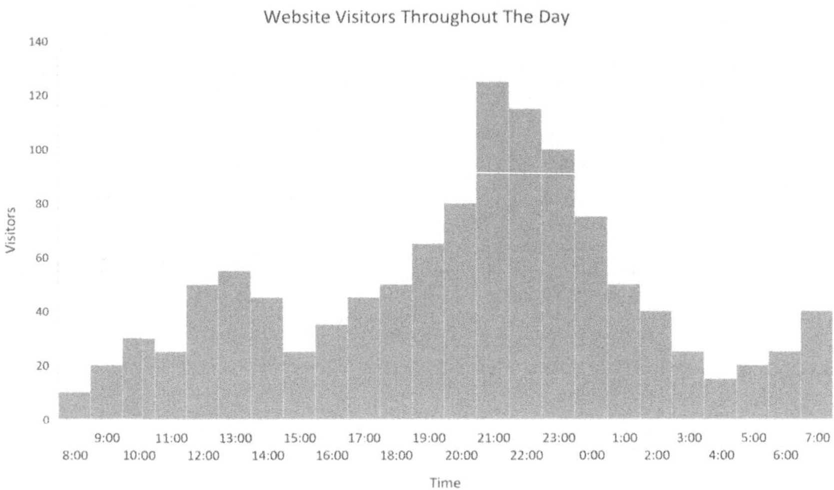

FIGURE 1.16- Histogram Showing website visitors over a 24 hour period.

FUNNEL CHART

Funnel charts are great for sequential data that moves through at least four stages.

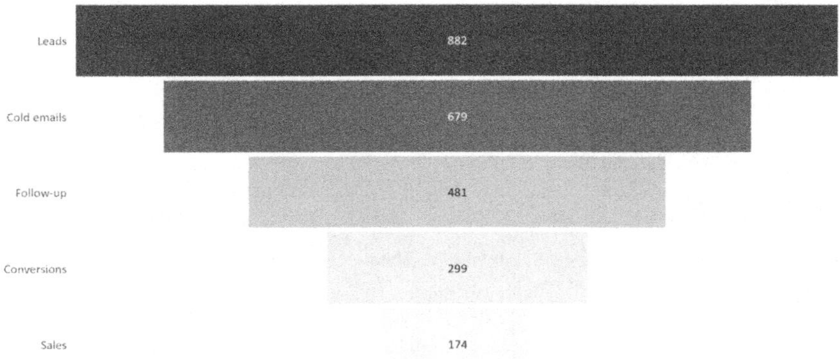

FIGURE 1.17- Funnel chart example.

How to Make Charts

Now that you have a better understanding of choosing the right charts to enhance your data story, you might run into *how* to create these charts. Although an in-depth guide will have to be saved for another book, I will point you in the right direction if you don't already have your tool of choice. Here are some top options:

- **Excel**

Excel is an industry-standard and my preferred method for creating visualizations. Data scientists working with code and more complex data sets might prefer programs like Tableau as it easily syncs with more extensive databases. But for many business situations, Excel is more than adequate. Excel might be straightforward for many business professionals, but i'll give you a quick rundown on creating and customizing charts with excel. Feel free to skip this if you're an Excel expert.

. . .

Simply highlight (Select) your data, then select the lightning bolt icon in the corner. You can hover over the desired charts to preview them.

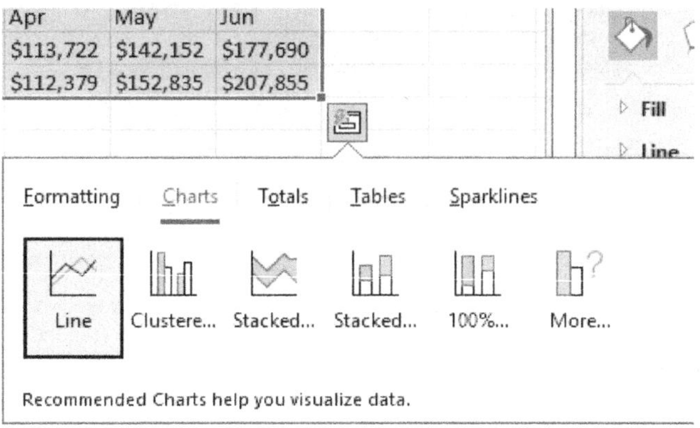

FIGURE 1.18

If you want to turn a set of data into a visualization easily, simply highlight your desired data, type ALT-F1, and it will auto-populate into a chart immediately.

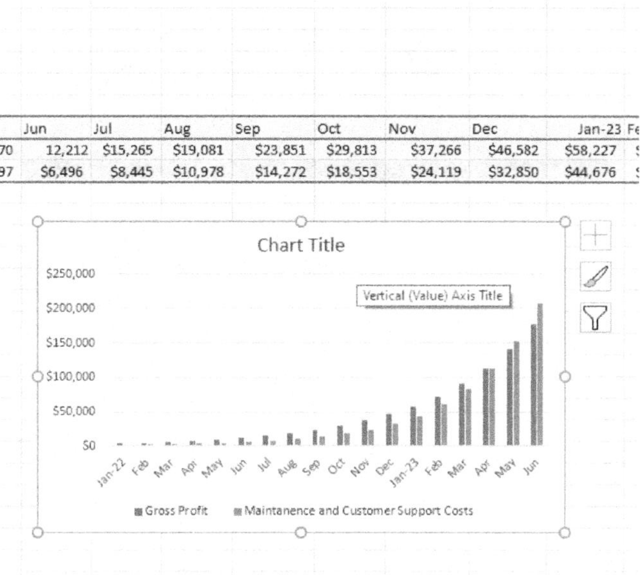

FIGURE 1.19

From there, under "Chart Design," you can select from many different chart types and design options to customize and make your own. You can also change the chart type by right-clicking on the middle of the chart.

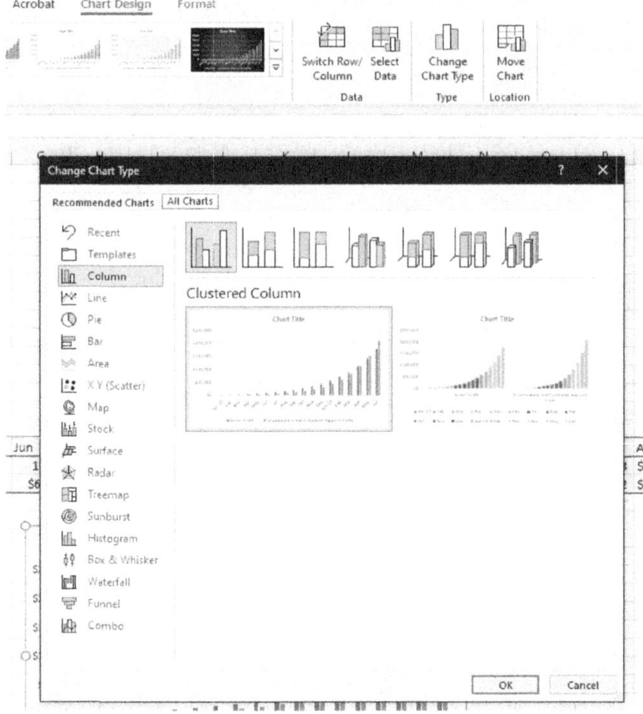

FIGURE 1.20

To add and customize data labels, titles, legend, or anything along these lines, simply use the "Add Chart Element" menu.

File
Home
Ins
Add Chart Element
Quick Layout
Axes
Axis Titles
Chart Title
Data Labels
Data Table
Error Bars
Gridlines
Legend
Lines
Trendline
Up/Down Bars

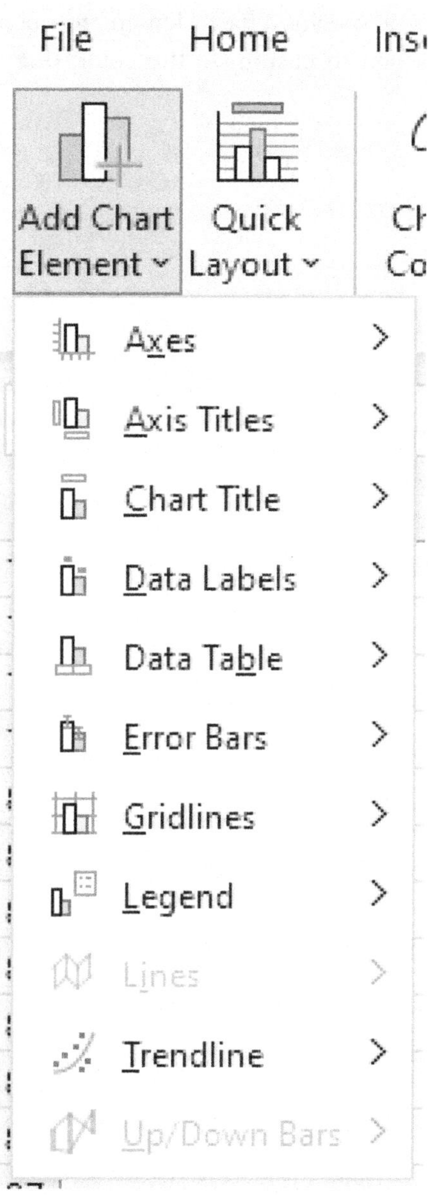

FIGURE 1.21

Double click on a specific chart element to open up the "format" menu. This allows you to customize the color, line weight, titles, and other details.

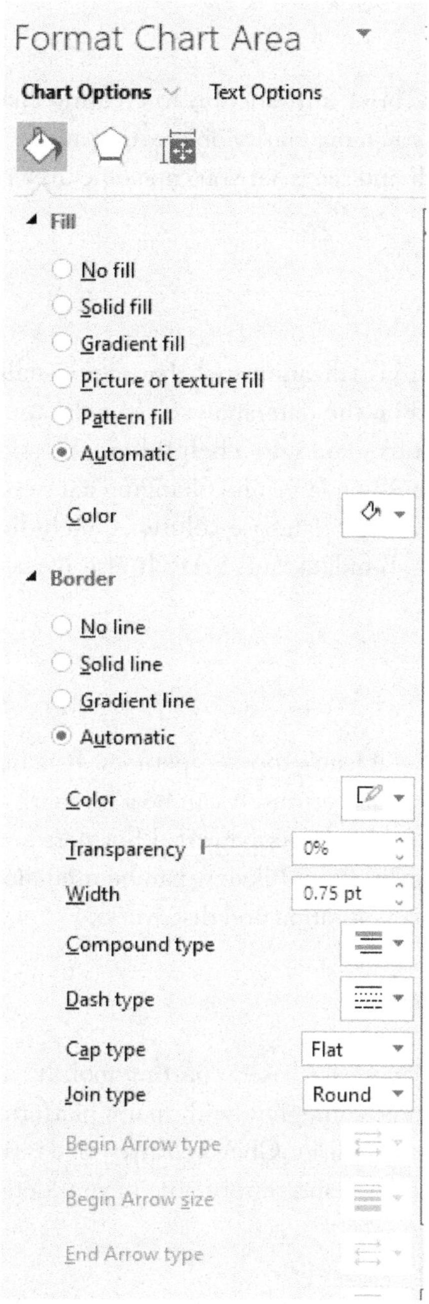

Format Chart Area

Chart Options Text Options

Fill

No fill
Solid fill
Gradient fill
Picture or texture fill
Pattern fill
Automatic

Color

Border

No line
Solid line
Gradient line
Automatic

Color
Transparency 0%
Width 0.75 pt
Compound type
Dash type
Cap type Flat
Join type Round
Begin Arrow type
Begin Arrow size
End Arrow type

FIGURE 1.23

That was a very brief introduction to creating charts through excel, and I hope it gives you more clarity on creating awesome visuals. Go and experiment yourself and see what you can come up with!

- **Tableau**

Tableau is a data visualization tool that can visualize data and get a clear opinion based on the data analysis. It is the top dog for visualization tools and can turn data into a helpful visualization very efficiently. It is proficient in handling large and changing datasets due to its integration with some advanced database solutions, including Amazon AWS, My SQL, Hadoop, Teradata, and SAP. It also has a very high level of security.

- **Qlikview**

Qlikview is one of Tableau's top competitors. It is highly customizable and has a wide range of features. It can be a bit more of a learning curve to get a feel for it. It also offers powerful business analytics and intelligence reporting capabilities. Qlikview can be used alongside Qlik Sense which handles data exploration and discovery.

- **FusionCharts**

FusionCharts is a javascript-based charting tool. It can prudence about 90 different chart types, integrate with many platforms, and has a lot of flexibility. What makes FusionCharts so attractive is that you can choose from many live templates and simply plug in your data sources.

It does not matter what tool you are using. What matters is that you follow the specific principles that allow your charts to be most effective when combined with the narrative of your data story. Therefore, I encourage you to explore and experiment with tools for chart creation to find the one that works best for you.

Now that we have gotten the basics of the visuals down, let's jump right into the next chapter, where we will define how you can refine your visuals for an even harder impact when presenting to your audience.

4
REFINING YOUR VISUALS - DEVELOPING A WINNING DESIGN

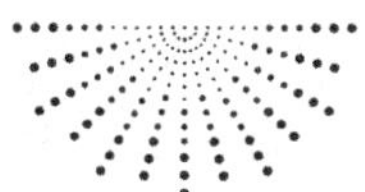

> "You can achieve simplicity in the design of effective charts, graphs, and tables by remembering three fundamental principles: restrain, reduce, emphasize."
>
> — *GARR REYNOLDS*

Having the right visualizations that enhance your narrative is a step in the right direction in hooking your audience before you even say a word. However, if these data visualizations aren't designed to appeal to the aesthetic this audience resonates with, all that effort beforehand would have been for nothing. Let's ensure that you are not wasting your time or your energy.

Always, and, I cannot stress this enough, always keep in mind that the data you are presenting is only as valuable as it is understandable to your audience. Deciding on the type of charts helpful in conveying your message is indeed an important one. Still, the work needs to be followed up, making it attractive and easy to digest mentally. With just one glance, you want to capture the attention of this audience. Remember how short the human attention span is currently. You need to make sure that this audience wants to learn more. Your aesthetic plays a vital role in developing that want. Therefore, while your chart might best represent the data, the audience can be pulled away from the message if the fonts interrupt the reading experiences, if the colors are too loud, or if the headings do not correspond with the delivered data.

With so many options when it comes to design, you can get caught up making the visual data pretty. But you must remember that the primary function of these visuals is to inform. The look must serve as a complement to that purpose. Even a visually unappealing chart that informs is better than a chart whose message gets lost in the quest to make the chart visually attractive.

Still, you want to hit your audience with a double whammy with charts that are both attractive and informative. You have taken care of the informative part with the development of the narrative and choosing the right type of charts. Next comes making decisions that make that data appealing to the eyes of the audience.

This part of this book focuses on how you can create clean and simple data visualizations that allow you to capture your audience's attention immediately. Only after you have hooked their attention can you deliver the key points precisely and with a resounding impact that increases the likelihood that your audience will be moved to act on your call-to-action. The winning design is free of clutter, has the proper use of color, is clean and precise, and is founded on design psychology. We will focus on each of these critical points and more now. Let's jump right in.

THE PSYCHOLOGY OF DESIGN

We have talked about visual perception and how it plays a part in how your audience perceives the data visualizations you deliver to them. Let's take a deeper look into how the brain relates what you see and how this plays a part in the success of your presentation.

There is a science as to why we find certain things visually appealing in comparison to others. That science extends to why your audience will be attracted to certain data visualizations instead of others, even when these charts display the same information.

Therefore, the first thing that needs to be addressed when developing a winning strategy for creating visuals that your audience wants to look at is not color schemes or font types. Instead, you need to delve into how humans mentally process images. Only then can you design and manipulate these mental pathways in your favor.

These mental pathways are known as artistic psychology. More precisely, it goes by the name of pre-attentive attributes. This is the process by which information catches a person's attention based on the visual images delivered to the brain so that the data delivered can be processed.

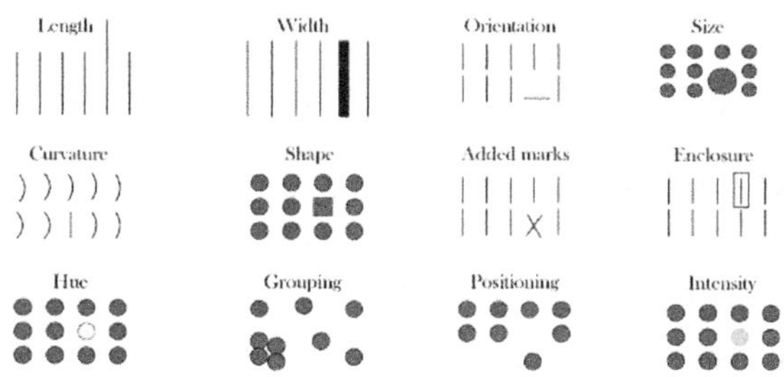

FIGURE 2- Pre-attentive attributes

Think of times that your eyes have been trained in a particular direction, but you do not remember a single time from that period of looking. This is because nothing during that time captures your attention visually. Therefore, the brain did not allocate resources to translate what that visual input might mean.

On the other hand, there are times when so much catches your attention visually that you do not know where to look next. That is pre-attentive attributes at work. That is the effect you want to stimulate when your audience looks at your graphs.

With the knowledge of pre-attentive attributes in your back pocket, you can design visuals that catch your audiences' attention. There are four qualities about an image that affect whether or not that image catches attention. These qualities are:

- Form
- Color
- Spatial position
- Movement

Let's take a look at what each of these elements means.

Movement refers to the use of flicker and motion elements related to images. A classic example of this is used in traffic lights. Banner ads also make frequent use of this element. These can, of course, be used in data visualizations; however, the use must be carefully weighed as it can be more distracting than aiding in capturing your audiences' attention. The audience may become captivated by the flickering effect rather than the information being relayed.

Spatial positioning speaks to the perception gained about an object's position relative to another object or one's self. It also refers to how a person might perceive that this object is turned relative to themselves. More specifically, does this person believe that the object is behind, in front of, left or right of, above, or below their person? 2D and 3D usage are examples of spatial positioning at work in data visualizations. The use of spatial positioning apart from 2D positioning can add depth to your data visualizations. Still, the use is not typically recommended because, just like flicker and motions usage, they can detract from the message rather than enhance it.

We will discuss color more in-depth later in this chapter. Let's take a deeper look at the element of form now.

Form refers to the structure of the elements that make up your visualizations. Therefore, this takes into account things like:

- Length

- Width
- Orientation
- Size
- Curvature
- Shape
- Added marks
- Enclosure
- Hue
- Grouping
- Positioning
- Intensity

...and more in relation to your chart. For example, the form would refer to the bars' height, width, degree of curvature, and hue in a bar chart. The wonderful thing about form is that it can help attract attention to certain parts of your data visualizations while detracting attention from other parts.

On the other hand, the improper use of form can make an element distracting. For example, if the tops of the bars in your bar charts are curved instead of straight, the audience may spend more time determining the actual value being represented instead of the connections you are trying to convey. You want to make it easy for your audience to extract information from your chart and move on swiftly. This will significantly increase your engagement and the incidence of the audience members being moved to the call-to-action.

The form also allows for creating uniformity in your charts. This makes for a straightforward interpretation of data as well as differentiation of differing elements. For example, each unit of a pie chart represents a certain percentage or fraction of the whole and allows for easier interpretation of the proportions of data being presented. Likewise, the height of each bar on a bar chart allows for that data to be mentally digested.

All of the qualities that contribute to the pre-attentive mental process do not happen on a conscious level. They are not things that you have to think that you have to process for them to happen. They just do, and it only takes fractions of milliseconds for human attention to be captured by such elements. Let's have a look at how we can use these to our advantage. As you can see in this horizontal bar chart there is valuable information, but someone seeing this chart for the first time won't necessarily understand the significance of it.

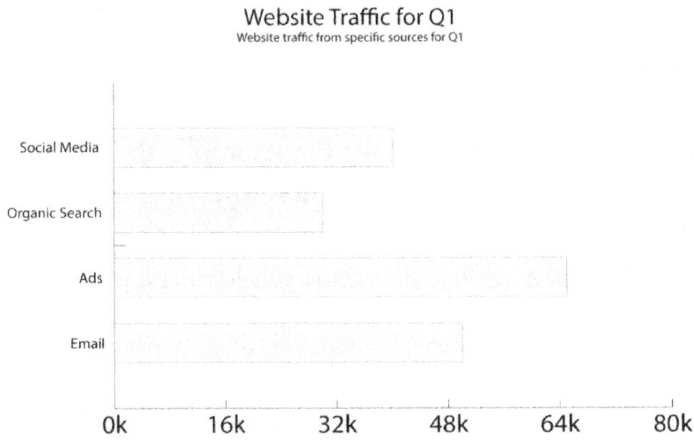

FIGURE 2.1 Not very memorable - Charted values with no known significance.

Rearranging the bars and highlighting specific information in green will better get your point across.

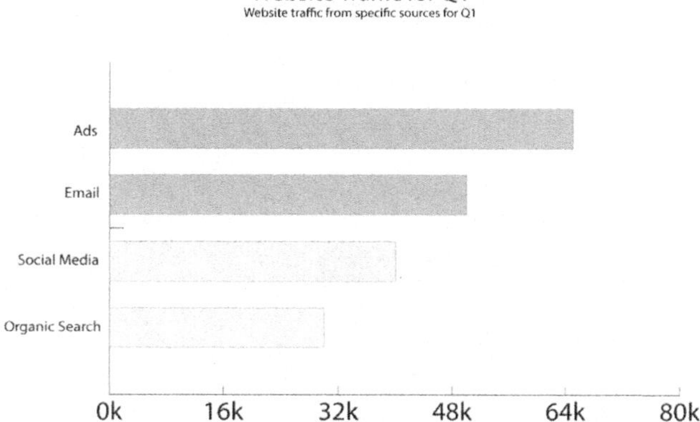

FIGURE 2.2 Use attributes to your advantage - Highlighting best performing sources in green to better understand the data. (Green tends to be a color representing something that is good)

The same can be done if you want to showcase the areas that didn't perform as well as expected.

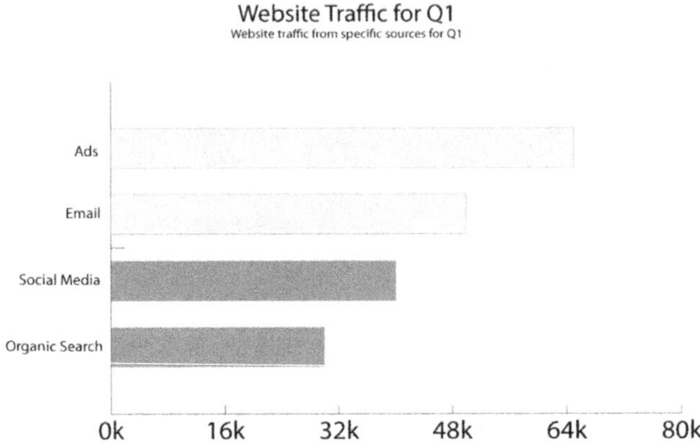

FIGURE 2.3 Using color to draw attention to specific values. (Use a color like red or yellow, these colors normally indicate something negative or slow.)

Adequately incorporating these elements into your data visualizations gets your audience's subconscious mind on board with the message you are trying to convey... once you do it the right way. Once performed well, though, incorporating these elements into the design of your data story allows for seamless interpretation of even the most complex data.

LET'S go back to the previous scenario we used in chapter 2 and have a look at another example.

FIGURE 2.4 Highlighting specific information like profit, cost, so it is easily distinguishable from the rest.

Although the other products' information is important, it is not what the audience wants. By initially showing them all of the products, then honing in on our main focus, they can easily distinguish the valuable information from the supporting information. We used similar tactics in the next visual.

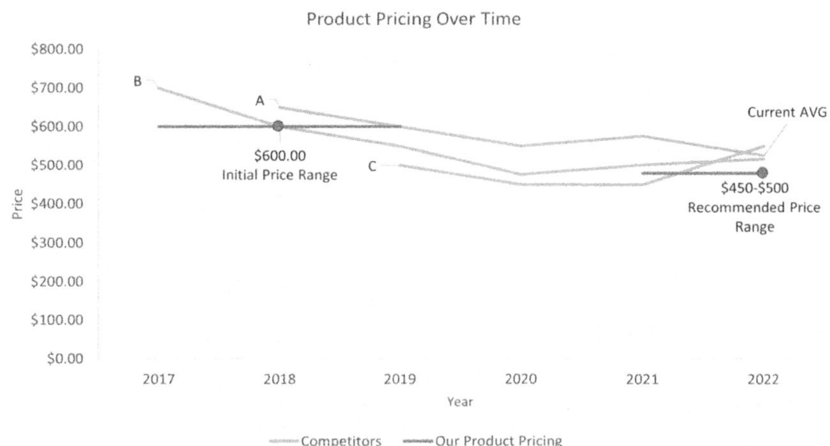

FIGURE 2.5 Utilizing color and text to signify our points.

As you see here, we want the competitors' data to support our validity, not undermine it. Adding our initial and recommended price point while showcasing the price range in a separate color emphasizes our point while showing the relevance to the competitors. Adding the "AVG" competitor price also helps reassure the reasoning for our price point.

At a glance, the audience can view all the valuable information without confusion.

The Gestalt Principles of Perception

Something worth familiarizing yourself with is the Gestalt Principles of Perception. At the Gestalt School of Psychology, they observed that humans naturally organize things in particular ways to try and make sense of it. The Gestalt theory emphasizes that the whole of anything is more significant than its parts. The theory consists of several principles that describe how we perceive visual information. They are:

Proximity: Objects close together are perceived as a group.

Proximity

FIGURE 2.6

Continuation: Objects that are aligned or in continuation of one and another are perceived as a group.

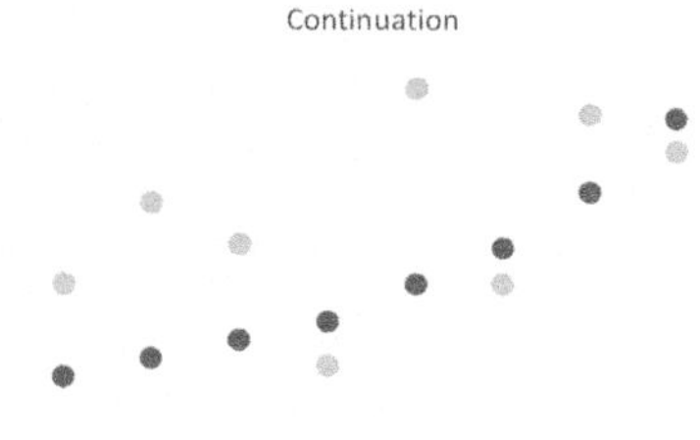

FIGURE 2.7

Similarity: Objects that share similar details such as color or shape are perceived as a group.

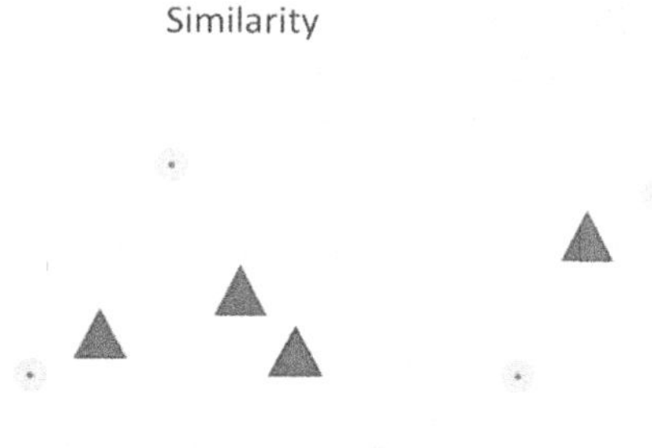

FIGURE 2.8

Connection: Objects connected (e.g., by a line) are perceived as a group.

FIGURE 2.9

Enclosure: Objects that have some sort of boundary enclosing them are perceived as a group.

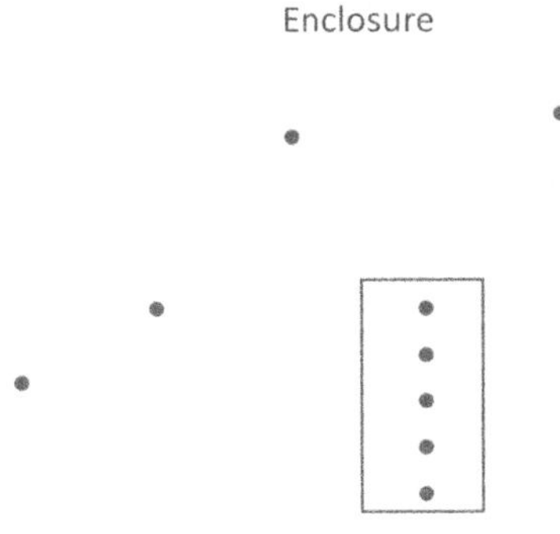

FIGURE 2.10

Closure: Our mind tends to add missing pieces of familiar shapes. When we are faced with objects that seem to be incomplete or open, we tend to perceive them as closed and complete. .(e.g., why a graph only needs an X and Y axis.)

FIGURE 2.11

The true purpose behind the Gestalt Principles is to understand how we perceive information. When applied correctly, we can deliver the information to our audience in the most effective way possible. Keep these principles in mind when creating data visualizations. Use these principles to highlight key insights in your visualizations.

COMMON MISTAKES MADE WHEN CREATING DATA VISUALIZATIONS

Often to get a good picture of how you should perform a task correctly, you need to know how *not* to perform that task. There are a few data visualizations mistakes that are common among business professionals. These mistakes can be off-putting to the audience and leave them with a bad taste in their mouth about that presentation. It might even leave them questioning the ethics of that analyst.

However, typically the data analyst does not make those mistakes out of malicious or destructive intent. They are simply honest mistakes born out of ignorance. You may find that even you have been guilty of making these same mistakes when utilizing data visualizations. If you are indeed guilty, note that this is not the end of the world, especially now that you are on a path to knowing better.

To set you on the right path, we will go over some of the top mistakes made when designing visualizations, how you can spot them, and how you can correct them.

Misleading Color Contrast

Color can add that special panache that your visuals need to convey accurate and adequate amounts of information to your audience when used correctly. The improper use of that color can lead to your audience being confused and deceived about what you are trying to convey with the information that you are presenting.

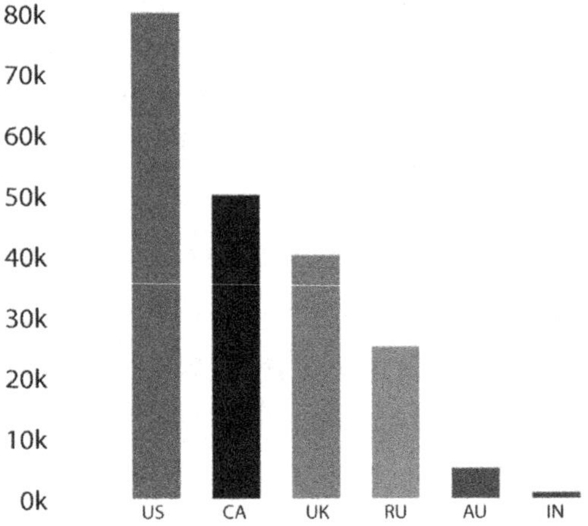

FIGURE 2.12 Unnecessary color - The use of color in this graph has no significance and may have your audience drawing conclusions that aren't warranted.

I chose to print the book in B+W to keep print costs down to ensure the book was as affordable as possible. If you would like the full-color PDF to view the visualizations as intended, sign up at ElizabethSClarke.com and respond to the first email. I will happily send you the full-color version. Thank you for your patience.

Color is not just used for purely aesthetic reasons, even though it can be pleasing to the eye. It is a persuasive element that shows degrees of contrast so that your audience notes disparities and differences in the information presented. If highlighting differences in values isn't necessary, avoid adding unnecessary colors.

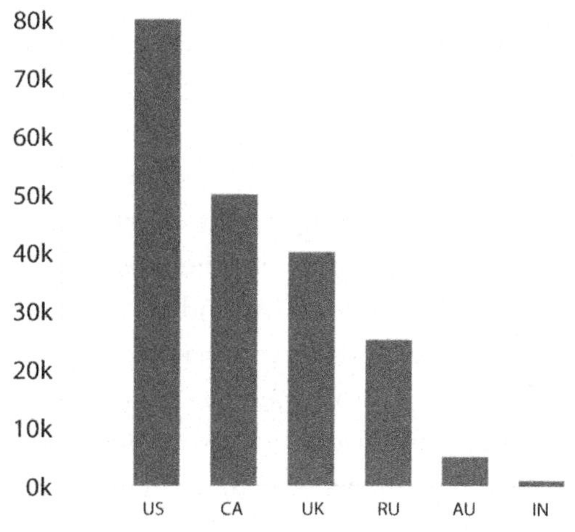

FIUGRE 2.13 Using color effectively - Keeping colors uniform and ordering graph appropriately will warrant a clear understanding of the data.

Highly contrasting color elements can cause the audience to believe that there is a greater degree of disparity than there really is. Therefore, it is best to use similar colors such as different shades of the same color for highlighting information with similarities and use higher levels of contrast like two completely different colors to show differences in the data presented.

Improper Use of 3D Graphics

Many data analysts are trying to adopt 3D data modeling but simply are not using it correctly. You should only use a 3D chart when a third dimension must be highlighted in your data story. While these graphics add visual interest, they do not always benefit the presentation. While data 3D graphics can be engaging, they can lead to confusion about the scale of differences and similarities between different datasets. They can also possibly obstruct how the audience perceives this data.

There is a simple way to avoid this potential mishap occurring in your presentation. Simply do not use 3D graphics unless there is a very good reason for doing so, which is the addition of dimensions that merely cannot be expressed effectively in 2D. The use of traditional 2D graphics eliminates these problems. The age-old saying of *don't fix it if it ain't broke* applies here.

Too Much Data

With so many bytes of data being produced about a business every single day, it can be challenging to determine what needs to be included in your presentations and visualizations and what does not need to be included. Being so close to your data, you may feel that every single byte of information is crucial to share to tell the entire story. However, too much information will simply overwhelm your audience. This overload of information makes the members of your audience zone out away from what you are trying to convey. This leads to less engagement and your call to action not being acted on.

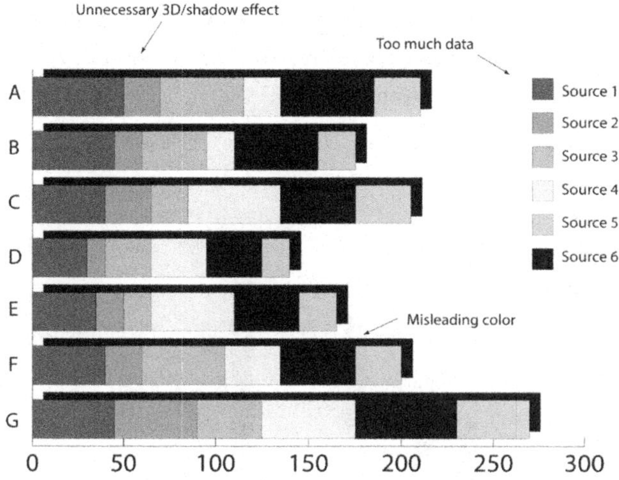

FIGURE 2.14 Too much data means clutter - Cluttering your graph with data and unnecessary elements will lead to confusion. Every element including the data must add significance to the graph so the viewer can easily understand what it is conveying.

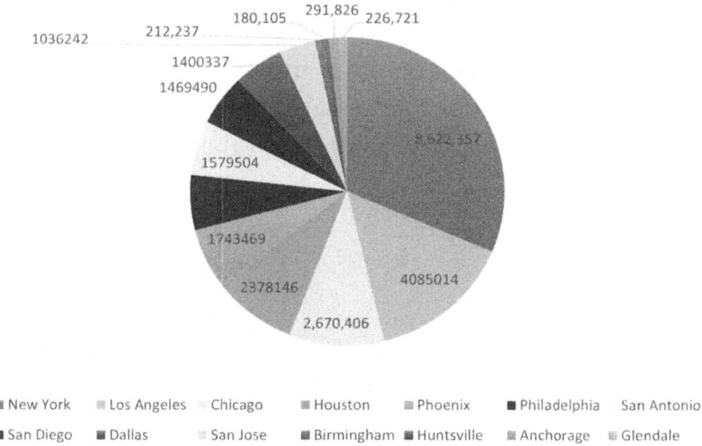

FIGURE 2.15 Another example of too much data.

The solution is to keep things as simple as possible. This means condensing the data into a limited number of visualizations or using multiple visualizations at different points in your presentation to present the audience with easier-to-digest information in smaller quantities. Lets have a look at another example:

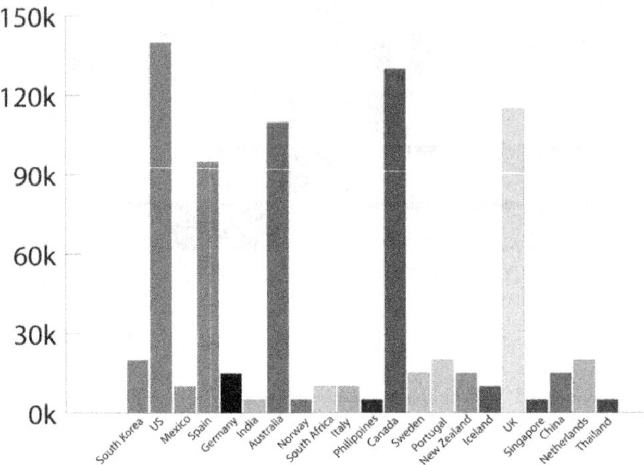

FIGURE 2.16 Overwhelming data - having too much data with no specific meaning will be confusing to most audiences.

When dealing with a data set similar to this one, try simplifying the data. Showcase the top five sets of values and mark the rest as "other". If your audience is needing more information about the "other" values you can create a few extra charts showcasing each specific point.

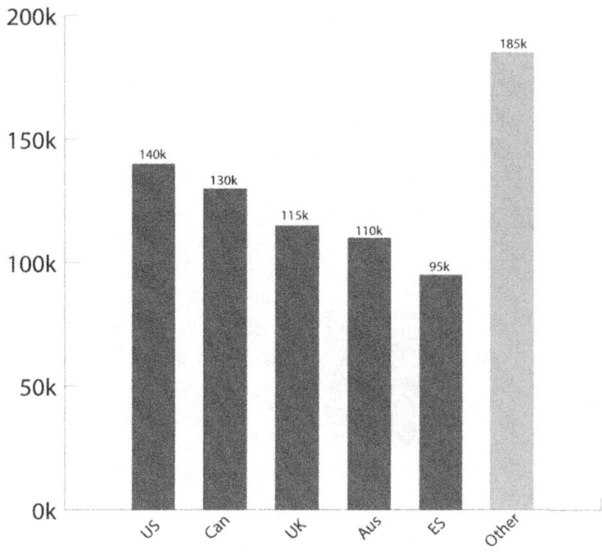

FIGURE 2.17 Simplifying the data - Simplify the data by showcasing the top five values in order. Expand upon any specific points or values if needed.

Omitting Baselines and Truncating Scale

To make data more digestible to the audience, some analysts choose to manipulate scales on charts. An example of this in action is to omit the baseline or start somewhere above the zero mark on the chart's Y-axis. This is typically done to make the differences in data more noticeable. Another example of this in action is replacing or shortening the X-axis value in datasets to be more comparable to lower values in that dataset.

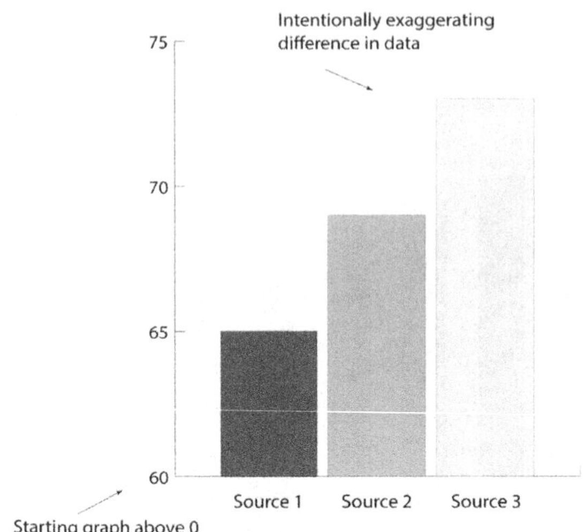

FIGURE 2.18 Starting graph above zero - Misleading your audience with an exaggerated scale may have viewers drawing conclusions that are inaccurate.

While these practices can indeed make it easier for some audiences to digest the data, they can also make it confusing and misleading to most. Essentially, these practices exaggerate or minimize the differences in datasets, which is unethical when presenting data to an audience. The solution here? Simply do not incorporate these practices in your data visualizations. Make sure to keep your visuals accurate and clear.

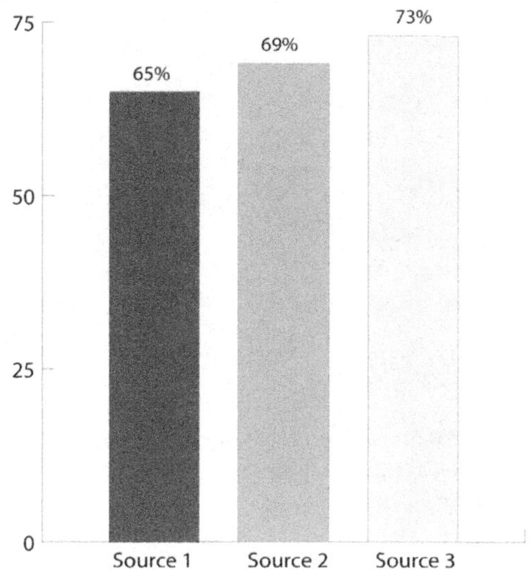

FIGURE 2.19 Proper scale - Compared to figure 2.17, you can see the values are closer to one another and do not warrant any serious action that figure 2.17 might have hinted to.

Choosing the Wrong Visualization Method

Choosing the right charts to support your presentation is not a game of eeny, meeny, miny, moe. There is an art and a science to this because data visualizations are not one size fits all. For example, using bar charts can make differences and similarities between different datasets more apparent. In contrast, when doing a simple parts of a whole analysis a pie chart might be well suited as long as you can easily distinguish the values.

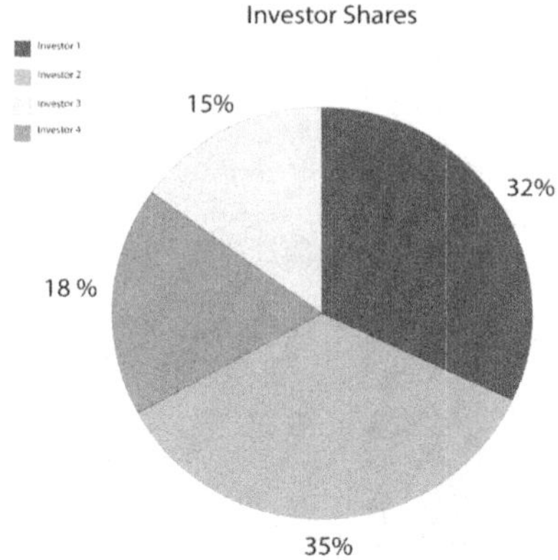

FIGURE 2.20 Not the best choice for this particular set of data. Your graph should enhance the meaning of the data, not make it more confusing.

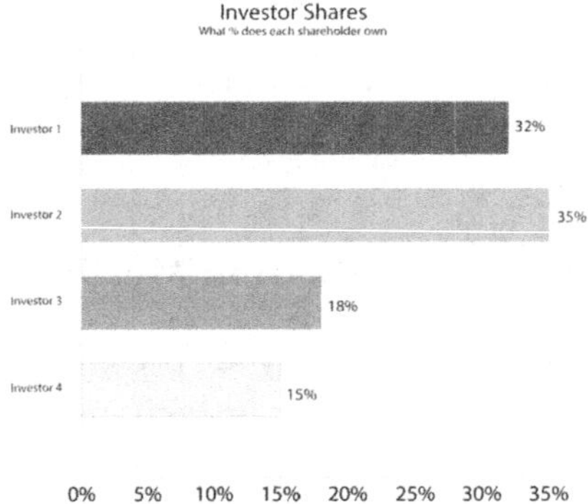

Figure 2.21 A better graph for this particular set of data.

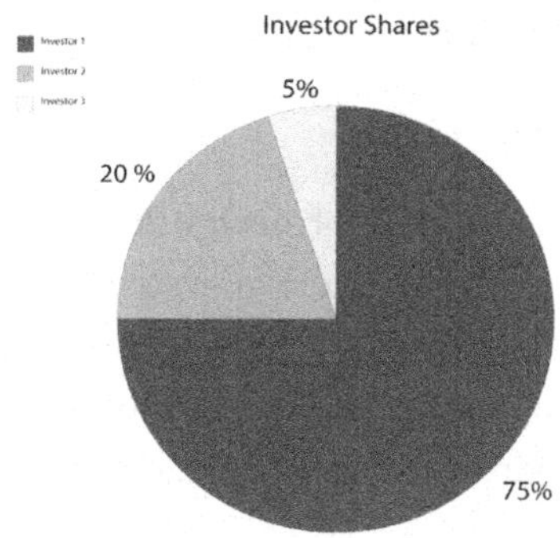

FIGURE 2.22 Using the proper chart allows for better interpretation of the data at first glance.

The type of data visualization you choose can get your audience on board with what you are trying to convey or make them more confused at first glance.

Avoiding that problem by taking the time to understand what your visuals must convey and then choosing the right charts to correlate with that ultimate vision.

Confusing Correlations

Using visuals to show correlations between different datasets is a helpful way of giving your audience a broader understanding of the data being presented. One of the best ways to show correlations is to overlay them in the same chart. However, having too many different datasets highlighted in one chart can lead to confusion. Instead of showing connections and inciting an "*aha*" moment, it can lead to the opposite effect, which is the "*huh?*" Moment. Too many data analysts try to use correlations to show the cause of what drives that data to be what it is. This will always fail because correlation is not synonymous with cause.

Instead of using what can be an unethical practice, it is better to use multiple visualizations to show how different datasets can be connected rather than overlaying them in a single chart. These multiple visualizations can still allow for that "*aha*" moment when the audience connects the relationships between different datasets.

Biased Text Descriptions

The inclusion of text is also part of designing your data visualizations. Just like everything else in the design process, the text needs to be considered carefully. All texts such as titles, captions, and labels need to support and provide an unbiased view of the data displayed in your charts. These texts are part of what persuades your audience to perform your call to action.

However, the problem lies in the fact that some business professionals use this text to manipulate how the audience perceives the data. This practice creates a bias towards a certain opinion or view. This is an unethical practice. Let's say you're visualizing The sales figures from Q1, showing a steady growth month over month. However, with this growth has come extra business costs, leaving profits smaller as revenue increases. Ignoring this important information may help you look good in the short term but will be detrimental in the long term. Our goal is to improve future trends and solve problems, not hide them. Don't focus solely on the good data. The bad can be just as important.

Cherry-picking Data

Cherry-picking data is when an analyst may only visualize specific data points to better support their narrative while leaving out crucial, contradictory evidence. For example, if sales are steady throughout Quarters 1-3, then dives Q4, they may only present quarters 1-3, claiming they are on a steady growth trajectory. In reality, the marketing methods working for them might need some adjusting due to the downturn.

DECLUTTERING YOUR DATA VISUALIZATIONS

Think about it. If you walk into a room with furniture, trash, all sorts of miss-matched pieces everywhere, you will be confused about what you should look at and how you should act in that room. This causes mental confusion. Most people are not able to be productive in a space that is cluttered like this.

The same analogy applies to your data visualizations. Data visualizations that are cluttered cause mental confusion, so your audience will not know where to look first or next. All that mental noise will cause most people to zone out and become less engaged with your presentation. Avoided that mental confusion by applying the apt saying, *less is more*.

Two different charts presenting the same data can have vastly different reactions because of the amount of information placed and how it is placed. Obviously, you want to be on the side of the fence where you present a good chart that is aesthetically pleasing and gives context to your audience. Lets look at a bad example, then figure out what we can do to redesign it:

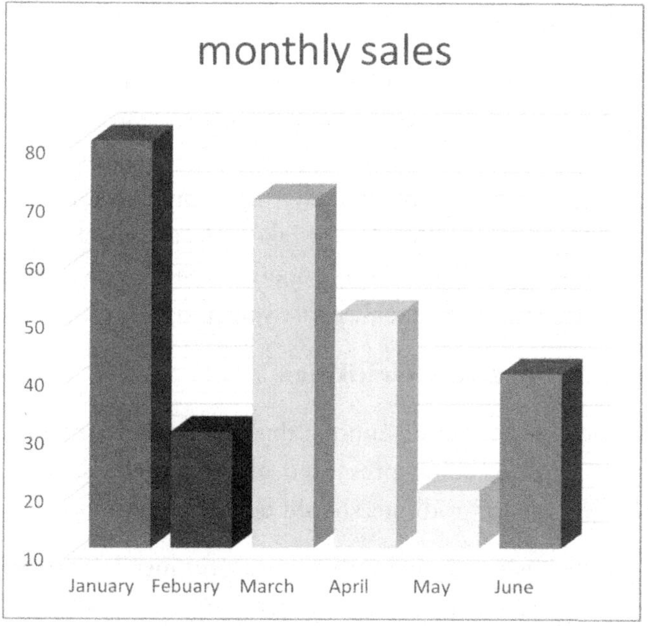

FIGURE 2.23 Example of a chart that needs a redesign

Start Your Bar Chart at Zero (0)

Think of the X and Y axis of your charts as the skeleton. Things will be skewed if you are missing bones from that skeleton. Zero is part of the makeup of the skeleton, and removing it will skew the look of that chart. Starting your chart above zero makes the bars of your chart misleading, and this skewed view will confuse your audience, and you would be representing the data inaccurately.

Ensure you have a "proper" decluttered chart by starting the origin as zero. Follow that up with ensuring that your axes are evenly scaled, placing uniformed spaces between the bars, and placing the bars in chronological order or in order of size.

Remove the Chart Border

Chart borders do not add information value to your visualizations. Often it is visually more appealing to watch white space rather than the clutter that these elements add.

Column Etiquette

As mentioned before, 3D charts can obstruct information and be misleading if they do not serve a very specific function. In addition, they can make charts harder to read and add clutter that is unnecessary to the presentation. 2D graphics are typically more suitable for effective data storytelling. Also, we should always take column width into account. Wide columns take away from the smooth visual flow we are going for. Consider medium/thinner stacks. Trust your judgment.

Steer Away from Dark Gridlines

Your charts need to be simple enough that the audience can note from a single glance what is being presented along each axis of your chart. Therefore, the need for gridlines should be zero or minimal.

The best practice is to eliminate the use of gridlines as they add unnecessary noise. In cases where they are necessary, use soft, grey gridlines instead of harsh, black gridlines.

Avoid Overuse of Bright, Bold Colors

Colors should be used to show similarities and differences and to provide context to your data story. Just as you should not use high color contrast to avoid misleading the audience, you need to also limit the amount of color you use. Bold, bright colors pull attention in several directions at once and make it hard to concentrate on specific elements of data visualizations.

Proper Use of Text

Ensure that the title properly describes the information given in the chart, and has the proper title case. The X and Y axis should be readable and easily understood. We will look deeper into text at the end of the chapter.

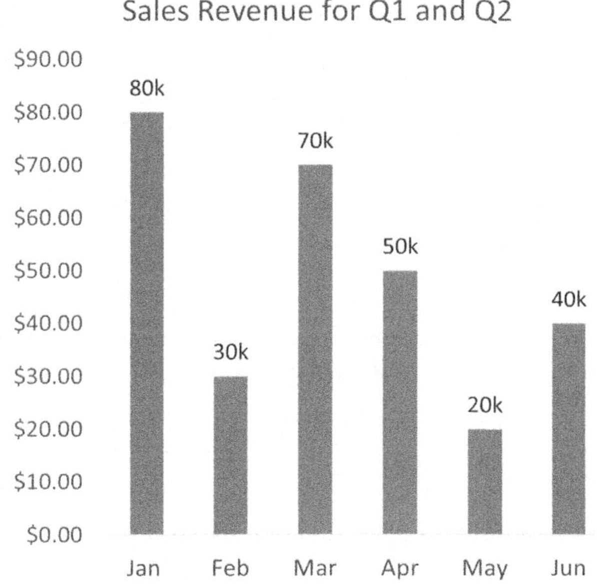

Figure 2.24 What it should look like - Bar graph with proper scale and removal of distracting elements such as gridlines, chart border, and unnecessary color. Clear and Descriptive title.

The best practice for using color is to use a single color and vary the shades to show similarities and differences or use a spectrum between two similar colors to show a range of data.

. . .

LET's walk through a full chart redesign together. How about we use our chart from chapter 2 and see how we got it to that point. This is where we started off after turning our data into an excel auto-populated chart. (You can do this by highlighting your data and selecting ALT-F1)

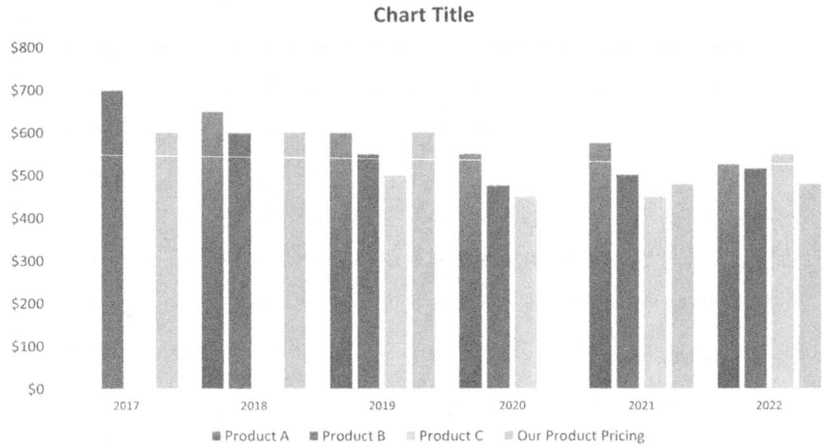

FIGURE 2.25 Confusing bar chart.

The first thing to decide is chart type. What would be best for this scenario? As you can see with the bar graph, It doesn't visually represent the data effectively. It's hard to distinguish the average price point without someone telling you what it is. We don't want that. Our main goal is for the audience to make the right conclusions independently through an effective visualization.

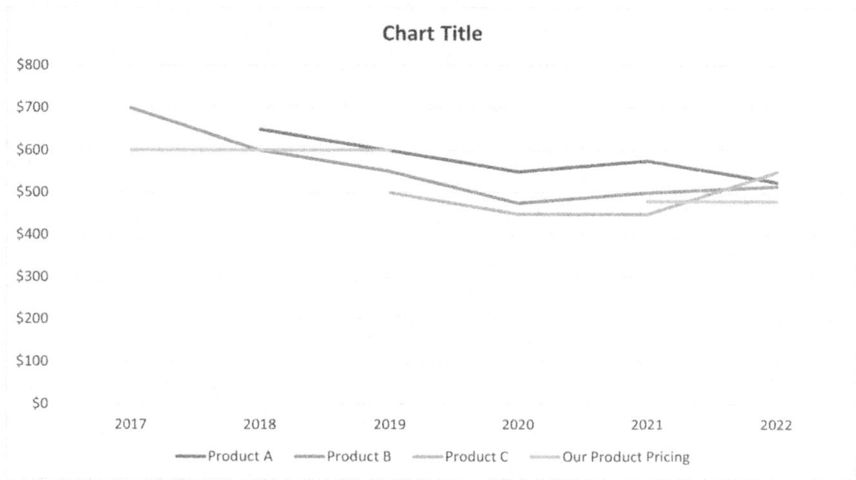

FIGURE 2.26 Line chart is better for recording trajectory over time.

A line graph is a lot more effective for this type of data as you can see determine the average without any information about it. There's still a lot to do before it becomes presentable.

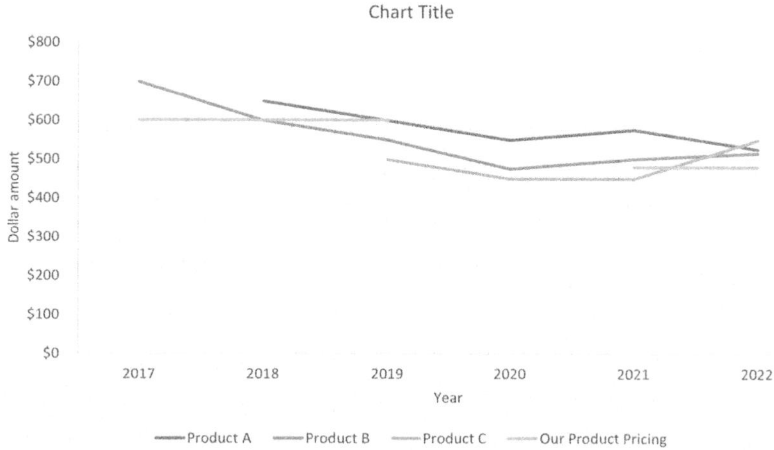

FIGURE 2.27 Adjusting text and lines

Let's start with the text and lines. A more subtle title and removal of gridlines looks very clean for this specific chart. I also removed the chart border to keep the visual flow. The legend has a few extra unnecessary elements, but we will get back to that. Let's do our axis labels. I kept it simple with "Dollar amount" and "Year" in this case.

That's all they need to know in terms of axis labels. The title is a bit more critical. Keeping it simple yet effective is what we should strive for.

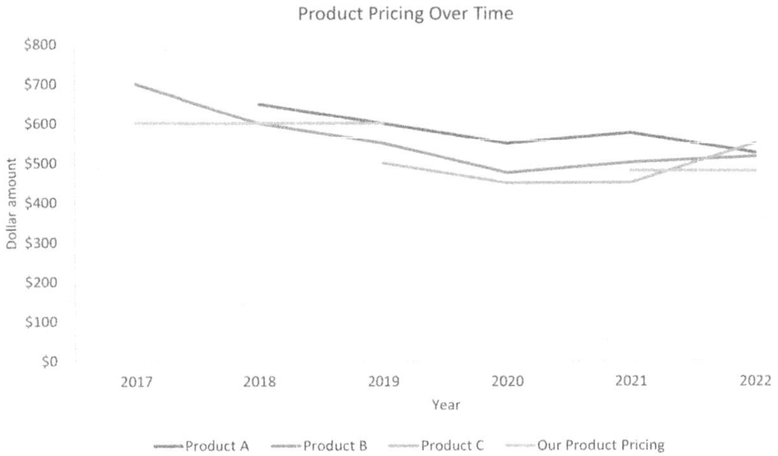

FIGURE 2.28

What exactly are we showing our audience? We shouldn't complicate it. In this scenario, "product pricing over time" should do the trick. We don't want them humming and hawing trying to understand the title and what's being presented to them. We want their eyes to go right to the relevant information available in the visual.

LET's address the color and legend. In this case, the competitors add valuable supporting information, to show the average product price and where we should be in relation. They don't need to be the star of the show. Let's make them all neutral and make our product something easy to see, and pleasant on the eyes. Let's also change the legend to be "competitors" to categorize them as one.

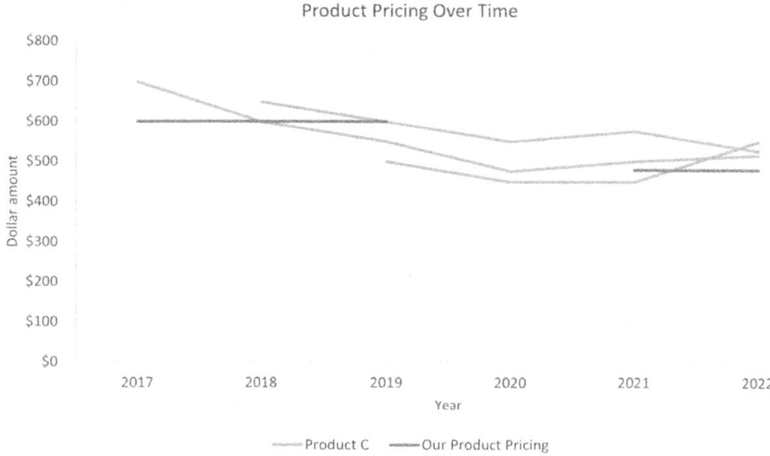

FIGURE 2.29

Now I THINK it's time to add some attributes to emphasize the main points. What exactly needs to be showcased?

1. What each line represents(Products)
2. What our initial price range was, what our new price range is, and why we changed it.
3. What the new average product price point is (so it's relatable to our price).

Let's add these. If you're using excel, these are called "Data Labels" and can be added by right-clicking middle of chart > Add data labels. Simply remove, reposition, and edit them as desired.

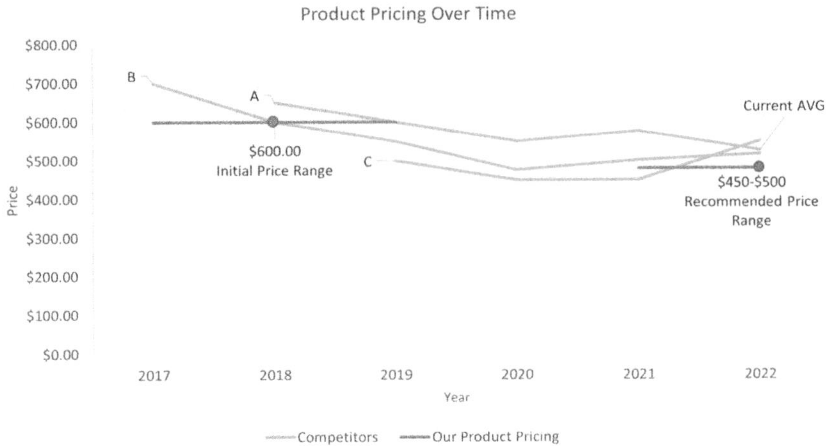

FIGURE 2.30

Here we have added our initial price point, the competitor average, and the new price point in relation to the competitors. Right away, you can see we are just below the competitors to remain competitive. Pair this with the "Product Profit Margins" chart from chapter 2, and you can easily show that we are the most competitive option while hitting our target for profitability.

USE the tips above to create charts that quiet the noise and steer your audience to the message you convey. Loud, cluttered charts tend to push audiences away rather than draw them in, but your data visualizations will be a lot more impactful if you apply the above principles to create clean concise charts.

Here is a quick tip if you are having trouble designing charts that stun - visit ElizabethSClarke.com or scan the QR and download my free data visualization checklist. This tool can be a game changer for new data analysts as you can adequately assess your charts to make sure all the elements are correctly executed and set up for success. Its absolutely free and a lot better than memorizing this whole section!

THE COLOR EXPERIENCE

A compelling data story is memorable and easy to digest. The same can be said about effective data visualization. Color is one element that makes it easier to achieve that memorability and easy digestion of information.

However, while color can add depth and dimension to your data visualization, it can also distract your audience from the information you were trying to convey. Unfortunately, most data storytellers have a distracted audience because of the improper use of color when designing data visualizations. That poor association is often the result of not understanding color theory and how to use color palettes when creating aesthetically pleasing yet informative visuals. You cannot just throw colors together and hope for the best. You have to be strategic about how, why, and when you use them.

We have touched on several aspects of color theory above. It is time to dive into how you can choose a color palette that compliments the intentions of your visualizations rather than distracts from it. While you can, of course, stick to one color in your charts, using a limited range of colors can add something unique to the same information. This range of colors is your color palette.

This range is not thrown together randomly, though, if you want that color to be effective. There are three color palette types that you can fall back on to make your charts pop in a good way, even if you do not have a design bone in your body. These types are:

Qualitative Palettes

With such a color palette, the colors used are distinctive. For example, if four colors are used in a line chart, they may be green, purple, orange, and yellow. Qualitative palettes are typically used when the variables are categorical and clearly different. For example, a line chart may be designed to show the unemployment rate in different countries over five years. Each line would represent a different country, which is a different category. This is distinct, and so each line would be colored differently.

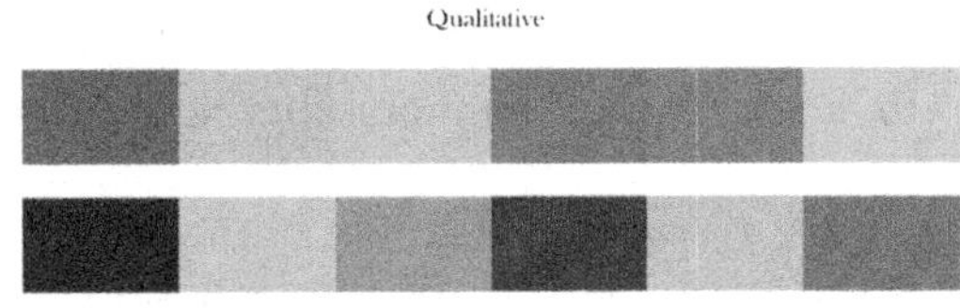

FIGURE 2.31 Qualitative color palette.

When using a qualitative color palette to design your chart, you may be tempted to go buck wild with the color input, but this is a temptation that you need to resist. Ideally, you should limit the number of colors used to 6. On the far end, you may go up to 10 colors but no further. The use of too many colors brings up the audience's inability to distinguish between the colors used as the chart becomes cluttered. This leaves far too much room for misinterpretation. If you find that your categories exceed ten total, the alternative is to bundle similar categories together or bundle categories with smaller values together and label this as "other."

Here are a few rules to stick by when using a qualitative color palette to design your charts:

- Ensure that the colors are used to complement each other so that the chart remains visually appealing.
- Ensure that different categories are distinct by ensuring different colors are used. This can be done by adjusting color saturation and lightness.
- Ensure that the color differences are not too significant, as this can lead the audience into thinking that some categories carry more importance than others.
- Do not use the same colors more than once, unless the categories have a relationship of some kind and a similar hue can be used.

Sequential Palettes

This type of color palette makes use of color by adding variations with different saturation. For example, there may be six variations that need to be presented on a chart. The color used on this chart to show these data variations is pink. Each of these variations will have its value represented by a different shade of pink.

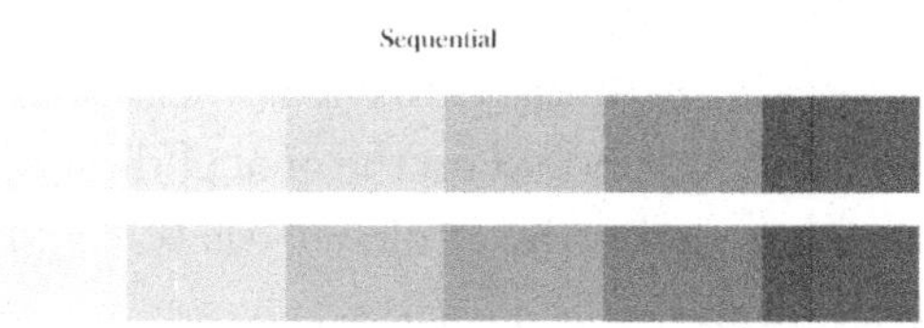

FIGURE 2.32 Sequential color palette.

Sequential color palettes are typically used when the variable values are numeric or ordered. For example, a chart showing wage changes in different companies over the four quarters of a year may be designed with a sequential palette. On the other hand, a diagram showing the percentage variables of a whole may also use a sequential palette.

Here are a few tips for gaining the most value when using a sequential color palette when designing your charts:

- Use lighter colors to depict lower values and darker shades to depict higher values when your chart is plotted on a white or light-colored background. Plot the variations from lighter to darker.
- Use darker colors to depict lower values and lighter colors to depict higher values when your chart is plotted on a dark background. Plot the variations from darker to lighter.
- More than one color may be used as well. This is done by also playing with the saturation of the colors used. For example, a chart may show the increasing temperature in a region by designing a chart that moves from a color hue like shades of blue to a warmer hue like shades of yellow and, finally, a hotter hue like shades red.
- The visual designer can use a discrete or continuous color gradient when plotting the values with this color palette. A discrete palette is one where there is a clear distinction between the color saturations. Discrete color palettes may even make use of text-like number values to highlight that distinction. On the other hand, with continuous palettes, the saturation appears to merge into each other. The use of either type of palette is dependent on the goal of the visual designer. A discrete palette helps the audience easily digest the data. So, this is great for times when there is a greater range of data. Discrete palettes are also great for use when the variable ranges are vastly unequal in size. Continuous palettes are better when the varying ranges are relatively equal in size and when the range of data is shorter.

Diverging Palettes

When plotting variables with a central value like zero, divergent palettes are typically the go-to color palette. Two different sequential palettes are combined to show the movement of values. Values on either side of that central value are assigned a different color gradient. One of the most common situations where divergent color palettes are used is when negative and positive values are highlighted in one chart. The same rules for designing when using a sequential palette apply when creating charts with diverging palettes.

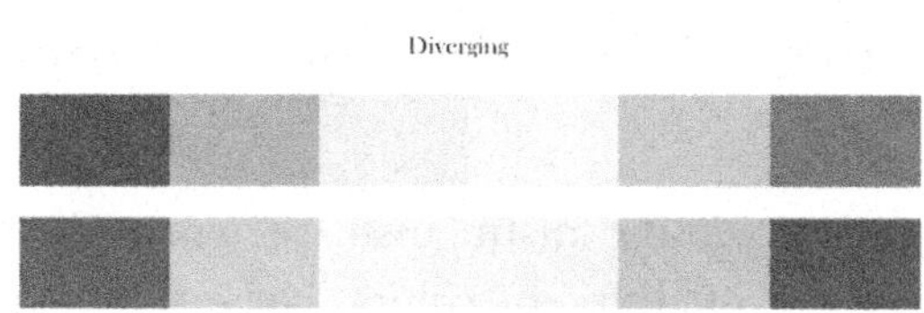

FIGURE 2.33 Diverging color palette.

The data color picker by Learn UI Design is an excellent tool to help you pick sequential and diverging palettes. Check it out here: https://learnui.design/tools/data-color-picker.html

BEST PRACTICES WHEN USING COLOR

In addition to keeping in mind the type of palette you use, here are a few tips for ensuring that your charts remain visually appealing to your audience.

Use Colors to Create Associations

Human beings have particular associations with color. For example, we see red and think stop or danger. Likewise, green is typically associated with nature and safety. These color associations invoke certain emotions within us. You can use these associations when designing your data visual to your advantage. Keep such associations in mind when you pick color palettes. For example, you may be presenting a data story to people from a certain university. When designing your visualizations, using their university flag colors can immediately invoke camaraderie in the audience and make them more receptive to your message.

Use a Single Color to Show Continuous Data

In situations where it is not permitted that your audience knows exact figures but rather that they recognize a trend, the use of continuous sequential and diverging palettes may be best. This allows the audience to grasp the trend quickly, whether increasing, decreasing, or unchanging so that you can link other information to that movement.

Use Contrasting Colors to Show Comparison and Contrast

Help your audience easily distinguish between datasets that are different with the use of different colors. For example, a social media analysis can easily distinguish the conversion rate of using organic traffic versus ads on Facebook with the help of the metrics being colored green and blue. On the other hand, if both metrics were colored the same, it would be harder to determine this at a single glance.

Use Color to Highlight Important Information

If you want your audience to focus on a particular piece of information, use a brighter color or a higher saturation of the single color used for that data set. This makes the information stand out from the rest. You can also choose to only color that set of information and leave the rest, less pertinent information, colored grey.

Do Not Pick Colors that Easily Merge Into Each Other

Once your audience starts to squint at your chart, you have failed to make the information easy to interpret with a glance. Avoid this situation by making the colors used when designing your chart easy to distinguish from each other. For example, if you are designing a line chart, using different shades of one color will incite that squinting effect. On the other hand, using a qualitative palette will allow for easier interpretation of the separate data trends with one look.

Keep Your Color Count at a Minimum

The colors of the rainbow are at your disposal when you design your charts. That does not mean that you should pick every color to infuse into your chart design. Make the colors relevant and also keep the color count down to avoid clutter. The maximum number of colors used should be kept at six. Any more and you risk your audience becoming overwhelmed and unable to interpret the information easily. If necessary, try and separate the data into two visuals.

Account for Accessibility

Color vision deficiencies are more prominent than most people realize. Some people can distinguish between separate colors. For example, orange and purple may look the same to some people. This is called color blindness. It is more common than you would think. Approximately once in twelve men are color blind. As a data storyteller, you need to account that some of your audience may suffer from such difficulties, and you need to cater to them as well. Be sure to research whether anyone in your audience faces visual challenges so that you can factor that into the development of your color palette. Sometimes, this information is not easy to source, so consider simply just designing every chart with this in mind.

THE PROPER USE OF TEXT

A problem that many new analysts run into is that they feel the need to explain every part of the data visualizations with the inclusion of excessive amounts of text. The thing that you do not realize to avoid repeating this mistake is that the data visualizations need to be strong enough to speak for themselves with a minimal amount of text.

When text is included, it needs to be done in a clean, concise manner that does not include lengthy paragraphs or unnecessary descriptions. Compelling text usually only consists of the labeling of axes if required and memorable, effective titles.

In keeping with the element of text inclusion, be sure to use a font that is appropriate for the presentation style and visualizations that you have chosen. If the font style and overall feel of the data presented do not mesh well, the audience will be put off from that experience.

While you should keep the use of text to a minimum in your data visualization, there is no denying that text does play an essential role in conveying the right message to your audience. Common text elements in data visualizations include captions, labels, titles, legends, and labeled icons. Despite their scarce use, the proper implementation of text in your data visualizations is a must. Lets look at a bad example of text, and what we can do to improve it.

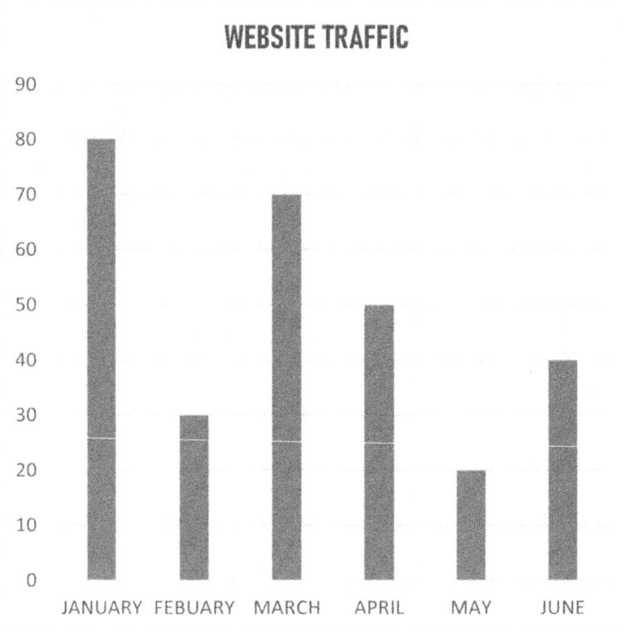

FIGURE 2.34 Ineffective title and text - the title should effectively state the values seen in the graph. X and Y axis should be easily interpreted while still being aesthetic.

Limit the Use of Uppercase Text

We live in a day and age when uppercase text can be perceived as a rude expression such as shouting. You certainly do not want your audience to feel that you are shouting data at them. Therefore, the use of uppercase text needs to be limited and carefully implemented when used. If you decide to use uppercase texts, do so in a manner that calls attention to a particular element.

Keep Chart Captions Short And Clear

Chart captions are used to summarize the data being portrayed in your charts. You need to analyze this text with an eagle eye, and any word that does not add value needs to be cut off swiftly. This means you need to chop all adjectives. Articles like *the*, *a*, and *an* should be removed where they are not required. All words that have a shorter synonym need to be replaced. Think short and crisp when you use captions.

So, what should be included in your chart captions? The first notable item is the units of measurement to represent the data in the chart. This should, of course, correspond with the data plotted in the chart. For example, you cannot have inches as the measurement in your chart and have centimeters in your caption. They need to be the same. Time periods should also be included if they are relevant to your chart. These are typically added in brackets. As for location, as a safe bet, center your caption as this generally is the most visually appealing. As a final note on this, ensure that you use sentence-style capitalization when creating captions that end those sentences with a period.

Shorten Data Labels

Labels help your audience identify the categories represented in your charts. They allow those categories to be associated with the corresponding value. These labels need to align with the categories represented in your chart. They need to be as short as possible for easy reading, especially if your chart factors in several variables. It is acceptable to use abbreviations to ensure this short length.

Suppose you find that it is not possible to shorten the length of your labels past a point where the labels do not run into each other, slant them. This diagonal view is still easily legible to most audiences. Do not rotate them as this will be hard for the audience to read.

Data Legends Must Match the Data Plotted

A legend acts as the key that clues your audience in on what you are conveying with the elements added to your charts. For example, the legend may indicate what each color in your chart represents. The first thing that you must do is ensure that the legend indeed corresponds to the data being represented. The order also needs to correspond to the order that these elements appear on the chart. For example, if red is the first color depicted on your chart, the first item in the legend needs to indicate what red represents. Lastly, the legend must be placed outside of the information plotted on the chart to ensure the chart remains uncluttered.

Titles Should Be Clear and Straightforward

Just like captions need to be kept minimally worded, so too do titles and headings. Do not confuse a title for a caption. The title of your chart needs to hold a lot less information compared to a caption. Ensure that the graph is titled in the shortest, crispest way. Those words are meant to draw the audience by capturing attention. Titles should also be void of jargon and be easy for any audience to interpret.

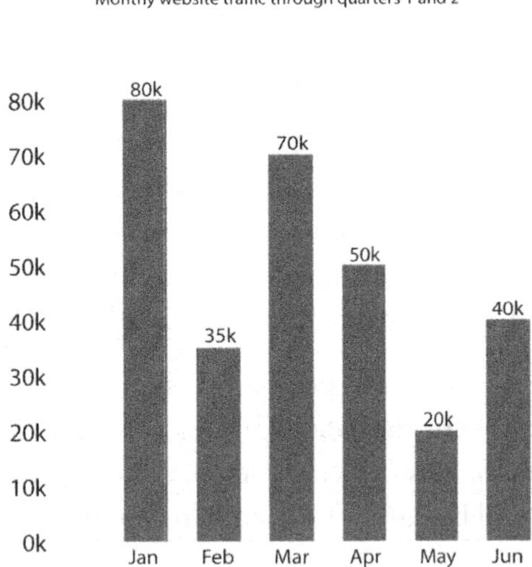

FIGURE 2.35 Proper use of text - Clear and effective title explaining what the chart is representing. Abbreviated x-axis for clean look. Additional values on top of bars can make it easy to read when specific values are required.

Just Keep It Simple

You want to wow your audience with a clear explanation of complex information. Your font is not where you want to get fancy. When in doubt, keep it simple, clear, and descriptive.

You've figured out your audience, selected the right charts, and designed them for success. Now, lets craft a winning data story.

5
CRAFTING A WINNING DATA STORY

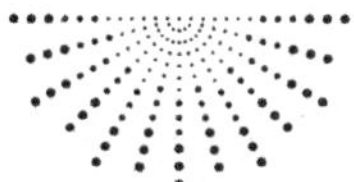

"Visualizations act as a campfire around which we gather to tell stories."

— *AL SHALLOWAY*

Movies, novels, and even data stories. They are modern examples of storytelling. However, storytelling is not new to humanity. Cave paintings show that our cavemen ancestors have been doing it a millennium back. In fact, there are cave paintings found that date back between 17,000 and 15,000 BCE.

Of course, with verbal communication came oral story storytelling, and with written language arose written storytelling. Written stories have been found dated back as far as 3,400 BCE. Those stories were written on clay tablets.

Luckily, some of the stories we find most precious are not written on such fragile things. With technological advancement, we can now listen to, read, and tell stories on radios, televisions, tablets, computers, and even on the go with our smartphones. What a way we have come!

To have withstood millennia of human changes, storytelling must be powerful indeed, and it has been shown that its powers are unlimited. Storytelling has the power to shape how we view the world and ourselves. This one thing has the ability to determine the prejudices that we develop (and yes, we all have biases) and the values and morals that we hold. It helps us understand and remember valuable information. It helps us cohabitate with each other via communication. Of course, we can deliver communication via hard facts, but stories give us context and deliver valuable insight that would have otherwise been lost.

All of these powers and more are yours to harness because by using storytelling, you can translate data into something understandable, relatable, and actionable. Through storytelling, data analysts can turn numbers that mean nothing to an audience, into a vehicle to drive change.

Just as there are steps and processes involved in creating a magnificent story through a novel or a movie, there are also steps and processes involved in creating a magnificent data story. Winging it will not do. Just as the human body is composed of specific parts to make complete anatomy, your data story needs to hold certain features for it to be complete and deliver value to your audience. Without these components, you will have a poorly executed data story.

This book was written to ensure that your data story has complete anatomy. It was written to give you the steps and processes necessary for developing a magnificent data story each and every time. This part of this book shows you how to bring all the steps and processes together beautifully.

HOW TO PRESENT YOUR DATA

It is all good and well to understand the steps and processes that go into creating a magnificent data story. However, you also need to know how to put these steps and processes together to have a well-oiled data storytelling machine. Such a machine has eight main components. These components are:

The Data Is Clearly Visible to the Audience

This component can seem obvious, but it is often the case where audiences need to squint to make out figures and texts on visualizations. What can seem clearly visible to you during the design phase of your data story can be hard to make out for your audience.

Avoid the embarrassment by getting a second opinion as to how visible the information on your charts is before you put it in front of the eyes of your audience.

The Data Illustrates the Key Points

Remember that your data means nothing to your audience until you slice it, dice it, and spice it up with the proper condiments. Then it becomes something tasty that your audience wants to digest.

Always uphold the structure of the main point of your data story, which is supported by key insights that are then further supported by points of relevant data. If your presentation does not follow that hierarchy, you need to go back to the drawing board. Anything else leaves far too much up to the interpretation of your audience. You are the one who needs to provide a clear path to solutions for your audience.

The Data Analyst Only Shares 1 Key Point from Each Chart at a Time

Each chart you develop as part of your data story has one function: to give context to a key insight. Some data analysts try to take the lazy way out and stuff several key insights into one chart. The only thing such an action will achieve is to confuse your audience.

The charts in your presentation need to be strategically aligned with the narrative you develop. The narrative needs to be paced well so that your audience does not become overwhelmed. The charts help maintain that strategic pace.

The Components of Each Chart Are Clearly Labelled

Your audience needs to gain as much information from a glance as possible without being overwhelmed. As a result, every component of your chart needs to be clearly and simply labeled. They also need to be visually impactful. Avoid that dreaded squinting effect from the audience.

Also, try to avoid abbreviations when possible in component labels as their extension might not be obvious to all audience members.

Lastly, add the component labels to each chart. Never assume that the audience will remember from viewing a previous chart.

The Data Visualizations Guide the Audience to Pre-planned 'Aha' Moments

An effective data story is a guided path to a conclusion. Think about any good tour that you have been on. There are stops along the way for you to marvel and point at before you reach that big finish. You need to provide the same experience with your data story. The conclusion is your big finish, but you also need to provide stops along the way that wow your audience. Those stops are your 'aha' moments. They are the key insights.

Make them special by verbally pointing them out as well as adding them to your charts. While you, of course, want to gently guide the audience to such moments and make the realization themselves, assume that it will fly over the heads of at least some of the audience members. Ensure that this does not happen by clearly stating these moments.

The Chart Titles Reinforce the Key Points

Another tool that leads your audience to their key insights (AKA the 'aha' moments) is the title of your charts. Just like those special stops along a guided tour spell out what the visitors will be seeing, you need to provide that part of the experience for your audience.

Ensure that the title complements the charts so that your audience is not confused. Imagine being on a tour and stopping at the "mango trees" attraction only to see apple trees. You will doubt everything else to come on that tour. The same analogy applies to titling your charts. This may seem obvious to some, but I have seen one too many titles that make little to no correlation with the data.

The Data Analyst Presents to the Audience Rather Than to the Data

Eye contact. It is a nonverbal communication method that can do a lot of things. It can intimidate. It can tell of interest without a word. It can express delight. Among the many other things it can do is that it can build a connection. Use that nonverbal communication device to your advantage when you present your data story.

Of course, there is nothing wrong with glancing at your visualizations to make references. However, far too many data analysts keep their eyes trained on the charts that they are presenting rather than their audience and miss that opportunity to form a human connection with these people. Not only that, but they also give up the chance to observe cues from the audience as to whether the audience is captivated or bored. Observing this allows the data analyst to keep on the current path or make changes on the spot to develop and maintain the connection.

HOW TO EXPLAIN YOUR CHART

As great as your visuals may be with aesthetic colors, appropriate titles and labels, and all the like, they need to be followed up with verbal communication that reinforces what is seen and adds relevant context.

I get it. Verbal presentations may not be some of our strong suits. And left to our own devices, we tend to make a muck of things. But that will not be the case. You can fall back on a methodology to make the most out of explaining your charts, and it is called Schneiderman's mantra.

Ben Schneiderman developed this mantra. Born in 1947, he is an American computer scientist and a professor at the University of Maryland. He proposed his mantra as a way for data analysts to understand how people visually engage content. An overview of this visual engagement goes like this:

1. Overview of the information
2. Zoom and filter specific parts of the information
3. Look for relevant details on demand

This mantra is used highly in interactive visualizations, but the principles are still applicable when static charts are used.

His mantra is the fifth step of developing chart presentations that wow and that are effective.

The five steps are:

1. Think about everything necessary to be included in your charts.
2. Label everything from the titles and legends to the X and Y axes.
3. Provide the context of how the data was processed to develop the charts.
4. Be intentional about the visual encoding, such as the colors and text used to develop your charts.
5. Use Schneiderman's mantra to explain the charts to the audience.

Steps 1, 2, and 4 are done before you start making your presentation. We have covered the bases as to how to do these steps. Step 3 is a matter of courtesy and allows you to avoid confusion. Simply outline your process for assimilating your data into the charts briefly in the introductory part of your presentation.

Now let's focus on step five, which outlines Schneiderman's mantra. By knowing how human beings tend to engage visual content, you can approach explaining your visualizations in a way that aligns with this natural flow. Here is a step-by-step guide to exactly how you can do this.

Provide the Overview First

You feel it when you are confronted with something visually for the first time. Your eyes move back and forth, trying to take in as much as possible in one glance. We often describe the motion as not knowing where to look first. The reason for this is because our brains are trying to decipher exactly what we are looking at. The brain has enlisted the function of the eyes to go on this fact-finding mission.

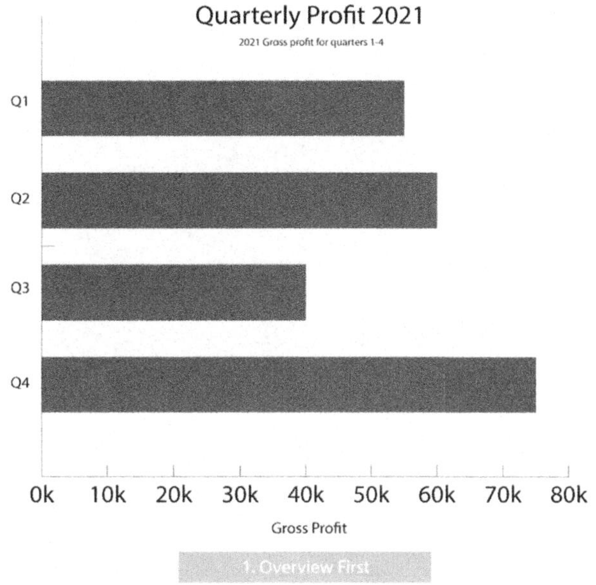

FIGURE 3 Overview of graph first - Overview of graph lets audience have a general understanding of values before making any conclusions.

Take advantage of the audience's natural inclination and aid the eyes' mission to decipher what is being visually presented to them by explaining exactly what they are looking at in the form of your visualization. This does not have to be long-winded. You only need to provide a sentence or two to describe what the chart is about. In essence, you are giving a slightly more detailed version of the title of your chart. And remember, your title is the showcase of the key insight highlighted by that chart.

Zoom and Filter

The next thing the brain is inclined to do after getting an overview of visual information is narrow in on specific things that are particularly attention-catching. It filters through all the information that is being presented and zooms in on specific details.

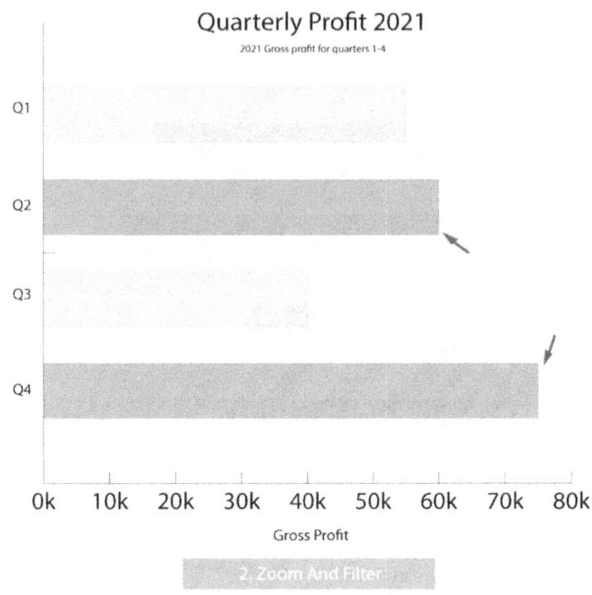

FIGURE 3.1 Zoom and filter - Highlight key points to better get your message across. Slowly lead your audience to your conclusion.

As an effective data analyst, you would have provided visual cues that are particularly attention-catching. For example, these may be the only colored bars in your bar graph or the highlighted trends in your line graph. These attention-grabbing details are what you will use to provide that 'aha' moment. Such details point your audience in a particular direction to reach the conclusion, which is the main point of your data story. Think back to our guided tour analogy, and you know what I mean. Those details support your insight (the stop before reaching the end of the tour).

This is where visual cues such as the colors you use can be of aid. For example, you may want to point out a specific line on your line chart to expand on that data. In that case, all you would have to do is say something like, "Notice this red line here..." and follow that up with your explanation.

Provide Details on Demand

Once the brain has drilled down on specific details that it finds interesting, curiosity is aroused. Therefore, it will want to know more about these particular details.

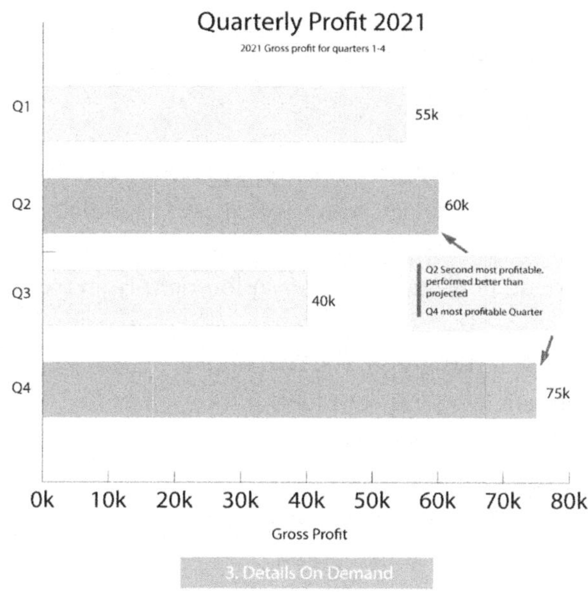

FIGURE 3.2 Details on demand - Explain key information in your chart related to specific highlighted points.

Again, this is something that you can capitalize on while delivering your data story. After you have made sure that your audience has been thoroughly captivated by the highlighted key insights, provide them with more data about them. Give them the relevant information about why this insight is relevant to the ultimate conclusion of your data story.

. . .

The best thing about using Schneiderman's mantra is that this three-step approach can be applied to explain any type of chart for any kind of situation. It is a solid approach that helps the audience understand what has been presented to them and allows data analysts to have a foolproof method of giving the audience relevant context to what is being visually presented to them. Always have this manta in the forefront of your mind when explaining your charts - overview first, zoom and filter, and finally, provide details on demand.

USING THE RIGHT VOCABULARY

From the beginning

Now that you've chosen an effective graph and designed it to work in your favour, it's time to get an idea of what vocabulary you should use when describing graphs, charts, and diagrams. Here are some phrases I like to use to catch my audience's attention right from the start.

- If you look at this graph, you will notice...
- To illustrate my point, let's look at some charts...
- Let's turn to this diagram...
- I'd like you to look at...
- If you look at this graph, you will notice...
- Let me show you this bar graph...
- Let's have a look at this pie chart...

Describing important elements

When you are describing any form of visual information, it is important to guide your audience to the key points you are trying to make. Some examples would be:

- The colored segment is for...
- The vertical axis shows...
- The shaded area describes...
- The horizontal axis represents...
- The curve here illustrates...

- The solid line shows...
- The green bar indicates....

ALWAYS HAVE SUPPORTING INFORMATION

Although a picture-perfect presentation is what we strive for, it is common to get hit with rebuttals and questions. Depending on your audience, this might be more or less prominent. Although healthy discussion is imminent and recommended, it is always good to keep some extra information on the back burner to further enhance the data's insights. Put yourself in the shoes of your audience. What areas allow for concern? What will they most likely be skeptical toward or want to know more about? It's always a good idea to have some extra insights and visualizations to fall back on, usually related to the main insights of the presentation. Supporting data is vital.

Some common questions that audiences tend to ask are:

- Is this our only course of action?
- Do you have any other figures so we can better understand the depth of your point?
- What exactly are you telling us?
- If we stay on this course, what will be the outcome?
- Do you have any concrete ideas for improvement in these areas?

Driving effective business growth is a difficult task. That's why so many businesses fail. Expect the amount of discussion to vary based on your audience and the significance of the data. A quick overview of the last quarter will be less intense than a yearly review of a failing product. Be strategic and prepare accordingly. This can make a huge impact on your presentation.

PERFORMING A GREAT EXECUTION

One of the best storytelling tactics is to give real-life examples, and I will show you what this looks like by giving you an example of what an effective data story looks like in this section. This section is a run-through of what an effective data story looks like in a real-world setting.

For such a scenario to work, you need to have gone through the steps previously outlined in this book. There is no skipping the creative process that ultimately leads you to the presentation of your charts. You would have needed to develop an engaging narrative, compile data that is relevant that aligns with that narrative and design visually appealing charts to support this relevant data. Without these supporting aspects, there is no hope of executing an excellent presentation.

With those aspects in the bag, you are prepared for the big day. You will prove your mettle as an engaging storyteller supported by data visualizations. Again, this is not something that you have to develop a new method for. There is a methodology that you can fall back on to tell great data stories.

An engaging data story has four main sections, and they are:

- The Introduction
- The rising action
- The climax
- Conclusion

How about we walk through an example and bring it all together.

Let's say you launched a new software at the beginning of 2022, and you're analyzing the profit margins for the year (you're a software company that sells payroll software to help businesses streamline their payroll processes through automated payments and calculations). You realize that your profit margins are smaller than projected due to higher customer support and software maintenance costs than anticipated. As you acquire more customers and costs go up, it will result in smaller profit margins, and eventually losses. You need to find a possible solution to the problem and present the whole story. Let's walk through the steps to make it as straightforward as possible.

Step 1: Some questions you need to ask before you start. There are multiple options here regarding who you're presenting to and a possible solution to the problem.

The Narrative: The product/service you offer had an excellent launch and is performing well. However, the profit margins are smaller than we projected due to higher customer support and software maintenance costs. Over time you will be in the negative if action is not taken for 2023

The Players: Who exactly is in charge of making a big decision? Is it the VP of product? The Product manager? Curate your presentation to cater to this person. What do they know, what don't they know? Refer to Chapter 2 to find out who you're talking to.

For this example, we are talking to the product manager. They have some in-depth knowledge of the product and its pricing but aren't familiar with the issue you are bringing to light. We can categorize them as a "manager" and an "analytical" audience type.

The Solution: How will we solve the problem? What is the solution? It is the product manager who will make the call. But as the one analyzing the data, you have the in-depth knowledge and need to present possible solutions to the problem. How can we raise the price or add extra costs without losing customers? Can we also cut costs to enhance the profit margins?

In this case, some solutions could be:

- Raise the monthly price gradually throughout the next six months
- Increasing perceived value by marketing a new feature as an "upgrade"(then raising the price).
- Decreasing maintenance/labor costs.
- Increase the value by adding additional services/features/upgrades, then raising the price.
- Raise/Add in an additional monthly "maintenance fee" or cost for upgrades/customer support.
- Or even just raise your prices with confidence.

In this case, the best option seems to add an additional monthly "maintenance fee." While reducing costs where you can. Label this as a "Version upgrade" with a minor price increase to improve customer relations and future maintenance/updates.

Step 2: How to choose and optimize your visual strategy.

We've created a visualization representing profit and maintenance costs for 2022.

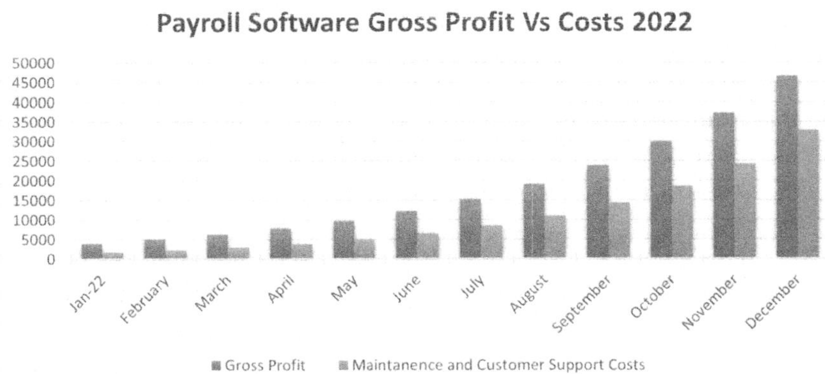

FIGURE 3.3

This is pretty standard of how most people would visualize this data. However, a line chart is a much more effective option when looking at a trajectory over time. As you can see with the 2022 numbers, profits are still fine, and although lower than expected, small tweaks should correct this. It even looks like profits could correct over time. Let's look at the same data in a line chart.

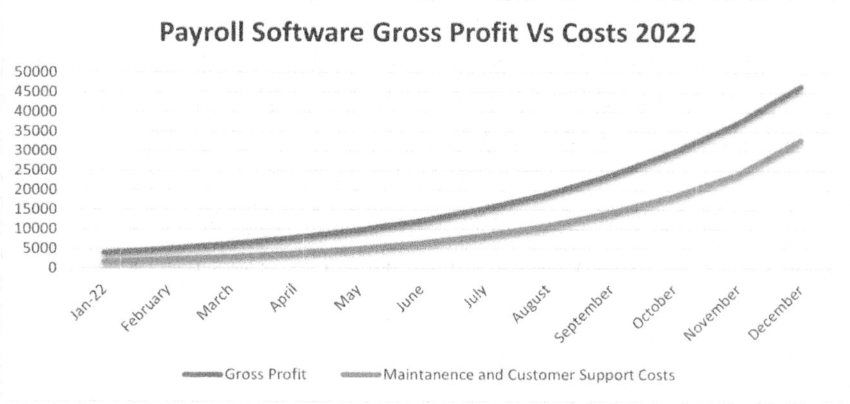

FIGURE 3.4

However, this doesn't tell the full story. After analyzing the data, we have a steady 25% growth month over month in profit. But a 30% growth month over month in costs. If you are accounting for inflation (wage increases, business cost increases, etc), Costs will be closer to 36% month over month come 2023. We can project that by April of 2023, the software will not be profitable.

Let's have a look at this in a bar chart.

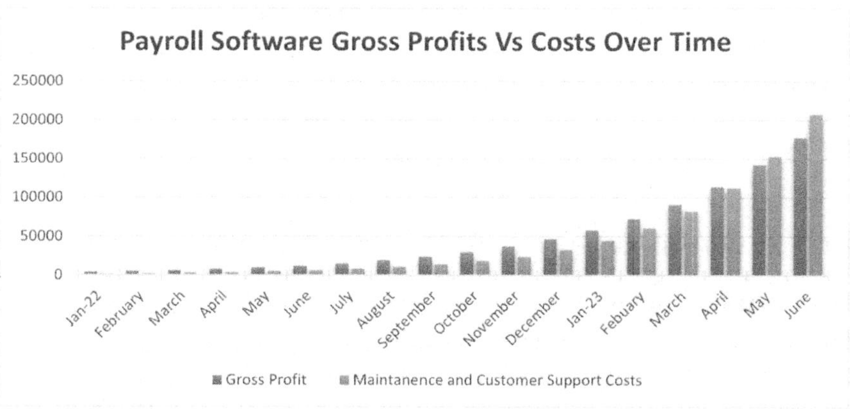

FIGURE 3.5

Some people will argue this is an effective way to visualize this data. However, it comes across as more stagnant figures than the trajectory over time. It's not easily distinguishable that the costs surpass the profits. At first glance, you might not even notice that one bar surpasses the other. It just looks like some ordinary data. Just like before, a line chart will be the most effective option.

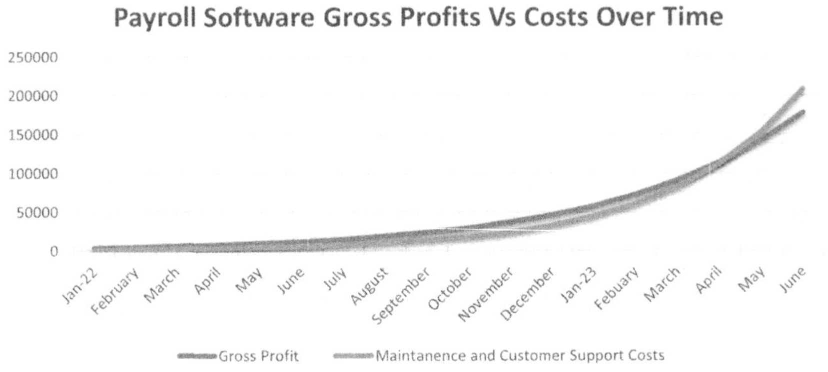

FIGURE 3.6

Now, we can easily see that as we acquire more businesses using our software, the rise in maintenance/customer support costs while considering inflation leaves us in the negative. We are rendering the software unprofitable by April of 2023. The product manager can now easily see the trajectory on their own and can visualize the detrimental outcome if action is not taken.

Step 3: Optimize your visual for maximum effectiveness

Now that we are representing our data in the most effective way possible, we must make it visually appealing to the audience. Let's revisit some essential ways to reduce clutter from chapter 4.

- Remove the chart Border.
- No Unnecessary effects (shadowing/3D, etc).
- Remove Gridlines.
- Overuse of bright/unnecessary colors.

- Shorten data labels.

This chart can be our "overview" of the initial data.

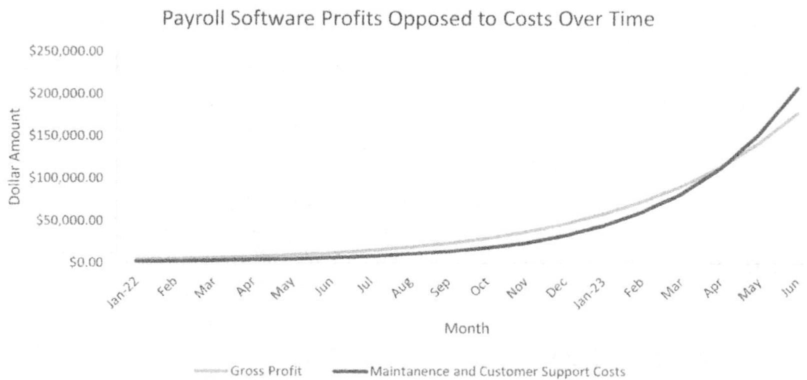

FIGURE 3.7

Now to increase the clarity of our point, let's introduce a second slide with some attentive attributes. I have labeled and highlighted the point where the maintenance/support costs outweigh the profits, Showing that we will start to make significant losses after this time frame if something isn't changed.

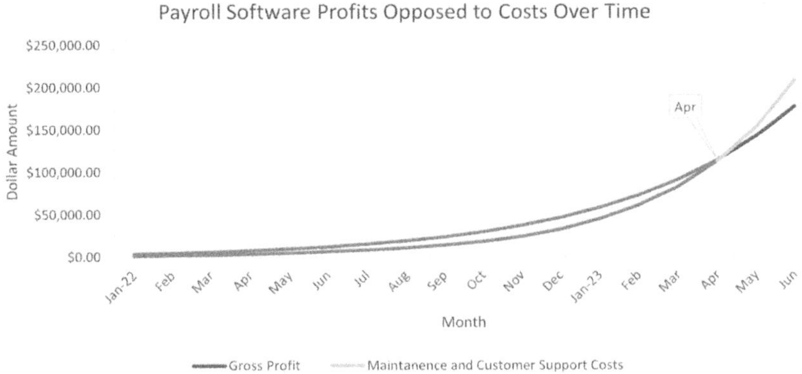

FIGURE 3.8

Step 4: Present the visual effectively.

Properly present the visual with presentation tactics used in this book, such as the sandwich approach and Schneiderman's mantra. Pair this with some specific techniques based on your audience type. You want the audience to come to a conclusion on their own. *they can see the profit margins are smaller than anticipated and will become unprofitable over time because of high maintenance/support costs. They'll need to adjust the price point or add additional maintenance fees to make up for the extra costs.*

Step 5: Present a Solution

If you did everything right, you would've known a possible solution before you even created a chart. However, if you have to relay a complicated and drastic solution, give them multiple options to consider. Explain some flaws in the other options, and then finally end up on the solution we think is the most effective and streamlined as if it is the only option. Or, potentially keep the options open and discuss the best direction. (this is only necessary with more complex problems you have to find a solution for)

In this case, the best option seems to add an additional monthly "maintenance fee." the best way to go about this is as a "Version upgrade" with a minor price increase to improve customer relations and future maintenance/updates. Show that they're receiving an upgraded and improved product overall. The original monthly subscription people pay for the software is $200. After analyzing the margins, Adding $25 per month for the subscription is enough to increase profits drastically without losing any customers. Now that we also know how high our maintenance and support costs can be with this particular software, we must do what we can to trim as much of that as possible. Suppose we can reduce costs by 10% in 2023, with the additional $25/month per customer. We are setting ourselves up for an excellent 2023. If we can make some changes at the beginning of the year, here are our projected numbers:

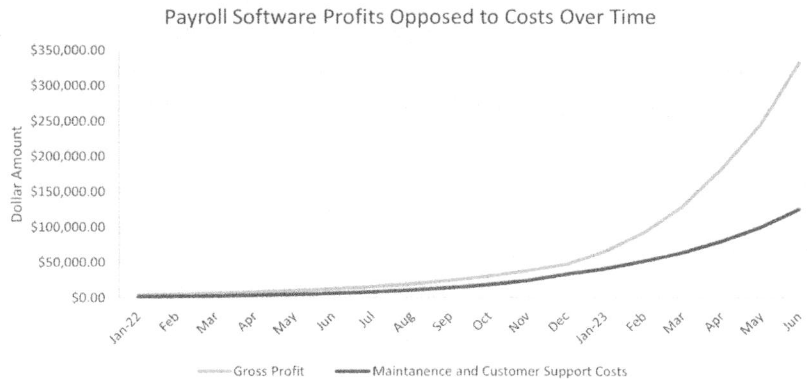

FGURE 3.9

Step 6: Bringing everything together.

Now let's bring this together as if we were presenting. By spending the extra effort doing research and creating proper charts, we can keep our presentation simple and let the charts and data speak for themselves.

Lets organize our data story like we stated before. The Introduction, The Rising Action, The Climax, The Conclusion.

THE INTRODUCTION

In a book or film, this section is a representation of the main characters going about their daily lives before they are ultimately thrown through the wringer to come out as a changed person. It is the setup to show where this character is now so that the audience has context as to how they will move through the main parts of the story. It is what allows the audience reading or watching to develop a connection with this character. When the audience cares, the introduction has performed its function and hooked these people.

In data storytelling, the introduction has the same function. It is a setup meant to give context and hook the audience. This is where the analyst will show the audience what problem brought everyone to that setting on that day, the benefits to solving that issue, and possible solutions to solving the problem. The audience needs to care about moving through the guided tour that starts with the problem and ends with the solution.

"We've analyzed the numbers for 2022, and we've noticed some issues with the long-term trajectory. As you can see, profit margins are smaller than we anticipated due to higher customer support and software maintenance costs."

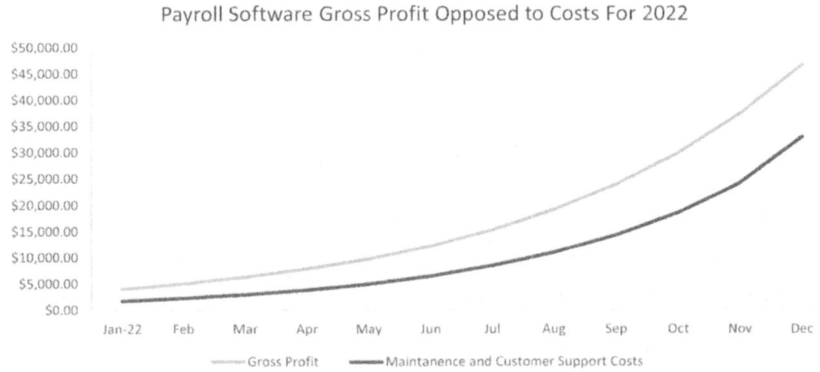

FIGURE 3.10

"Although it seems to be quite manageable, there are some more significant issues that need to be addressed with the long term trajectory.

We have set the stage by showcasing the norm and highlighting the problem that led to this data story's need. They also alluded to finding the cause of the problem and the delivery of a solution to the problem.

They have provided context and delivered the hook.

THE RISING ACTION

In books and films, this is where the main character's life changes. A catalyst causes this change and ensures no turning back from the path ahead of this person. The introduction has gotten the audience to care about this person, but this part will have the audience at the edge of their seats wanting to know what happens next.

In data storytelling, again, the analogy applies. The catalyst that incites change is the delivery of analyzed data to support the findings that highlight the problem. Many junior data analysts make a mistake here: they throw data point after data point after point at the audience. The function of this part of the story is to build anticipation of the solution to the problem. Continue to give context to the problem and support this with only relevant details. Do not be stingy but build anticipation by leaving the audience wondering where you are leading them. Keep that image of the guided tour in your mind. You do not want to see everything the tour has to offer upfront. Otherwise, what would there be for you to look forward to?

We have a steady 25% growth month over month in gross profit. But a 30% growth month over month in costs. If you are accounting for inflation (wage increases, business expenses, etc.) our costs will be closer to 36% come 2023.

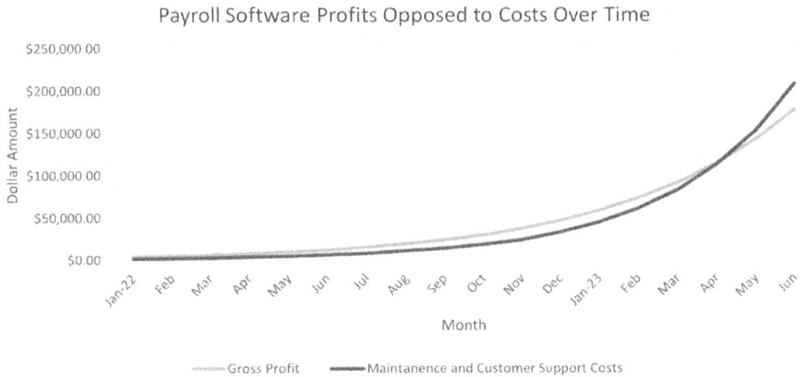

FIGURE 3.11

As can be seen, by this explanation, we are giving more context to data. At this point, they are also showcasing charts that support this context. Notice that their wording gives more details and leads the audience's focus to a particular point, which is why this problem has arisen and how it can be solved.

THE CLIMAX

This step in storytelling represents that turning point in the story where the changes that will come to fruition become clear. It is the highest point of tension in the story. It is the height of the anticipation built in the rising action step. Remember that this part will not serve its purpose unless you set the foundation with a good introduction and the anticipation developed in the rising action.

In data storytelling, the climax is your 'aha' moment. It finally reveals the things that the presenter was alluding to in the introduction and rising action portions. Things should become clear to the audience then, leaving them with a sense of fulfillment.

"As more businesses use our software, We can project that the costs will outweigh our profits by April of 2023 if no major changes are made. Rendering the software unprofitable"

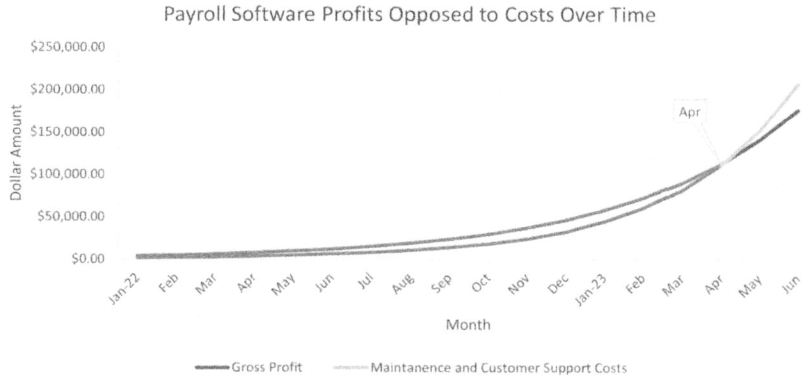

FIGURE 3.12

This speech has revealed the why of the problem that was stated from the introduction and given context in the rising action. The audience should feel relieved to know the cause of the problem and look forward to the conclusion which leads the way forward.

CONCLUSION

In a book or movie, this is the part that gives closure to the audience as it shows how the main character is settling in with the new changes. Data storytelling summarizes the entire presentation in as brief a language as possible and defines the steps that should be taken next.

The following steps can be hypothetical, a solution to how the situation can turn out if certain actions were taken or avoided, or recommendations for future action.

"After analyzing the numbers, I believe the best way to fix the trajectory is to issue a "Version upgrade" to improve customer relations and future maintenance/updates. Adding $25 per month to the subscription is more than enough to increase profits drastically without losing any customers. Now that we also know how high our maintenance and support costs can be with this particular software, it is important to do what we can to trim as much of that as possible."

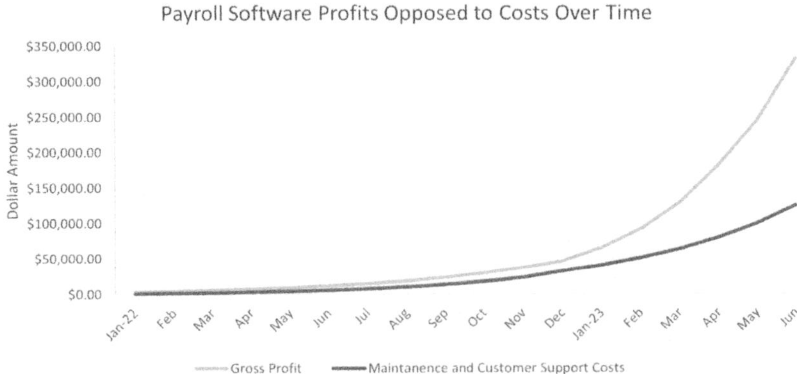

FIGURE 3.13

"AS YOU CAN SEE, If we can manage to reduce costs by 10%, paired with the additional $25/month per customer. We are setting ourselves up for an excellent 2023 and beyond."

Overview

To create an effective data story, it starts with understanding the narrative. What do we need to present, and why? Once you figure this out, you can determine who you're presenting to and what solution you need to guide them towards. When creating visuals, we have to make sure we choose the most effective way of presenting that data to our specific audience. Is it just visually showing some values or driving conclusions in an easy to interpret manner? When you've found the best chart for the data, designing to win is a crucial step. Eliminate any unwanted clutter and make the information as clear as possible. Once your visuals are up to par, presenting the data in an effective and structured manner is the key to winning over your audience. Start with an overview of the information you've analyzed. Slowly work your way through the supporting evidence and possible solution to the problem. Ask the right questions and properly design the visuals so the audience can come to your desired conclusion with as little persuasion as possible. Let's have a look at where we started and where we ended up.

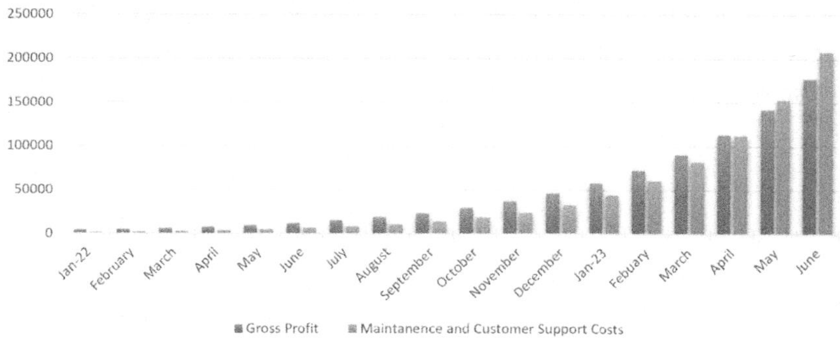

Payroll Software Profits Opposed to Costs Over Time

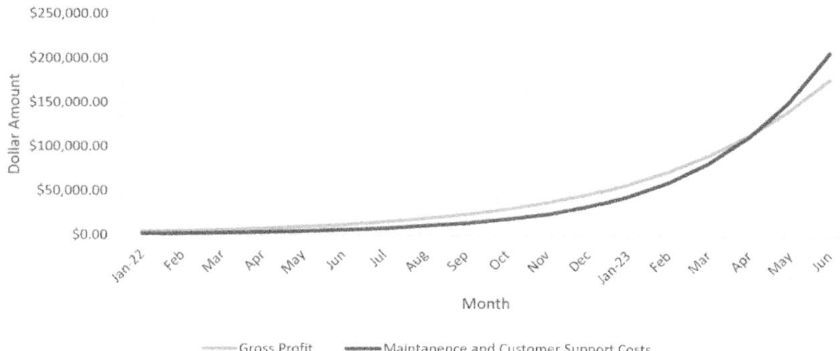

FIGURE 3.14

By utilizing the six steps above, you will be on track to create a winning data story. If you want to get some hands-on practice, try creating a scenario from a situation at work or your imagination. Create the visuals and structure them to present them to someone important.

Like everything else with data storytelling, you do not have to reinvent the wheel to explain your charts right. The template has already been prepared for you. First, introduce the problem that has warranted the need for the development of this data story. Get your audience anticipating a solution by giving them context and hinting why this problem has developed with the rising action. Provide the 'aha' moment in the climax of the data story by plainly explaining the *why* that has been anticipated. And finally, leave the audience fulfilled with a conclusion that outlines possible solutions to solving this problem.

CONCLUSION

> "The effectiveness of data visualization can be gauged by its simplicity, relevancy, and its ability to hold the users hand during their data discover journey."
>
> — JAGAT SAIKIA

Every single day, data, so much of it, is being created. It would all look like nonsensical babble if not for people like you. Data analysts and business professionals are the translators of data, and without them, so many audiences would not know how to proceed with this data influx.

However, there is an art and a science to delivering data to an audience in an understandable, relatable, and actionable way, and that is data storytelling. You have gotten to this part of this book, and I commend you for that dedication to mastering data storytelling. You have all the tools necessary for delivering a powerful data story to your audience each and every time. From here, you can continue to expand upon your knowledge and grow your expertise to translate more complex and compelling data.

As a quick reference, here is a brief summary of what it takes to create a data story that wows and informs:

The Foundation, The Narrative

This is the narrative of your data story. The entire structure will depend on how effectively you develop the narrative. Your goals will be established here. You will also drill down on the context of your data story here. The context gives the why of this data story - why it is necessary that this data story be told. What is the problem that needs solving, and how can it be solved in actionable steps? Developing the narrative also allows you to develop an understanding of who the key players are and what information is already at their disposal. Figuring out such details will also help you to develop an introduction that hooks your audience and keeps them captivated throughout the presentation.

Captivating Your Audience

The narrative, the chart development, and all other effort and time you have put into developing a data story will be for nothing if you fail to connect with the audience you are delivering to. These people rely on you to clearly state the problem that needs to be addressed and provide possible solutions. Therefore, how to present data to them should always be at the forefront of your mind. You need to become familiar with the needs of these people, their familiarity with the subject, the best ways of communicating with them, and the best methods of influencing them in taking action after all is said and done.

Refining Your Visuals: Choosing the Right Chart

With the narrative developed and the audience figured out, you need to recreate the details in visual form. This is the function of your charts. However, not just any chart will do. You need to create naturally paced charts and designed visuals to keep your audiences informed but not overwhelmed.

This phase also means choosing the right charts to showcase data in the best light. This choice is dependent on the type of data that needs to be highlighted during your presentation. Just because some data has been put into a pie graph doesn't mean it's any more valuable than raw numbers. Make sure the chart effectively depicts the information you are presenting. The charts are intended to make the data easily understood.

Refining Your Visuals: Developing a Winning Design

Chart development is not just about having relevant data presented. Charts must also be visually appealing to your audience. This is a delicate balance that you must achieve to keep your audience engaged and interested in seeing your data story to the end. The psychology of design is something that you must fall back on to choose colors, textures, texts, and other design details that positively capture the attention of the audience and help them understand the key insights being delivered. To make your charts clean and easy to interpret, eliminate elements that don't add any informative value. Highlight key insights with attentive attributes to put your audience's attention exactly where you want it so they can quickly drive the correct conclusions on their own.

Crafting a Winning Data Story

You have all it takes to execute a winning data story once you follow the steps outlined above. These tools guide you to crafting a presentation that fulfills its purpose. The last step is execution. Luckily, Schneiderman's mantra allows you to clearly explain your charts with these steps:

1. Overview the information
2. Zoom and filter specific parts of the information
3. Look for relevant details on demand

A data story being effectively delivered has 4 main sections, and they are:

- The introduction
- The rising action
- The climax
- Conclusion

Follow that structure, and you will have this in the bag!

If there is one thing that I want you to take away after reading this book, it is that anyone can craft an engaging data story. The steps and tools have already been clearly laid out for you. This book was written in plain language to show you step by step how this methodology plays out so that you have the best chances of creating winning data stories every time. This last bit only you can perform, putting these steps and tools into good use. Don't overthink it. Just follow the methodology, expand upon it, and become an awesome data storyteller. What are you waiting for?

RESOURCES

Boyd B. (2018). The evolution of stories: from mimesis to language, from fact to fiction. *Wiley interdisciplinary reviews. Cognitive science*, 9(1), e1444. https://doi.org/10.1002/wcs.1444

Boyd, R. L., Blackburn, K. G., & Pennebaker, J. W. (2020). The narrative arc: Revealing core narrative structures through text analysis. *Science advances*, 6(32), eaba2196. https://doi.org/10.1126/sciadv.aba2196

Dettori, J. R., & Norvell, D. C. (2018). The Anatomy of Data. *Global spine journal*, 8(3), 311–313. https://doi.org/10.1177/2192568217746998

Elliot A. J. (2015). Color and psychological functioning: a review of theoretical and empirical work. *Frontiers in psychology*, 6, 368. https://doi.org/10.3389/fpsyg.2015.00368

Hattab, G., Rhyne, T. M., & Heider, D. (2020). Ten simple rules to colorize biological data visualization. *PLoS computational biology*, 16(10), e1008259. https://doi.org/10.1371/journal.pcbi.1008259

Lee, J. C., & Livesey, E. J. (2018). Rule-based generalization and peak shift in the presence of simple relational rules. *PloS one*, 13(9), e0203805. https://doi.org/10.1371/journal.pone.0203805

Li Q. (2020). Overview of Data Visualization. *Embodying Data: Chinese Aesthetics, Interactive Visualization and Gaming Technologies*, 17–47. https://doi.org/10.1007/978-981-15-5069-0_2

Marković S. (2012). Components of aesthetic experience: aesthetic fascination, aesthetic appraisal, and aesthetic emotion. *i-Perception*, 3(1), 1–17. https://doi.org/10.1068/i0450aap

Martinez-Conde, S., Alexander, R. G., Blum, D., Britton, N., Lipska, B. K., Quirk, G. J., Swiss, J. I., Willems, R. M., & Macknik, S. L. (2019). The Storytelling Brain: How Neuroscience Stories Help Bridge the Gap between Research and Society. *The Journal of neuroscience: the official journal of the Society for Neuroscience*, 39(42), 8285–8290. https://doi.org/10.1523/JNEUROSCI.1180-19.2019

Mastandrea, S., Fagioli, S., & Biasi, V. (2019). Art and Psychological Well-Being: Linking the Brain to the Aesthetic Emotion. *Frontiers in psychology*, 10, 739. https://doi.org/10.3389/fpsyg.2019.00739

Midway S. R. (2020). Principles of Effective Data Visualization. *Patterns (New York, N.Y.)*, 1(9), 100141. https://doi.org/10.1016/j.patter.2020.100141

Plante, T. B., & Cushman, M. (2020). Choosing color palettes for scientific figures. *Research and practice in thrombosis and hemostasis*, 4(2), 176–180. https://doi.org/10.1002/rth2.12308

Ranganathan, P., & Gogtay, N. J. (2019). An Introduction to Statistics - Data Types, Distributions, and Summarizing Data. *Indian journal of critical care medicine: peer-reviewed, official publication of Indian Society of Critical Care Medicine*, 23(Suppl 2), S169–S170. https://doi.org/10.5005/jp-journals-10071-23198

Suzuki, W. A., Feliú-Mójer, M. I., Hasson, U., Yehuda, R., & Zarate, J. M. (2018). Dialogues: The Science and Power of Storytelling. *The Journal of neuroscience: the official journal of the Society for Neuroscience*, 38(44), 9468–9470. https://doi.org/10.1523/JNEUROSCI.1942-18.2018

Wolfe, J. M., & Utochkin, I. S. (2019). What is a preattentive feature?. *Current opinion in psychology*, 29, 19–26. https://doi.org/10.1016/j.copsyc.2018.11.005

L.C.T. (2020, July 7). *How to Tell a Story With Data.* Lucidchart. Retrieved November 2, 2021, from https://www.lucidchart.com/blog/how-to-tell-a-story-with-data

Goldmeier, J. M. (2019, November 12). *The only data visualization guide you'll ever need (in 5 principles).* LinkedIn. Retrieved November 2, 2021, from https://www.linkedin.com/pulse/only-data-visualization-guide-youll-ever-need-5-jordan-goldmeier

Goldmeier, J. M. (2019, November 12). *The only data visualization guide you'll ever need (in 5 principles).* LinkedIn. Retrieved November 2, 2021, from https://www.linkedin.com/pulse/only-data-visualization-guide-youll-ever-need-5-jordan-goldmeier

Infogram. (n.d.). *How to Choose the Right Chart for Your Data.* https://infogram.com/page/choose-the-right-chart-data-visualization

Gulbis, J. B. (n.d.). *Data Visualization – How to Pick the Right Chart Type?* EazyBI. Retrieved November 2, 2021, from https://eazybi.com/blog/data-visualization-and-chart-types

Yi, M. (2019, August 23). *A Complete Guide to Bar Charts.* Chartio. Retrieved November 2, 2021, from https://chartio.com/learn/charts/bar-chart-complete-guide/

Yi, M. (2019b, September 24). *A Complete Guide to Stacked Bar Charts.* Chartio. Retrieved November 2, 2021, from https://chartio.com/learn/charts/stacked-bar-chart-complete-guide/

Yi, M. (2019b, August 29). *A Complete Guide to Pie Charts.* Chartio. Retrieved November 2, 2021, from https://chartio.com/learn/charts/pie-chart-complete-guide/

Marr, B. (2021, July 13). *Why You Shouldn't Use Pie Charts In Your Dashboards And Performance Reports.* Bernard Marr. Retrieved November 2, 2021, from https://bernardmarr.com/why-you-shouldnt-use-pie-charts-in-your-dashboards-and-performance-reports/?contentID=1779#:%7E:text=From%20a%20design%20point%20of,data%20more%20complicated%20than

%20before.

Yi, M. (2019c, September 13). *A Complete Guide to Line Charts*. Chartio. Retrieved November 2, 2021, from https://chartio.com/learn/charts/line-chart-complete-guide/

Yi, M. (2019d, September 16). *A Complete Guide to Area Charts*. Chartio. Retrieved November 2, 2021, from https://chartio.com/learn/charts/area-chart-complete-guide/#:%7E:text=An%20area%20chart%20combines%20the,like%20in%20a%20bar%20chart.

R. (2020b, March 8). *Presenting data visualization to engage your audience*. Medium. Retrieved November 2, 2021, from https://uxdesign.cc/presenting-data-visualization-to-engage-your-audience-815eb6a43a62

Yi, M. (2019f, October 16). *A Complete Guide to Scatter Plots*. Chartio. Retrieved November 2, 2021, from https://chartio.com/learn/charts/what-is-a-scatter-plot/

Brown, L. (n.d.). *Wondershare Fotophire Online Support Center*. Wondershare. Retrieved November 2, 2021, from https://photo.wondershare.com/graph-maker/best-graphing-software.html

Verma, R. (2021, February 26). *Data Visualization: Top 5 Most Important Things to Know*. Loginworks. Retrieved November 2, 2021, from https://www.loginworks.com/blogs/data-visualization-top-5-most-important-things/

V. (2019, February 13). *Preattentive Attributes in Visualization - An Example*. Daydreaming Numbers. Retrieved November 2, 2021, from http://daydreamingnumbers.com/blog/preattentive-attributes-example/

Preattentive Visual Properties and How to Use Them in Information Visualization. (2018, October 2). The Interaction Design Foundation. Retrieved November 2, 2021, from https://www.interaction-design.org/literature/article/preattentive-visual-properties-and-how-to-use-them-in-information-visualization

Horne, J. (2020, June 5). *Neuroaesthetics and Informative Art | iDashboards Blog*. IDashboards |. Retrieved November 2, 2021, from https://www.idashboards.com/blog/2017/08/23/neuroaesthetics-and-informative-art/

Baltusevičius, G. (2021, February 2). *How to Do Storytelling with Data Using Visualizations*. Blog | Whatagraph. Retrieved November 2, 2021, from https://whatagraph.com/blog/articles/data-using-visualizations

Bowers, M. (2020, October 20). *Numbers Shouldn't Lie – An Overview of Common Data Visualization Mistakes*. Toptal Design Blog. Retrieved November 2, 2021, from https://www.toptal.com/designers/ux/data-visualization-mistakes

I. (2018, November 29). *Dos and Don'ts: Data Visualization Tips Before and After*. Medium. Retrieved November 2, 2021, from https://medium.com/@Infogram/dos-and-donts-data-visualization-tips-before-and-after-f1d65a7b6402

M. (2021, June 17). *7 Best Practices for Using Color in Data Visualizations*. Sigma Computing. Retrieved November 2, 2021, from https://www.sigmacomputing.com/blog/7-best-practices-for-using-color-in-data-visualizations/#:%7E:text=Why%20color%20use%20in%20data%20visualization%20matters&text=Using%20color%20strategically%20helps%20viewers,visualization%20is%20trying%20to%20tell.

Makulec, A. (n.d.). *Identifying Your Audience*. Slideshare. Retrieved November 2, 2021, from https://www.slideshare.net/AmandaMakulec/identifying-your-audience-40086476

Sleeper, R. (2021, January 2). *Vital Question 1: Who is the Audience?* Playfair Data. Retrieved November 2, 2021, from https://playfairdata.com/vital-question-1-who-is-the-audience/

S. (2018b, May 25). *Presenting complex data? Engage your audience with these 10 tips*. Medium. Retrieved November 2, 2021, from https://speakerhubhq.medium.com/presenting-complex-data-engage-your-audience-with-these-10-tips-232509301a4d

INDEX

EVERYTHING DATA ANALYTICS: A BEGINNERS GUIDE TO DATA LITERACY

BEGINNERS GUIDE TO DATA VISUALIZATION

HOW TO WIN WITH YOUR DATA VISUALIZATIONS

Made in the USA
Coppell, TX
12 February 2024